Kraken Latin 3

Student Edition

Published by Canon Press
P.O. Box 8729, Moscow, Idaho 83843
800.488.2034 | www.canonpress.com

Natali H. Monnette, *Kraken Latin for the Logic Years 3: Student Edition*

Cover design by Rachel Rosales (orangepealdesign.com). Cover illustration by Forrest Dickison. Interior design by Phaedrus Media and Valerie Anne Bost. Typesetting by Laura Storm and Valerie Anne Bost.

Printed in the United States of America.

Library of Congress Cataloging-in-Publication Data forthcoming.

19 20 21 22 23 24 25 26 27 28 29 10 9 8 7 6 5 4 3 2 1

BOOK 3

Kraken Latin *for the* Logic Years

by NATALI H. MONNETTE

canonpress
Moscow, Idaho

CONTENTS

INTRODUCTION

Discipulī Discipulaeque,

If you are reading this, you have successfully completed your first two years of *Kraken Latin* and are poised to begin another. At this point I really should give you some inspiring Latin quotes such as *ad astra per aspera*, "to the stars through difficulties"; *citius, altius, fortius*, "faster, higher, stronger" (the motto of the Olympics, incidentally), or perhaps simply *excelsior!*, "[ever] higher!" You have, after all, competently navigated the shallows of Latin grammar, mastering the entire indicative verb system and all declensions of nouns, not to mention adjectives and other little words along the way. So perhaps your battle cry should be *ālea iacta est*, "the die has been cast"—for now, after last year's taste of Latin, you must inevitably progress to the delightful grammatical banquet before you. However, I've always had a sneaking fondness for old Lucius Accius' phrase *ōderint dum metuant*, "let them hate, provided they fear." (It became a favorite saying of the Emperor Caligula, an unpleasant and insane man by most accounts, but let us disregard that for the moment.) Now of course I do not wish for any of you to hate Latin, but realistically I know that not all of you approach your Latin lessons with dances of joy. So for those of you who find Latin a struggle, a challenge, even a battle with a thrashing sea monster—you are hereby permitted not to love Latin if you must, provided that you respect and appreciate her beauty and utility.

And for those of you who are quivering with anticipation about this next voyage, it promises to be a wild ride. You will learn more complex grammatical concepts, particularly delving deeper into verbs and coming to grips with the remaining moods (infinitive, participle, and subjunctive). You will also add to your knowledge of pronouns, adjectives, and nouns. But most importantly, you will begin to translate increasingly unadapted Latin texts as you transition out of this last year of logic-stage Latin. Memorizing a few Latin words to improve your English vocabulary was never the goal (although it is a side benefit). Reading, savoring, and feasting upon Latin history, poetry, speeches, and theology can all be yours. It's just a few battles away.

Ex animō,
Natali H. Monnette,
Magistra Discipulaque

Pronunciation Guide

By now you have settled in to your own Latin pronunciation. The following is meant to serve as a reminder of the classical pronunciation, although keep in mind that there are other schools of thought. The main thing is to ensure the Latin sounds beautiful as you say or read it.

Vowels

Vowels in Latin have only two pronunciations, long and short. When speaking, long vowels are held twice as long as short vowels. Long vowels are marked with a "macron" or line over the vowel (e.g., ā). Vowels without a macron are short vowels.

When spelling a word, including the macron is important, as it can clarify the meaning of the word (e.g., *liber* is a noun meaning "book," and *līber* is an adjective meaning "free").

LONG VOWELS		SHORT VOWELS	
ā	like a in father: *frāter, suprā*	a	like a in idea: *canis, mare*
ē	like e in obey: *trēs, rēgīna*	e	like e in bet: *et, terra*
ī	like i in machine: *mīles, vīta*	i	like i in this: *hic, silva*
ō	like o in holy: *sōl, glōria*	o	like o in domain: *bonus, scopulus*
ū	like oo in rude: *flūmen, lūdus*	u	like u in put: *sum, sub*
ȳ	like i in chip: *grȳps, cȳgnus*		

Diphthongs

A combination of two vowel sounds collapsed together into one syllable is a diphthong:

ae	like *ai* in aisle: *caelum, saepe*	eu	like eu in eulogy: *Deus*
au	like *ou* in house: *laudō, nauta*	oe	like oi in oil: *moenia, poena*
ei	like *ei* in reign: *deinde*	ui	like ew in chewy: *huius, huic*

Consonants

Latin consonants are pronounced like English consonants, with the following exceptions:

c	like *c* in come	never soft like city, cinema, or peace
g	like *g* in go	never soft like gem, geology, or gentle
v	like *w* in wow	never like Vikings, victor, or vacation
s	like *s* in sissy	never like easel, weasel, or peas
ch	like ch in chorus	never like church, chapel, or children
r	is trilled	like a dog snarling or a machine gun
i	like y in yes	when used before a vowel at the beginning of a word or between two vowels within a word (otherwise it's usually a vowel)

1 Unit One

UNIT 1: GOALS

Lessons 1–8

By the end of Unit 1, students should be able to . . .

- Form and use present, perfect, and future infinitives
- Understand, form, and translate impersonal verbs
- Understand, form, and translate the dative of reference
- Understand, form, and translate reflexive pronouns and adjectives
- Understand, form, and translate indirect statements (accusative and infinitive)
- Understand, form, and translate the supine
- Understand and form the subjunctive in the present, imperfect, perfect, and pluperfect in both active and passive
- Understand and form the subjunctive of irregular verbs *sum* and *possum*
- Understand and translate the hortatory/jussive subjunctive
- Understand and translate purpose clauses
- Understand and translate result clauses
- Understand and translate the prohibitive subjunctive
- Understand sequence of tenses
- Understand and translate *cum* clauses

LESSON 1

Verbs: Infinitives & Impersonal Verbs; Nouns: Dative of Reference

Word List

Nouns

1. cōgitātiō, -tiōnis (f) *thought, opinion*
2. daemonium, -iī (n) *demon, evil spirit*
3. iūdex, -dicis (m) *judge*
4. platēa, -ae (f) *street, broad way*
5. quisquam, quidquam/quicquam *anyone, anything, someone, something*
6. sabbatum, -ī (n) *the Sabbath (often plural with singular meaning)*

Verbs

7. coepī, coepisse, coeptum (defective) *I began, undertook*
8. decet, -ēre, decuit (impers. +acc.) *it is fitting, proper, suitable, right*
9. dīligō, -ere, -lēxī, -lēctum *I choose out, love; perf. pass. part.* dīlēctus, -a, -um *(adj.) beloved*
10. edō, -ere, ēdī, ēsum *I eat, devour*
11. ēligō, -ere, -lēgī, -lēctum *I pick out, choose, elect*
12. licet, -ēre, licuit, licitum (impers. +dat./acc.) *it is permitted, lawful, allowed*
13. oportet, -ēre, oportuit, -tuitum (impers. +acc.) *it is proper, necessary*
14. placeō, -ēre, -cuī, -citum *I please, am pleasing (often impers.* placet/placuit *[+dat.])*
15. spērō (1) *I hope, expect*

Adjectives

16. necesse (n, indecl.) *necessary, unavoidable;* necesse est (impers. +dat./acc.), *it is necessary*
17. impius, -a, -um *irreverent, wicked, impious*

Adverbs

18. at *yet, but*
19. haud *not at all, by no means*
20. pariter *equally*

Memorization

This unit's memorization is a familiar Bible passage, John 1:1–14. This lesson's portion is verses 1–3a. Verse numbers are provided to help, but you don't have to memorize them.

> **[1] In principio erat Verbum et Verbum erat apud Deum et Deus erat Verbum. [2] Hoc erat in principio apud Deum. [3] Omnia per ipsum facta sunt,**
>
> *[1] In the beginning was the Word and the Word was with God and the Word was God* [or, *God was the Word*]. *[2] This/He was in the beginning with God. [3] All things were made by/through Him,*

Grammar

Kraken Latin 2, Unit 2 focused heavily on the formation and usage of participles. In this unit, we will of course be continuing to use participles, but we will move on to two other verb moods. The first few lessons of the unit we will spend reviewing verbs and nouns, and then we will review and expand our use of the infinitive, and then we will move on to introducing the subjunctive (fear not; its name is more intimidating than its forms and usage!). Once you have mastered the subjunctive, you will basicaly know all Latin grammar.

Verbs—Infinitives

In this unit we will be continuing to use participles as we did in *Kraken Latin 2*, but we will also move on to two other verb moods. The first few lessons of the unit we will spend reviewing verbs and nouns, and then we will review and expand our use of the infinitive, and then we will move on to introducing the subjunctive (fear not; its name is more intimidating than its forms and usage!). Once you have mastered the subjunctive, you will basicaly know all Latin grammar.

In the "Latin Grammar Basics" introduction, an infinitive was initially defined as "The basic form of the verb in Latin—the 'to' form; so called because it is not bound by person and number and therefore is 'infinite'." Since we have progressed in our grammatical knowledge, we can enhance this definition by saying that *a Latin infinitive is a verbal noun not bounded by person or number; the second principal part of the verb.*

The phrase "verbal noun" should sound familiar; a gerund is a verbal noun while participles (including gerundives) are verbal adjectives. Like the gerund, then, the infinitive has qualities of both a noun and a verb. It can function as the subject of a sentence, for example: *To kill dragons is good.* Notice that in this example sentence it was also acting as a verb, because it took the direct object "dragons." Infinitives can also be modified by adverbs: *To kill dragons justly is good.*

Thus far we have only dealt with present infinitives, both active and passive (and deponent, of course). The Latin infinitive also exists in the perfect active and passive, as well as the future active and passive.

Let's review how to form the **present passive infinitive**. As with other verb moods in the present, you must find the present stem by going to the 2nd principal part (the present active infinitive) and removing the *–re*. Then for a passive infinitive, you simply add *–rī* to the stem in the 1st, 2nd, and 4th conjugations, and just an *–ī* for 3rd and 3rd *–iō* conjugations. We should be very familiar with this by now, and with the translations:

Oswaldus necāre hunc dracōnem debet. Oswald ought to kill this dragon.

Hic dracō necārī ab Oswaldō debet. This dragon ought to be killed by Oswald.

The **perfect active infinitive** is formed from the perfect active stem. Go to the 3rd principal part and remove the *–ī*. For example, the perfect stem of *necō* is *necāv-*. The only new form that you have to learn in this lesson is the ending *–isse*, which you add to the perfect stem to get *necāvisse*. The **perfect passive infinitive** is formed using the same principle as the perfect passive indicative. With the perfect passive indicative, you use the perfect passive participle plus the helping verb *sum* in the indicative (*necātus/a/um sum*). With the perfect passive infinitive, you take the perfect passive participle with the helping verb sum in the infinitive: *necātus/a/um esse*. To translate these, we must indicate past action while still using an infinitive form, and happily in English we use such past infinitives all the time:

Oswaldus necāvisse hunc dracōnem debet. Oswald ought to have killed this dragon.

Hic dracō necātum esse ab Oswaldō debet. This dragon ought to have been killed by Oswald.

The **future active infinitive** is formed similarly by taking the future active participle along with the infinitive of *sum*: *necātūrus/a/um esse*. You will not be required to know the future passive infinitive in this book; the Romans made do with the supine (see Ls. 19; basically looks like the neuter nominative singular of the perfect passive participle, as in *necātum*) plus the present passive (impersonal) infinitive of *eō*. Thus it would look like this: *necātum īrī*. However, this form is uncommon, so don't worry about it.

Latin Infinitive Endings

	INFINITIVE			
	LATIN ACTIVE	ENGLISH ACTIVE	LATIN PASSIVE	ENGLISH PASSIVE
PRES.	*-re* (2nd p.p.)	to X	*-rī/-ī*	to be Xed
PF.	perf. stem + *-isse*	to have Xed	4th p.p. + *esse*	to have been Xed
FUT.	fut. act. prt. + *esse*	to be about to X	(uncommon)	

Here are some sample verbs:

1st Conjugation: *amō, amāre, amāvī, amātum*

	INFINITIVE			
	LATIN ACTIVE	ENGLISH ACTIVE	LATIN PASSIVE	ENGLISH PASSIVE
PRES.	amāre	to love	amārī	to be loved
PF.	amāvisse	to have loved	amātus/a/um esse	to have been loved
FUT.	amātūrus/a/um esse	to be about to love	(uncommon)	

2nd Conjugation: *videō, vidēre, vīdī, vīsum*

	INFINITIVE			
	LATIN ACTIVE	ENGLISH ACTIVE	LATIN PASSIVE	ENGLISH PASSIVE
PRES.	vidēre	to see	vidērī	to be seen, to seem
PF.	vīdisse	to have seen	vīsus/a/um esse	to have been seen, to have seemed
FUT.	visūrus/a/um esse	to be about to see	(uncommon)	

3rd Conjugation: *dūcō, dūcere, dūxī, ductum*

	INFINITIVE			
	LATIN ACTIVE	ENGLISH ACTIVE	LATIN PASSIVE	ENGLISH PASSIVE
PRES.	dūcere	to lead	dūcī	to be led
PF.	dūxisse	to have led	ductus/a/um esse	to have been led
FUT.	ductūrus/a/um esse	to be about to lead	(uncommon)	

3rd *-iō* Conjugation: *capiō, capere, cēpī, captum*

	INFINITIVE			
	LATIN ACTIVE	ENGLISH ACTIVE	LATIN PASSIVE	ENGLISH PASSIVE
PRES.	capere	to capture	capī	to be captured
PF.	cēpisse	to have captured	captus/a/um esse	to have been captured
FUT.	captūrus/a/um esse	to be about to capture	(uncommon)	

4th Conjugation: *audiō, audīre, audīvī, audītum*

	INFINITIVE			
	LATIN ACTIVE	ENGLISH ACTIVE	LATIN PASSIVE	ENGLISH PASSIVE
PRES.	audīre	to hear	audīrī	to be heard
PF.	audīvisse	to have heard	audītus/a/um esse	to have been heard
FUT.	audītūrus/a/um esse	to be about to hear	(uncommon)	

Review of Infinitive Usage

Thus far we have seen the complementary infinitive, which completes the meaning of the main verb, as in one of the previous examples: *Oswaldus necāre hunc dracōnem debet.* "Oswald ought to kill this dragon." What exactly ought Oswald to do? The verb *debet* is completed by explaining that he ought to kill the dragon.

The infinitive can also be used instead of the gerund as the subject or direct object of a sentence:

Necāre malōs dracōnēs est bonum. To slay (Slaying) evil dragons is good.

Oswaldus malōs dracōnēs necāre amat. Oswald loves to slay (slaying) evil dragons.

Enjoy these simple review usages and make sure you are thoroughly familiar with the various tenses and forms. One way to ensure this familiarity is of course our old friend the synopsis. We have now expanded it to include all the infinitives. As with participles, an infinitive doesn't have a person, so just give the basic infinitive form (plural in the case of the compound infinitives in the perfect passive and future active).

Synopsis of *ēligō* in the 1st person plural: *ēligō, ēligere, ēlēgī, ēlectum*

		LATIN ACTIVE	ENGLISH ACTIVE	LATIN PASSIVE	ENGLISH PASSIVE
INDICATIVE	PRES.	ēligimus	we choose	ēligimur	we are chosen
	IMPF.	ēligēbāmus	we were choosing	ēligēbāmur	we were (being) chosen
	FUT.	ēligēmus	we will choose	ēligēmur	we will be chosen
	PF.	ēlēgimus	we chose/have chosen	ēlectī/ae/a sumus	we were/have been chosen
	PLPF.	ēlēgerāmus	we had chosen	ēlectī/ae/a erāmus	we had been chosen
	FT. PF.	ēlēgerimus	we will have chosen	ēlectī/ae/a erimus	we will have been chosen
PART.	PRES.	ēligentēs, -ntium	choosing		
	PF.			ēlectī, -ae, -a	(having been) chosen
	FUT.	ēlectūrī, -ae, -a	about to choose	ēligendī, -ae, -a	(about) to be chosen
INF.	PRES.	ēligere	to choose	ēligī	to be chosen
	PF.	ēlēgisse	to have chosen	ēlectī/ae/a esse	to have been chosen
	FUT.	ēlectūrī/ae/a esse	to be about to choose		
IMP.	SG.	ēlige!	choose!	ēligere!	be chosen!
	PL.	ēligite!	choose! (pl.)	ēligiminī!	be chosen! (pl.)

Verbs—Impersonal Verbs

Several entries in this lesson's word list may look a little odd. Instead of ending in the standard *–ō* or deponent *–r*, these verbs arrive in 3rd person singular (*placeō* is talented and can do both). They are called "impersonal verbs" precisely because they do not have a specific person as their subject. We have a few of these in English: "It's raining" (and other weather phrases); "One could eat heaps of this cake." In the first example, we all know that really the clouds are raining, and we could also say, "The clouds are raining," but the idiomatic way of discussing the weather is to use the impersonal "it." Sometimes we can use the pronoun "one" when we don't need to specify a subject (as in the second example). Nowadays it's probably more common to say "You could eat heaps of this cake," where we don't mean "you personally" (the person to whom we are speaking) but a nebulous, undefined subject.

Latin uses impersonal verbs more readily than English. The "weather usage" (as in "it's raining, it's snowing," etc.) is also found in Latin, but we won't be touching on weather words in this chapter. Often impersonal verbs are accompanied by an infinitive that is actually the subject of that impersonal verb:

> *Decet hunc dracōnem necāre.* It is right to slay this dragon. To slay this dragon is right.
>
> *Oportuit hunc dracōnem necāre.* It was necessary to slay this dragon. To slay this dragon was necessary.

Here is a list of the common impersonal verbs that you will need to add to your vocabulary repertoire this lesson:

8. *decet, -ēre, decuit, ——* (*impers.* +acc.) it is fitting, proper, suitable, right

12. *licet, -ēre, licuit, licitum* (*impers.* +dat./acc.) it is permitted, lawful, allowed

13. *oportet, -ēre, -tuit, -tuitum* (*impers.* +acc.) it is proper, necessary

14. *placeō, -ēre, -cuī, -citum* I please, am pleasing (often impers. *placet/placuit* [+dat.])

16. *necesse est* (*impers.* +dat./acc.) it is necessary

I was unable to find an example of a fourth principal part for *decet*, so I'm assuming it either does not exist or is so uncommon that it isn't worth including for our purposes here. As mentioned before, *placeō* is a verb that can be used personally or impersonally. *Necesse* is a neuter indeclinable adjective, but often appears with *est* and is used impersonally. These verbs take a word in the dative or accusative, or sometimes both. Here are some examples of these impersonal verbs in action:

Sīc enim decet nōs implēre omnem iūstitiam. For thus it is fitting for us to fulfill all righteousness. (from Mattt. 3:15)

Nōn licet tibi habēre eam. It is not lawful for you to have her. (from Matt. 14:4)

Oportet Fīlium hominis multa patī. It is necessary for the Son of Man to suffer many things. Or, The Son of Man must suffer many things. (from Mark 8:31)

Tunc placuit apostolīs...ēligere virōs ex eīs. Then it pleased the apostles to choose men from them. (from Acts 15:22)

Nāvigāre necesse est; vivere nōn est necesse. It is necessary to sail; it is not necessary to live. Or, To sail is necessary; to live is not necessary. (According to Plutarch, Pompey, a member of the first triumvirate, said this to his soldiers when ordering them to bring food from Africa to Rome during a storm.)

Notice that these impersonal verbs, while remaining in the 3rd person singular, can change tenses and appear as infinitives too. Below is a summary of the possible forms for our vocabulary words:

PRES. INDIC.	decet	licet	oportet	placet	vidētur
IMPF. INDIC.	decēbat	licēbat	oportēbat	placēbat	vidēbātur
FUT. INDIC.	decēbit	licēbit	oportēbit	placēbit	vidēbitur
PF. INDIC.	decuit	licuit, licitum est	oportuit	placuit	vīsum est
PLUPF. INDIC.	decuerat	licuerat	oportuerat	placuerat	vīsum erat
FUT. PF. INDIC.	decuerit	licuerit	oportuerit	placuerit	vīsum erit
PRES. SUBJ.*	deceat	liceat	oporteat	placeat	videat
IMPF. SUBJ.*	decēret	licēret	oportēret	placēret	vidēret
PERF. SUBJ.*	decerit	licuerit	oportuerit	placuerit	vīderit
PLUPF. SUBJ.*	decuisset	licuisset	oportuisset	placuisset	vīdisset
PRES. INFIN.	decēre	licēre	oportēre	placēre	vīdērī
PF. INFIN.	decuisse	licuisse	oportuisse	placuisse	vīdisse
FUT. INFIN.	——	licitūrum esse	——	placitūrum esse	vīsūrum esse

*Although the subjunctive hasn't been introduced yet (see Lesson 4), I'm including these forms here for future reference.

So far, so good. Even though we may not use impersonal verbs a whole bunch in English, we can understand what the Latin is getting at. But there is one more interesting feature to impersonal verbs in Latin. Why do *vidētur* and other 3rd person passive forms of *videō* appear in our chart above? Well, sometimes intransitive verbs in the passive are used impersonally. Thus *vidētur* means "it seems . . . ." Another one which might seem strange is *ventum est*, literally meaning "it was come"—but idiomatically meaning "one came" or "they came" depending on the context.

Nouns—Dative of Reference

We now have several uses of the dative in our repertoire: 1. dative as indirect object (*Dedī id tibi*, "I gave it to you"); 2. dative of possession (*Quod tibi nōmen est?* "What is your name?"—literally, "What is the name to you?"); and 3. dative of agent (*Hoc tibi faciendum est*, "You must do this"—literally, "This must be done by you"). Today we add another dative to the list: The Dative of Reference.

Unlike the other dative usages listed above, the dative of reference relies upon the whole meaning of the sentence or clause, rather than hanging upon one word. For instance, in the second example above, *Quod tibi nōmen est?*, the dative *tibi* depends on *nomen*. A dative of reference would look more like one of these examples:

1. *Tibi hunc dracōnem necās.* "You are killing this dragon for yourself." (The "for yourself" refers to the rest of that entire sentence "You are killing this dragon.").

2. *Oswaldus erit mihi semper rēx.* "Oswald will always be a king to me [in my opinion]." This type of dative of refence expresses a person's point of view. We can say something similar in English, as in "Everyone else likes vanilla, but me, I prefer chocolate." The "me" emphasizes that "in my opinion" or "as far as I'm concerned" chocolate is better.

3. The demon-possessed man called Legion says: *"Quid mihi et tibi, Iesu Filī Deī Summī?"* Literally, "What to me and to you, Jesus Son of God Most High?" More idiomatically, "What do you have to do with me, Jesus Son of God Most High?" (Mark 5:7). This dative of reference is a Latin idiom and is used in questions and exclamations.

Now you may have noticed that even though this is a new use of the dative, we are still often translating it with the prepositions "to/for" as we did way back in the day for indirect objects. However, when you see a "for" in English, do not automatically translate the object of that preposition into the Latin dative. Think about what that phrase means as a whole. Thus if we have the sentence "Oswald killed the dragon for me!", the "for me" actually means "for my sake." In this instance, you may not use the dative but should use *prō* plus the ablative, *Oswaldus dracōnem prō mē necāvit.* Another example would be "Jesus died for me" (instead of *mihi*), *Iesus prō mē mortuus est.*

Review

Be sure to review the words *volō, nōlō,* and *mālō.* Also, practice putting a few words in locative, just to keep it fresh in your mind.

Worksheet 1

A. Vocabulary

1. dīligō, dīligere, dīlēxī, ________________: ________________
2. sabbath: ________________
3. at: ________________
4. alius, -ia, -iud (adj.): ________________
5. impius: ________________
6. street: ________________
7. I began: ________________
8. almost: ________________
9. judge: ________________
10. ēligō, ________________, ēlēgī, ēlectum: ________________
11. afterwards: ________________
12. placeō, __________, __________ placitum: ________________
13. haud: ________________
14. necesse (n, indecl.): ________________
15. oportet, oportēre, oportuit (impers. _____): ________________
16. alter, -era, -erum (adj.): ________________
17. it is fitting: ________________
18. equally: ________________
19. licet, licēre, ________, licitum (impers. ____________): ________________
20. occupō:________________
21. demon: ________________
22. I hope: ________________
23. I eat: ________________
24. cōgitātiō: ________________
25. quisquam, quidquam/quicquam (adj.): ________________

B. Grammar

1. Do a synopsis of *dīligō* in the 3rd person plural, first giving principal parts:

____

		LATIN ACTIVE	ENGLISH ACTIVE	LATIN PASSIVE	ENGLISH PASSIVE
INDICATIVE	PRES.				
	IMPF.				
	FUT.				
	PF.				
	PLPF.				
	FT. PF.				
PARTICIPLE	PRES.				
	PF.				
	FUT.				
INFINITIVE	PRES.				
	PF.				
	FUT.				
IMPERATIVE	SG.				
	PL.				

2. Translate these phrases from Latin into English or English into Latin as appropriate, using your new impersonal verbs.

   oportuit nōs iūrāre: ______________________________

   it is fitting for her to love: ______________________________

   necesse tibi spērāre est: ______________________________

   licēbat vōs edere: ______________________________

   it pleases him to cross over: ______________________________

   it will be necessary to decide: ______________________________

   licuit mihi parcere tibi: ______________________________

C. Memorization

Fill in the blanks in John 1:1–3a in Latin.

____ ____________ ______ __________ ____ Verbum _______ _______ Deum ___ _____ ____ Verbum. Hoc ____ __ principio _____ ______. _______ ____ ipsum ______ sunt,

D. Translation

English to Latin

Translate these sentences into Latin, using participles or gerunds where *italicized.*

1. It was fitting for Jesus to cast out very many demons in streets and beside tombs *by speaking* a word to them.

   ____

   ____

   ____

2. The impious judge expects you to have already given him money, and then he will want to hand over mercy to you.

   ____

   ____

   ____

3. It pleases the gods to eat a hundred cookies, and therefore we must offer them on the altar, once they *have been made* by certain mothers equally in our city. (Translate the underlined phrase first with an impersonal verb, and then with a passive periphrastic.)

4. My companions ought not to have spoken [their] true thoughts about the king's *beloved* sheep; yet someone told the king while he *was feeding* them.

5. "What are your names? And what do you have to do with us? What things *must* you *do* here?" the man *enslaved* by the demons began to ask us.

E. Latin to English

Adapted from Matthew 12:1-32

In illo tempore abiit Iesus sabbatis per agros; discipuli autem eius *esurierunt* et coeperunt *vellere spicas* et manducare. *Pharisaei* autem videntes dixerunt ei: "Ecce discipuli tui faciunt, quod non licet facere sabbato." At ille dixit eis: "Non legistis de David? Quid fecit quando *esuriit* et qui cum eo erant? Quomodo intravit in domum Dei et panes propositionis* *comedit*, quod non licebat ei edere neque his, qui cum eo erant, nisi solis sacerdotibus? Aut non legistis in Lege quia sabbatis sacerdotes in templo sabbatum *violant* et sine *crimine* sunt? Dico autem vobis quia templo maior est hic. Scite autem hoc: 'Misericordiam volo et non sacrificium.' Dominus est enim Filius hominis sabbati."

Et inde transiens, venit in *synagogam* eorum; et ecce homo manum habens aridam. Et interrogabant eum dicentes: "Licet sabbatis curare*?", quia *accusare* eum voluerunt. Ipse autem dixit illis: "Qui erit ex vobis homo, qui habens ovem unam et, si ceciderit haec sabbatis in *foveam*, nonne tenebit et *levabit* eam? *Quanto* igitur melior est homo ove! Itaque licet sabbatis bene facere." Tunc ait homini: "*Extende* manum tuam." Et *extendit*, et *restituta est sana* sicut altera. Exeuntes autem Pharisaei consilium faciebant *adversus* eum, quod eum perdere volebant.

Iesus autem sciens *secessit* inde. Et secuti sunt eum multi, et curavit eos omnes et *comminatus est* eis: "Nolite *manifestum* me facere"—et ideo *adimpletus est*, quod dictum est per *Isaiam prophetam* dicentem: "Ecce puer meus, quem elegi, dilectus meus, in quo bene placuit animae meae; ponam Spiritum meum super eum, et iudicium gentibus nuntiabit. Non *contendet* neque clamabit, neque audiet aliquis in plateis vocem eius. *Arundinem quassatam* non franget et *linum fumigans* non *exstinguet*, sed eiciet ad victoriam iudicium; et in nomine eius gentes sperabunt."

Tunc oblatus est ei daemonium habens, caecus et *mutus*, et curavit eum, et *mutus* locutus est et vidit. Et miratae sunt omnes turbae et dicebant: "Numquid hic est filius David?" Pharisaei autem audientes dixerunt: "Hic non eicit daemones nisi in *Beelzebul*, principe daemonum."

Sciens autem cogitationes eorum dixit eis: "Omne regnum *divisum* contra *se desolatur*, et omnis civitas vel domus divisa contra se non stabit. Et si *Satanas Satanam* eicit, *adversus* se *divisus* est; quomodo ergo stabit regnum eius? Et si ego in *Beelzebul* eicio daemones, filii vestri in quo eiciunt? Ideo ipsi iudices erunt vestri. Si autem in Spiritu Dei ego eicio daemones, igitur pervenit in vos regnum Dei. Aut quomodo potest quisquam intrare in domum fortis et *vasa* eius *diripere*, nisi prius *alligaverit* fortem? Et tunc domum illius *diripiet*. Qui non est mecum, contra me est; et, qui non congregat mecum, *spargit*. Ideo dico vobis: Omne *peccatum* et *blasphemia* dimittetur hominibus, Spiritus autem *blasphemia* non dimittetur. Et quicumque dixerit verbum contra Filium hominis, dimittetur ei; qui autem dixerit contra Spiritum Sanctum, non dimittetur ei neque in hoc saeculo neque in *futuro*."

Notes:
* *pānēs:* can also mean "loaf," which works better here
* *prōpositiōnis: prōpositiō* a setting forth, proposition. Here with ***pānēs***, the "loaves of the setting forth" are of course the "showbread" (a much shorter and snappier way to put it)
* *cūrāre: cūrō* can also mean "I heal, cure"

Glossary:
accūsō (1): I accuse
adimpleō, -ēre, -ēvī, -ētum: I fill up, fulfill
adversus (+acc.): against
alligō (1): I bind up, tie up
arundō, -inis (f): reed
Beelzebul, -ulis (m) (sometimes indecl.): Beelzebub
blasphēmia, -ae (f): blasphemy, slander
comedō, -ere, -ēdī, -ēsus: I eat up, consume (compound of *edō*)
comminor, -ārī, -ātus sum: I threaten
contendō, -ere, -tendī, -tentum: I strive, stretch out
crīmen, -minis (n): crime, fault, offence
dēsōlō (1): I leave alone, forsake
dīripiō, -ere, -ripuī, -reptum: I tear apart, plunder
dīvidō, -ere, -vīsī, -vīsum: I divide, separate
ēsuriō, -īre, -iī, -ītum: I hunger, desire food
exstinguō, -ere, -stinxī, -stinctum: I put out, quench, extinguish
extendō, -ere, extendī, extensum: I stretch out
fovea, -ae (f): pit, snare
fūmigō (1): I smoke
futūrum, -ī (n): the future
Isaias, -ae (m): Isaiah (either the prophet or the book)
levō (1): I lift up, raise
līnum, -ī (n): flax
manifestus, -a, -um: manifest, evident
mūtus, -a, -um: mute
peccātum, -ī (n): sin, fault
Pharisaeus: Pharisee
prophēta, -ae (m): prophet, soothsayer
quantō: by how much
quassō (1): I shake violently, batter
restituō, -ere, -stituī, -stitutus: to replace, restore
sānus, -a, -um: whole, healthy
Satanās, -ae (m): Satan
sēcēdō, -ere -cessī, -cessum: I withdraw, go apart
spargō, -ere, sparsī, sparsum: I scatter
spīca, -ae (f): point, head (of grain), ear (of corn)
suī, sibi, sē, sē (reflexive pronoun): himself, herself, itself
synagōga, -ae (f): synagogue
vās, vāsis; pl. vāsa, -ōrum (n): vessel, equipment
vellō, -ere, vulsī/vellī, vulsum: I pluck, pull
violō (1): I violate, profane, dishonor

Lesson 2

Nouns/Adjectives: Reflexive Pronouns and Adjectives; Verbs: Indirect Statement (Accusative and Infinitive)

Word List

Nouns/Pronouns

1. collis, collis (m) *hill*
2. fās (n, indecl.) *divine law;* (usu. transl. as adj.) *lawful, permitted, possible*
3. memoria, -ae (f) *memory, remembrance*
4. nefās (n, indecl.) *sin, crime;* (when transl. as adj.) *forbidden*
5. numerus, -ī (m) *number*
6. pecus, -coris (n) *cattle, herd*
7. quisque, quaeque, quidque (pron.) and quodque (adj.) *each (one), every(one)*
8. ——, suī (3rd person reflexive pron.) *himself, herself, itself, themselves*

Adjectives

9. crēber, -bra, -brum *thick, frequent, numerous*
10. īdem, eadem, idem *the same*
11. suus, -a, -um (3rd person reflexive possessive adj.) *his (own), her (own), its (own), their (own)*

Verbs

12. consūmō, -ere, -sūmpsī, -sūmptum *I consume, spend, invest*
13. incolō, -ere, -coluī, -cultum *I dwell in, inhabit, cultivate*
14. inferō, -ferre, intulī, illātum (+dat. or +ad/in+acc.) *I bring in, carry in*
15. intellegō, -ere, -lēxī, -lēctum *I understand, perceive*
16. iubeō, -ēre, iūssī, iūssum *I order, command*
17. redeō, -īre, -iī, -itum *I go back, come back, return*
18. resistō, -ere, -stitī, —— *I stand back/still, halt*
19. ūtor, ūtī, ūsus sum (+abl.) *I use, enjoy*

Adverbs

20. eōdem (adv.) *in the same place, to the same place/purpose*

Memorization

John 1:1–5

> [1] In principio erat Verbum et Verbum erat apud Deum et Deus erat Verbum. [2] Hoc erat in principio apud Deum. [3a] Omnia per ipsum facta sunt, **[3b] et sine ipso factum est nihil quod factum est. [4] In ipso vita erat et vita erat lux hominum. [5] Et lux in tenebris lucet et tenebrae eam non conprehenderunt.**
>
> *[3b] and without Him nothing was made that was made. [4] In Him was life and the life was the light of men. [5] And the light shines in the darkness, and the darkness did not understand it.*

Grammar

Reflexive Pronouns and Adjectives

A reflexive pronoun or adjective is one that "points back" (*reflectō, -ere, -flēxī, -flexum*, "I turn back") to the subject. In the sentence "Oswald wounded it" (meaning the dragon), the "it" is a regular old pronoun referring to the dragon, but in "Oswald wounded himself," the "himself" is referring to Oswald, the subject. In English we usually indicate a reflexive pronoun by adding that suffix *-self/-selves* to personal pronouns:

> I wounded myself.
>
> You wounded yourself. (2nd person singular)
>
> He wounded himself. She wounded herself. It wounded itself.
>
> We wounded ourselves.
>
> You wounded yourselves. (2nd person plural)
>
> They wounded themselves.

Happily, you already know the reflexive pronouns for 1st person (I, we) and 2nd person (you, you [pl.]), because they are the same as the 1st and 2nd personal pronouns. Thus:

> *Is* mē *vulnerāvit.* He wounded me. *[Ego]* mē *vulnerāvī.* I wounded myself.
>
> *Is* nōs *vulnerāvit.* He wounded us. *[Nōs]* nōs *vulnerāvimus.* We wounded ourselves.
>
> *Is* tē *vulnerāvit.* He wounded you. *[Tū]* tē *vulnerāvistī.* You wounded yourself.
>
> *Is* vōs *vulnerāvit.* He wounded you all. *[Vōs]* vōs *vulnerāvistis.* You all wounded yourselves.

The first sentence of each example above uses a personal pronoun as the direct object; in the second sentence that same pronoun becomes reflexive because now it refers back to the subject. If you are the sort of person who must have a chart to visualize these reflexives, here you go:

Reflexive Pronoun

	1ST PERSON		2ND PERSON	
	SING.	PL.	SING.	PL.
NOM.	——	——	——	——
GEN.	meī	nostrī	tuī	vestrī
DAT.	mihi	nōbīs	tibi	vōbīs
ACC.	mē	nōs	tē	vōs
ABL.	mē	nōbīs	tē	vōbīs

You may have noticed that these reflexive pronouns do not have a nominative. Before you start to fret, just think about it for a minute: since a reflexive pronoun by its very nature must point back to the subject, it cannot be the subject. (In the example sentences above, I gave the personal subject pronouns in brackets to illustrate the personal pronoun side by side with the reflexive.)

There is a new pronoun to learn for the 3rd person reflexive pronoun, but it's quite simple. As a reminder, we use *is, ea, id* as the 3rd person personal pronoun, and it declines in all three genders in the singular and plural. The reflexive only has four forms to learn:

Reflexive Pronoun (3rd Person)

	SG. OR PL.
NOM.	——
GEN.	suī
DAT.	sibi
ACC.	sē
ABL.	sē

Note that it is the same in the singular and plural. If the subject is singular, then the reflexive will be singular (since it points back to that subject); if the subject is plural, it will be plural. Here are a few examples:

[Is] ***sē*** *vulnerāvit.* He wounded himself. *[Ea]* ***sē*** *vulnerāvit.* She wounded herself. *[Id]* ***sē*** *vulnerāvit.* It wounded itself.

[Eī/Eae/Ea] ***sē*** *vulnerāvērunt.* They wounded themselves.

For 1st and 2nd person, the reflexive possessive adjectives are also the same as the possessive adjectives that we have already learned: *meus, tuus, noster,* and *vester.* For example, you already know how to say "I killed the dragon with my (own) sword": *[Ego] dracōnem meō gladiō necāvī.* In English we can either use "my sword" or make the reflexive possession a bit stronger by saying "my own sword." For 3rd person, the reflexive possessive adjective is *suus, -a, -um,* and declines just like any regular *–us, –a, –um* adjective.

Oswaldus dracōnem suō gladiō necāvit. Oswald killed the dragon with his (own) sword.

Equitēs dracōnem suīs gladiīs necāvērunt. The knights killed the dragon with their (own) swords.

Notice how the Latin possessive pronouns here are far clearer than the English ones. If we simply say, "Oswald killed the dragon with his sword," we might assume that it is Oswald's sword (depending on the context), but it could very well be someone else's sword. In Latin we distinguish the two by using *suus* to refer back to the subject as the possessor, and *eius* or *eōrum* to point to a possessor other than the subject:

Oswaldus dracōnem suō gladiō necāvit. Oswald killed the dragon with his (own) sword.

Oswaldus dracōnem gladiō eius necāvit. Oswald killed the dragon with his [someone else's; e.g., Julius's] sword.

Equitēs dracōnem suīs gladiīs necāvērunt. The knights killed the dragon with their (own) swords.

Equitēs dracōnem gladiīs eōrum necāvērunt. The knights killed the dragon with their [someone else's; e.g., the priests'] swords.

It is important to make sure that you see another difference between these two possessives: *suus, -a, -um* is an adjective and therefore declines to match the noun it is modifying. However, *eius* and *eōrum* are pronouns and are in the genitive case when they are acting as possessives. You should also be forewarned that as neat and tidy as this all seems, sometimes ancient authors use "improper" grammar and might use an *eius* to refer back to the subject, etc. Flow with the context and you will be just fine.

Indirect Statement (Accusative and Infinitive)

And now we come to something completely different. We have already been using direct statement or discourse for quite some time. "I killed the dragon," said Oswald—*"Ego," inquit Oswaldus, "dracōnem necāvī."* But now we need to move on to indirect statement (also called indirect discourse), where one is quoting something that was said or reporting on something that was done: "Oswald said that he killed the dragon," or "The princess hoped that he would kill the dragon." The underlined portions are the indirect statements. The words *said, thought, hoped, wished,* and so forth mean that whatever follows is not itself affirmed by the sentence: it is only asserted or believed by someone else.

In English we show that we are using indirect statement (rather than direct) by not using quotation marks, putting in a "that" (although it can be left out as well), and sometimes changing the tense of the verb (saying ". . . that Oswald would kill the dragon" rather than "Oswald will kill" in direct statement). **In Latin, the subject of the indirect statement is put into the accusative case and the verb into the infinitive mood.** Some examples of this are definitely in order! Here are the two sentences from earlier in this paragraph alongside their direct statement equivalents.

TYPE OF STATEMENT	ENGLISH	LATIN
DIRECT	Oswald said, "I killed the dragon."	*Oswaldus dīxit, "Ego dracōnem necāvī."*
INDIRECT	Oswald said that he killed the dragon.	*Oswaldus dīxit sē dracōnem necāre.*
DIRECT	The princess hoped, "He will kill the dragon."	*Fīlia rēgis sperāvit, "Dracōnem necābit."*
INDIRECT	The princess hoped that he would kill the dragon.	*Fīlia rēgis sperāvit eum dracōnem necātūrum esse.*

A few things to observe. First off, notice how helpful our new reflexive pronoun is going to be. In the first indirect example, *sē* is used because the "he" refers back to the subject of the main clause, Oswald. In the second example, we use *eum* because it refers to Oswald, not to the subject of the main sentence, the princess. Also, notice that a literal translation will usually make no sense in English. *Oswaldus dīxit sē dracōnem necāre* would word-for-word be "Oswald said himself to kill the dragon," while *Fīlia rēgis sperāvit eum dracōnem necātūrum esse* would be "The princess hoped him to be about to kill the dragon." Neither of these makes good English sense!

One way to practice translating these accusative and infinitive statements is to bracket the clause off, and automatically insert a "that." So, when confronted with the sentence *Oswaldus dīxit sē dracōnem necāre,* you should read through the whole thing, and when you see that infinitive at the end, preceded by an accusative, you should bracket that clause off: *Oswaldus dīxit [sē dracōnem necāre].* Then you should translate the main sentence: "Oswald said." Next insert the English "that" to indicate an indirect statement: "Oswald said that . . . ." Now you can look at the indirect statement clause, *sē dracōnem necāre*, and figure out which accusative should be the subject of that infinitive (often it comes first, but context will help out as well).

In our example sentences, we have already seen that the tense of the infinitive, like the tense of participles, is relative to the main verb. In our first example, *Oswaldus dīxit sē dracōnem necāre,* that present infinitive *necāre* occurs at the same time as *dīxit*: "Oswald said that he killed the dragon." But in the next example, *Fīlia rēgis sperāvit eum dracōnem necāturum esse,* the future infinitive *necātūrum esse* indicates action in the future of that perfect tense main verb *sperāvit*: "The princess hoped that he would kill the dragon." To make sure we are all on the same page, here it is all spelled out (just like participles!):

Present Infinitive: happens at the same time as the main verb

Perfect Infinitive: happens before the main verb does (in the main verb's past)

Future Infinitive: happens after the main verb does (in the main verb's future)

And here is a chart with examples of each tense of the infinitive paired with a present, past, and future main verb:

Sequence of Tenses

INFINITIVE	LATIN SENTENCE	ENGLISH TRANSLATION(S)
PRESENT	Fīlia rēgis Oswaldum dracōnem necāre scit.	The princess knows that Oswald is killing the dragon.
	Fīlia rēgis Oswaldum dracōnem necāre scīvit.	The princess knew that Oswald killed/was killing the dragon.
	Fīlia rēgis Oswaldum dracōnem necāre sciet.	The princess will know that Oswald will kill the dragon.
PERFECT ACTIVE	Fīlia rēgis Oswaldum dracōnem necāvisse scit.	The princess knows that Oswald (has) killed the dragon.
	Fīlia rēgis Oswaldum dracōnem necāvisse scīvit.	The princess knew that Oswald had killed the dragon.
	Fīlia rēgis Oswaldum dracōnem necāvisse sciet.	The princess will know that Oswald (has) killed the dragon.
PERFECT PASSIVE	Fīlia rēgis Oswaldum ab dracōne nōn necātum esse scit.	The princess knows that Oswald was/has not been killed by the dragon.
	Fīlia rēgis Oswaldum ab dracōne nōn necātum esse scīvit.	The princess knew that Oswald had not been killed by the dragon.
	Fīlia rēgis Oswaldum ab dracōne nōn necātum esse sciet.	The princess will know that Oswald was/has not been killed by the dragon.
FUTURE ACTIVE	Fīlia rēgis Oswaldum dracōnem necātūrum esse scit.	The princess knows that Oswald will kill the dragon.
	Fīlia rēgis Oswaldum dracōnem necātūrum esse scīvit.	The princess knew that Oswald would kill the dragon.
	Fīlia rēgis Oswaldum dracōnem necātūrum esse sciet.	The princess will know that Oswald will kill the dragon.

Remember that the future passive infinitive is uncommon and so is not included in this book. However, the future passive participle (gerundive) plus *sum* in the infinitive does occur. Here are some examples of this passive periphrastic construction (with dative of agent, naturally) combined with indirect statement:

Fīlia rēgis Oswaldō dracōnem necandum esse scit. The princess knows that Oswald must/ought to/should kill the dragon. [Lit., "The princess knows that the dragon should be killed by Oswald."]

Fīlia rēgis Oswaldō dracōnem necandum fuisse scit. The princess knows that Oswald ought to have/should have killed the dragon. [Lit., "The princess knows that the dragon ought to have been/should have been killed by Oswald."]

What sorts of verbs can be followed by indirect statement? As illustrated in previous examples, verbs having to do with speech, feelings or perception, knowledge, and thought are all commonly followed by accusative and infinitive.

Here is a list of verbs you've already learned (although this is certainly not an exclusive list):

Verbs of speaking or saying: *āiō, dēclārō, dīcō, doceō, cantō, iubeō, iūrō, narrō, nuntiō, moneō, ōrō, petō, respondeō, scribō* [N.B.: capitalize *Inquam* is generally only used with direct quotations.]

Verbs of feeling or perceiving: *audiō, gaudeō, mīror, memoriā teneō, videō* in active or passive (e.g., *vidētur*, "it seems that...")

Verbs of knowing: *cognōscō, intelligō, noscō, sciō*

Verbs of thinking: *cogitō, crēdō, exspectō, spērō*

Impersonal verbs: *decet, licet, oportet*

At the end of this list I threw in impersonal verbs, which (as already discussed) can be translated in English a couple of ways: *Oportet Oswaldum dracōnem necāre*, "It is necessary for Oswald to kill the dragon," or "It is necessary that Oswald kill the dragon."

Review

Be sure to review the forms for *aliquis/aliquī, quīdam,* and *quīcumque.* Also, make a few sentences with the dative of reference in there.

Worksheet 2

A. Vocabulary

1. numerus: ______________________________
2. hill: ______________________________
3. īdem, eadem, idem: ______________________________
4. intellegō, __________, __________, __________: ______________________________
5. fās (n, indecl. or adj.): ______________________________
6. quando: ______________________________
7. consūmō, __________, consūmpsī, __________: ______________________________
8. eōdem (adv.): ______________________________
9. ——, suī (3rd person reflexive pron.): ______________________________
10. aedificō (1): ______________________________
11. incolō, __________, __________, incultum: ______________________________
12. iubeō, iubēre, __________, __________: ______________________________
13. ūtor, ūtī, ūsus sum (____): ______________________________
14. inferō, inferre, __________, __________ (____ or ____ ____): ______________________________
15. nūllus, -a, -um: ______________________________
16. suus, -a, -um (adj.): ______________________________
17. memory: ______________________________
18. quoniam: ______________________________
19. quisque, quaeque, quidque (pron.) and quodque (adj.): ______________________________
20. nefās (n, indecl. or adj.): ______________________________
21. redeō, redīre, rediī, reditum: ______________________________
22. sapiēns, -entis: ______________________________
23. resistō, -ere, -stitī, ——: ______________________________
24. cattle: ______________________________
25. crēber: ______________________________

B. Grammar

1. Rewrite these sentences in English, turning the *italicized* personal pronouns into reflexive pronouns.

   The man aimed for the fly but hit *him* instead.

   ____

   My aunt saw *her* in the mirror.

   ____

   We did not want to find *them* here.

   ____

   After buying the shoes, they were very happy with *them*.

   ____

   ____

   You really do love *her* more than anything in the whole world.

   ____

   I wasn't talking to *him*; I was just talking.

   ____

   The small child just wanted to give *him* a present.

   ____

2. Parse these verbs. For Indicatives, give Person, Number, Tense, Voice, Mood; for Participles, give Gender, Number, Case, Tense, Voice, Mood; and for Infinitives, give Tense, Voice, Mood. Then for each form provide the 1st principal part of the verb it comes from, and translate the form.

VERB	PNTVM OR GNCTVM OR TVM	1ST PRINC. PT.	TRANSLATION
intellēxisse			
consūmptīs			
oportuit			
iubēbimus			

rediēns			
incultūrōs esse			
ūsī ērunt			
inferre			
dīlecta esse			
resistiterās			

3. Do a synopsis of *inferō* in the 2nd person plural, first giving principal parts:

____

		LATIN ACTIVE	ENGLISH ACTIVE	LATIN PASSIVE	ENGLISH PASSIVE
INDICATIVE	PRES.				
	IMPF.				
	FUT.				
	PF.				
	PLPF.				
	FT. PF.				
PARTICIPLE	PRES.				
	PF.				
	FUT.				

INFINITIVE	PRES.				
	PF.				
	FUT.				
IMPERATIVE	SG.				
	PL.				

4. Decline "the same hill."

	LATIN SINGULAR	LATIN PLURAL
NOM.		
GEN.		
DAT.		
ACC.		
ABL.		
VOC.		

*As with other demonstratives, you probably won't find this in the vocative.

C. Memorization

Fill in the blanks in John 1:1-5 in Latin.

____ ____ ____ ____ ____ Verbum ____ ____ ____ ____
____ ____ Verbum. ____ ____ ____ principio ____ ____. ____ ____
ipsum ____ ____, ____ sine ____ ____ ____ nihil ____ factum ____. ____
____ vita ____ ____ ____ erat ____ ____. ____ lux ____ ____ lucet __
____ eam ____ ____.

D. Latin to English

Put brackets around the indirect statement(s) in both English and Latin, and translate these short sentence sets, paying particular attention to the tense of the infinitives.

1. Is sē eam amāre dēnique intellegit.

   Is sē eam amāvisse dēnique intellegit.

   Is sē eam amātūrum esse dēnique intellegit.

   Is sē eam amāre dēnique intellēxit.

   Is sē eam amāvisse dēnique intellēxit.

   Is sē eam amātūrum esse dēnique intellēxit.

2. Audīmus vōs eadem consumere.

   Audīmus vōs eadem consūmpsisse.

   Audīmus vōs eadem consūmptūrōs esse.

Audiēbāmus vōs eadem consumere.

Audiēbāmus vōs eadem consūmpsisse.

Audiēbāmus vōs eadem consūmptūrōs esse.

3. Dīcisne mē impium esse?

Dīcisne mē impium fuisse?

Dīcisne mē impium futūrum esse?

Dīxistīne mē impium esse?

Dīxistīne mē impium fuisse?

Dīxistīne mē impium futūrum esse?

4. Eōs pecore ūtī mīrantur.

Eōs pecore ūsōs esse mīrantur.

Eōs pecore ūsūrōs esse mīrantur.

Eōs pecore ūtī mīrātī sunt.

Eōs pecore ūsōs esse mīrātī sunt.

Eōs pecore ūsūrōs esse mīrātī sunt.

5. Vidētur eās crēbra inferre.

Vidētur eās crēbra intulisse.

Vidētur eās crēbra illatūrās esse.

Vidēbatur eās crēbra inferre.

Vidēbatur eās crēbra intulisse.

Vidēbatur eās crēbra illatūrās esse.

You get a break from participles this lesson. Translate these short little indirect statements into English.

6. It was necessary that each one dwell in the same place.

7. The demons perceived that He would throw them out.

8. He believes that he (himself) was not born there.

9. I heard that his memory was pleasing to you.

10. They say that they'll eat their own cattle.

E. Latin to English

Adapted from Caesar's *Commentarii de Bello Gallici (Gallic Wars)*, Book VI.11ff. This passage describes part of Caesar's invasion of Britain, beginning with a storm that destroyed many of his ships soon after their arrival.

His rebus cognitis, Caesar *legiones equitatumque revocari* atque in itinere resistere iubet; ipse ad naves revertitur. *Perspicit,* amissis circa XL navibus, reliquas tamen *refici* posse magno labore visas esse. Itaque ex legionibus *fabros* eligit et ex *continenti* alios mitti iubet. Ipse, *etsi* res erat multae operae ac laboris,* tamen *commodissimum* esse constituit omnes naves *subduci* et cum castris una *munitione coniungi.* In his rebus circa dies X consumit, et deinde ipse eodem unde redierat proficiscitur.

Britanniae pars *interior* ab eis incolitur quos natos esse in insula ipsi memoria traditum esse dicunt*; pars *maritima* ab eis qui praedae ac belli inferendi causa ex *Belgio* transierunt, et bello illato ibi permanserunt atque agros colere coeperunt. Hominum est *infinita* multitudo creberrimaque *aedificia Gallicis* simillima, et pecorum magnus numerus. Nascitur ibi *plumbum* album in *mediterraneis regionibus,* in maritimis ferrum, sed eius *exigua* est copia; *aere* utuntur *importato. Materia* cuiusque generis ut in Gallia est, praeter *fagum* atque *abietem. Leporem* et *gallinam* et *anserem* edere fas esse non putant; haec tamen *alunt voluptatis* causa.

Ex his omnibus longe sunt *humanissimi* qui *Cantium* incolunt, quae regio est maritima omnis, neque multum a Gallico *differunt* more. Interiores plurimi frumenta non *serunt,* sed lacte et carne vivunt *pellibusque* sunt induti. Omnes vero se *Britanni vitro* inficiunt, quod caeruleum efficit *colorem,* atque hoc horrendiores sunt in proelio conspectus*; capilloque sunt promisso* atque omni parte corporis rasa* praeter caput et *labrum* superius. Uxores habent *deni duodēnique* inter se *communes* et maxime fratres cum fratribus *parentesque* cum liberis.

Equites hostium *essedariique acriter* proelium cum *equitatu* nostro in itinere pugnaverunt, tamen nostri omnibus partibus superiores fuerunt atque eos in silvas collesque coegerunt; sed multis interfectis *cupidius* secuti aliquos ex suis *amiserunt.* At illi post hoc subito se pro castris congregati acriter pugnaverunt. Novo genere *pugnae* territis nostris per medios *audacissime* ruperunt seque inde *incolumes* in silvas *receperunt.* Illi pluribus missis *cohortibus* dēnique *repelluntur.*

Toto hoc in genere pugnae intellectum est nostros propter *gravitatem* armorum minus *aptos* esse ad huius generis hostem; equites autem magno cum periculo proelio pugnare. Hostes etiam numquam *conferti* sed *rari* magnisque *intervallis* pugnabant, atque alios alii *deinceps excipiebant, integrique defatigatis succedebant.*

Notes:

* *multae operae ac laboris:* This construction is called a genitive of quality (see, the genitive can be used for expressing things other than possession!).

* Notice the sweet indirect statement within indirect statement (with words reordered): *incolitur ab eīs quōs ipsī dīcunt [memoria traditum esse {nātōs esse in insulā}]*

* *cōnspectus:* acc of respect

* *capillōque...prōmissō:* ablative of quality; lit., "They are with hair having been grown out"="They have long hair."

* *omnī parte...rāsā:* another ablative of quality

Glossary:

abiēs, -etis (f): fir (tree)
ācriter (adv.): from *ācer, ācris, ācre*
aedificium, -iī: building, structure
aes, aeris (n): copper, bronze; money
alō, alere, aluī, altum/alītum: I nourish, feed, cherish
āmittō, -ere, -mīsī, -missum: I send away, lose
ānser, -eris (m): goose
aptus, -a, -um: suitable, suited, fitted
audacissimē (superl. adv.): from *audāx, -ācis* bold, daring
Belgium, -iī (n): Belgium (territory of the Belgae tribe in northern Gaul)
Britannia, -ae (f): Britain
Brittanī, -ōrum (m, pl): the Britons
Cantium, -iī: Kent (county in the southeast corner of Britain)
capillus, -ī (m): hair
cohors, -hortis (f): cohort, Roman military unit usually consisting of 480 footsoldiers; a tenth part of a legion
color, -ōris (m): color
commodus, -a, -um: suitable, convenient
commūnis, -e: common
confertus, -a, -um: crowded, close (together)
coniungō, -ere, -iūnxī, -iūnctum: I join (together), unite, connect
continēns, -entis (f): continent, mainland
cupidius: comp. adv. from *cupidus, -a, -um* eager, zealous
dēfatīgō (1): I tire (out), exhaust
deinceps: successively, in turn
dēnī, -ae, -a: ten at a time, ten each
differō, -ferre, distulī, dīlātum: I separate, differ
duodēnī, -ae, -a: twelve at a time, twelve each
efficiō, -ere, -fēcī, -fectum: I effect, cause, accomplish
equitātus, -ūs (m): cavalry
essedarius, -ī (m): charioteer (fighter in a war-chariot, not just a driver); gladiator
etsi: although, though
excipiō, -ere, -cēpī, -ceptum: I take out, relieve
exiguus, -a, -um: meager, scanty
faber, -brī (m): worker, carpenter, smith
fāgus, -ī (f): beech (tree)
Gallicus, -a, -um: Gallic, of/belonging to the Gauls
gallīna, -ae (f): hen
gravitās, -tātis (f): weight, heaviness
hūmānus, -a, -um: human, humane, cultured
importō (1): I carry in, import
incolumis, -e: safe, unharmed
inficiō, -ere, -fēcī, -fectum: I put/dip in, dye
infīnītus, -a, -um: boundless, infinite
integer, -tēgra, -tēgrum: whole, fresh, untouched
interior, -ius (gen. –teriōris): inner, interior
intervāllum, -ī (n): interval, distance (of space or time)
lābrum, -ī (n): lip
legiō, -ōnis (f): legion (usually consisting of 10 cohorts, each with 480 footsoldiers; plus 300 horsemen), army
lepus, -oris (m): hare
maritimus, -a, -um: of/belonging to the sea
māteria, -ae (f): material, timber
mediterrāneus, -a, -um: inland
mūnītiō, -ōnis (f): fortification, bulwark
parēns, -entis (m/f): parent
pellis, -is (f): skin, hide
perspiciō, -ere, -spēxī, -spectum: I perceive, ascertain
plumbum, -ī (n): lead
prōmittō, -ere, -mīsī, -missum: I send forth, let grow
pugna, -ae (f): fight, battle
rādō, -ere, rāsī, rāsum: I shave
rārus, -a, -um: thin, scattered
recipiō, -ere, -cēpī, -ceptum: I take back; with *sē*, I withdraw, retreat
reficiō, -ere, -fēcī, -fectum: I remake, repair
regiō, -ōnis (f): boundary, territory, region
repellō, -ere, reppulī, repulsum: I drive back, push back, repel
revocō (1): I call back, call again
serō, -ere, sēvī, satum: I sow, plant
subdūcō, -ere, -dūxī, -ductum: I draw up, haul up
succedō, -ere, -cessī, -cessum: I succeed, replace
vitrum, -ī (n): woad (the plant Isatis tinctoria and the blue dye derived from its leaves)
voluptās, -tātis (f): pleasure, enjoyment

Lesson 3

Supine; Review of Indirect Statement

Word List

Nouns

1. aura, -ae (f) *breeze, air, heaven*
2. custōs, -ōdis (m/f) *guard, watch(man), defender*
3. līmen, -minis (n) *threshold, doorway, house*
4. onus, oneris (n) *burden, load*
5. umbra, -ae (f) *shadow, shade, ghost*

Adjective

6. mīrābilis, -e *marvelous, wonderful*

Verbs

7. absum, -esse, āfuī, āfutūrum *I am absent, am away (from)*
8. adsum, -esse, adfuī, adfutūrum *I am present, am at/near*
9. custōdiō, -īre, -iī/-īvī, -ītum *I guard, watch, defend, keep*
10. for, fārī, fātus sum *I say, speak, prophesy*
11. negō (1) *I say no, deny (often used instead of* nōn dīcō*)*
12. nesciō, -īre, -iī/-īvī, -ītum *I do not know, am ignorant (of)*
13. putō (1) *I consider, think, suppose*
14. sentiō, -īre, sēnsī, sēnsum *I feel, realize, perceive*

Adverbs

15. ferē *nearly, almost*
16. frustrā *in vain, in error*
17. longē *a long way off, far off*
18. rursum/rursus *back(wards), again*
19. subitō/subitum *suddenly, unexpectedly, immediately*
20. vix, *scarcely, hardly*

Memorization

John 1:1–7

[1] In principio erat Verbum et Verbum erat apud Deum et Deus erat Verbum. [2] Hoc erat in principio apud Deum. [3] Omnia per ipsum facta sunt, et sine ipso factum est nihil quod factum est. [4] In ipso vita erat et vita erat lux hominum. [5] Et lux in tenebris lucet et tenebrae eam non conprehenderunt. **[6] Fuit homo missus a Deo cui nomen erat Iohannes. [7] Hic venit in testimonium ut testimonium perhiberet de lumine ut omnes crederent per illum.**

[6] There was a man sent from God whose name was John. [7] He came for a witness, to bear witness about the light so that all might believe through him.

Grammar

Supine

You may still be reeling from the non-literal translating of the accusative and infinitive. Thus you have another lesson to allow this concept to settle, while we introduce a very minor new grammatical tidbit: the supine. The supine may sound intimidating, but it is quite easily dealt with. The supine is a verbal noun (like the gerund), having qualities of both verbs and nouns. It is a 4th declension noun derived from the 4th principal part of the verb, and—this is the very joyous part—only has two forms, the accusative and ablat

	LATIN SINGULAR	LATIN PLURAL
NOM.	—	—
GEN.	—	—
DAT.	—	—
ACC.	-um	—
ABL.	-ū	—

To find the proper stem to form the supine, go to the 4th principal part and remove the *-um* (which as you remember is short for *-us, -a, -um*). Then add the *-um* for the accusative supine and *-ū* for the ablative supine. Here are example verbs from each conjugation:

amō, -āre, -āvī, -ātum → amāt- → amātum, amātū

videō, -ēre, vīsī, vīsum → vīs- → vīsum, vīsū

dīcō, -ere, dīxī, dictum → dict- → dictum, dictū

faciō, -ere, fēcī, factum → fact- → factum, factū

inveniō, -īre, -vēnī, -ventum → invent- → inventum, inventū

(You've probably noticed that the accusative supine comes out looking exactly the same as the 4th principal part, a.k.a. the perfect passive participle. You will be able to tell these two apart by—what else?—context!)

As promised, the formation of the supine was a cinch. It is also an easy matter to translate this beast:

1. The Supine in the Accusative (*-um*): Expresses purpose after verbs of motion.
2. The Supine in the Ablative (*-ū*): Expresses an ablative of specification. We'll unpack this with examples.

The accusative supine, being a verbal noun, can be followed by an object in whatever case that particular verb takes.

Examples of the Supine in the Accusative

LATIN	ENGLISH
Oswaldus necātum dracōnem vēnit.	"Oswald has come to kill the dragon." Here is an instance where it is easy to tell that *necātum* is the supine and not the perfect passive participle, since you can't translate it as such without saying "the dragon having been killed," which should be an ablative absolute anyway (*necātō dracōne*).
Sacerdōs vīsum suum domum redierat.	"The priest had returned to see his home."
Capta fēmina servītum rēgī aliēnō ībit.	"The captured woman will go to serve the foreign king." Note that since *serviō* takes dative, its supine *servītum* is also followed by the dative *rēgī aliēnō.*

Examples of the Supine in the Ablative

LATIN	ENGLISH
Tum Oswaldus dracōnem—horrendum visū!—volantem suprā spectāvit.	"Then Oswald looked at the dragon—horrible to see!—flying above." Often the ablative supine will appear in this interjectory fashion.
Hoc est nefās dictū.	"This is forbidden to speak of." Or, "It is forbidden to speak of this."
Mīrābile audītū, carmen pīrātae erat pucherrimum trīstissimumque.	"Marvelous to hear, the pirate's song was very beautiful and sad."

You may have noticed that in all of the example sentences, the supine (whether accusative or ablative) was translated with an English infinitive "to X." This will generally work, but feel free to get creative and poetic as needed to make your translation sound better.

The ablative supine most commonly appears with a handful of adjectives as well as a few nouns (*fās, nefās,* and *opus*). Unlike the accusative supine, which can be followed by an object, the ablative supine never takes an object. In addition, not every verb occurs in the ablative supine in the corpus of Latin literature. Some common ones from verbs that you have already learned are *audītū, dictū, factū, inventū, nātū,* and *vīsū*. Other verbs do appear in the ablative supine (such as *cognītū, intellectū, inventū,* and *scītū*, along with a few others), but not as frequently.

Finally, remember that *ad* + gerund/gerundive can also indicate purpose. So now we have two different ways to show purpose (three if you include that occasional use of the future active participle), although of course the accusative supine must be accompanied by a verb of motion.

Review

Be sure to review how to form all your infinitives, and put the reflexive in all four available cases.

Worksheet 3

A. Vocabulary

1. suddenly: ____________________
2. adsum, adesse, __________, ______________: ____________________
3. putō (1): ____________________
4. guard: ____________________
5. ferē: ____________________
6. I do not know: ____________________
7. absum, __________, āfuī, ______________: ____________________
8. a long way off: ____________________
9. for, fārī, fātus sum: ____________________
10. negō (1): ____________________
11. apud (+acc.): ____________________
12. breeze: ____________________
13. often: ____________________
14. sentiō, __________, __________, __________: ____________________
15. threshold: ____________________
16. cōnor, -ārī, cōnātus sum: ____________________
17. trādō, -ere, -didī, -ditum: ____________________
18. mīrābilis, -e: ____________________
19. again: ____________________
20. I guard: ____________________
21. vix: ____________________
22. sīc: ____________________
23. in vain: ____________________
24. burden: ____________________
25. shadow: ____________________

B. Grammar

1. Translate these supine phrases.

   dictū mīrābile ______________________________

   profecta ēs quaesītum ______________________________

   horrendus vīsū ______________________________

   dictū nefās ______________________________

   consūmptum exeunt ______________________________

   vīsū facilis ______________________________

   ascendētis cāntum ______________________________

2. Decline these noun-adjective pairs in Latin by way of review.

   thick shadow

	LATIN SINGULAR	LATIN PLURAL
NOM.		
GEN.		
DAT.		
ACC.		
ABL.		
VOC.		

   marvelous threshold

	LATIN SINGULAR	LATIN PLURAL
NOM.		
GEN.		
DAT.		
ACC.		
ABL.		
VOC.		

3. Do a synopsis of *adsum* in the 2nd person plural, first giving principal parts:

____

		LATIN ACTIVE	ENGLISH ACTIVE	LATIN PASSIVE	ENGLISH PASSIVE
INDICATIVE	PRES.				
	IMPF.				
	FUT.				
	PF.				
	PLPF.				
	FT. PF.				
PARTICIPLE	PRES.				
	PF.				
	FUT.				
INFINITIVE	PRES.				
	PF.				
	FUT.				
IMPERATIVE	SG.				
	PL.				

C. Memorization

Fill in the blanks in John 1:1-7 in Latin.

_____ ______________ _______ ___________ _____ ___________ _______ ________ ________ ________

________ _______ _____________. _______ _______ _____ _________________ ________ ___________.

___________ ______ ___________ ________ ______, _____ _______ ________ ___________ ______

________ _______ ____________ ______. _____ ________ _______ _______ _____ _______ ______ _____

_______________. ______ ______ _____ ____________ _______ _____ _____________ _______ _______

________________________. _______ ________ ___________ ___ _______ ______ __________ ________

_____________. _____ ________ _____ ____________________ _____ ________________

_______________ _____ ____________ _____ __________ ______________ _______ ____________.

D. Translation

English to Latin

Translate these sentences into Latin. (Hint: translate *italicized* verbs with Latin participles/gerunds, <u>underlined</u> with infinitives, and **bold** with supines.)

1. Yesterday I suddenly realized that I <u>had</u> never <u>seen</u> a ghost.

   ____

2. The Son of Man came to serve and to give His life for many.

   ____

   ____

3. Once the hill has been captured, we think that the guards will defend their king in vain.

   ____

   ____

4. The same women were prophesying in the streets and then, marvelous to say, the cattle began to fly through the air.

   ____

   ____

5. The impious judge ordered that you <u>*must deny*</u> Christ or you <u>will die</u>.

   ____

   ____

6. When *asked*, each boy told his teacher that he had been at home, but we knew that they had all been away a long way off in the Cave of Plunder.

7. This is the same man who says that ________ for you ________ as many loads as possible.

8. I lifted myself up by *climbing* the wall but could scarcely see the priests *bringing*—forbidden **to speak of**!—burnt offerings to demons.

9. Is it not permitted to walk on this threshold, the god of stone *having fallen* and *breaking* there?

10. Dragons enjoy *burning* things and *eating* sheep and cattle, and understand that they are nearly the greatest and most evil animals in the world.

E. Latin to English

The Escape from Troy, adapted from the *Aeneid* II.671-795

Hinc dexterā* ferrum sumō rursus *clipeumque* sinistrā* mēque domum ferēbam*. Ecce autem *complexa* mē in līmine mea coniunx *Creūsa* parvum mihi tradēbat *Iūlum*: "Si moritūrus abis, et nōs rape in omnia tēcum, sed hanc prīmum servā domum!" Haec loquēbātur et *subitum* dīctūque oritur mīrābile *mōnstrum*. Nam inter manūs trīstēsque vultūs nostrōs, ecce vīsa est ignis *fundere* in capite *Iūlī*, *innoxiaque lambere comās* et caput. Nōs timentēs *comam* torrentem *excutere* et *restinguere* sanctōs aquā ignēs conātī sumus.

At pater *Anchīsēs* laetus ad caelum manūs cum voce tetendit: "*Iuppiter omnipotēns*, spectā nōs, dā deinde auxilium, pater, atque haec sīgna *firmā*." Vix ea fātus erat, subitōque *intonuit* in sinistrō, et dē caelō lapsa per umbrās stella multā cum lūce cucurrit. Vidēmus illam labentem super tecta *clāram* sē occultāre in silvā *Īdaeā sīgnantemque* viam nostram.

Et iam per moenia clārior ignis audītur, propiusque flammae *volvunt*. "Ergo age, cāre pater, circā *cervīcem* meam pōne tua *bracchia*; ipse tē portabō *umerīs*. Mihi parvus *Iūlus* erit comes, et sequētur nostra *vestīgia* coniūnx mea. Vōs, servī, quae dīcam audīte. Est praeter urbem *tumulus* templumque antīquum *Cereris*. Hūc undique congregābimus unā. Tū, pater, cape sacra manū *penātēsque*; mē, ēgressum ex bellō et sanguine tangere nefās est, *donec* mē flūminē vivō lāverō."

Haec fātus, tollō onus et dextram meam parvus *Iūlus* capit; sequitur coniunx. Vadimus per tenēbrās, et mē nunc omnēs terrent *aurae*. Dēnique *propinquābam* portīs, et subitō *sonītum* multōrum *pedum* audīmus. Pater per umbram spectāns, "Nāte," exclamat, "Fuge, nāte; *propinquant*! Ardentēs clipeōs atque *aera micantia* videō!" Hīc forte aliquod mālum nūmen ēripuit meum *confūsum* animum. Nam ex urbe dum ēgredior, heu—aut miserō fatō ērepta est Creūsa, aut errāvit ab viā, seu *lassa* sedit—incertum est. Nec eam *amissam* rēspēxī, sed ad tumulum antiquae Cereris vēnīmus, et hīc, congregatīs omnibus sōla āfuit.

Ascanium Anchīsenque patrem penātēsque tradō sociīs; deinde ipse urbem rursus micantibus armīs petō. Omnia vestīgia nostra *retrō* sequor per noctem, et inde domum—forte, forte illūc reversa erat. Sed videō *Graecōs* vēnisse et tectum omne tenēre; flammae surgunt ad aurās. Deinde arcem ascendō et iam in templō *Iunōnis* custōdēs lectī* *Phoenix* et ferus *Ulixēs* praedam custōdiēbant. Hūc undīque *Troiae* dīvitiae, ex cremātīs ereptae templīs congregantur, et puerī terrītaeque longō ōrdine mātrēs stant circum.

Ausus etiam vocāre per umbram implēvī clāmōre viās, miserque Creūsam frustrā iterumque iterumque vocāvī. Subitō īnfēlix umbra ipsius *Creūsae* mihi quaerentī vīsa est. Mīrātus sum, steteruntque comae et vōx *faucibus haesit*. Tum sīc fāta est hīs dictīs: "Quid tibi placet habēre hunc *insānum dolōrem*, O dulcis coniūnx? Nōn haec sine nūmine deōrum *ēveniunt*; nec tē comitem hinc portāre Creūsam fās est. Longa tibi *exsilia* ferenda sunt, et vastum mare nāvigandum est, et terram *Ītaliae* veniēs. Illīc rēs laetae rēgnumque et rēgīna data est* tibi; *lacrimās* dilēctae dīmitte *Creūsae*. Nōn egō terrās superbās Graecōrum spectābō nec Graecīs servītum* mātribus ibō. Iamque valē et custōdī amōrem nātī* nostrī." Haec ubī dicta dedit, exit in tenuēs aurās *Ter* conātus sum pōnere mea bracchia circum eam; ter frustrā meās manūs *effūgit* umbra Sīc dēnique ad sociōs consūmptā nocte redeō.

Notes:

* *dexterā...sinistrā:* Whenever you see these two adjectives, used in the feminine, they are most likely referring to an implied *manus*, and can be translated simply as "right hand" or "left hand."

* *mē...ferēbam:* When any form of *ferō* appears with a reflexive pronoun (or even in the passive), it basically means "I come/go"; literally it would be "I carry myself" (like the archaic English "I betake myself").

* *lectī:* from legō, -ere, lēxī, lectum (*KL1*, Wk. 28), I choose

* *data est:* Agrees in number and gender with its nearest subject, *rēgina*

* *servitum:* Hey! Look! It's a supine in its natural habitat!!!

* *nātī:* Remember that *nātus* (lit., "one born") can also mean "son."

Glossary:

aes, aeris (n): copper, bronze; money
āmittō, -ere, -mīsī, -missum: I send away, lose
Anchīsēs, -ae (m): Anchises, father of Aeneas
bracchium, -iī (n): arm, forearm
Cerēs, -eris (f): Ceres, Roman goddess of grain and agriculture (Demeter to the Greeks)
cervīx, -vīcis (f): neck
clārus, -a, -um: bright, clear
clipeus (clypeus), -ī (m): shield (a round bronze one; as opposed to the oval *scūtum* made of wood and hide)
coma, -ae: hair
complector, -plectī, -plexus sum: I embrace, hug
confundō, -ere, -fūdī, -fūsum: I pour together, confound, confuse
Creūsa, -ae (f): Creusa, wife of Aeneas and daughter of King Priam of Troy
dolor, -ōris (m): pain, grief
dōnec: until; as long as, while
effugiō, -ere, -fūgī, -fugitum: I escape, flee away
ēveniō, -īre, -vēnī, -ventum: I come to pass, happen
excutiō, -ere, -cussī, -cussum: I shake out/off
exsilium, -iī (n): exile, banishment
faucēs, -ium (f, pl): throat, gullet
firmō (1): I confirm, strengthen
fundō, -ere, fūdī, fūsum: I pour (out), shed
Graecus, -a, -um: Greek
haereō, -ēre, haesī, haesum: I cling, stick
Īdaeus, -a, -um: of (Mount) Ida, a mountain outside of Troy
incertus, -a, -um: uncertain [here used impersonally with *est*]
innoxius, -a, -um: harmless
insānus, -a, -um: insane
intonō, -āre, -uī/-āvī, ——: I thunder, make a noise
Ītalia, -ae (f): Italy
Iūlus, -ī (m): Iulus, also called Ascanius; son of Aeneas and Creusa
Iūno, -ōnis (f): Juno, queen of the gods and wife of Jupiter (called Hera by the Greeks)
Iuppiter, Iovis (m): Jupiter/Jove, king of the gods (called Zeus by the Greeks)
lācrima, -ae (f): tear
lambō, -ere, lambī, lambitum: I lick (up), touch
lassus, -a, -um: tired, weary, faint
micō, -āre, -uī, ——: I glitter, flash
mōnstrum, -ī (n): omen, portent
omnipotēns, -tentis: omnipotent, all-powerful, almighty
penātēs, -ium (m, pl): the Penates, Latin deities of the home/family; household gods
pēs, pedis (m): foot
Phoenīx, -nīcis (m): Phoenix, son of Amyntor, a Greek warrior
propinquō (1) (+dat./acc.): I approach, come near
rēstinguō, -ere, -stinxī, -stinctum: I put out, exstinguish
rētrō: back(ward), behind
sīgnō (1): I mark out, point out
sonitus, -ūs (m): noise, sound
subitus, -a, -um: sudden, unexpected
ter: three times, thrice
Trōius, -a, -um: Trojan
tumulus, -ī (m): tomb, grave mound
Ulixēs, -is (m): Ulysses, a Greek leader (a.k.a. Odysseus)
umerus, -ī (m): shoulder, upper arm
vestīgium, -iī (n): footstep, footprint, track
volvō, -ere, volvī, volūtum: I roll, turn around/over

F. For Fun: Latin Cryptogram

Crack the code of this simple substitution cipher, then translate the various Latin words you have deciphered. Each letter of the alphabet has been substituted for another letter, and you'll be able to figure it out faster if you can discover the code word. I've selected the name of a grammatical concept to serve as the code word, which means its letters will be swapped out for the letters at the beginning of the alphabet, and then the remaining letters of the alphabet will follow in their usual order, omitting letters found in the code word. For example, if the code word were ADVERB, this is how it would look:

A	B	C	D	E	F	G	H	I	J	K	L	M	N	O	P	Q	R	S	T	U	V	W	X	Y	Z
A	D	V	E	R	B	C	F	G	H	I	J	K	L	M	N	O	P	Q	S	U	V	W	X	Y	Z

In this example, A=A, B=D, C=V, and so on. If you were asked to decipher the coded word LRVALS, it would be NECANT, "they kill."

Use this table to work out the key for the exercises below:

A	B	C	D	E	F	G	H	I	J	K	L	M	N	O	P	Q	R	S	T	U	V	W	X	Y	Z

1. ICPRT: ______________________________
2. KLKORTCR: ______________________________
3. GCPNR: ______________________________
4. PKNLCQQN: ______________________________
5. CJENOON: ______________________________
6. JNQPCVCQQN: ______________________________
7. ONICRTH: ______________________________
8. ICGCANON: ______________________________
9. SUNQQN: ______________________________
10. PKJQTHLQCQQN: ______________________________

Lesson 4

Verbs: Present Active & Passive Subjunctive; Present Subjunctive of Irregular Verbs *sum* and *possum*; Hortatory/Jussive Subjunctive

Word List

Nouns

1. auris, -is (f) *ear*
2. dēserta, -ōrum (n, pl) *desert places, wilderness*
3. imāgō, -ginis (f) *image, likeness*
4. prīncipium, -iī (n) *beginning, origin*
5. sīgnum, -ī (n) *sign, signal, miracle*
6. prophēta, -ae (m) *prophet, soothsayer*

Adjectives

7. dēsertus, -a, -um *deserted, solitary, forsaken*
8. ūniversus, -a, -um *all together, whole, entire*

Verbs

9. appāreō, -ēre, -uī, -itum (+dat.) *I appear, am visible (impers.* apparet, *"it is evident/apparent that")*
10. arbitror, -ārī, -ātus sum *I judge, think, suppose*
11. benedīcō, -ere, -dīxī, -dictum (+dat.) *I speak well, bless, praise*
12. cōnfiteor, -fitērī, -fessus sum (+dat./acc.) *I confess, admit*
13. ineō, -īre, -iī (-īvī), -ītum *I go in(to), enter, begin*
14. maledīcō, -ere, -dīxī, -dictum (+dat.) *I speak ill of, curse, slander*
15. requiēscō, -ere, -quiēvī, -quiētum *I rest*
16. ruō, -ere, ruī, rutum [*but* ruitūrus] *I fall down (violently), rush (down), hurl down*
17. sanctificō (1) *I make holy, sanctify*

Adverbs, Conjunctions, and Prepositions

18. nē (adv.) *not, no;* (conj.) *that not, lest*
19. nimis (adv.) *too (much), excessively*
20. usque (adv.) *continuously, constantly;* (prep. + acc.) *all the way up to, as far as*

Memorization

John 1:1–9

> [1] In principio erat Verbum et Verbum erat apud Deum et Deus erat Verbum. [2] Hoc erat in principio apud Deum. [3] Omnia per ipsum facta sunt, et sine ipso factum est nihil quod factum est. [4] In ipso vita erat et vita erat lux hominum. [5] Et lux in tenebris lucet et tenebrae eam non conprehenderunt. [6] Fuit homo missus a Deo cui nomen erat Iohannes. [7] Hic venit in testimonium ut testimonium perhiberet de lumine ut omnes crederent per illum. **[8] Non erat ille lux, sed ut testimonium perhiberet de lumine. [9] Erat lux vera quae inluminat omnem hominem venientem in mundum.**
>
> *[8] He was not the light, but [came] to bear witness concerning the light. [9] This was the true light which shines upon every man coming into the world.*

Grammar: Present Active and Passive Subjunctive

Definition and Formation

This is a momentous lesson. The time has finally come to introduce the final Latin verb mood, the subjunctive. Once you are familiar with the subjunctive, you will be equipped to tackle any passage of real Latin!

Remember that the attributes of the Latin verb: person, number, tense, voice, and mood. The persons are 1st, 2nd, and 3rd, number is singular and plural, the tenses are present, imperfect, future, perfect, pluperfect, and future perfect, voice is active and passive. Thus far the moods we have learend are indicative, imperative, infinitive, participle, and, finally, subjunctive.

English does indeed have a subjunctive, but it is not used as extensively as the Latin subjunctive. Here are some examples of the subjunctive in English, with the indicative verbs given in parentheses to show the difference:

> The king desires that Oswald **kill** the dragon. (Indicative: Oswald **kills** the dragon.)
>
> It is necessary that they **be** brave for this ordeal. (Indicative: They **are** brave.)
>
> I **would say** something else if I **were** you. (Indicative: I say; I was.)

In English, indicative statements are generally statements of fact or questions, while subjunctive statements are about hypothetical, potential, or indirect action. Notice that the English subjunctive is often accompanied by helping verbs such as *would, were, may, might, could, should,* etc. These examples above illustrate the subjunctive in English; the Latin subjunctive will behave somewhat differently.

Subsequent chapters will reveal new ways to express these various flavors of the subjunctive. The Latin subjunctive only comes in four tenses: present, imperfect, perfect, and pluperfect, and in both moods, active and passive. This presents a fantastic opportunity to pull out the chart showing which tense-voice-mood combinations are possible in Latin:

	necō	necāre	necāvī	necātum
DEFINITION/ FUNCTION → FORMATION OF MOODS ↓	1st Sg. Pres. Act. Indic.—*I kill*; helps identify conjug. & shows if pres. stem vowel has contracted	Pres. Act. Infin.—*to kill*; Pres. Stem: necā-	1st. Sg. Pf. Act. Indic.—*I killed, have killed*; Pf. Act. Stem: necav-	Neut. Sg. Nom. Pf. Pass. Pple.—*killed, having been killed*; forms Pf. Passives, so in that sense may be considered Pf. Pass. "Stem"
INDICATIVE		Present Active Present Passive Imperfect Active Imperfect Passive Future Active Future Passive	Perfect Active Pluperfect Active Future Perfect Active	Perfect Passive Pluperfect Passive Future Perfect Passive
IMPERATIVE		Present Active Present Passive Future Active Future Passive		
INFINITIVE		Present Active Present Passive Future Passive	Perfect Active	Perfect Passive Future Active
SUBJUNCTIVE		Present Active Present Passive Imperfect Active Imperfect Passive	Perfect Active Pluperfect Active	Perfect Passive Pluperfect Passive
PARTICIPLE		Present Active Future Passive		Perfect Passive Future Active

In this lesson we will only cover the present subjunctive in the active and passive, but note that all the subjunctives are formed from the same stems as their indicative counterparts: present and imperfect active and passives from the Present Stem (2nd principal part); perfect and pluperfect active from the Perfect Active Stem (3rd principal part); and perfect and pluperfect passives from the Perfect Passive Stem (4th principal part). Nothing new here.

To form the present subjunctive, we first (as always) go to the second principal part to find our present stem. But then we must do something radical to this stem, which has thus far gone untouched. The stem vowel of each conjugation changes to a new vowel or vowels (involving an *ā*, except in the first conjugation). This is how these new vowels shake out:

Subjunctive Stem Vowel Changes/Additions

1st Conjugation: ā → ē

2nd Conjugation: ē → eā

3rd Conjugation: e → ā

3rd -iō Conjugation: e → iā

4th Conjugation: ī → iā

The difference in the present stem for each conjugation will then look like this:

CONJUGATION	PRESENT STEM FOR INDICATIVE, INFINITIVE, IMPERATIVE, AND PARTICIPLE	PRESENT STEM FOR SUBJUNCTIVE
1ST	amāre → amā-	amē-
2ND	vidēre → vidē-	videā-
3RD	dūcere → duce-	ducā-
3RD -IO	capere → cape-	capiā-
4TH	audīre → audī-	audiā-

To this new vowel stem we will then add the usual present endings: *-m* (not *-ō*), *-s*, *-t*, *-mus*, *-tis*, *-nt* for the active and *-r*, *-ris*, *-tur*, *-mur*, *-minī*, *-ntur* for the passive. Below are charts for each conjugation showing the difference between the present active and passive indicative and the present active and passive subjunctive.

First Conjugation: *amō, -āre, -āvī, -ātum*

	PRESENT ACTIVE INDICATIVE		PRESENT ACTIVE SUBJUNCTIVE	
	SG.	PL.	SG.	PL.
1ST	am**ō**	am**ā**mus	am**em**	am**ē**mus
2ND	am**ās**	am**ā**tis	am**ēs**	am**ē**tis
3RD	am**at**	am**ant**	am**et**	am**ent**
	PRESENT PASSIVE INDICATIVE		**PRESENT PASSIVE SUBJUNCTIVE**	
	SG.	**PL.**	**SG.**	**PL.**
1ST	am**or**	am**ā**mur	am**er**	am**ē**mur
2ND	am**ā**ris	am**ā**minī	am**ē**ris	am**ē**minī
3RD	am**ā**tur	am**an**tur	am**ē**tur	am**en**tur

Second Conjugation: *videō, -ēre, vīdī, vīsum*

	PRESENT ACTIVE INDICATIVE		PRESENT ACTIVE SUBJUNCTIVE	
	SG.	PL.	SG.	PL.
1ST	vid**eō**	vid**ē**mus	vid**eam**	vid**eā**mus
2ND	vid**ēs**	vid**ē**tis	vid**eās**	vid**eā**tis
3RD	vid**et**	vid**ent**	vid**eat**	vid**eant**
	PRESENT PASSIVE INDICATIVE		**PRESENT PASSIVE SUBJUNCTIVE**	
	SG.	**PL.**	**SG.**	**PL.**
1ST	vid**eor**	vid**ē**mur	vid**ear**	vid**eā**mur
2ND	vid**ē**ris	vid**ē**minī	vid**eā**ris	vid**eā**minī
3RD	vid**ē**tur	vid**en**tur	vid**eā**tur	vid**ea**ntur

Third Conjugation: *dūcō, -ere, dūxī, dūctum*

	PRESENT ACTIVE INDICATIVE		PRESENT ACTIVE SUBJUNCTIVE	
	SG.	PL.	SG.	PL.
1ST	dūc**ō**	dūc**i**mus	dūc**a**m	dūc**ā**mus
2ND	dūc**i**s	dūc**i**tis	dūc**ā**s	dūc**ā**tis
3RD	dūc**i**t	dūc**u**nt	dūc**a**t	dūc**a**nt
	PRESENT PASSIVE INDICATIVE		PRESENT PASSIVE SUBJUNCTIVE	
	SG.	PL.	SG.	PL.
1ST	dūc**o**r	dūc**i**mur	dūc**a**r	dūc**ā**mur
2ND	dūc**e**ris	dūc**i**minī	dūc**ā**ris	dūc**ā**minī
3RD	dūc**i**tur	dūc**u**ntur	dūc**ā**tur	dūc**a**ntur

Third *-iō* Conjugation: *capiō, -ere, cēpī, captum*

	PRESENT ACTIVE INDICATIVE		PRESENT ACTIVE SUBJUNCTIVE	
	SG.	PL.	SG.	PL.
1ST	cap**iō**	cap**i**mus	cap**ia**m	cap**iā**mus
2ND	cap**i**s	cap**i**tis	cap**iā**s	cap**iā**tis
3RD	cap**i**t	cap**i**unt	cap**ia**t	cap**ia**nt
	PRESENT PASSIVE INDICATIVE		PRESENT PASSIVE SUBJUNCTIVE	
	SG.	PL.	SG.	PL.
1ST	cap**io**r	cap**i**mur	cap**ia**r	cap**iā**mur
2ND	cap**e**ris	cap**i**minī	cap**iā**ris	cap**iā**minī
3RD	cap**i**tur	cap**iu**ntur	cap**iā**tur	cap**ia**ntur

Fourth Conjugation: *audiō, -īre, -īvī, -ītum*

	PRESENT ACTIVE INDICATIVE		PRESENT ACTIVE SUBJUNCTIVE	
	SG.	PL.	SG.	PL.
1ST	aud**iō**	aud**ī**mus	aud**ia**m	aud**iā**mus
2ND	aud**ī**s	aud**ī**tis	aud**iā**s	aud**iā**tis
3RD	aud**i**t	aud**iu**nt	aud**ia**t	aud**ia**nt
	PRESENT PASSIVE INDICATIVE		PRESENT PASSIVE SUBJUNCTIVE	
	SG.	PL.	SG.	PL.
1ST	aud**io**r	aud**ī**mur	aud**ia**r	aud**iā**mur
2ND	aud**ī**ris	aud**ī**minī	aud**iā**ris	aud**iā**minī
3RD	aud**ī**tur	aud**iu**ntur	aud**iā**tur	aud**ia**ntur

Important Note: The 1st person present active and passive subjunctives in the 3rd, 3rd -iō, and 4th conjugations look identical to their future active and passive indicatives: *dūcam/ dūcar, capiam/capiar, audiam/audiar.* Again, our old friend context will usually distinguish them for us. If context doesn't clarify which one it is, go with whichever one makes more sense (and if it happens to be a sentence in this book, both translations will be accepted). It won't be a big deal, really.

Translation of the Subjunctive

In the new synopsis including the subjunctive, I do not require an English translation of subjunctive, but have put in "depends on context." As each new subjunctive usage is introduced, we will discuss how best to translate it. Sometimes we will use an English indicative or infinitive or even imperative; sometimes we will use English helping verbs (would, were, may, might, could, should, etc., as mentioned above). Occasionally we will translate a Latin subjunctive with an English subjunctive. Again, we need to remember the two languages are very different.

And now, without further ado, here is an example of how your new complete synopsis will look with the subjunctive added. I have also given a synopsis with a deponent verb.

Synopsis with Subjunctive (in other words, the Full and Complete Synopsis)

amō in the 1st Person Plural

		LATIN ACTIVE	ENGLISH ACTIVE	LATIN PASSIVE	ENGLISH PASSIVE
INDICATIVE	PRES.	amāmus	we love	amāmur	we are loved
	IMPF.	amābāmus	we were loving	amābāmur	we were (being) loved
	FUT.	amābimus	we will love	amābimur	we will be loved
	PF.	amāvimus	we (have) loved	amātī/ae/a sumus	we were/have been loved
	PLPF.	amāverāmus	we had loved	amātī/ae/a erāmus	we had been loved
	FT. PF.	amāverimus	we will have loved	amātī/ae/a erimus	we will have been loved
SUBJUNCTIVE	PRES.	amēmus	[depends on context]	amēmur	[depends on context]
	IMPF.	T.B.A.	[depends on context]	T.B.A.	[depends on context]
	PF.	T.B.A.	[depends on context]	T.B.A.	[depends on context]
	PLPF.	T.B.A.	[depends on context]	T.B.A.	[depends on context]
PARTICIPLE	PRES.	amantēs, -ium	loving		
	PF.			amātī, -ae, -a	(having been) loved
	FUT.	amātūrī, -ae, -a	about to love	amandī, -ae, -a	(about) to be loved
INFINITIVE	PRES.	amāre	to love	amārī	to be loved
	PF.	amāvisse	to have loved	amātī/ae/a esse	to have been loved
	FUT.	amātūrī/ae/a esse	to be about to love		
IMP.	SG.	amā!	love!	amāre!	be loved!
	PL.	amāte!	love! (pl.)	amāminī!	be loved! (pl.)

Synopsis of a Deponent Verb, Including the Subjunctive

arbitror, -ārī, -ātus sum in the 1st Person Plural

		LATIN ACTIVE	ENGLISH ACTIVE	LATIN PASSIVE	ENGLISH PASSIVE
INDICATIVE	PRES.	—	—	arbitrāmur	we judge
	IMPF.	—	—	arbitrābāmur	we were judging
	FUT.	—	—	arbitrābimur	we will judge
	PF.	—	—	arbitrātī/ae/a sumus	we (have) judged
	PLPF.	—	—	arbitrātī/ae/a erāmus	we had judged
	FT. PF.	—	—	arbitrātī/ae/a erimus	we will have judged
SUBJUNCTIVE	PRES.	—	[depends on context]	arbitrēmur	[depends on context]
	IMPF.	T.B.A.	[depends on context]	T.B.A.	[depends on context]
	FUT.	T.B.A.	[depends on context]	T.B.A.	[depends on context]
	PF.	T.B.A.	[depends on context]	T.B.A.	[depends on context]
PARTICIPLE	PRES.	arbitrantēs, -ium	judging		
	PF.			arbitrātī, -ae, -a	(having) judged
	FUT.	arbitrātūrī, -ae, -a	about to judge	arbitrandī, -ae, -a	(about) to be judged
INFINITIVE	PRES.	—	—	arbitrārī	to judge
	PF.	—	—	arbitrātī/ae/a esse	to have judged
	FUT.	arbitrātūrī/ae/a esse	to be about to judge		
IMP.	SG.	—	—	arbitrāre!	judge!
	PL.	—	—	arbitrāminī!	judge! (pl.)

Irregular Subjunctives: *Sum* and *Possum*

Not surprisingly, our favorite irregular verb *sum* has an irregular present subjunctive. And this of course means its compound verbs (*absum, adsum, possum,* etc.) will be similarly irregular. Basically the present indicative vowels *-u-* and *-e-/-ē-* become *-i-* or *-ī-*.

sum, esse, fuī, futūrum

	PRESENT INDICATIVE		PRESENT SUBJUNCTIVE	
	SG.	PL.	SG.	PL.
1ST	sum	sumus	sim	sīmus
2ND	ēs	estis	sīs	sītis
3RD	est	sunt	sit	sint

possum, posse, potuī, ——

	PRESENT INDICATIVE	
	SG.	PL.
1ST	possum	possumus
2ND	potes	potestis
3RD	potest	possunt

PRESENT SUBJUNCTIVE	
SG.	PL.
possim	possīmus
possīs	possītis
possit	possint

Hortatory/Jussive Subjunctive

Latin subjunctives can be divided into independent and dependent uses. As the names suggest, an independent subjunctive is a main, stand-alone verb in the sentence, while a dependent subjunctive appears in a subordinate clause in an indicative sentence.

The primary independent usage discussed in this book is the hortatory or jussive subjunctive. "Hortatory" comes from the deponent verb *hortor*, "I encourage, urge, exhort"; while "jussive" derives from *iubeō*, "I order, command" (Lesson 2). Thus the hortatory or jussive subjunctive is an encouragment, exhortation, or command.* Most often it can be translated with the English helping verbs "may" or "let." Here are some examples of verbs in isolation:

LATIN	ENGLISH
amem	let me love, may I love
amer	let me be loved, may I be loved
videāmus	let us see, may we see
videāmur	let us be seen, may we be seen (or let us seem, may we seem)
dūcat	let him lead, may he lead
dūcātur	let him be led, may he be led
audiant	let them hear, may they hear
audiantur	let them be heard, may they be heard

I did not include any 2nd person examples, because 2nd person jussive subjunctives usually occur in poetry and early Latin. Therefore, although 2nd person jussives do appear in Latin, I will for the most part stick to the 1st and 3rd person.

And now for some examples in the context of a sentence:

> *Dracōne necātō, fīlia rēgis Oswaldum amet.* Since the dragon has been killed, let the princess love Oswald.
>
> *Benedīcāmus Deō semper!* May we always bless God!
>
> *Cētus subitō necētur.* Let the kraken be killed immediately.

* Technically, the term "hortatory" applies to 1st person, while "jussive" is used with 2nd and 3rd persons. But since the usage and translation are the same, the terms can be used interchangeably. I will endeavor to use them in their technical and appropriate sense.

If we desire to make a jussive or hortatory subjunctive negative, we will not use our old friend *nōn*, but rather a new word, *nē*: *Oswaldus ab dracōne nē necētur,* "Let Oswald not be killed by the dragon."

If you want a few more examples, go look up the *Pater Noster* from Unit 1 in *KL1*. There are several nice jussive subjunctives in it:

Sanctificētur nōmen tuum. May/let Your name be made holy.

Adveniat rēgnum tuum. May/let your kingdom come.

Fiat voluntās tua. May/let your will be done.

A final note on the trickiness of English. We have been using the helping verbs "let" and "may" to translate our hortatory/jussive subjunctives. However, both of these words can have other meanings as well. "Let" can also mean "allow," as in, "Let me carry that box for you," or "Let the little children come unto me." In Latin, if we are intending to say "allow," we would use the verb *sinō* plus an accusative and infinitive construction. The word "may" can also be used as a polite way to ask permission: "May I be excused?" or to indicate a possibility: "It may rain tomorrow."

Review

We are going to be learning ways to use the subjunctive to talk about time. However let's not forget how to use participles to talk about time: make some sentences with the ablative absolute (present and past). Also, practice putting a few verbs in the supine, just to shake things up.

Worksheet 4

A. Vocabulary

1. sīgnum: ____________________
2. prīncipium: ____________________
3. ruō, ruere, ______, rutum: ____________________
4. war: ____________________
5. usque (adv.): ____________________ (prep. ____) ____________________
6. appāreō, ___________, ___________ apparitum _____: ____________________
7. nē: ____________________
8. prophet: ____________________
9. sēū/sīve: ____________________
10. mīror, mīrārī, mīrātus sum: ____________________
11. imāgō: ____________________
12. maledīcō, maledīcere, ___________, ____________________
13. enough: ____________________
14. ear: ____________________
15. lābor, -ī, lapsus sum: ____________________
16. benedīcō, ____________, ___________benedictum ____________________
17. arbitror, arbitrārī, arbitrātus sum: ____________________
18. sanctificō (1): ____________________
19. dēsertus: ____________________
20. cōnfiteor, cōnfitērī, confessus sum ____________________
21. I rest: ____________________
22. dēserta: ____________________
23. ineō, inīre, iniī (inīvī), inītum: ____________________
24. ūniversus: ____________________
25. too much: ____________________

B. Grammar

1. Give the subjunctive equivalents for these indicatives.

INDICATIVE	SUBJUNCTIVE
Example: apparēmus	*Example:* appareāmus
arbitrantur	
sentīs	
fātur	
cōnfitēminī	
ūtimur	
requiēscit	
iubētis	
cōnsūmor	
ruō	
sanctificāmus	

2. Translate these jussive/hortatory subjunctives.

LATIN	ENGLISH
Example: benedīcat	*Example:* let him bless
cōnfiteantur	
ruat	
negēmur	
nē absit	
arbitrēmur	
edāmus	
incolant	
nē appaream	
oporteat	
custōdiāmus	

3. Do a synopsis of *benedīcō* in the 1st person singular, first giving principal parts:

____

		LATIN ACTIVE	ENGLISH ACTIVE	LATIN PASSIVE	ENGLISH PASSIVE
INDICATIVE	PRES.				
	IMPF.				
	FUT.				
	PF.				
	PLPF.				
	FT. PF.				
SUBJUNCTIVE	PRES.				
	IMPF.	T.B.A.		T.B.A.	
	PF.	T.B.A.		T.B.A.	
	PLPF.	T.B.A.		T.B.A.	
PARTICIPLE	PRES.				
	PF.				
	FUT.				
INFINITIVE	PRES.				
	PF.				
	FUT.				
IMP.	SG.				
	PL.				

C. Memorization

Fill in the blanks in John 1:1-9 in Latin.

____

__________ ___ ____ _____ ________ ___ _____

_____ _______ ____ ___ _____ _____ _____ ___ ____ _____ _____

__________. ___ ____ ___ ________ ______ ___ ________ _____ _____

__________ _____ ______ _______ __ _____ cui _______ _____ Iohannes.

_____ ______ ____ ____________ ___ testimonium __________ ___

_______ _ ________ crederent ____ ______. _____ _____ ille ____, ____ ___

testimonium __________ ___ lumine. _____ _____ vera ______ __________

omnem ________ venientem ___ ________.

D. Translation

English to Latin

Translate these sentences into Latin. (Hint: Translate *italicized* verbs with Latin participles/gerunds, **bold** with subjunctives, <u>underlined</u> with infinitives, and SMALL-CAPPED with supines.)

1. It is apparent that man <u>was made</u> in the image of God, amazing **to say**!

____

____

2. **May I speak** the whole truth to the judge, and then I will speak nearly everything that happened.

____

____

3. **Let** them **wear** their best garments since the ghosts *are guarding* the threshold in vain.

____

____

4. Who is the priest who said, "**May** he not **rest** in peace"? **Let** this same man **be handed over**!

____

____

5. **Let** us **bless** the Lord by continuously *praising* His name and *singing* of all His noble works.

6. You *must consume* these cookies and enjoy them, or the queen will be very angry.

7. **May** it **please** the judge to send the worst men *to bear* the greatest burdens on the road to Rome.

8. **Let** them not **suppose** that the prophet went into the wilderness <u>to prophesy</u> numerous things.

9. Although my ears scarcely *heard* the breezes, trees and cattle unexpectedly kept falling down on the hills, didn't they?

10. **Let**'s not **put** our faces in our food while we *are eating.*

E. Latin to English

Adapted from Genesis 1:1-2:3

In principio creavit Deus caelum et terram. Terra autem erat *inanis* et *vacua*, et tenēbrae erant super faciem *abyssi*; et Spiritus Dei ferebatur super aquas.

Dixitque Deus, "Fiat lux." Et facta est lux. Et vidit Deus lucem esse bonam: et *divisit* lucem a tenēbris. Appellavitque lucem Diem, et tenēbras Noctem: factumque est vespere et mane, dies unus.

Dixit quoque Deus, "Fiat *firmamentum* in medio aquarum; et dividat aquas ab aquis." Et fecit Deus firmamentum, divisitque aquas, quae erant sub firmamento, ab his quae erant super firmamentum. Et factum est ita. Vocavitque Deus firmamentum, Caelum: et factum est vespere et mane, dies secundus.

Dixit vero Deus, "Congregentur aquae, quae sub caelo sunt, in locum unum: et appareat *arida*." Et factum est ita. Et vocavit Deus *aridam* Terram, *congregationes*que aquarum appellavit Maria. Et vidit Deus id esse bonum. Et ait, "*Germinet* terra gramen viride, et faciens *semen*, et lignum *pomiferum* faciens fructum iuxta* genus suum. Et factum est ita. Et germinavit terra gramen viride, et faciens semen iuxta genus suum, lignumque faciens fructum, et habens quidque semen secundum* *speciem* suam. Et vidit Deus id esse bonum. Et factum est vespere et mane, dies tertius.

Dixit autem Deus, "Fiant *luminaria* in firmamento caeli, et dividant diem ac noctem, et sint in signa et tempora, et dies et annos; et luceant in firmamento caeli, et *illuminent* terram." Et factum est ita. Fecitque Deus duo *luminaria* magna: *luminare* maius, quod regit diem; et *luminare* minus, quod regit noctem; et stellas. Et posuit eas in firmamento caeli, et lucebant super terram, et regebant diem ac noctem, et dividebant lucem ac tenēbras. Et vidit Deus id esse bonum. Et factum est vespere et mane, dies quartus.

Dixit etiam Deus, "*Producant* aquae *reptile* animae viventis,* et *volatile* super terram sub firmamento caeli." Creavitque Deus cetos* magnos, et omnem animam viventem atque moventem, quam *produxerant* aquae in species suas, et omne volatile secundum genus suum. Et vidit Deus id esse bonum. *Benedixit*que eis, dicens, "Crescite, et *multiplicamini*, et implete aquas maris: avesque *multiplicentur* super terram." Et factum est vespere et mane, dies quintus.

Dixit quoque Deus, "*Producat* terra animam viventem in genere suo, *iumenta*, et reptilia, et bestias terrae secundum *species* suas." Factumque est ita. Et fecit Deus bestias terrae iuxta *species* suas, et *iumenta*, et omne *reptile* terrae in genere suo. Et vidit Deus id esse bonum.

Et ait, "Faciamus hominem ad* imaginem et *similitudinem* nostram: et regat pisces maris, et volatiles caeli, et bestias, universamque terram, omneque reptile, quod movet in terra." Et creavit Deus hominem ad imaginem suam; ad imaginem Dei creavit illum*, *masculum* et *feminam* creavit eos. Benedixitque illis Deus, et ait, "Crescite *et multiplicamini*, et implete terram, et *subicite* eam, et regite pisces maris, et *volatiles* caeli, et omnes viventes, quae movent super terram." Dixitque Deus, "Ecce, dedi vobis omne gramen ferens semen super terram, et omnia ligna quae habent in ipsis *semen* generis sui, et erunt vobis cibus; et cunctis viventibus terrae, omnique *volatili* caeli, et universis quae movent in terra, et in quibus est anima vivens, et habebunt ad *vescendum*." Et factum est ita. Viditque Deus cuncta quae fecerat, et erant valde bona. Et factum est vespere et mane, dies sextus.

Igitur *perfecti sunt* caeli et terra, et omnis *ornatus* eorum. Complevitque Deus die septimo opus suum quod fecerat; et requievit die septimo ab universo opere quod *patraverat*. Et benedixit die septimo, et sanctificavit illum, quia in ipso *cessaverat* ab omni opere suo quod creavit Deus et fecit.

Notes:
* *ille, illa, illum*: Feel free to translate as a simple pronoun ("he, she, it, they"), rather than a demonstrative ("that man," "that woman," etc.).
* *iūxtā* (*KL1*, Wk. 28): can also mean "according to"
* *secundum:* This is the preposition, not the adjective.
* *animae viventis:* genitive of quality; can translate with "of" or "with"
* *cētus, -ī (m):* can also mean simply "sea creature"
* *ad:* can also mean "according to"

Glossary:
abyssus, -ī (m): the deep, sea, bottomless pit, abyss
ārida, -ae (f): dryness, dry place, dry land
cessō (1): I cease from, stop
compleō, -ēre, -plēvī, -plētum: I fill up, complete
congregātiō, -ōnis (f): assembling, union, gathering
dīvidō, -ere, -vīsī, -vīsum: I divide, separate
fēminus, -a, -um: female
firmāmentum, -ī (n): support, prop; the firmament, the sky
germinō (1): I sprout forth, bud, put forth
illūminō (1): I light up, give light, illuminate
inānis, -e: empty, void
iūmentum, -ī (n): beast (of burden)
lūmināre, -āris (n): light(-giver), heavenly body, luminary
masculus, -a, -um: male
multiplicō (1): I multiply, increase
ornātus, -ūs (m): preparation, furnishing, adornment, ornament
pātrō (1): I bring to pass, accomplish
perficiō, -ere, -fēcī, -fectum: I finish, complete, perfect
pōmifer, -era, -erum: fruit-bearing
prōdūcō, -ere, -dūxī, -ductum: I lead forth, bring forth, produce
reptilis, -e: creeping, reptile
sēmen, -minis (n): seed
similitūdō, -dinis (f): likeness, resemblance
speciēs, -ēī (f): appearance, likeness, species
sūbiciō, -ere, -iēcī, -iectum: I throw/place under, subdue
vacuus, -a, -um: empty, vacant, void
vescor, vesc, —— (+ abl.): I eat, feed (on)
volātilis, -e: flying, winged

Lesson 5

Verbs: Imperfect Active and Passive Subjunctive; Purpose and Result Clauses

Word List

Nouns

1. carcer, -ceris (m) *jail, prison*
2. concilium, -iī (n) *council, meeting*
3. doctrīna, -ae (f) *teaching, instruction*
4. peccātor, -ōris (m)/peccātrix, -trīcis (f) *sinner*
5. salvātor, -ōris (m) *savior, redeemer*
6. testis, -is (m) *witness*
7. vīs, vīs (f) *strength, force, power, violence*

Adjectives

8. immundus, -a, -um *[or* inm-, *etc.] unclean, dirty, foul*
9. mundus, -a, -um *clean, neat, elegant*
10. senior, -ōris *older, elder;* as noun, *an elder [comparative of* senex*]*
11. tālis, -e *such*
12. tantus, -a, -um *so great, of such size*

Verbs

13. afferō (adf-), -ferre (adf-), attulī (adt-), allātum (adl-) *I bring (to), carry (to)*
14. ēdūcō, -ere, -dūxī, -ductum *I lead out/forth, bring out*
15. mundō (1) *I clean, cleanse*
16. ostendō, -ere, -dī, -sum/-tum *I show, point out, declare*
17. rēpleō, -ēre, -plēvī, -plētum *I fill (up), fill again, complete*

Conjunctions and Adverbs

18. omnīno *altogether, wholly, at all*
19. tam *so, so much;* tam…quam *so…as*
20. ut (conj. +indic.) *as, when, how;* (+subj.) *(so) that, in order that/to, to*

Memorization

John 1:1–12a

[1] In principio erat Verbum et Verbum erat apud Deum et Deus erat Verbum. [2] Hoc erat in principio apud Deum. [3] Omnia per ipsum facta sunt, et sine ipso factum est nihil quod factum est. [4] In ipso vita erat et vita erat lux hominum. [5] Et lux in tenebris lucet et tenebrae eam non conprehenderunt. [6] Fuit homo missus a Deo cui nomen erat Iohannes. [7] Hic venit in testimonium ut testimonium perhiberet de lumine ut omnes crederent per illum. [8] Non erat ille lux, sed ut testimonium perhiberet de lumine. [9] Erat lux vera quae inluminat omnem hominem venientem in mundum. **[10] In mundo erat et mundus per ipsum factus est et mundus eum non cognovit. [11] In propria venit et sui eum non receperunt. [12] Quotquot autem receperunt eum,**

[10] He was in the world and the world was made through Him and the world did not know Him. [11] He came to His own [things], and His own [people] did not receive Him. [12] But however many received Him,

Grammar

Imperfect Active and Passive Subjunctive

In this lesson we advance to the second out of our four subjunctive tenses, the imperfect. The formation of the imperfect subjunctive, whether active or passive, is quite simple: Take the whole present active infinitive (2nd principal part), and add on the basic endings (*-m, -s, -t, -mus, -tis, -nt* for active; *-r, -ris, -tur, -mur, -minī, -ntur* for passive).*

1st Conjugation: *amāre* → *amārem* (active); *amārer* (passive)

2nd Conjugation: *vidēre* → *vidērem* (active); *vidērer* (passive)

3rd Conjugation: *dūcere* → *dūcerem* (active); *dūcerer* (passive)

3rd Conjugation *-iō*: *capere* → *caperem* (active); *caperer* (passive)

4th Conjugation: *audīre* → *audīrem* (active); *audīrer* (passive)

These example verbs are fully conjugated in the imperfect subjunctive on the Lesson's Wordlist sheet. For additional examples, here are some of the verbs from this lesson's list, *mundō*, *rēpleō*, and *ostendō*.

First Conjugation: *mundō, -āre, -āvī, -ātum*

	IMPERFECT ACTIVE SUBJUNCTIVE	
	SG.	PL.
1ST	mundārem	mundārēmus
2ND	mundārēs	mundārētis
3RD	mundāret	mundārent

IMPERFECT PASSIVE SUBJUNCTIVE	
SG.	PL.
mundārer	mundārēmur
mundārēris	mundārēminī
mundārētur	mundārentur

* When these endings are added to it, the final *-e* of the infinitive will become long where you'd expect: in the active, 2nd person singular, 1st person plural, and 2nd person plural; in the passive, 2nd and 3rd person singular, and 1st and 2nd person plural. See the charts of the example verbs in the appendices.

Second Conjugation: *repleō, -ēre, -plēvī, -plētum*

	IMPERFECT ACTIVE SUBJUNCTIVE	
	SG.	PL.
1ST	replērem	replērēmus
2ND	replērēs	replērētis
3RD	replēret	replērent

IMPERFECT PASSIVE SUBJUNCTIVE	
SG.	PL.
replērer	replērēmur
replērēris	replērēminī
replērētur	replērentur

Third Conjugation: *ostendō, -ere, -dī, -sum/tum*

	IMPERFECT ACTIVE SUBJUNCTIVE	
	SG.	PL.
1ST	ostenderem	ostenderēmus
2ND	ostenderēs	ostenderētis
3RD	ostenderet	ostenderent

IMPERFECT PASSIVE SUBJUNCTIVE	
SG.	PL.
ostenderer	ostenderēmur
ostenderēris	ostenderēminī
ostenderētur	ostenderentur

With the imperfect subjunctive added, our synopsis will look like this:

Synopsis of *amō* in the 2nd person plural: *amō, amāre, amāvī, amātum*

		LATIN ACTIVE	ENGLISH ACTIVE	LATIN PASSIVE	ENGLISH PASSIVE
INDICATIVE	PRES.	amātis	you (all) love	amāminī	you (all) are (being) loved
	IMPF.	amābātis	you (all) were loving	amābāminī	you (all) were (being) loved
	FUT.	amābitis	you (all) will love	amābiminī	you (all) will be loved
	PF.	amāvistis	you (all) (have) loved	amātī/ae/a estis	you (all) were/have been loved
	PLPF.	amāverātis	you (all) had loved	amātī/ae/a erātis	you (all) had been loved
	FT. PF.	amāveritis	you (all) will have loved	amātī/ae/a eritis	you (all) will have been loved
SUBJUNCTIVE	PRES.	amētis		amēminī	
	IMPF.	amārētis		amārēminī	
	FUT.	T.B.A.		T.B.A.	
	PF.	T.B.A.		T.B.A.	
PARTICIPLE	PRES.	amantēs, -ium	loving		
	PF.			amātī, -ae, -a	(having been) loved
	FUT.	amātūrī, -ae, -a	about to love	amandī, -ae, -a	(about) to be loved
INFINITIVE	PRES.	amāre	to love	amārī	to be loved
	PF.	amāvisse	to have loved	amāti/ae/a esse	to have been loved
	FUT.	amātūrī/ae/a esse	to be about to love		
IMP.	SG.	amā!	love! (sg.)	amāre!	be loved! (sg.)
	PL.	amāte!	love! (pl.)	amāminī!	be loved! (pl.)

Although the basic idea behind the formation of the imperfect subjunctive is simple, you have to get a little creative when it comes to deponent verbs. Since deponents don't have that present active infinitive, you have to imagine what it would be if the deponent were a normal verb, and then form the imperfect subjunctive off of that imaginary infinitive.

First Conjugation: *arbitror, -ārī, -ātus sum*

	IMPERFECT PASSIVE DEPONENT SUBJUNCTIVE	
	SG.	PL.
1ST	arbitrārer	arbitrārēmur
2ND	arbitrārēris	arbitrārēminī
3RD	arbitrārētur	arbitrārentur

Second Conjugation: *cōnfiteor, -fitērī, -fessus sum*

	IMPERFECT PASSIVE DEPONENT SUBJUNCTIVE	
	SG.	PL.
1ST	cōnfitērer	cōnfitērēmur
2ND	cōnfitērēris	cōnfitērēminī
3RD	cōnfitērētur	cōnfitērentur

Third Conjugation: *loquor, -quī, locūtus sum*

	IMPERFECT PASSIVE DEPONENT SUBJUNCTIVE	
	SG.	PL.
1ST	loquerer	loquerēmur
2ND	loquerēris	loquerēminī
3RD	loquerētur	loquerentur

Third *-iō* Conjugation: *patior, patī, passus sum*

	IMPERFECT PASSIVE DEPONENT SUBJUNCTIVE	
	SG.	PL.
1ST	paterer	paterēmur
2ND	paterēris	paterēminī
3RD	paterētur	paterentur

Fourth Conjugation: *mōlior, -īrī, mōlītus sum*

	IMPERFECT PASSIVE DEPONENT SUBJUNCTIVE	
	SG.	PL.
1ST	mōlīrer	mōlīrēmur
2ND	mōlīrēris	mōlīrēminī
3RD	mōlīrētur	mōlīrentur

And now apply this knowledge on the formation of the imperfect subjunctive of deponent verbs to a synopsis of one:

Deponent Synopsis: *arbitror* in the 2nd person plural: *arbitror, arbitrārī, arbitātum sum*

		LATIN ACTIVE	ENGLISH ACTIVE	LATIN PASSIVE	ENGLISH PASSIVE
INDICATIVE	PRES.			arbitrāminī	you (all) judge
	IMPF.			arbitrābāminī	you (all) were judging
	FUT.			arbitrābiminī	you (all) will judge
	PF.			arbitrātī/ae/a estis	you (all) (have) judged
	PLPF.			arbitrātī/ae/a erātis	you (all) had judged
	FT. PF.			arbitrātī/ae/a eritis	you (all) will have judged
SUBJUNCTIVE	PRES.			arbitrēminī	
	IMPF.			arbitrārēminī	
	PF.	T.B.A.		T.B.A.	
	PLPF.	T.B.A.		T.B.A.	
PARTICIPLE	PRES.	arbitrantēs, -ium	judging		
	PF.			arbitrātī, -ae, -a	(having) judged
	FUT.	arbitrātūrī, -ae, -a	about to judge	arbitrandī, -ae, -a	(about) to be judged
INFINITIVE	PRES.			arbitrārī	to judge
	PF.			arbitrātī/ae/a esse	to have judged
	FUT.	arbitrātūrī/ae/a esse	to be about to judge		
IMP.	SG.			arbitrāre!	judge! (sg.)
	PL.			arbitrāminī!	judge! (pl.)

Imperfect Subjunctive of Irregular Verbs *Sum* and *Possum*

Although *sum* and *possum* have irregular principal parts, their imperfect subjunctives are formed regularly. Take the whole infinitive, even if it be irregular, and add on the endings—*ecce*!

sum, esse, fuī, futūrum

	IMPERFECT SUBJUNCTIVE	
	SG.	PL.
1ST	essem	essēmus
2ND	essēs	essētis
3RD	esset	essent

possum, posse, potuī, ——

	IMPERFECT SUBJUNCTIVE	
	SG.	PL.
1ST	possem	possēmus
2ND	possēs	possētis
3RD	posset	possent

Purpose Clauses and Result Clauses

Our next two usages of the subjunctive are fairly straightforward and self-explanatory. The Purpose Clause, as you might suppose from its name, **expresses the purpose of the main verb**, and is introduced by a new word from this lesson's list, *ut*. Now *ut* can also appear with indicative verbs, in which case it means "as, when, how"; but when it introduces a subjunctive clause, then it means "(so) that, in order that/to, to."

ut + indicative: *Dracō necātur ut Oswaldus in spēluncam init.* The dragon is killed when Oswald enters the cave.

ut + subjunctive: *Oswaldus in spēluncam init ut dracōnem necet.* Oswald enters the cave in order that he may kill the dragon. Oswald enters the cave in order to kill the dragon. Oswald enters the cave to kill the dragon.

A negative purpose clause is introduced by the conjunction *nē*: *Dracō pugnat nē necētur.* "The dragon fights lest he be killed." Note that both positive and negative purpose clauses describe a hypothetical action, and can therefore be translated with English helping verbs such as "may" and "might." Several possible translations are given in the *ut* + subjunctive example above.

(The last option, "Oswald enters the cave to kill the dragon," uses an English infinitive. However, good Latin (almost) never uses an infinitive to express purpose. Never say something like *Oswaldus in speluncam init dracōnem necāre.*)

While a purpose clause describes intent and hypothetical or future action, **the result clause expresses an actual action that occurs as a result of the main verb**. It is also introduced by *ut*, but often is preceded with words in the main clause such as *tam*, *tālis*, *tantus*, *ita*, and *sīc*.

Oswaldus dracōnem tam bene pugnat ut eum necet. Oswald fights the dragon so well that he kills it.

Oswaldus tantus vir est ut rēx fiat. Oswald is such a great man that he becomes king.

Since the result clause describes actual action, a negative result clause is NOT introduced by *nē* but rather with *ut* plus a negative word we'd also use with an indicative, such as *nōn, nēmō, nūllus, numquam,* etc.: *Oswaldus dracōnem tam bene pugnat ut nōn necētur.* "Oswald fights the dragon so well that he is not killed." Why, if a result clause expresses actual action, does it need to be in the subjunctive and not in the indicative? Recall that a subjunctive expresses hypothetical, potential, or indirect action—and by "indirect action" I mean subordinate action. Just as Latin uses the infinitive mood to show indirect discourse, it will use the subjunctive mood to describe other indirect actions.

At this point, it may be easy to confuse purpose and result clauses, so here is a handy chart to highlight their differences and similarities.

	PURPOSE	RESULT
EXPRESSES	why the action of the main verb is or was taking place	the consequence of the action of the main verb
CLAUSE INTRODUCED BY...	*ut*	*ut* (often with *tam, tālis, ita, sīc, adeō, ūsque eō,* etc. in the main clause)
NEGATIVE CLAUSE INTRODUCED BY...	*nē*	*ut* + *nōn, nēmō, nūllus, numquam* etc. [NOT *nē*]
TRANSLATED BY...	English subjunctive (may, might, etc.), indicative, or infinitive	English indicative (usually no helping verb like may or might)
EXAMPLES	*Oswaldus drācōnem necat ut filiam rēgis servet.* Oswald kills the dragon so that he may save the princess.	*Oswaldus tālem fērum dracōnem ut filiam rēgis servet.* Oswald kills such a fierce dragon that he saves the princess.
	Oswaldus in spēluncam iniit ut dracōnem necāret. Oswald entered the cave in order that he might kill the dragon.	*Oswaldus tam celeriter in spēluncam iniit ut dracōnem terrēret.* Oswald entered the cave so quickly that he frightened the dragon.
	Deus Suum Fīlium mīsit ut nostrum Salvātōrem esset. God sent His Son in order that He might be our Savior.	*Sic dīlēxit Deus mundum ut Suum Fiium mitteret.* God so loved the world that He sent His Son.

Quick Introduction to Sequence of Tenses

More will be said about this in the next two lessons, but just as we use different tenses of the infinitive in indirect statement to show when the action occurred relative to the main verb, so we will also with the subjunctive. Present subjunctive is used with a present or future main verb to express the same time as or future of the main verb; imperfect subjunctive with past main verbs (imperfect, perfect, or pluperfect).

MAIN VERB	SUBJUNCTIVE	ACTION RELATIVE TO MAIN VERB
PRESENT OR FUTURE	Present	same time/future
	Perfect	before
PAST (IMPERFECT, PERFECT, OR PLUPERFECT)	Imperfect, Pluperfect	same time/future, before

Purpose Constructions Thus Far

Try to think of all the ways we can express Latin in purpose thus far, and then look at the chart below.

CONSTRUCTION	LATIN	ENGLISH
1. AD + GERUND/GERUNDIVE	Oswaldus ad necandum dracōnem ex castellō ēgressus est.	Oswald left the castle to kill the dragon.
2. CAUSĀ + GERUND/GERUNDIVE	Oswaldus necandō dracōne causā ex castellō ēgressus est.	Oswald left the castle to kill the dragon [*Lit.*, "for the sake of killing the dragon."].
3. FUTURE ACTIVE PARTICIPLE	Oswaldus necātūrus dracōnem ex castellō ēgressus est.	Oswald left the castle to kill the dragon [*Lit.*, "about to kill…"].
4. ACCUSATIVE SUPINE WITH VERB OF MOTION	Oswaldus necātum dracōnem ex castellō ēgressus est.	Oswald left the castle to kill the dragon.
5. PURPOSE CLAUSE WITH SUBJUNCTIVE	Oswaldus ex castellō ēgressus est ut dracōnem necāret.	Oswald left the castle to kill the dragon [*or*, "in order to kill, so that he might kill," etc.].

Review

Be sure to practice the present subjunctive this lesson so you don't lose it. Also, if you can, get a notebook or a few sheets of paper to keep track of the various examples of the subjunctive. There's over ten that we will learn in this book (thus far we have learned *Hortatory/Jussive, Result Clause,* and *Purpose Clause*), and you will want to keep track of the sequence of tenses. At the end of these lessons there is a list of subjunctives and all the ways you can use them. Feel free to flip to that if anything is confusing.

Worksheet 5

A. Vocabulary

1. witness: ______________________________
2. afferō, __________, __________allātum: ______________________________
3. vīs: ______________________________
4. ēdūcō, ________________, ēdūxī, ēductum: ______________________________
5. heart: ______________________________
6. tālis, -e: ______________________________
7. mundō (1): ______________________________
8. ut (+indic.): ____________ (+subj.) ______________________________
9. īta ______________________________
10. dīvitiae: ______________________________
11. tam: ______________________________
12. senior: ______________________________
13. __________, ____________, ____________, rēplētum: ______________________________
14. peccātor/peccātrix: ______________________________
15. clean: ______________________________
16. unclean: ______________________________
17. council: ______________________________
18. patior, -ī, passus sum: ______________________________
19. savior: ______________________________
20. ____________, ____________, ostendī, ostensum/ostentum: ______________________________
21. I follow: ______________________________
22. jail: ______________________________
23. doctrīna: ______________________________
24. tantus: ______________________________
25. omnīno: ______________________________

B. Grammar

1. Decline "foul force" in Latin.

	LATIN SINGULAR	LATIN PLURAL
NOM.		
GEN.		
DAT.		
ACC.		
ABL.		
VOC.		

2. Give the subjunctive equivalents for these indicatives.

INDICATIVE	SUBJUNCTIVE
Example: mundābāmus	*Example:* mundārēmus
sentiunt	
rēplēbant	
ēducēbāris	
arbitrābatur	
oportet	
ostendēbātis	
adsum	
aberam	
cōnfitēbāminī	
ruēbat	
apparētis	
sanctificābar	
benedīcō	
maledīcēbātis	
iubēs	

3. Do a synopsis of *ēdūcō* in the 3rd person plural, first giving principal parts:

____

		LATIN ACTIVE	ENGLISH ACTIVE	LATIN PASSIVE	ENGLISH PASSIVE
INDICATIVE	PRES.				
	IMPF.				
	FUT.				
	PF.				
	PLPF.				
	FT. PF.				
SUBJUNCTIVE	PRES.				
	IMPF.				
	PF.	T.B.A.		T.B.A.	
	PLPF.	T.B.A.		T.B.A.	
PARTICIPLE	PRES.				
	PF.				
	FUT.				
INFINITIVE	PRES.				
	PF.				
	FUT.				
IMP.	SG.				
	PL.				

C. Memorization

Fill in the blanks in 1 John 1:1-12a in Latin.

____

____

____

____

____

_____ _____ _____ _____ _____ _____ _____ _____ _____. _____

_____ _____ _____ _____ _____ _____ _____ _____ _____

_____ _____ _____ _____ _____. _____ _____ ille _____, _____ _____

_____ _____ _____ lumine. _____ _____ _____ _____ _____

omnem _____ _____ _____ _____. _____ _____ erat _____

_____ per _____ factus _____ _____ _____ eum _____ _____. _____

propria _____ _____ sui _____ _____ receperunt. Quotquot _____ _____ eum,

D. English to Latin

Translate these sentences into Latin. (Hint: Translate *italicized* verbs with Latin participles/gerunds, **bold** with subjunctives, <u>underlined</u> with infinitives, and SMALL-CAPPED with supines.)

1. (a) The older priests, *having been made* unclean, went to the well **to cleanse** themselves.

   ____

   ____

   (b) The older priests, *having been made* unclean, went to the well *to cleanse* themselves.

   ____

   ____

   (c) The older priests, *having been made* unclean, went to the well to cleanse themselves.

   ____

   ____

2. The very evil witnesses declared so many things against the prophet that the judge also **slandered** him.

   ____

   ____

3. **May** it **please** the Savior to bring us sinners out of darkness in order that we **may confess** His holy name.

4. *Use a dative of reference in this sentence:*
In my opinion, some ghost, not a breeze, suddenly attacked me with such force that I **fell down**.

5. All excessively elegant women *must dwell* in the best houses on the best streets, lest they **appear** to be without money.

6. Who told you that we were staying in Rome after the meeting *had been* altogether *completed*?

7. **Let** us not **suppose** that, the walls of the jail *having been broken*, any wicked men were led out.

8. As they brought such a great herd to the wilderness, seven watchmen were given instructions lest someone **snatch** the animals.

E. Latin to English

Adapted from Acts 5:12-42

Per manus autem apostolorum fiebant signa et *prodigia* multa in multitudine. Et erant una omnes in *porticu Salomonis.* Autem augebatur credentium in Domino multitudo virorum ac mulierum, ita ut in plateas eicerent *infirmos*, et ponerent in *lectulis* et *grabatis*, ut, veniente *Petro*, *saltem* umbra illius *obumbraret* quemquam illorum, et liberarentur ab *infirmitatibus* suis. Congregabat autem et multitudo civitatum prope *Ierusalem*, afferentes aegros, et vexatos a spiritibus immundis: qui curabantur omnes.

Surgens autem princeps sacerdotum, et omnes qui cum illo erant, repleti sunt *zelo*; et *iniecerunt* manus in apostolos, et posuerunt eos in carcere. *Angelus* autem Domini per* noctem aperiens portas carceris, et educens eos, dixit, "Ite,* et stantes loquimini* in templo multitudini omnia verba vitae huius." Hoc audito, intraverunt mane in templum, et docebant. Veniens autem princeps sacerdotum, et qui cum eo erant, *convocaverunt* concilium, et omnes seniores filiorum *Israel*; et miserunt ad carcerem ut *adducerentur.* Autem venerunt *ministri*, et aperto carcere non invenerunt illos; et reversi nuntiaverunt, dicentes: "Carcerem quidem invenimus *clausum*, et custodes stantes ante portas: aperientes autem neminem intra invenimus."

Ut autem audiverunt hos sermones *magistratus* templi et principes sacerdotum, quaerebant, "De illis quidnam fiebat?" Perveniens autem quidam nuntiavit eis: "Ecce, viri, quos posuistis in carcerem, sunt in templo stantes, et docentes populum." Tunc abiit *magistratus* cum *ministris*, et *adduxit* illos sine vi: timebant enim populum ne *lapidarentur.* Adductis illis, statuerunt in concilio: et interrogavit eos princeps sacerdotum, dicens, "*Praecipiendo praecepimus* vobis, 'Nolite docere in nomine isto'; et ecce replevistis Ierusalem *doctrina* vestra; et vultis *adducere* super nos sanguinem hominis istius."

Respondens autem Petrus, et apostoli, dixerunt, "*Obedire* oportet Deo magis quam hominibus. Deus patrum nostrorum *suscitavit* Iesum, quem vos cecidistis, *suspendentes* in ligno. Hunc principem et salvatorem Deus *exaltavit* dextera sua ad dandam *paenitentiam Israeli*, et *remissionem peccatorum*: et nos sumus *testes* horum verborum, et Spiritus Sanctus, quem dedit Deus omnibus *obedientibus* sibi."

His auditis, *dissecabantur*, et cogitabant interficere illos. Surgens autem quidam in concilio *Pharisaeus*, nomine *Gamaliel*, *legisdoctor*, iussit *foras breviter* homines fieri, dixitque ad illos: "Viri *Israelis*, audite mihi. *Discedite* ab hominibus istis, et *sinite* illos: quoniam si est ex hominibus consilium hoc, aut opus, *dissolvetur*: si vērō ex Deo est, non poteritis *dissolvere* illud, ne forte et contra Deum pugnare inveniamini."

Consenserunt autem illi. Et *convocantes* apostolos, illis caesis iusserunt, "Nolite omnino loqui in nomine Iesu," et dimiserunt eos. Et illi quidem ibant gaudentes a conspectu concilii, quoniam digni putati sunt pro nomine Iesu *contumeliam* pati. Omni autem die non cessabant in templo, et circa domos docentes, et *evangelizantes* Christum Iesum.

Notes:

* *per:* can also mean "by"

* *Īte, loquiminī:* imperatives (remember?); *īte* is the plural imperative of *eō*, and *loquiminī* is the deponent plural imperative of *loquor*

Glossary:

addūcō, -ere, -dūxī, -ductum: I lead (to), bring (to)
aeger, -gra, -grum: sick, diseased, ill
angelus, -ī (m): angel, messenger
breviter: shortly, for a short time
cessō (1): I cease (from), stop
claudō, -ere, clausī, clausum: I close, shut (up)
cōnsentiō, -īre, -sensī, -sensum (+dat.): I agree (with), consent (to)
contumēlia, -ae (f): insult, reproach, abuse
convocō (1): I call together, assemble
dignus, -a, -um: worthy, deserving
discēdō, -ere, -cessī, -cessum: I separate, go away from
dissecō (1): I cut (to the heart)
dissolvō, -ere, -solvī, -solūtum: I dissolve, destroy
ēvangelīzō (1): I preach/proclaim (the Gospel)
exaltō (1): I raise, exalt
forās: out(side), out of doors
Gamaliel, -elis (m): Gamaliel
grabātus, -ī (m): pallet, mat, low couch
Ierusalem (n, indecl.): Jerusalem
Israel (m, indecl.) or Israel, -is (m): Israel
īnfīrmitās, -tātis (f): infirmity, sickness, weakness
īnfīrmus, -a, -um: feeble, weak, infirm
īniciō, -ere, -iēcī, -iectum: I throw in/on, put in/on
lapidō (1): I stone, throw stones at
lectulus, -ī (m): bed, small couch
lēgisdoctor, -ōris (m): teacher/doctor of the law
magistrātus, -ūs (m): magistrate
minister, -strī (m): attendant, servant, minister
oboediō [obediō], -īre, -īvī, -ītum (+dat.): I obey, serve, heed
obumbrō (1): I overshadow, cover, cast a shadow (on)
paenitentia, -ae (f): repentance, penitence
paenitentiam agō: I repent
Petrus, -ī (m): Peter
Pharisaeus, -ī (m): Pharisee
porticus, -ūs (f): portico, porch, colonnade
praecipiō, -ere, -cēpī, -ceptum: I anticipate, warn, command
prōdigium, -iī (n): prophetic sign, wonder, portent
remissiō, -ōnis (f): remission, forgiveness
Salomon, -mōnis (m): Solomon
saltem: at least, anyhow
sinō, -ere, sīvī, situm: I let, allow, permit
suscitō (1): I raise up [from the dead], awaken, stir up
suspendō, -ere, -pendī, -pensum: I hang (up), suspend
zēlus, -ī (m): zeal, jealousy

LESSON 6

Verbs—Subjunctive: Perfect and Pluperfect Active and Passive; Prohibitive Subjunctive

Word List

Nouns

1. aequor, -oris (n) *sea, level surface*
2. āgmen, -minis (n) *movement, course; army (on the march)*
3. dolus, -ī (m) *deceit, fraud*
4. latus, -eris (n) *side, flank*
5. mendācium, -iī *lie, falsehood, counterfeit*
6. mendāx, -dācis (m/f) *liar*
7. scelus, -leris (n) *crime, sin*
8. simulācrum, -ī (n) *likeness, image, idol*
9. sors, -rtis (f) *lot, oracle, chance, destiny*
10. tēlum, -ī (n) *weapon*
11. tergum, -ī (n) *back*

Adjectives

12. certus, -a, -um *certain, sure;* (adv.) certe, *certainly*
13. Graecus, -a, -um *Greek;* (as noun) *a Greek*
14. gravis, -e *heavy, burdensome*

Verbs

15. careō, -ēre, -uī, -itum (+abl.) *I lack, am without*
16. mentior, -īrī, -ītus sum *I lie, deceive, say falsely*
17. ōdī, ōdisse, (fut. prt.) ōsūrum [defective] *I hate, dislike*

Adverbs/Conjunctions/Prepositions

18. bis *twice, twofold*
19. forās *out(side), out of doors, forth*
20. scīlicet *of course, naturally, it is clear*

Memorization

John 1:1–13

[1] In principio erat Verbum et Verbum erat apud Deum et Deus erat Verbum. [2] Hoc erat in principio apud Deum. [3] Omnia per ipsum facta sunt, et sine ipso factum est nihil quod factum est. [4] In ipso vita erat et vita erat lux hominum. [5] Et lux in tenebris lucet et tenebrae eam non conprehenderunt. [6] Fuit homo missus a Deo cui nomen erat Iohannes. [7] Hic venit in testimonium ut testimonium perhiberet de lumine ut omnes crederent per illum. [8] Non erat ille lux, sed ut testimonium perhiberet de lumine. [9] Erat lux vera quae inluminat omnem hominem venientem in mundum. [10] In mundo erat et mundus per ipsum factus est et mundus eum non cognovit. [11] In propria venit et sui eum non receperunt. [12] Quotquot autem receperunt eum **dedit eis potestatem filios Dei fieri, his qui credunt in nomine eius, [13] qui non ex sanguinibus neque ex voluntate carnis neque ex voluntate viri sed ex Deo nati sunt.**

to them He gave power to become sons of God, to those who believe in His name, [13] who were not born of bloods nor of the will of the flesh nor of the will of man but of God

Grammar

Perfect and Pluperfect Active and Passive Subjunctive

This is a big lesson. You get to learn your *very last* new verb chant forms! After this, you will only need to learn a few more ways to use all the verb chants you have studied. Our final chants to learn are the perfect and pluperfect subjunctive in the active and passive. These will be conveniently formed off of the same stems as their perfect and pluperfect indicative equivalents.

This seems a good time to review the chart from the very beginning of *KL3*, which laid out each principal part and the tenses and moods formed from it. This time pay special attention to the subjunctive row, and recall how we form the present and imperfect subjunctives (both active and passive) from the 2nd principal part.

	necō	*necāre*	*necāvī*	*necātum*
DEFINITION/ FUNCTION → FORMATION OF MOODS ↓	1st sg. Pres. Act. Indic.—I kill; helps identify conjug. & shows if pres. stem vowel has contracted	Pres. Act. Infin.—to kill; Pres. Stem: *necā-*	1st. sg. Pf. Act. Indic.—I killed, have killed; Pf. Act. Stem: *necāv-*	Neut. Sg. Nom. Pf. Pass. Pple.—killed, having been killed; forms Pf. Passives, so in that sense may be considered Pf. Pass. "Stem": *necāt-*
INDICATIVE		Present Active Present Passive Imperfect Active Imperfect Passive Future Active Future Passive	Perfect Active Pluperfect Active Future Perfect Active	Perfect Passive Pluperfect Passive Future Perfect Passive
IMPERATIVE		Present Active Present Passive Future Active		

INFINITIVE		Present Active Present Passive	Perfect Active	Perfect Passive Future Active
SUBJUNCTIVE		Present Active Present Passive Imperfect Active Imperfect Passive	Perfect Active Pluperfect Active	Perfect Passive Pluperfect Passive
PARTICIPLE		Present Active Future Passive		Perfect Passive Future Active

The perfect and pluperfect active subjunctive, like the indicative, are formed off the 3rd principal part. We will take the perfect stem, plus a few letters (see the box below), and then add our basic *-m, -s, -t, -mus, -tis, -nt* endings. So, first remove the *-ī* from the 3rd principal part, *necāv-*, just like we always do for the perfect tenses. Then we add the following letters: -e-r-i- for the perfect and -i-s-s-e- for the pluperfect

Now we have this: *necāveri-* (perfect active subjunctive) and *necāvisse-* (pluperfect active subjunctive). To these new "stems" we can then add our faithful old active endings and get the following:

necō, -āre, -āvī, -ātum

	PERFECT ACTIVE SUBJUNCTIVE	
	SG.	PL.
1ST	necāverim	necāverīmus
2ND	necāverīs	necāverītis
3RD	necāverit	necāverint

FUTURE PERFECT ACTIVE INDICATIVE	
SG.	PL.
necāvissem	necāvissēmus
necāvissēs	necāvissētis
necāvisset	necāvissent

If you are keeping track of long and short vowels, note that the -i- (perfect) and the -e- (pluperfect) become long in the 2nd person singular, 1st person plural, and 2nd person plural. You might have noticed by now that the perfect active subjunctive looks remarkably like the future perfect active indicative. Old standby context will usually make clear which is intended—and if for some reason the Latin is ambiguous, you should go with the one that sounds best in translation. Here are the two side by side for reference:

	PERFECT ACTIVE SUBJUNCTIVE	
	SG.	PL.
1ST	necāverim	necāverīmus
2ND	necāverīs	necāverītis
3RD	necāverit	necāverint

FUTURE PERFECT ACTIVE INDICATIVE	
SG.	PL.
necāverō	necāverimus
necāveris	necāveritis
necāverit	necāverint

Now, the perfect and pluperfect passive subjunctives are truly a thing of beauty and a joy forever (especially the pluperfect passive subjunctive, which I here confess is my favorite

Latin verb tense). The formation of these is so simple, so logical, so . . . Roman. Start with the perfect and pluperfect passive indicatives—in our example verb *necō*, these would be *necātus sum* and *necātus eram*. Remember, the perfect is formed using the perfect passive participle (4th principal part) with the helping verb *sum* in its present tense. The pluperfect uses that same participle plus *sum* in the imperfect. For the subjunctive (and here's where it gets really exciting), all you need to do is use the present subjunctive of your helping verb *sum*, along with that same perfect passive participle, and *voilà!* you have the perfect passive subjunctive. Then for the pluperfect passive subjunctive, take the participle plus the imperfect subjunctive of *sum*. Told you it was beautiful!

	PERFECT ACTIVE SUBJUNCTIVE	
	SG.	PL.
1ST	necātus/a/um sim	necātī/ae/a sīmus
2ND	necātus/a/um sīs	necātī/ae/a sītis
3RD	necātus/a/um sit	necātī/ae/a sint

PERFECT PASSIVE SUBJUNCTIVE	
SG.	PL.
necātus/a/um essem	necātī/ae/a essēmus
necātus/a/um essēs	necātī/ae/a essētis
necātus/a/um esset	necātī/ae/a essent

To solidify these, try predict what these forms will be in perfect and pluperfect subjunctive from the following common verbs

Second Conjugation: *videō, -ēre, vīdī, vīsum*

	PERFECT ACTIVE SUBJUNCTIVE	
	SG.	PL.
1ST	vīderim	vīderīmus
2ND	vīderīs	vīderītis
3RD	vīderit	vīderint

PERFECT PASSIVE SUBJUNCTIVE	
SG.	PL.
vīsus/a/um sim	vīsī/ae/a sīmus
vīsus/a/um sīs	vīsī/ae/a sītis
vīsus/a/um sit	vīsī/ae/a sint

	PLUPERFECT ACTIVE SUBJUNCTIVE	
	SG.	PL.
1ST	vīdissem	vīdissēmus
2ND	vīdissēs	vīdissētis
3RD	vīdisset	vīdissent

PLUPERFECT PASSIVE SUBJUNCTIVE	
SG.	PL.
vīsus/a/um essem	vīsī/ae/a essēmus
vīsus/a/um essēs	vīsī/ae/a essētis
vīsus/a/um esset	vīsī/ae/a essent

Third Conjugation: *dūcō, -ere, dūxī, dūctum*

	PERFECT ACTIVE SUBJUNCTIVE	
	SG.	PL.
1ST	dūxerim	dūxerīmus
2ND	dūxerīs	dūxerītis
3RD	dūxerit	dūxerint

PERFECT PASSIVE SUBJUNCTIVE	
SG.	PL.
dūctus/a/um sim	dūctī/ae/a sīmus
dūctus/a/um sīs	dūctī/ae/a sītis
dūctus/a/um sit	dūctī/ae/a sint

	PLUPERFECT ACTIVE SUBJUNCTIVE		PLUPERFECT PASSIVE SUBJUNCTIVE	
	SG.	PL.	SG.	PL.
1ST	dūxissem	dūxissēmus	dūctus/a/um essem	dūctī/ae/a essēmus
2ND	dūxissēs	dūxissētis	dūctus/a/um essēs	dūctī/ae/a essētis
3RD	dūxisset	dūxissent	dūctus/a/um esset	dūctī/ae/a essent

Third *-iō* Conjugation: *capiō, -ere, cēpī, captum*

	PERFECT ACTIVE SUBJUNCTIVE		PERFECT PASSIVE SUBJUNCTIVE	
	SG.	PL.	SG.	PL.
1ST	cēperim	cēperīmus	captus/a/um sim	captī/ae/a sīmus
2ND	cēperīs	cēperītis	captus/a/um sīs	captī/ae/a sītis
3RD	cēperit	cēperint	captus/a/um sit	captī/ae/a sint

	PLUPERFECT ACTIVE SUBJUNCTIVE		PLUPERFECT PASSIVE SUBJUNCTIVE	
	SG.	PL.	SG.	PL.
1ST	cēpissem	cēpissēmus	captus/a/um essem	captī/ae/a essēmus
2ND	cēpissēs	cēpissētis	captus/a/um essēs	captī/ae/a essētis
3RD	cēpisset	cēpissent	captus/a/um esset	captī/ae/a essent

Fourth Conjugation: *audiō, -īre, -īvī, -ītum*

	PERFECT ACTIVE SUBJUNCTIVE		PERFECT PASSIVE SUBJUNCTIVE	
	SG.	PL.	SG.	PL.
1ST	audīverim	audīverīmus	audītus/a/um sim	audītī/ae/a sīmus
2ND	audīverīs	audīverītis	audītus/a/um sīs	audītī/ae/a sītis
3RD	audīverit	audīverint	audītus/a/um sit	audītī/ae/a sint

	PLUPERFECT ACTIVE SUBJUNCTIVE		PLUPERFECT PASSIVE SUBJUNCTIVE	
	SG.	PL.	SG.	PL.
1ST	audīvissem	audīvissēmus	audītus/a/um essem	audītī/ae/a essēmus
2ND	audīvissēs	audīvissētis	audītus/a/um essēs	audītī/ae/a essētis
3RD	audīvisset	audīvissent	audītus/a/um esset	audītī/ae/a essent

Now that we have complete knowledge of verb endings, our synopsis is now complete as well. Here is an example of a normal verb synopsis followed by a deponent verb synopsis.

rēpleō, rēplēre, rēplēvī, rēplētum in the 1st person plural

		LATIN ACTIVE	ENGLISH ACTIVE	LATIN PASSIVE	ENGLISH PASSIVE
INDICATIVE	PRES.	rēplēmus	we complete	rēplēmur	we are (being) completed
	IMPF.	rēplēbāmus	we were completing	rēplēbāmur	we were (being) completed
	FUT.	rēplēbimus	we will complete	rēplēbimur	we will be completed
	PF.	rēplēvimus	we (have) completed	rēplētī/ae/a sumus	we were/have been completed
	PLPF.	rēplēverāmus	we had completed	rēplētī/ae/a erāmus	we had been completed
	FT. PF.	rēplēverimus	we will have completed	rēplētī/ae/a erimus	we will have been completed
SUBJUNCTIVE	PRES.	rēpleāmus	[depends on context]	rēpleāmur	[depends on context]
	IMPF.	rēplērēmus	[depends on context]	rēplērēmur	[depends on context]
	PF.	rēplēverimus	[depends on context]	rēplētī/ae/a simus	[depends on context]
	PLPF.	rēplēvissēmus	[depends on context]	rēplētī/ae/a essēmus	[depends on context]
PARTICIPLE	PRES.	rēplentēs, -ium	completing		
	PF.			rēplētī, -ae, -a	(having been) completed
	FUT.	rēplētūrī, -ae, -a	about to complete	rēplendī, -ae, -a	(about) to be completed
INFINITIVE	PRES.	rēplēre	to complete	rēplērī	to be completed
	PF.	rēplēvisse	to have completed	rēplētī/ae/a esse	to have been completed
	FUT.	rēplētūrī/ae/a esse	to be about to complete		
IMP.	SG.	rēplē!	complete! (sg.)	rēplēre!	be completed! (sg.)
	PL.	rēplēte!	complete! (pl.)	rēplēminī!	be completed! (pl.)

mentior, mentīrī, mentītus sum in the 3rd person singular

		LATIN ACTIVE	ENGLISH ACTIVE	LATIN PASSIVE	ENGLISH PASSIVE
INDICATIVE	PRES.	—	—	mentītur	he lies
	IMPF.	—	—	mentiēbātur	he was lying
	FUT.	—	—	mentiētur	he will lie
	PF.	—	—	mentītus/a/um est	he (has) lied
	PLPF.	—	—	mentītus/a/um erat	he had lied
	FT. PF.	—	—	mentītus/a/um erit	he will have lied
SUBJUNCTIVE	PRES.	—	—	mentiātur	[depends on context]
	IMPF.	—	—	mentīrētur	[depends on context]
	PF.	—	—	mentītus/a/um sit	[depends on context]
	PLPF.	—	—	mentītus/a/um esset	[depends on context]
PARTICIPLE	PRES.	mentiēns, -ntis	lying		
	PF.			mentītus, -a, -um	having lied
	FUT.	mentītūrī, -ae, -a	about to lie	mentiendī, -ae, -a	(about) to be lied [to]

INFINITIVE	PRES.	—	—	mentīrī	to lie
	PF.	—	—	mentītus/a/um esse	to have lied
	FUT.	mentītūrus/a/um esse	to be about to lie		
IMP.	SG.	—	—	mentīre!	lie! (sg.)
	PL.	—	—	mentīminī!	lie! (pl.)

Perfect and Pluperfect Subjunctives of *sum* and *possum*

Even though *sum* and *possum* are irregular verbs, their perfect and pluperfect subjunctives are formed regularly. As with other verbs, go to the 3rd principal part, remove the *-ī* for the perfect stem, add *-eri-* for the perfect and *-isse-* for the pluperfect, then the endings *-m, -s, -t, -mus, -tis, -nt.* And remember that these verbs do not have passive forms!

sum, esse, fuī, futūrum

	PERFECT ACTIVE SUBJUNCTIVE		PLUPERFECT ACTIVE SUBJUNCTIVE	
	SG.	PL.	SG.	PL.
1ST.	fuerim	fuerīmus	fuissem	fuissēmus
2ND.	fuerīs	fuerītis	fuissēs	fuissētis
3RD.	fuerit	fuerint	fuisset	fuissent

possum, posse, potuī, —,

	PERFECT ACTIVE SUBJUNCTIVE		PLUPERFECT ACTIVE SUBJUNCTIVE	
	SG.	PL.	SG.	PL.
1ST.	potuerim	potuerīmus	potuissem	potuissēmus
2ND.	potuerīs	potuerītis	potuissēs	potuissētis
3RD.	potuerit	potuerint	potuisset	potuissent

Sequence of Tenses

Again, this will be officially covered next in *KL2*, Lesson 7, but I bring it up here so that you can see where our new subjunctive tenses fit in. In order to let the forms sink in some more, I will not emphasize the perfect and pluperfect subjunctives in the translations until the next lesson. For now, keep in mind that the perfect subjunctive shows action happening before a present or future main verb, while pluperfect indicates previous action for a verb in one of the past tenses.

MAIN VERB	SUBJUNCTIVE	ACTION RELATIVE TO MAIN VERB
Present or Future	Present	same time/future
	Perfect	before
Past (Imperfect, Perfect, or Pluperfect)	Imperfect	same time/future
	Pluperfect	before

Prohibitive Subjunctive; Summary of Various Prohibitions/Negative Commands

We have actually already learned how to do a negative command (also called a prohibition) in the 1st and 3rd persons, by using *nē* with a hortatory or jussive subjunctive: *Nē hoc malum faciāmus.* "Let us not do this evil." *Nē hoc malum faciat.* "Let him not do this evil." There are several ways to form negative commands for the 2nd person. You have also already learned the most common way to do this, by using *nōlī* or *nōlīte* plus an infinitive: *Nōlī hoc malum facere!* "Do not do this evil!"

There are two ways to use the subjunctive in a prohibition. First, you can use *cavē/cavēte* ("beware") or occasionally *vidē/vidēte* or another verb of similar meaning, plus *nē* plus a present subjunctive.*

Ō Oswalde, cavē nē ā dracōne necēris. O Oswald, beware lest you be killed by the dragon. O Oswald, do not be killed by the dragon.

Equitēs, vidēte nē ā dracōne necēminī. Knights, see that you are not killed by the dragon. Knights, do not be killed by the dragon.

Another prohibitive subjunctive (considered back in the Latinic day to be more informal) uses *nē* with a 2nd person perfect subjunctive.†

Ō Oswalde, nē a dracōne necātus sis. O Oswald, do not be killed by the dragon.

Ō Dracōnēs, nē Oswaldum necāveritis. O Dragons, do not kill Oswald.

Below is a summary of these various ways to form prohibitions (which you may feel at liberty to call negative commands if you so desire):

PERSON	TYPE OF PROHIBITION	EXAMPLE
1ST (SING. OR PL.)	*nē* + hortatory subjunctive	*Nē hunc dracōnem necēmus.* Let us not kill this dragon.
3RD (SING. OR PL.)	*nē* + jussive subjunctive	*Nē hunc dracōnem necet.* Let him not kill this dragon.
2ND (SING. OR PL.)	*nōlī/nōlīte* + infinitive	*Nōlīte hunc dracōnem necāre!* Do not kill this dragon!
	cavē/cavēte, vidē/vidēte, etc. + *nē* + 2nd person present subjunctive	*Cavēte nē hunc dracōnem necētis!* Beware lest you kill this dragon! Do not kill this dragon! *Vidē nē hunc dracōnem necēs!* See that you do not kill this dragon! Do not kill this dragon!
	nē + 2nd person perfect subjunctive	*Nē hunc dracōnem necāverīs!* Do not kill this dragon!

* In older Latin sometimes you will see *cavē, vidē*, etc. with a perfect subjunctive; in this text I will use the present only. Also, occasionally with *cavē* the *nē* will be left out without changing the meaning, but in this book I will always include it for clarity.

† Again, older Latin writers and also poets will sometimes use *nē* plus the 2nd person present subjunctive (*nē necēs* rather than *nē necāveris*). Those tricky fellows will also sometimes simply use *nē* plus our regular old imperative (*nē necā/necāte*).

Review

Be sure to review how to put *sum* and *possum* in the subjunctive; they're very important words. Also, be sure to review the imperfect subjunctives (watch out especially for passive subjunctives—they can slip through the cracks). Also add to your sequence of tenses in your notebook, and add the *Prohibitive* to your list of subjunctives.

Worksheet 6

A. Vocabulary

1. twice: ______
2. certus: ______
3. deceit: ______
4. aequor: ______
5. sermō: ______
6. I lie: ______
7. lie: ______
8. snow: ______
9. āgmen: ______
10. simulācrum: ______
11. sors: ______
12. side: ______
13. I hate: ______
14. tēlum: ______
15. outside: ______
16. gignō, gignere, genuī, genitum: ______
17. vel: ______
18. scīlicet: ______
19. careō, ______, ______, caritum (+abl.): ______
20. back: ______
21. dulcis, -e: ______
22. heavy: ______
23. scelus: ______
24. Greek (adj.): ______
25. liar: ______

B. Grammar

1. Parse the following verbs. For Indicative or Subjunctive, give Person, Number, Tense, Voice, and Mood. For Participles, give Gender, Number, Case, Tense, Voice, and Mood. For Infinitives, give Tense, Voice, and Mood. For any mood, provide the 1st Principal Part of the verb it comes from. For the translation of subjunctive, you may write "depends on context" rather than attempting to translate the verb in isolation.

VERB	PNTVM (INDIC./SUBJ.), GNCTVM (PRT.), OR TVM (INFIN.)	1ST PRINCIPAL PART	TRANSLATION
ruat			
mundāverim			
arbitrāta sit			
maledīcentēs			
affertis			
adessēs			
ūtenda			
fātī essēmus			
rēplētibus			
ostendisset			
sanctificārer			
ineuntem			
oporteat			
requiēsciēbātis			

sentīrī			

2. Do a synopsis of *ostendō* in the 1st person plural, first giving principal parts:

____

		LATIN ACTIVE	ENGLISH ACTIVE	LATIN PASSIVE	ENGLISH PASSIVE
INDICATIVE	PRES.				
	IMPF.				
	FUT.				
	PF.				
	PLPF.				
	FT. PF.				
SUBJUNCTIVE	PRES.				
	IMPF.				
	PF.				
	PLPF.				
PARTICIPLE	PRES.				
	PF.				
	FUT.				
INFINITIVE	PRES.				
	PF.				
	FUT.				

IMP.	SG.				
	PL.				

C. Memorization

Fill in the blanks in 1 John 1:1-13 in Latin.

____ ____ ____ ____, ____ ____ ____ ____ ____

____. ____ ____ ____ ____ ____ ____

____ ____ ____ ____. ____ ____ erat ____

____ ____ ____ factus ____ ____ ____ ____ ____

____. ____ propria ____ ____ ____ ____ ____ receperunt. Quotquot

____ ____ ____, ____ ____ potestatem ____ ____ fieri, ____

____ credunt ____ nomine ____, ____ ____ ____ sanguinibus ____

____ voluntate ____ neque ____ ____ viri ____ ____ ____ nati ____

D. English to Latin

Prohibitions: Translate the following sentence into Latin using various ways to express prohibition: a) *Nōlī(te)* + infinitive, b) *cavē(te)* + *nē* + 2nd person present subjunctive, and c) *nē* + 2nd person perfect subjunctive.

1. Do not attack dragons from the side; it is better to attack them with force from the rear. [N.B.: for "from," use *ā* or *ab*.]

Purpose Sentences: Translate the following sentences into Latin using various ways to express purpose: a) *ad* + gerund(ive), b) *causā* + gerund(ive), c) future active participle, d) accusative supine with verb of motion, and e) purpose clause (subjunctive).

2. By chance, we heard that the enemy's army had set out to crush our kingdom with all their weapons.

Translate these remaining sentences into Latin. (Hint: Translate *italicized* verbs with Latin participles/gerundives, **bold** with subjunctives, <u>underlined</u> with infinitives, and SMALL-CAPPED with supines.)

3. That liar slandered you with so many deceits that the elders **believed** him, and of course now they hate you for crimes that you never did.

4. Which Greek will deceive them *by speaking* elegant words about the very large image of the horse?

____

____

5. Certainly fate has showed me twice that these burdensome commands *should be kept* lest I **be consumed** by the Forsaken Sea.

____

____

____

6. God *willing*, we will have our meeting in the agreed upon place because it will be necessary to speak about such things there.

____

____

____

E. Latin to English

Laocoön Warns against the Trojan Horse in Vain (Adapted from Vergil's *Aeneid*, Book II.40-253)

Laocoön's Warning

Prīmus ibī ante omnēs, magnā congregātā multitūdine, *Laōcoōn* ardēns currit dē summā arce, et procul clāmat: "Ō miserī cīvēs, quae tanta *īnsānia* est haec? Crēditis nāvigātōs esse hostēs? Aut ūlla putātis dōna carēre dolīs *Danaōrum*? Nōnne vōbīs nōtus est *Ulixes*? Aut hōc *inclūsī* lignō occultantur Graecī, aut haec in nostrōs facta est *machina* mūrōs, spectūra domōs ventūraque contrā urbem. Equō nē crēdiderītis, Teucrī. Quidquid id est, timeō Danaōs et dōna ferentēs."

Sīc fātus, potentibus ingentem vīribus hastam in latus equī iēcit. Stetit illa *tremēns*, *uterō*que percussō *insonuērunt cavae gemitum*que dedērunt *cavernae*. Et, si fāta deōrum fuisset,* sī mēns nōn laeva fuisset,* Laōcoōn coēgisset* nōs ferrō Danaum delēre equum, Troiaque nunc starēs,* Priamīque arx alta manērēs.*

Sinon's Story

Ecce, intereā pastōrēs Teucrī magnō ad rēgem clamōre trahēbant adulescentem manibus vinctibus, quī sē consiliō,* ut mentīret Troiamque aperīret Danaīs, obtulerat. Accipe nunc Danaōrum īnsidiās et crīmine ab ūnō disce omnis.

"Heu, quae nunc tellūs," inquit, "quae mē aequōra possunt accipere? Aut quid mīserō mihi dēnique manet, cui nōn apud Danaōs iam locus est, et ipsī Teucrī meum sanguinem quaerunt?" Flēvit magnoperē, et nōs eius miserērī coepimus. "Cuncta quidem tibi, rēx, fābor vēra," inquit; "neque mē Graecā dē gente negābō. Fātum *Sinonem* miserum sed nōn mendācem fēcit.

"Ulixem semper egō ōderam quod iste interfēcit meum dominum, et Ulixēs, hōc inventō, mē etiam ōdit. *Pallade laesā*, Graecī autem diū voluērunt domum nāvigāre, sed ventī aut aequōra horrenda nolēbant. Dēnique nōs ab prophētā quaerimus, quī fātur vīta hominis in altāribus offerenda esse. Mē scīlicet quam sacrificium Ulixes ēligit. Illā nocte ex castrīs Danaīs fūgī et mē occultāvī; illī sine mē offerendō māne nāvigāvērunt."

Deinde Rēx *Priamus*, "Cur," inquit, "hunc equum ingentem relīquistis?" Iste mendāx, Sinon, locūtus est, "Nōs *Danaī* Athēnam nōbīs victōriam datūram esse sperāverant, sed simulācrō eius ex templō vestrō ab *Ulixe Diomēdeque* ēreptō, īrātissima nōbīscum erat. Prophēta fātus est nōbīs hunc ingentem equum līgneī quam sacrificium aedificandum esse ut īram eius plācārēmus. Sed *Danaī* volunt subitō, eā *plācātā*, redīre vōs rursum pugnātum."

Laocoön's Demise

Tālibus īnsidiīs Sinōnis crēdita est rēs, captīque sumus dolīs *lacrimīs*que coāctīs—[nōs] quōs neque Diomēdēs nec Achillēs, nōn annī superāvērunt decem, nōn mīlle nāvēs.

Laōcoōn interim, factus Neptūnō sorte sacerdōs, sacra taurum ingentem offerēbat ad altāria. Ecce autem geminī *anguēs*, pervenientēs ā *Tenedī* per undās, nant (horridum vīsū!) super aequōra ūnāque ad lītora tendunt. Fit *sonitus spūmante sālō*; iamque agrōs tenēbant, ardentēsque oculōs implentēs sanguine et ignī, ōra *sībila lambēbant* linguīs *vibrantibus*.

Nōs fugimus *exsanguēs*, sed illī agmine certō Laōcoōnta petunt; et prīmum parva duōrum corpora fīliōrum serpēns *amplexus* quisque *implicat*, et miserōs ōre edit *artūs*. Deinde Laōcoōnta ipsum euntem ut auxilium det ac tēla ferentem rapiunt, *spirīs*que vinciunt ingentibus; et iam *bis* mēdium amplēxī, bis *cōllum squāmeīs tergīs*, superant illum capitibus altīs. Laōcoōn simul* manibus tendit rumpere *spīrās*, capite *perfūsō* sanguine atrōque *venēnō*, et clāmōrēs simul* horrendōs ad caela tollit. At geminī lapsī templum ad summum dracōnēs fugiunt *saevae*que petunt Palladis arcem, sub pedibusque deae et sub *clipeō* occultantur.

The Trojans' Fate Sealed

Tum vērō cunctī māgnoperē verentur, et scelus expendisse merentem Laōcoōnta dīcunt, quod sacrum līgnum pessimā percusserat hastā. Ducendum esse ad templum simulācrum orandaque esse deae nūmina clamant. Dīvidimus mūrōs et moenia aperīmus urbis. Laborant omnēs ut equum līgnī trahant; ascendit fatālis machina per mūrōs fēta armīs. Puerī circum puellaeque sacra carmina canunt equumque manū tangere gaudent; illa machina init mediamque mināns labitur in urbem. Ō pātria, Ō deōrum domus Īlium! Quater equus ipsō in līmine portae substitit atque ex uterō sonitum quater arma dedērunt; instāmus tamen immemores caecīque furōre. Tunc etiam futūrīs fātīs aperit Cassandra ōra deī mandatō, nōn umquam crēdita ab Teucrīs. Nōs miserī, quibus ultimus esset* ille diēs, templa deōrum induimus festā fronde per urbem. Vertitur intereā caelum et ruit ex Oceanō nox involvēns umbra magna terramque caelumque Danaōrumque dolōs; fusī per moenia Teucrī conticuērunt; sopor fessōs amplectitur artūs.

Notes:

* *Et sī...fuisset, sī...fuisset, ...coēgisset, ...starēs, ...manērēs:* Subjunctives in a condition (see Lesson 10); translate as, "And if... had been, if...had been, ...he would have compelled, ...you would stand, ...you would remain."

* *consiliō:* The ablative can mean "intentionally, on purpose."

* *simul...simul:* "not only...but at the same time"

* *esset:* Technically this is called an "adversative relative clause" or a "relative clause of characteristic with accessory notion of cause," but for our purposes, see how it's a subordinate verb? That's why it's subjunctive!

Glossary:

amplector, -ī, -plexus sum: I embrace, encircle
anguis, -is (m): serpent, snake
artus, -ūs (m): joint, limb
Cassandra, -ae (f): Cassandra, a daughter of Priam; she was cursed by Apollo with the gift of prophecies that no one believed
caverna, -ae (f): cavity, cavern
cavus, -a, -um: hollow, empty
clipeus [or clypeus], -ī (m): shield
cōllum, -ī (n): neck
conticescō, -ere, -ticuī: I become silent, fall silent
Danaus, -a, -um: Greek, Danaan, a descendant of Dandaus, founder of Argos; (as noun) a Greek
Diomēdēs, -is (m): Diomedes, Greek warrior
dīvidō, -ere, -vīsī, -vīsum: I divide, separate
expendō, -ere, -dī, -sum: I pay for, suffer
exsanguis, -e: bloodless, pale
fatālis, -e: fatal, fated, deadly
fessus, -a, -um: weary, tired, exhausted
fēstus, -a -um: festal, festive, joyful, merry
fētus, -a, -um: pregnant, filled
frōns, frondis (f): foliage, garland, greenery
furor, -ōris (m): madness, fury, rage
fūsus, -a, -um: spread out, scattered
futūrus, -a, -um: future, about to be
gemitus, -ūs (m): groan, complaint
Īlium, -iī (n): Ilium, Troy
inclūdō, -ere, -clūsī, -clūsum: I shut in/up, enclose
insānia, -ae (f): insanity, madness
Laōcoōn, -ontis (m) [acc. Laōcoōnta]: Laocoön, Trojan priest of Neptune
laedō, -ere, laesī, laesus: I wound, offend
immemor, -ōris: unmindful, heedless, not thinking
implicō (1): I entwine, entangle
īnsonō, -āre, -uī, -ītum: I resound, echo
īnstō, -āre, -stitī, -stātum: I press on, urge forward
involvō, -ere, -volvī, -volūtum: I roll up, wrap (in), envelop
lācrima, -ae (f): tear
lambō, -ere, lambī, -bitum: I lick
māchina, -ae (f): machine, device, (military) engine
mereō, -ēre, -uī, -itus: I deserve, merit, earn
minor, -ārī, -ātus sum: I threaten, menace
Neptūnus, -ī (m): Neptune, god of the sea
Ōceanus, -ī (m): ocean, [the deity] Ocean
Pallas, -adis (f): (Pallas) Athena, identified with Roman goddess Minerva
perfundō, -ere, -fūdī, -fūsus: I pour over, drench
plācō (1): I appease, pacify
Priamus, -ī (m): Priam, last king of Troy
quater (adv.): four times
saevus, -a, -um: savage, fierce, cruel
sālum, -ī (n): the (salt) sea
sībilus, -a, -um: hissing, whistling
Sinon, -ōnis (m): Sinon, the Greek left behind to deceive the Trojans regarding the horse
sonitus, -ūs (m): sound, noise
sopor, -ōris (m): (deep) sleep
spīra, -ae (f): coil, fold
spūmō (1): I foam, froth, spray
squāmeus, -a, -um: scaly
subsistō, -ere, -stitī, ——: I halt, stand still, pause
Tenedos, -ī (f): Tenedos, small island near Troy where the Greeks had sailed and hidden their ships until the horse was taken into the city
Teucrus, -a, -um: Teucrian, Trojan; (as noun) a Trojan [Teucer was considered the first king of Troy]
tremō, -ere, -uī, ——: I shake, quiver, tremble
Ulixēs, -is (m): Ulysses (Odysseus)
uterus, -ī (m): belly, womb
venēnum, -ī (n): venom, poison
vibrō (1): I vibrate, flicker

F. For Fun

Match the Latin names of these Roman weapons with their meanings.

ANCIENT NAME	MODERN NAME
arcus g	a. a round shield made of bronze
ballista q	b. a helmet (usually of leather)
cassis i	c. a catapult siege engine used for hurling large stones
clipeus a	d. an arrow
dolābra s	e. a light throwing javelin
galea b	f. a catapult-type weapon used for hurling darts, stones, and other missiles
gladius Hispaniensis m	g. a bow
hasta vēlitāris e	h. lead-weighted throwing dart
hasta r	i. a helmet (usually of metal)
onager c	j. a half-sword or dagger
parma k	k. a small circular shield
pīlum t	l. spiked instrument thrown down to hinder marching armies and animals
plumbāta sagitta h	m. a short sword used by Roman legionaries
pūgiō p	n. usually a long sword, broad and two-edged without a point
sagitta d	o. oblong shield made of wood and leather
scorpiō f	p. dagger
scūtum o	q. a large ancient type of cross-bow used for hurling stones and missiles
semispatha j	r. a thrusting spear, lance
spatha n	s. a pickaxe
tribulus l	t. a heavy throwing javelin

LESSON 7

Verbs: Subjunctive: *Cum* Clauses; Sequence of Tenses

Word List

Nouns/Pronouns

1. fīdūcia, -ae (f) *trust, faith, confidence*
2. generātiō, -ōnis (f) *generation*
3. īdōlum, -ī (n) *image, form, idol*
4. initium, -iī (n) *beginning, commencement, entrance*
5. laetitia, -ae (f) *joy, gladness*
6. -met (intensifying suffix on personal pronouns) *-self*
7. modus, -ī (m) *measure, way, manner, sort*
8. salūs, -ūtis (f) *salvation, deliverance, health, safety*

Adjectives

9. immānis, -e *enormous, monstrous, immense*
10. iūstus, -a, -um *just, righteous, upright*
11. tūtus, -a, -um *safe, secure*

Verbs

12. adnūntiō (1) [annūntiō, etc.] *I announce, make known*
13. dēscendō, -ere, -scendī, -scensum *I come down, descend, fall (down)*
14. permaneō, -ēre, -mansī, -mansum *I remain, continue, abide (in)*
15. polliceor, -ērī, pollicitus sum *I promise, offer, declare*
16. temptō (1) *I attempt, try, test*

Adverbs, etc.

17. cum (prep. + abl.) *with;* (conj.) *when, while, since, after, although*
18. nōndum (adv.) *not yet*
19. potius (adv.) *more, rather*
20. sōlum (adv.) *only, alone, merely*

Memorization

John 1:1–14

[1] In principio erat Verbum et Verbum erat apud Deum et Deus erat Verbum. [2] Hoc erat in principio apud Deum. [3] Omnia per ipsum facta sunt, et sine ipso factum est nihil quod factum est. [4] In ipso vita erat et vita erat lux hominum. [5] Et lux in tenebris lucet et tenebrae eam non conprehenderunt. [6] Fuit homo missus a Deo cui nomen erat Iohannes. [7] Hic venit in testimonium ut testimonium perhiberet de lumine ut omnes crederent per illum. [8] Non erat ille lux, sed ut testimonium perhiberet de lumine. [9] Erat lux vera quae inluminat omnem hominem venientem in mundum. [10] In mundo erat et mundus per ipsum factus est et mundus eum non cognovit. [11] In propria venit et sui eum non receperunt. [12] Quotquot autem receperunt eum dedit eis potestatem filios Dei fieri, his qui credunt in nomine eius, [13] qui non ex sanguinibus neque ex voluntate carnis neque ex voluntate viri sed ex Deo nati sunt. **[14] Et Verbum caro factum est et habitavit in nobis et vidimus gloriam eius, gloriam quasi unigeniti a Patre plenum gratiae et veritatis.**

[14] And the Word became flesh and dwelt among us and we saw His glory, the glory as of the Only-Begotten from the Father, full of grace and truth.

Grammar

Cum Clauses

We have long been acquainted with *cum* the preposition, which takes the ablative case and means "with" (*KL1*, Lesson 9). We have used this to show what Latin grammarians call ablative of accompaniment: *Oswaldus cum suō amicō ad spēluncam dracōnis iit*, "Oswald went to the dragon's cave with his friend." *Cum* can also appear in the ablative of manner: *Dracō eum cum timōre spectāvit*, "The dragon looked at him with fear." This usage is also very familiar to us in the phrases *summā cum laude* and *magnā cum laude*. These honor roll titles actually illustrate an important *cum* phenomenon. Basically, just remember that *cum* is a coward. Whenever it can, it likes to hide behind or between words. So, when this ablative of manner includes an adjective, *cum* prefers to go in the middle. Thus we say *cum laude*, but *summā cum laude* (not *cum summā laude* or *cum laude summā*). And, just so you know, sometimes with that adjective the *cum* is left out altogether (or you could think of it as hiding so well in its cowardice that it cannot be seen at all): *summā laude*.

Another way the preposition *cum* is a coward is that when it is used with personal and reflexive pronouns (*ego, tū, nōs, vōs,* and *suī*), it will run behind its object pronoun (which is in the ablative case of course) and attach onto it as an enclitic: *mēcum*, "with me"; not *cum mē*. With the other pronouns it will appear as *tēcum, nōbīscum, vōbīscum,* and *sēcum*. *Cum* can also do this with relative pronouns, although it doesn't have to. Thus you will see either *quōcum* or *cumquō*; *quibuscum* or *cum quibus*.

So much for *cum* as preposition. Before we head into *cum*'s very important role as conjunction, I want to mention briefly that *cum* also appears as the prefix *com-* (especially on verbs, nouns, and adjectives). Depending on the initial letter of the word it is attaching to, that *com-* can change to *con-*, *cor-*, *col-*, or *co-*. This prefix can mean either the expected "with, together", or indicates completeness, or simply intensifies the meaning of the word it attaches to (and sometimes that intensity can't be adequately translated). For example, *conferō, conferre, contulī, collātum* [or *conlātum*] means either "I bring together," or something like "I bring [something] in some sort of intensified way" (exact translation depends on context—such as "I'm bringing it in a hurry"). Likewise, *consurgō, consurgere, consurrēxī, consurrectum* can mean either "I rise up together," or simply, "I rise up."

In addition to being a prefix and a preposition, *cum* can also be a conjunction, introducing a subordinate clause. This clause can either have an indicative or a subjunctive verb. **When *cum* introduces a clause with an indicative verb, it is called a temporal *cum* clause,** and describes a simple relation of time between the subordinate and main clauses:

Cum dracō īrātus est, tum ululat. When a dragon is angry, then he howls.

Cum Oswaldus Rōmae erat, dracōnem pugnāvit. When Oswald was in Rome, he fought a dragon.

Any tense of the indicative can appear in this type of *cum* clause, and the *cum* is usually translated as "when." However, sometimes you will see *tum* in the main clause, and together *cum . . . tum* can mean "not only . . . but also" or "both . . . and" (although they can also just mean "when . . . then"). Again, notice that the temporal *cum* clause (with indicative) simply defines the time period in which the main action is occurring. A negative temporal *cum* clause uses *nōn.*

***Cum* can also introduce a subordinate clause with a subjunctive verb.** Different Latin grammars give slightly varying names, although they generally agree on three basic types:

1. **Circumstantial or Historical *Cum* Clause:** Describes the general circumstances of an (usually past) action. Translate with "as, when, while, after."
2. **Causal *Cum* Clause:** Relates the cause of the main action. Translate with "since, because, as, whereas."
3. **Concessive or Adversative *Cum* Clause:** Describes a circumstance that interferes in some way with the main action. Translate with "although, whereas." Sometimes *tamen* appears in the main clause.

These may sound more complicated than they actually are. Here are some examples to clarify them.

SUBJUNCTIVE *CUM* CLAUSES	EXAMPLES
CIRCUMSTANTIAL/ HISTORICAL	*Cum Oswaldus rēx esset, multōs dracōnēs pugnāvit.* When Oswald was king, he fought many dragons. *Cum Oswaldus dracōnem necet, filiam rēgis servābit.* After Oswald kills the dragon, he will save the princess.
CAUSAL	*Cum tū dracōnem nōn necārēs, Oswaldō eum necāre necesse erat.* Since you did not kill the dragon, it was necessary for Oswald to kill it. *Dracō subito mortuus est cum nimis multās ovēs ēdisset.* The dragon suddenly died after it had eaten too many sheep.

CONCESSIVE/ ADVERSATIVE	*Cum dracō fortiter pugnāverit, Oswaldus nunc nōn vulnerātur.* Although the dragon fought bravely, nevertheless Oswald is now not wounded. *Equitēs currēbat cum dracōnem vidēre nōn possent.* The knights kept running although they couldn't see the dragon.

Note that in all of these examples, the *cum* clause verb is in the subjunctive and it is generally translated by an English indicative. Also notice that a good deal of the time, context will have to help us figure out which type of *cum* clause we are dealing with. Take the first example under Circumstantial/Historical *Cum* Clause—seen in isolation, it would be hard to know which translation to go with:

Cum Oswaldus rēx esset, multōs dracōnēs pugnāvit.

(a) When Oswald was king, he fought many dragons.

(b) Since Oswald was king, he fought many dragons.

(c) Although Oswald was king, he fought many dragons.

You can easily imagine a context in which each of these translations could work. So consider the meaning of the whole passage and how each particular *cum* clause fits with it in order to choose the best translation. These *cum* clauses really are simple to work with in real Latin, trust me.

When translating from English to Latin, there are a few things to keep in mind. The English word "when" has different possibilities that may not work in Latin. For example, if you see the English sentences "When is he coming?" and "I asked him when he is coming," both of these whens are interrogative, and CANNOT be translated with a *cum* clause; they need to be translated by "quando." A *cum* clause must always be governed by a finite verb (in the indicative or subjunctive), and not a participle. The sentence "Oswald, when killing dragons, always prays first" would use a Latin participial phrase for "when killing dragons" and NOT a *cum* clause.

What follows is a chart illustrating the varied and beauteous ways of *cum*.

Summary of Cum Usages

PART OF SPEECH	DESCRIPTION OF USAGE	MEANING/EXAMPLES
PREFIX	*cō-/col-/com-/con-/cor-*	"together, with"; indicates completeness or for emphasis/intensity
PREPOSITION	+ ablative	"with"
	Abl. of Manner	*cum timōre,* "with fear"
	Abl. of Accompaniment	*cum amicō,* "with a friend"
	enclitic on personal, reflexive, & sometimes relative pronouns	*mēcum, tēcum, nōbīscum, vōbīscum, sēcum, quōcum (cum quō), quibuscum (cum quibus)*

CONJUNCTION + INDICATIVE	Temporal *Cum* Clause	*Cum dracō īrātus est, tum ululat.* When a dragon is angry, then he howls.
CONJUNCTION + SUBJUNCTIVE	Circumstantial/Historical *Cum* Clause	*Cum Oswaldus rēx esset, multōs dracōnēs pugnāvit.* When Oswald was king, he fought many dragons.
	Causal *Cum* Clause	*Cum tū dracōnem nōn necārēs, Oswaldō eum necāre necesse erat.* Since you did not kill the dragon, it was necessary for Oswald to kill it.
	Adversative *Cum* Clause	*Cum dracō fortiter pugnāverit, Oswaldus nunc nōn vulnerātur.* Although the dragon fought bravely, nevertheless Oswald is now not wounded.

Sequence of Tenses

After all the hinting, it's finally time to officially discuss Sequence of Tenses. Remember that a subjunctive portrays hypothetical, indirect, or subordinate action. Different tenses of the infinitive in indirect statement show when that subordinate action occurred relative to the main verb. For instance, if we use the *-ere* ending, it means it happened in the same tense as the main verb. If, however, we use the *-isse* ending, it means it happened before the tense of the main verb. And if we used *-ūrum esse*, it means that it happened relative to the future.

Similarly, we will change the tense of the subjunctive depending on its relationship with the main verb. The present subjunctive is used with a present or future main verb to express the same time as or future of the main verb; imperfect subjunctive shows the same time as main verbs in one of the past tenses (imperfect, perfect, or pluperfect). To indicate action occurring before that of the main verb, we will use a perfect subjunctive when the main verb is a present or future, and a pluperfect subjunctive if the main verb is in the past. Here is a chart that should make this clear:

MAIN VERB	SUBJUNCTIVE	ACTION RELATIVE TO MAIN VERB
PRESENT OR FUTURE	Present	same time/future
	Perfect	before
PAST (IMPERFECT, PERFECT, OR PLUPERFECT)	Imperfect	same time/future
	Pluperfect	before

Here are some examples (some of them are a little stilted for purposes of illustration):

Cum dracōnem necet, Oswaldus fīliam rēgis servābit. When/Since he kills [*or,* will kill] the dragon, Oswald will save the princess.

Cum dracōnem necāverit, Oswaldus fīliam rēgis servābit. When/Since he (has) killed the dragon, Oswald will save the princess.

Cum dracōnem necāret, Oswaldus fīliam rēgis servābat. When/Since he was killing the dragon, Oswald was saving the princess.

Cum dracōnem necāvisset, Oswaldus fīliam rēgis servābat. When/Since he had killed the dragon, Oswald saved [*or,* was saving] the princess.

Sequence of Tenses is something that might seem a little intimidating at first, but it is really only a bit challenging when you are translating from English to Latin. When reading in Latin, you will probably be able to translate sequence of tense without even thinking about it, and the various tenses will just make sense.

Review

Be sure to review the perfect and pluperfect subjunctives; don't forget how the perfect subjunctive is slightly different from the future perfect. Review the differences carefully. Be sure to add the *Cum Clauses* to your list of subjunctives and expand your sequence of tenses. At this point you have learned them all, so you should practice using it on all the different subjunctives you've learned.

Worksheet 7

A. Vocabulary

1. army: ______________________________
2. immānis: ______________________________
3. bibō, -ere, bibī, potum: ______________________________
4. easy: ______________________________
5. adnūntiō (1): ______________________________
6. modus: ______________________________
7. laetitia: ______________________________
8. fīdūcia: ______________________________
9. polliceor, pollicērī, pollicitus sum: ______________________________
10. initium: ______________________________
11. īdōlum: ______________________________
12. salvation: ______________________________
13. potius: ______________________________
14. -met: ______________________________
15. not yet (adv.): ______________________________
16. temptō (1): ______________________________
17. just: ______________________________
18. safe: ______________________________
19. ______________, ______________, permansī, ______________: ______________________________
20. generation: ______________________________
21. sumō, -ere, sūmpsī, sūmptum: ______________________________
22. I come down: ______________________________
23. sōlum: ______________________________
24. I buy: ______________________________
25. cum (prep. ________ or ________): ______________________________

B. Grammar

1. Translate these *cum* snippets into English.

   a. pāx vōbīscum: ____________________

   b. cum descenderēs: ____________________

   c. māximā cum laetitiā: ____________________

   d. vīdimus eōs quibuscum permanēmus: ____________________

   e. cum adnuntiāvissem: ____________________

   f. cum īdōlīs: ____________________

   g. vade mēcum: ____________________

   h. cum pollicētur: ____________________

2. Parse the following verbs. For Indicative or Subjunctive, give Person, Number, Tense, Voice, and Mood. For Participles, give Gender, Number, Case, Tense, Voice, and Mood. For Infinitives, give Tense, Voice, and Mood. Also give the 1st principal part, and indicate if the verb is a deponent, no matter what its mood is. For the translation of subjunctive, you may write "depends on context" rather than attempting to translate the verb in isolation.

VERB	PNTVM (INDIC./SUBJ.), GNCTVM (PRT.), *OR* TVM (INFIN.)	1ST PRINCIPAL PART	TRANSLATION
incolendum			
coepisse			
putentur			
ēdūcentur			
carērēris			
ēstis			

consūmptī			
sentiātis			
adsumus			
decuit			

3. Do a synopsis of *polliceor* in the 2nd person singular, first giving principal parts:

____

		LATIN ACTIVE	ENGLISH ACTIVE	LATIN PASSIVE	ENGLISH PASSIVE
INDICATIVE	PRES.				
	IMPF.				
	FUT.				
	PF.				
	PLPF.				
	FT. PF.				
SUBJUNCTIVE	PRES.				
	IMPF.				
	PF.				
	PLPF.				

PARTICIPLE	PRES.				
	PF.				
	FUT.				
INFINITIVE	PRES.				
	PF.				
	FUT.				
IMP.	SG.				
	PL.				

C. Memorization

Fill in the blanks in 1:1-14 in Latin.

____ ____ ____ ____ ____ ____ ____ ____ ____ ____ ____

____ ____ ____ ____. ____ ____ ____ ____ ____ ____

____ ____. ____ ____ ____ ____, ____

____ ____ ____ ____ fieri, ____ ____ ____ ____ nomine ____,

____ ____ ____ sanguinibus ____ ____ ____ ____ neque ____

____ ____ ____ ____ ____ nati ____. ____ ____ caro ____

____ ____ habitavit ____ ____ ____ vidimus ____ ____, gloriam ____

____ ____ Patre ____ gratiae ____ ____.

D. English to Latin

Translate these sentences into Latin. (Hint: Translate *italicized* verbs with Latin participles/gerunds, **bold** with subjunctives, <u>underlined</u> with infinitives, and SMALL-CAPPED with supines.)

1. Although the herd **was** safe on the enormous mountain, nevertheless, *descending* to the sea it rushed into the deserted waters.

2. When my clothes become dirty, I myself wash them, much water *having been carried* here.

3. While the enemy's army **was attempting** <u>to attack</u> our flank, we used deceit and came upon them suddenly from the rear.

4. Since the righteous woman **had** a strong faith in God, she will remain in prison in Rome.

5. After the Greeks **had promised** that they <u>would depart</u>, we did not lack any joy, *saying*, "**Let** us **thank** the gods!"

6. The princess does not yet understand that I *must sing* these songs of love under her tower so that she *may love* me.

7. Although this generation only **loves** its idols, I still will announce that all *must receive* salvation.

8. When the older guard was in Athens, at that time he thought he saw either a demon or a ghost *hiding* in a doorway there.

9. **Do** not **work** well in the beginning of a work but badly later.

10. Since your soldiers **had lost** all their weapons, they wanted to go home rather than to war lest **they be killed** or **defeated**.

E. Latin to English

Adapted from Sulpicius Severus, *Vīta Sanctī Martinī*, 13.1-14.7

St. Martin and the Pine Tree

Etiam, cum in oppidō quōdam *Martinus* templum *antīquissimum* sustulisset et *aggressus esset* caedere* arborem *pīnum*, quae templō* erat proxima, tum vērō sacerdōtēs locī illīus cēteraque *gentīlium* turba coepērunt *obsistere*. Et cum īdem illī, dum templum *ēvertitur*, iubente Dominō *quiēvissent*, tamen caedī arborem non volēbant. *Martinus* eōs valde monuit, nihil esse *religiōnis* in līgnō; potius, eōs sequī Deum, cui servīret ipse; arborem illam caedī oportere, quia *esset* daemoniō *dedicāta*.

Tum ūnus ex illīs quī erat fortior cēterīs, "Sī habēs," inquit, "aliquam fīdūciam dē Deō tuō, quem dīcis tē cōlere, nōsmet ipsī caedēmus hanc arborem, et tū, eam ruentem accipe; et sī tēcum* est tuus, ut dīcis, Dominus, ēvadēs." Tum ille *intrepidē confisus* in Dominō sē factūrum esse hoc *pollicētur.* Hīc vērō ad istius modī *condiciōnem* omnis illa gentīlium turba *consensit,* facilemque arboris suae putāvērunt *iactūram,* ut inimīcum sacrōrum suōrum casū eius delērent.

Itaque, cum ūnam in partem pīnus illa esset *acclīnis,* ut non esset *dubium,* quam in partem caesa rueret*, eō locī vinctus *statuitur* cōgitātiōne *rusticōrum,* quō arborem esse casūram nēmō *dubitābat.* Caedere igitur ipsī suam pīnum cum ingentī gaudiō laetitiāque coepērunt. Aderat procul turba mīrantium. Iamque *paulātim nutāvit* pīnus casūra.

Pallēbant procul *monachī* et perīculō iam propiōre territī spem omnem fīdūciamque perdiderant, sōlam *Martinī* mortem exspectantēs. At ille *confīsus* in Dominō *intrepidē* exspectāns, cum iam *fragōrem* suī pīnus caedēns dedisset, iam arborī cadentī, iam super sē ruentī, sublātā *obviam* manū, sīgnum *salūtis* fēcit. Tum vērō *dīversam* in partem ruit, tam ut rusticōs, quī tutō in locō steterant, paenē strāverit.

Tum vērō, in caelum clamōre sublatō, *gentīlēs* mīrātī sunt sīgnum, *monachī* flēvērunt ob gaudium, et Christī nōmen ab omnibus *praedicātum est:* satisque cōnstituitur eō diē salūtem illī vēnisse *regiōnī.* Nam nēmō ferē ex immānī illā multitūdine *gentīlium* fuit, quī nōn *impositiōne* manus cupītā Dominum Iēsum, relictō *impietātis errōre,* crēdiderit. Et vērō ante *Martinum* paucissimī, *immō* paene nūllī in illīs regiōnibus Christī nōmen *recēperant;* quod tam virtutibus* suīs *exemplōque convaluit,* ut iam ibī nūllus locus sit, quī nōn aut ecclesiīs crebērrimīs aut *monasteriīs* sit replētus*. Nam ubī templa delēvit, statim ibī aut ecclesiās aut monastēria aedificābat.

Assassination Attempts on Martin

Quid ētiam in terrā *Aeduōrum* actum sit*, narrābō. Dum templum illīc tolleret, *furēns gentīlium rusticōrum* in eum ruit multitūdō. Cumque unus fortior cetērīs *strictō* eum gladiō peteret, *Martinus reiectō palliō nūdam cervicem* percussūrō* *praebuit.* Nec *cunctātus* percutīre *gentīlis,* sed cum dexteram altius sustulisset, *resupinus* ruit, *cōnsternātus*que *divinō* metū *veniam* petēbat. Nec dissimile huic fuit illud: cum eum īdōla *dēstruentem cultrō* quidam percutīre voluisset, in ipsō *ictū* ferrum eī dē manibus *excussum* nōn appāruit. *Plērumque* autem contrā dicentibus sibi rusticīs, nē eōrum templa delēret, īta sermōne sanctō *gentīlēs* animōs *mitigābat,* ut lūce eīs vēritātis ostensā, ipsī sua templa *subverterent.*

Notes:

* *caedere:* infinitive of purpose (found in later Latin and not considered "proper" Latin)

* *templō:* dative with *proxima*

* *-cum:* Remember that *cum* can attach onto personal pronouns; *tēcum,* therefore, is the same as *cum tē.*

* *rueret:* This is a subjunctive because it is a relative clause within a purpose clause (fancy name, *ōrātiō oblīqua,* "indirect discourse").

* *virtūtibus: virtūs* can also mean "virtue, miracle"

* *replētus sit:* see note on *rueret* above

* *actus sit:* Subjunctive in Informal Indirect Discourse, but notice how easy it is to translate!

* *percussūrō:* dative, referring to the *unus fortior*

Glossary:

acclīnis, -e: leaning (on), inclined (to/toward)
Aeduī, -ōrum (m, pl): the Aedui, a Gallic tribe from central France
aggredior, -ī, -gressus sum: I approach, attack
cervīx, -īcis (f): neck
condiciō, -ōnis (f): condition, agreement, terms
confīdō [-fideō], -ere, -fisus sum: [semi-deponent] I trust (in), have confidence (in)
cōnsentiō, -īre, -sensī, -sensum: I feel together, agree
cōnsternō (1): I bring to confusion, terrify, dismay
convalēscō, -ere, -valuī, -valitus: I grow strong, gain strength
culter, -trī (m): knife
cunctor, -ārī, -ātus sum: I delay, hesitate
dēdicō (1): I dedicate, consecrate
dēstruō, -ere, -xī, -ctum: I destroy, tear down

dīversus, -a, -um: diverse, opposite
dīvīnus, -a, -um: divine
dubitō (1): I doubt, am uncertain, question
dubius, -a, -um: doubtful, dubious, uncertain; *dubium est* = it is doubtful
error, -ōris (m): error, mistake
ēvādō, -ere, -vāsī, -vāsum: I go out/forth, escape
ēvertō, -ere, -tī, -sum: I overturn, overthrow, destroy
excutiō, -īre, -cussī, -cussum: I shake out/off, cast out
exemplum, -ī: example
fragor, -ōris (m): a crashing, crash, noise, din
furō, -ere, -uī, ——: I rage, rave, am furious
gentīlis, -is (m/f): Gentile, pagan, heathen
iactūra, -ae (f): a throwing (away/over); here = "trajectory"
ictus, -ūs (m): blow, stroke
immō: nay rather, on the contrary, no indeed
impietās, -tātis (f): impiety, irreverence, ungodliness
impositiō, -ōnis (f): a putting on, laying on
intrepidē: without trembling, intrepidly
Martinus, -ī (m): Martin
mītigō (1): I calm, soothe, pacify
monachus, -ī (m): monk
monastērium, -iī (n): monastery
nūdus, -a, -um: naked, bare, exposed
nūtō (1): I nod, shake, sway to and fro
obsistō, -ere, -stitī, -stitum: I oppose, withstand, resist
obviam (adv.): in the way, against
palleō, -ēre, -uī, ——: I am/grow pale
pallium, -ī (n): cloak, cover(ing)
paulātim: little by little, gradually
pīnus, -ī (f): pine (tree), fir (tree)
plērumquē (adv.): generally, for the most part
praebeō, -ēre, -uī, -ītum: I give, show, expose
praedīcō (1): I proclaim, preach, declare
quiēscō, -ere, quiēvī, quiētum: I rest, keep quiet
recipiō, -ere, -cēpi, -ceptum: I take back/again, receive
regiō, -ōnis (f): region, territory, boundary
rēiciō, -ere, -iēcī, -iectum: I throw back, fling back
religiō, -ōnis (f): religion, reverence
resupīnus, -a, -um: backwards, lying on one's back, supine
rusticus, -a, -um: of the county, rustic, rural; (as noun) a countryman, rustic, peasant
statuō, -ere, -uī, -ūtum: I cause to stand, set (up), place
stringō, -ere, strinxī, strictum: I draw (out), pull
subvertō, -ere, -vertī, -versus: I overturn, overthrow, ruin
venia, -ae (f): mercy, pardon, forgiveness

LESSON 8

Review and Test

Word List

No new words this lesson. Review vocabulary, including brushing up on any old words from *KL1* and *KL2* as necessary.

Grammar

No new grammar this lesson. Review previous lessons.

Worksheet 8

A. Vocabulary

1. jail: ______
2. aequor: ______
3. āgmen: ______
______
4. prīncipium: ______
5. ear: ______
6. līmen: ______
______
7. cōgitātiō: ______
8. wilderness: ______
9. collis: ______
10. custōs: ______
______
11. generation: ______
12. daemonium: ______
13. pecus: ______
14. prophet: ______
15. imāgō: ______
16. teaching: ______
17. dolus: ______
18. fās: ______
(adj.) ______
19. aura: ______
20. concilium: ______
21. fīdūcia: ______
______
22. īdōlum: ______
23. joy: ______
24. initium: ______
______
25. decet: ______
______
26. latus: ______
27. judge: ______
28. peccātor/peccātrix: ______
29. cōnfiteor: ______
30. ineō: ______
31. lie: ______
32. liar: ______
33. -met: ______
34. immundus: ______
35. modus: ______
______
36. I lie: ______
37. consūmō: ______
______
38. necesse: ______
39. nefās: ______
40. arbitror: ______
41. number: ______
42. memoria: ______
43. placeō: ______
44. onus: ______
45. platēa: ______
46. sabbātum: ______
47. salvātor: ______

48. ūniversus: ______________________________

____

49. crime: ______________________________

50. appareō: ______________________________

51. sign: ______________________________

52. simulācrum: ______________________________

____

53. sors: ______________________________

____

54. iubeō: ______________________________

55. custōdiō: ______________________________

____

56. tēlum: ______________________________

57. witness: ______________________________

58. shadow: ______________________________

59. ēdūcō: ______________________________

____

60. vīs: ______________________________

____

61. mīrābilis: ______________________________

____

62. absum: ______________________________

____

63. impius: ______________________________

____

64. I announce: ______________________________

65. tantus: ______________________________

66. I rest: ______________________________

67. tergum: ______________________________

68. I make holy: ______________________________

69. adsum: ______________________________

70. afferō: ______________________________

71. salvation: ______________________________

72. benedīcō: ______________________________

____

73. quisque: ______________________________

74. I lack: ______________________________

75. coepī: ______________________________

76. I come down: ______________________________

77. iūstus: ______________________________

78. dīligō: ______________________________

79. oportet: ______________________________

80. putō: ______________________________

81. crēber: ______________________________

____

82. īdem, eadem: ______________________________

83. suus: ______________________________

____

84. tam: ______________________________

85. haud: ______________________________

86. edō: ______________________________

87. ēligō: ______________________________

88. resistō: ______________________________

89. sentiō: ______________________________

90. for: ______________________________

91. incolō: ______________________________

____

92. intellegō: ______________________________

93. ūtor, ūtī, ūsus sum: ______________________________

94. polliceor: ______________________________

95. licet: ______________________________

____

96. temptō: ______________________________

97. maledīcō: ______________________________

____

98. mundō: ______________________________

99. redeō: ______________________________
____

100. dēsertus: ______________________________
____

101. heavy: ______________________________

102. I fall down: ______________________________

103. negō: ______________________________

104. I do not know: ______________________________

105. I hate: ______________________________

106. inferō: ______________________________

107. I show: ______________________________

108. permaneō: ______________________________
____

109. rēpleō: ______________________________
____

110. I hope: ______________________________

111. certain: ______________________________

112. dīlēctus: ______________________________

113. Greek: ______________________________

114. immānis: ______________________________
____

115. mundus: ______________________________

116. senior: ______________________________
____

117. safe: ______________________________

118. such: ______________________________

119. at: ______________________________

120. usque (adv. or prep +a________): ____________
____
____

121. twice: ______________________________

122. certe: ______________________________

123. in vain: ______________________________

124. cum (prep. +__________ or conj.): __________
____
____

125. eōdem (adv.): ______________________________
____

126. ferē: ______________________________

127. forās: ______________________________
____

128. longē: ______________________________

129. nē (adv.): ______________________________
(conj.) ______________________________

130. subitō/subitum: ______________________________
____

131. nimis (adv.): ______________________________
____

132. not yet: ______________________________

133. omnīno: ______________________________
____

134. pariter: ______________________________

135. potius: ______________________________

136. quisquam, quidquam/quicquam: ____________
____
____

137. rursum/rursus: ______________________________

138. scīlicet: ______________________________
____

139. sōlum (adv.): ______________________________

140. —— , suī: ______________________________
____

141. ut (conj. +indic.): ______________________________
(+subj.) ______________________________

142. vix: ______________________________

B. Grammar

1. Noun-Adjective Combos: Identify gender, number, and case (any possible options) of the following noun and adjective combinations, then translate them.

LATIN PHRASE	GENDER NUMBER CASE	LITERAL ENGLISH TRANSLATION
īdōlīs Graecīs		
mīrābilis umbrae		
aequōra dēserta		
tantōrum numerōrum		
vim immānem		
onus grave		
prophētae iūstō		
ūniversīs sabbatīs		
certa salūs		
mendācum crēbrārum		
pecōrī tūtō		
tālēs aurēs		

cuique carcerī		
fīdūciae impiae		
eiusdem daemoniī		

2. Decline *each witness* (include Locative, just for practice, even though it's highly unlikely this particular noun would appear in the Locative).

	LATIN SINGULAR	LATIN PLURAL
NOM.		
GEN.		
DAT.		
ACC.		
ABL.		
VOC.		
LOC.		

3. Decline *sure strength* (include Locative—again, just for practice).

	LATIN SINGULAR	LATIN PLURAL
NOM.		
GEN.		
DAT.		
ACC.		
ABL.		
VOC.		
LOC.		

4. Parse the following verbs. For Indicative or Subjunctive, give Person, Number, Tense, Voice, and Mood. For Participles, give Gender, Number, Case, Tense, Voice, and Mood. For Infinitives, give Tense, Voice, and Mood. Also provide 1st principal part, and indicate if the verb is a deponent, no matter what its mood is. For the translation of subjunctive, you may write "depends on context" rather than attempting to translate the verb in isolation.

VERB	PNTVM (INDIC./SUBJ.), GNCTVM (PRT.), OR TVM (INFIN.)	1ST PRINCIPAL PART	TRANSLATION
ōderāmus			
attulissēs			
custōdītīs			
adnūntiāverimus			
sanctificāverīmus			
spēranda			
mentīrēminī			
redībō			
placitūrum esse			
temptantis			
fārī			

rēplētūrōs			
iūssa sint			
ruētis			
oporteat			
ūsae sumus			
pollicear			
illātārum			
requiēscis			
licet			
negantibus			
āfuisse			
ēlēgerim			
maledīcī			

restituērunt			
mundēminī			
intellectī essēmus			
dīligentēs			
permanent			
nesciēbāris			
ostenta esse			
inīre			

5. Conjugate *benedīcō* in full in all its possible tenses, voices, and moods!

____

	PRESENT ACTIVE INDICATIVE			
	LATIN SINGULAR	ENGLISH SINGULAR	LATIN PLURAL	ENGLISH PLURAL
1ST				
2ND				
3RD				

	PRESENT PASSIVE INDICATIVE			
	LATIN SINGULAR	ENGLISH SINGULAR	LATIN PLURAL	ENGLISH PLURAL
1ST				
2ND				
3RD				

	IMPERFECT ACTIVE INDICATIVE			
	LATIN SINGULAR	ENGLISH SINGULAR	LATIN PLURAL	ENGLISH PLURAL
1ST				
2ND				
3RD				

	IMPERFECT PASSIVE INDICATIVE			
	LATIN SINGULAR	ENGLISH SINGULAR	LATIN PLURAL	ENGLISH PLURAL
1ST				
2ND				
3RD				

	FUTURE ACTIVE INDICATIVE			
	LATIN SINGULAR	ENGLISH SINGULAR	LATIN PLURAL	ENGLISH PLURAL
1ST				
2ND				
3RD				

	FUTURE PASSIVE INDICATIVE			
	LATIN SINGULAR	ENGLISH SINGULAR	LATIN PLURAL	ENGLISH PLURAL
1ST				
2ND				
3RD				

	PERFECT ACTIVE INDICATIVE			
	LATIN SINGULAR	ENGLISH SINGULAR	LATIN PLURAL	ENGLISH PLURAL
1ST				
2ND				
3RD				

	PERFECT PASSIVE INDICATIVE			
	LATIN SINGULAR	ENGLISH SINGULAR	LATIN PLURAL	ENGLISH PLURAL
1ST				
2ND				
3RD				

	PLUPERFECT PASSIVE INDICATIVE			
	LATIN SINGULAR	ENGLISH SINGULAR	LATIN PLURAL	ENGLISH PLURAL
1ST				
2ND				
3RD				

	PLUPERFECT PASSIVE INDICATIVE			
	LATIN SINGULAR	ENGLISH SINGULAR	LATIN PLURAL	ENGLISH PLURAL
1ST				
2ND				
3RD				

	FUTURE PERFECT ACTIVE INDICATIVE			
	LATIN SINGULAR	ENGLISH SINGULAR	LATIN PLURAL	ENGLISH PLURAL
1ST				
2ND				
3RD				

	FUTURE PERFECT PASSIVE INDICATIVE			
	LATIN SINGULAR	ENGLISH SINGULAR	LATIN PLURAL	ENGLISH PLURAL
1ST				
2ND				
3RD				

	PRESENT ACTIVE SUBJUNCTIVE			
	LATIN SINGULAR	ENGLISH SINGULAR	LATIN PLURAL	ENGLISH PLURAL
1ST				
2ND				
3RD				

	PRESENT PASSIVE SUBJUNCTIVE			
	LATIN SINGULAR	ENGLISH SINGULAR	LATIN PLURAL	ENGLISH PLURAL
1ST				
2ND				
3RD				

	IMPERFECT PASSIVE SUBJUNCTIVE			
	LATIN SINGULAR	ENGLISH SINGULAR	LATIN PLURAL	ENGLISH PLURAL
1ST				
2ND				
3RD				

	IMPERFECT PASSIVE SUBJUNCTIVE			
	LATIN SINGULAR	ENGLISH SINGULAR	LATIN PLURAL	ENGLISH PLURAL
1ST				
2ND				
3RD				

	PERFECT ACTIVE SUBJUNCTIVE			
	LATIN SINGULAR	ENGLISH SINGULAR	LATIN PLURAL	ENGLISH PLURAL
1ST				
2ND				
3RD				

	PERFECT PASSIVE SUBJUNCTIVE			
	LATIN SINGULAR	ENGLISH SINGULAR	LATIN PLURAL	ENGLISH PLURAL
1ST				
2ND				
3RD				

	PLUPERFECT ACTIVE SUBJUNCTIVE			
	LATIN SINGULAR	ENGLISH SINGULAR	LATIN PLURAL	ENGLISH PLURAL
1ST				
ND				
3RD				

	PLUPERFECT PASSIVE SUBJUNCTIVE			
	LATIN SINGULAR	ENGLISH SINGULAR	LATIN PLURAL	ENGLISH PLURAL
1ST				
2ND				
3RD				

		LATIN ACTIVE	ENGLISH ACTIVE	LATIN PASSIVE	ENGLISH PASSIVE
PARTICIPLE	PRES.				
	PF.				
	FUT.				
INFINITIVE	PRES.				
	PF.				
	FUT.				
IMP.	SG.				
	PL.				

C. Memorization

Fill in the blanks in John 1:1-14 in Latin. The first two words of each verse have been supplied for you.

In principio ______________________________

____

Hoc erat ______________________________

Omnia per ______________________________

____

In ipso ______________________________

Et lux ______________________________

____

Fuit homo ______________________________

Hic venit ______________________________

____

Non erat ______________________________

Erat lux ______________________________

____

In mundo ______________________________

____

In propria ______________________________

Quotquot autem ______________________________

____

qui non ______________________________

____

Et Verbum ______________________________

____

D. English to Latin

Translate this sentence into five different possible ways of expressing purpose in Latin:

The prophet descended from the holy hill to prophesy his burdensome oracle to everyone in the streets.

Translate this sentence into three different possible ways of expressing prohibition (negative command) in Latin:

My son, do not frighten a dragon from the rear while he is eating.

E. Latin to English

First translate these sentence sets reviewing Indirect Discourse. Pay particular attention to the tenses of the verbs.

1. a) Rōmānus Graecō adnuntiat sē cētum necāre.

   b) Rōmānus Graecō adnuntiat sē cētum necāvisse.

   c) Rōmānus Graecō adnuntiat sē cētum necātūrum esse.

2. a) Rōmānus Graecō adnuntiāvit sē cētum necāre.

   b) Rōmānus Graecō adnuntiāvit sē cētum necāvisse.

   c) Rōmānus Graecō adnuntiāvit sē cētum necātūrum esse.

3. a) Rōmānus Graecō fātur eum omnia crūstula edere.

   b) Rōmānus Graecō fātur eum omnia crūstula ēdisse.

   c) Rōmānus Graecō fātur eum omnia crūstula ēditūrum esse.

4. a) Rōmānus Graecō fātēbatur eum omnia crūstula edere.

____

____

b) Rōmānus Graecō fātēbatur eum omnia crūstula ēdisse.

____

____

c) Rōmānus Graecō fātēbatur eum omnia crūstula ēsūrum esse.

____

____

Translate the following sentences into English, identify the listed nouns and parse the listed verbs, and then explain why the listed verb is in the mood that it is in (in other words, its particular type of usage or clause—*cum* clause, ablative absolute, jussive subjunctive, etc.).

Identifying Nouns: Give Gender (Masc./Fem./Neut.), Number (Sg./Pl.), and Case (Nom./Gen./Dat./Acc./Abl./Voc./Loc.). Also tell which noun it comes from (i.e., give the noun's nominative singular).

Parsing Verbs: For Indicatives and Subjunctives, give Person, Number, Tense, Voice, and Mood; for Infinitives, give Tense, Voice, and Mood; for Participles, give Gender, Number, Case, Tense, Voice, and Mood. For all the moods, give the first principal part of the verb in question, and identify deponents as such.

5. In prīncipiō rēgnī nostrī cum mendācibus ostendere rēgī suās doctrīnās licēret, tum diēs ātrae omnīnō erant et tempora mala usque erant.

   a. Translation: ____

   ____

   ____

   b. Identify *diēs*: ____

   c. Parse *ostendere*: ____

   licēret: ____

   erant: ____

   d. Why is *licēret* in the mood that it is in? ____

   ____

6. Meās cōgitātiōnēs īnfimās rursum ēdūcam ne vōs meam magnam sapientiam nesciātis.

   a. Translation: ____

   ____

   ____

b. Identify *cōgitātiōnēs*: ______

c. Parse *ēdūcam*: ______

nesciātis: ______

d. Why is *ēdūcam* in the mood that it is in? ______

______

What about *nesciātis*? ______

7. Sīgnīs mīrābilibus certē factīs, Deō tam crēdidimus ut ab Eō salūtem peterēmus et relinquere nostra scelera coepissēmus.

a. Translation: ______

______

______

b. Identify *salūtem*: ______

c. Parse *factīs*: ______

crēdidimus: ______

peterēmus: ______

relinquere: ______

coepissēmus: ______

d. Why is *factīs* in the mood that it is in? ______

What about *peterēmus* and *coepissēmus*? ______

8. Sabbatīs Rōmae mendācia peccātōrum dolīque testium iūdicī inconciliō audienda sunt, et tunc omnēs rēs pariter bene arbitrābitur.

a. Translation: ______

______

______

b. Identify *Rōmae*: ______

c. Parse *audienda*: ______

sunt: ______

arbitrābitur: ______

d. Why is *audienda* in the mood that it is in? ______

______

9. Habetne quisquam vestīmenta munda quibus ego ūtī possum? Mea immunda facta sunt cum crēbrōs porcōs in dēsertīs custōdiissem.

   a. Translation: ______________________________

   ____

   ____

   b. Identify ***dēsertīs:*** ______________________________

   c. Parse *habet*: ______________________________

   ūtī: ______________________________

   possum: ______________________________

   facta sunt: ______________________________

   ____

   custōdissem: ______________________________

   d. Why is *ūtī* in the mood that it is in? ______________________________

   ____

   What about *custōdiissem*? ______________________________

10. Bis camēlus suōrum onerum inferendōrum causā ad līmen ferē adiit; bis nōn intellegēns iubendum suī dominī subitum restitit.

   a. Translation: ______________________________

   ____

   ____

   b. Identify *līmen*: ______________________________

   iubendum: ______________________________

   c. Parse *inferendōrum*: ______________________________

   adiit: ______________________________

   intellegēns: ______________________________

   restitit: ______________________________

   d. Why is *inferendōrum* in the mood that it is in? ______________________________

   ____

11. Nē nimis consūmpserīs crūstula, nē odium omnium cēterōrum cibōrum sentiās et tē sōlum crūstula semper ēsūrum esse exspectēs.

    a. Translation: ______

    ______

    ______

    b. Identify *cibōrum*: ______

    c. Parse *consūmpserīs*: ______

    sentiās: ______

    ēsūrum esse: ______

    exspectēs: ______

    d. Why is *consumperīs* in the mood that it is in? ______

    ______

    What about *sentiās* and *exspectēs*? ______

    What about *ēsūrum esse*? ______

12. Rōmānus suam domum seniōrem—horrendum dictū!—memoriīs dēsertīs et impiīs daemoniīs incultam esse putāvit; ita eōdem redīre sperāvimus mundātum domum sanctificātumque eam pāce Salvatōris nostrī.

    a. Translation: ______

    ______

    ______

    ______

    ______

    b. Identify *memoriīs*: ______

    c. Parse *incultam esse*: ______

    putāvit: ______

    redīre: ______

    sperāvimus: ______

    d. Why is *incultam esse* in the mood that it is in? ______

    Tell me more about *dictū*: ______

    ______

    Tell me more about *mundātum* and *sanctificātum*: ______

    ______

13. Mihi aurēs istius imāginis tantae sunt ut haud appāreat esse idem nūmen quod dīligāmus et cuius in doctrīnīs requiēscāmus.

 a. Translation: ______________________________

 ____

 ____

 ____

 b. Identify *nūmen*: ______________________________

 c. Parse *sunt*: ______________________________

 appāreat: ______________________________

 esse: ______________________________

 dīligāmus: ______________________________

 requiēscāmus: ______________________________

 ____

 d. Why is *appāreat* in the mood that it is in? ______________________________

14. In colle altō adsimus cum ūllae aurae vix sint, at absimus cum sit forās magnus numerus aurārum.

 a. Translation: ______________________________

 ____

 ____

 b. Identify *colle*: ______________________________

 c. Parse *adsimus*: ______________________________

 sint: ______________________________

 absimus: ______________________________

 sit: ______________________________

 d. Why is *adsimus* in the mood that it is in? ______________________________

 What about *absimus*? ______________________________

 What about *sit*? ______________________________

15. Scīlicet satis vīs rēgīnae erat ad negandōs istōs eī mentientēs, et ad inveniendōs testēs eam frustrā maledīcentēs.

 a. Translation: ______________________________

 ____

 ____

b. Identify *rēgīnae* and explain why it is in that particular case: ______________________

____

c. Parse *erat*: ____

negandōs: ____

mentientēs: ____

inveniendōs: ____

maledīcentēs: ____

d. What are *negandōs* and *inveniendōs* doing in this sentence? ____________________

____

2 Unit Two

UNIT 2: GOALS

Lessons 9–16

By the end of Unit 4, students should be able to . . .

- Understand and translate the subjunctive in indirect questions
- Form and recognize the subjunctive of irregular verbs *eō*, *ferō*, *vōlō*, *nōlō*, and *malō*
- Understand and translate the subjunctive in indirect commands
- Recognize and translate syncopated perfects
- Understand and translate indicative and subjunctive conditions
- Understand and translate the subjunctive in relative clauses of characteristic
- Understand and translate optative subjunctives
- Understand and translate potential subjunctives
- Understand and translate deliberative subjunctives
- Understand and translate the subjunctive in fear clauses
- Understand and translate additional uses of the dative
- Understand and translate the subjunctive in *dum*/proviso clauses
- Understand and translate the genitive and ablative of description
- Translate all of 1 John, and identify various grammatical constructions used therein

Lesson 9

Subjunctive: Indirect Question; Subj. of Irregular Verbs *eō, ferō, volō, nōlō, mālō*

Word List 25

Nouns

1. homicīda, -ae (m/f) *murderer/murderess, homicide, man-slayer*
2. impetus, -ūs (m) *attack, onset, impetus*
3. lācrima, -ae (f) *tear*
4. sententia, -ae (f) *thought, opinion, sentence*

Adjectives

5. memor, -oris *mindful, remembering*
6. pauper, -eris *poor*
7. quālis (interrog. adj.) *of what sort, what kind of*; (rel. adj.) *of such a sort, such as, as*
8. tot (indecl. adj.) *so many, so great a number*
9. vīcīnus, -a, -um *neighbor(ing), near(by)*

Verbs

10. coniungō, -ere, -iūnxī, -iūnctum *I join (together), unite*
11. convertō, -ere, -vertī, -versum *I turn around/back, change, convert*
12. effundō, -ere, -fūdī, -fūsum *I pour out/forth, shed*
13. soleō, -ēre, solītus sum (semi-deponent) *I am accustomed (to), am in the habit of*

Adverbs/Conjunctions

14. amplius (adv.) *more, longer, further, besides*
15. an (introduces 2nd half of a question, often with *utrum*) *or, or whether*
16. quamdiu (adv.) *how long?; as long as, until*
17. quārē (adv.) *by what means? how? why? wherefore (?)*
18. quemadmodum (adv.) *how, in what manner*
19. usquam (adv.) *anywhere, at/in any place*
20. ūtrum (adv.) *whether* (translated by tone of voice in direct questions)

Memorization

This unit's memorization is the prologue of the *Aeneid.* This lesson's portion is lines 1–2.

Arma virumque canō, Troiae quī prīmus ab ōrīs
Ītaliam, fātō profugus, Lāvīnaque vēnit

Arms and the man I sing, who first came from the shores of Troy,
a fugitive from Fate, to Italy and the Lavinian [coasts]

Grammar

Indirect Question

We will add another subjunctive usage to our repertoire in this lesson. Remember that Latin often shows indirect or subordinate action in a different way than English. For example, English will simply show indirect statement by word order and often the word "that", whereas Latin uses the accusative and infinitive: "We said that Oswald had killed the dragon," *Nōs Oswaldum dracōnem necāvisse dīximus.* With an indirect question, English will again use word order but Latin will put the indirect question into the subjunctive to show that the clause is a subordinate one. Here are some English direct and indirect questions, just so we're clear on what these are.

DIRECT QUESTION	INDIRECT QUESTION
Who are you?	I know [who you are].
How did you escape?	We wondered [how you escaped].
Where is she?	No one is sure [where she is].

One obvious difference is that indirect questions will not have question marks, but they will be introduced by an interrogative word of some sort. If it helps makes the clause more obvious, you can put indirect questions in brackets before you translate into Latin.

When putting these indirect questions into Latin, it is important to observe the Sequence of Tenses learned in *KL2*, Lesson 7.

MAIN VERB	SUBJUNCTIVE	ACTION RELATIVE TO MAIN VERB
Present or Future	Present	same time
	Perfect	before
	Periphrastic Future	future
Past (Imperfect, Perfect, or Pluperfect)	Imperfect	same time/future
	Pluperfect	before
	Periphrastic Future	future

Often, to clarify that they are referring to the future of the main verb, Latin authors will use a periphrastic subjunctive construction. A "periphrastic" construction is simply a roundabout way of saying something, and since there is no future subjunctive, we will use the future active participle combined with either the present or imperfect subjunctive form of *sum*. Some examples will clarify this:

Rēx rogat quemadmodum Oswaldus dracōnem necet.
The king asks how Oswald is killing the dragon.

Rēx rogat quemadmodum Oswaldus dracōnem necāverit.
The king asks how Oswald killed the dragon.

Rēx rogat quemadmodum Oswaldus dracōnem necātūrus sit.
The king asks how Oswald will kill the dragon.

Rēx rogāvit quemadmodum Oswaldus dracōnem necāret.
The king asked how Oswald killed [was killing] the dragon.

Rēx rogāvit quemadmodum Oswaldus dracōnem necāvisset.
The king asked how Oswald had killed the dragon.

Rēx rogāvit quemadmodum Oswaldus dracōnem necātūrus esset.
The king asked how Oswald would kill the dragon.

Honestly, indirect questions are quite easy to translate from the Latin, and although it takes a little bit more mental effort to translate them from English into Latin, they are nonetheless not that complicated.

Subjunctive of Irregular Verbs *eō, ferō, volō, nōlō, mālō*

We have already considered the subjunctive of irregular verbs *sum* and *possum*, and will now examine some additional and very common irregular verbs.

***eō, īre, iī/īvī, itum* (and compounds *abeō, adeō, exeō, ineō, trānseō,* etc.)**
Since our old friend *eō* is such a short verb, some of its forms can be a bit tricky. First off, I thought it would be helpful to compare its present indicative side by side with the present subjunctive. This is a fourth conjugation verb, but an irregular one, so it does not have the usual *-ia-* vowel change that a regular fourth conjugation verb would.

	PRESENT INDICATIVE		PRESENT SUBJUNCTIVE	
	SG.	PL.	SG.	PL.
1ST	eō	īmus	eam	eāmus
2ND	īs	ītis	eās	eātis
3RD	it	eunt	eat	eant

Although it is irregular, *eō* forms its imperfect, perfect, and pluperfect subjunctives fairly regularly. Thus, just like any other verb, we take its whole infinitive plus the *-m, -s, -t* endings to form the imperfect subjunctive.

	IMPERFECT SUBJUNCTIVE	
	SG.	PL.
1ST	īrem	īrēmus
2ND	īrēs	īrētis
3RD	īret	īrent

The perfect subjunctive is the perfect stem (in this case, the very short one of *-i-*) plus *-eri-* plus the personal endings.

	PERFECT SUBJUNCTIVE	
	SG.	PL.
1ST	ierim	ierīmus
2ND	ierīs	ierītis
3RD	ierit	ierint

Finally, the pluperfect is that perfect stem *-i-* plus *-isse-* plus the personal endings. The two *i*'s will combine to form one long *-ī-*.

	PLUPERFECT SUBJUNCTIVE	
	SG.	PL.
1ST	īssem	īssēmus
2ND	īssēs	īssētis
3RD	īsset	īssent

***ferō, ferre, tulī, lātum* (and compounds *inferō, offerō,* etc.)**

The third conjugation irregular verb *ferō* also deserves a closer look, particularly in the present system. It does roughly follow the vowel patterns for ordinary third conjugation verbs: *ō, i, i, i, i, u* for the present indicative; *a, ē, e, ē, ē, e* for the future indicative, and the switch to *-a-* for all of the present subjunctive forms. Compare these three tenses below in the active and passive:

	PRES. ACT. INDIC.		FUT. ACT. INDIC.		PRES. ACT. SUBJ.	
	SG.	PL.	SG.	PL.	SG.	PL.
1ST	ferō	ferimus	feram	ferēmus	feram	ferāmus
2ND	fers	fertis	ferēs	ferētis	ferās	ferātis
3RD	fert	ferunt	feret	ferent	ferat	ferant

	PRES. PASS. INDIC.		FUT. PASS. INDIC.		PRES. PASS. SUBJ.	
	SG.	PL.	SG.	PL.	SG.	PL.
1ST	feror	ferimur	ferar	ferēmur	ferar	ferāmur
2ND	ferris	feriminī	ferēris	ferēminī	ferāris	ferāminī
3RD	fertur	feruntur	ferētur	ferentur	ferātur	ferantur

The other subjunctive tenses are straightforward. Although its principal parts are irregular, the subjunctives of *ferō* are formed regularly from those weird principal parts. For the imperfect subjunctive we will add the personal endings *-m, -s, -t, -mus, -tis, -nt* or *-r, -ris, -tur, -mur, -minī, -ntur* to the infinitive.

	IMPERFECT ACTIVE SUBJUNCTIVE		IMPERFECT PASSIVE SUBJUNCTIVE	
	SG.	PL.	SG.	PL.
1ST	ferrem	ferrēmus	ferrer	ferrēmur
2ND	ferrēs	ferrētis	ferrēris	ferrēminī
3RD	ferret	ferrent	ferrētur	ferrentur

Then for the perfect active subjunctive, as we might expect, we will add *-eri-* plus the personal endings *-m, -s, -t, -mus, -tis, -nt* to the perfect stem. The perfect passive is formed using the perfect passive participle plus the present subjunctive of *sum*.

	PERFECT ACTIVE SUBJUNCTIVE		PERFECT PASSIVE SUBJUNCTIVE	
	SG.	PL.	SG.	PL.
1ST	tulerim	tulerīmus	lātus/a/um sim	lātī/ae/a sīmus
2ND	tulerīs	tulerītis	lātus/a/um sīs	lātī/ae/a sītis
3RD	tulerit	tulerint	lātus/a/um sit	lātī/ae/a sint

Similarly, there are no surprises with the pluperfect active and passive, adding *-isse-* plus *-m, -s, -t, -mus, -tis, -nt* for the active, and the perfect passive participle plus the imperfect subjunctive of *sum* for the passive.

	PLUPERFECT ACTIVE SUBJUNCTIVE		PLUPERFECT PASSIVE SUBJUNCTIVE	
	SG.	PL.	SG.	PL.
1ST	tulissem	tulissēmus	lātus/a/um essem	lātī/ae/a essēmus
2ND	tulissēs	tulissētis	lātus/a/um essēs	lātī/ae/a essētis
3RD	tulisset	tulissent	lātus/a/um esset	lātī/ae/a essent

volō, velle, voluī, ——

The next three verbs, *volō*, *nōlō*, and *mālō*, are similar in their irregularity. The present subjunctive is the only truly tricky chant for all three, because the imperfect, perfect, and pluperfect subjunctives are all formed regularly from those irregular principal parts:

	PRESENT SUBJUNCTIVE		IMPERFECT SUBJUNCTIVE	
	SG.	PL.	SG.	PL.
1ST	velim	velīmus	vellem	vellēmus
2ND	velīs	velītis	vellēs	vellētis
3RD	velit	velint	vellet	vellent

	PERFECT SUBJUNCTIVE		PLUPERFECT SUBJUNCTIVE	
	SG.	PL.	SG.	PL.
1ST	voluerim	voluerīmus	voluissem	voluissēmus
2ND	voluerīs	voluerītis	voluissēs	voluissētis
3RD	voluerit	voluerint	voluisset	voluissent

nōlō, nolle, nōluī, ——

	PRESENT SUBJUNCTIVE		IMPERFECT SUBJUNCTIVE	
	SG.	PL.	SG.	PL.
1ST	nōlim	nōlīmus	nōllem	nōllēmus
2ND	nōlīs	nōlītis	nōllēs	nōllētis
3RD	nōlit	nōlint	nōllet	nōllent

	PERFECT SUBJUNCTIVE		PLUPERFECT SUBJUNCTIVE	
	SG.	PL.	SG.	PL.
1ST	nōluerim	nōluerīmus	nōluissem	nōluissēmus
2ND	nōluerīs	nōluerītis	nōluissēs	nōluissētis
3RD	nōluerit	nōluerint	nōluisset	nōluissent

mālō, malle, māluī, ——

	PRESENT SUBJUNCTIVE		IMPERFECT SUBJUNCTIVE	
	SG.	PL.	SG.	PL.
1ST	mālim	mālīmus	māllem	māllēmus
2ND	mālīs	mālītis	māllēs	māllētis
3RD	mālit	mālint	māllet	māllent

	PERFECT SUBJUNCTIVE	
	SG.	PL.
1ST	māluerim	māluerīmus
2ND	māluerīs	māluerītis
3RD	māluerit	māluerint

PLUPERFECT SUBJUNCTIVE	
SG.	PL.
māluissem	māluissēmus
māluissēs	māluissētis
māluisset	māluissent

Review

Be sure to add *Indirect Question* to your list of subjunctives, and also review the sequence of tenses. Write some sentences in the subjunctive with *cum* clauses to reinforce your knowledge of tense sequences.

Worksheet 9

A. Vocabulary

1. effundō, ______________, effūdī, effūsum: ______________________________
2. ūtrum: ______________________________
3. quemadmodum: ______________________________
4. vīcīnus: ______________________________
5. dum/dummodo: ______________________________
6. poor: ______________________________
7. amplius: ______________________________
8. frūmentum: ______________________________
9. ferō, ferre, tulī, lātum: ______________________________
10. coniungō, ______________, ______________, coniūnctum: ______________________________
11. sententia: ______________________________
12. murderer: ______________________________
13. usquam: ______________________________
14. soleō, solēre, ______________: ______________________________
15. impetus: ______________________________
16. quō: ______________________________
17. an: ______________________________
18. memor, -oris: ______________________________
19. tot (indecl. adj.): ______________________________
20. tear: ______________________________
21. fidēs: ______________________________
22. ______________, ______________, ______________, conversum: ______________________________
23. quārē: ______________________________
24. quamdiu: ______________________________
25. quālis (interrog. adj. or rel. adj.): ______________________________

B. Grammar

1. Give the subjunctive equivalents for these indicatives.

INDICATIVE	SUBJUNCTIVE
māvult	
ferēbāmur	
exiērunt	
estis	
voluī	
māluerās	
adībat	
lātae erāmus	

INDICATIVE	SUBJUNCTIVE
eunt	
erās	
obtulit	
fueram	
poterant	
nōlō	
māluistis	

2. Put each direct question into a sentence using it as an indirect question.

How long will you be gone?

____

Why didn't he say anything?

____

Where are they going?

She found out where they are going.

When does the picnic start?

Tell me when the picnic starts.

Who had started the fight?

The teacher asked who had started the fight.

How much does this strange sword cost?

He wants to know how much this strange sword costs.

Whose cookie did I just eat?

I asked them whose cookie I just ate.

3. Do a synopsis of *coniungō* in the 2nd person singular, first giving principal parts:

coniungō, coniungere, coniūnxī, coniūnctum

		LATIN ACTIVE	ENGLISH ACTIVE	LATIN PASSIVE	ENGLISH PASSIVE
INDICATIVE	PRES.				
	IMPF.				
	FUT.				
	PF.				
	PLPF.				
	FT. PF.				
SUBJUNCTIVE	PRES.				
	IMPF.				
	PF.				
	PLPF.				
PARTICIPLE	PRES.				
	PF.				
	FUT.				
INFINITIVE	PRES.				
	PF.				
	FUT.				

IMP.	SG.				
	PL.				

C. Memorization

Fill in in the blanks in *Aeneid* 1.1-2 in Latin.

Arma ____________ ________, Troiae _____ __________ ___ _______

Ītaliam, ______ ____________, ______________ vēnit

D. English to Latin

Translate these sentences into Latin. (Hint: Translate italicized verbs with Latin participles/gerunds, bold with subjunctives, underlined with infinitives, and circled with supines.)

1. The poor man does not know why the neighbor woman **is pouring forth** tears.

   ____

   The poor man does not know why the neighbor woman **poured forth** tears.

   ____

   The poor man does not know why the neighbor woman **will pour forth** tears.

   ____

2. We could not believe how long the pirates **were eating**.

   ____

   We could not believe how long the pirates **had eaten**.

   ____

   We could not believe how long the pirates *would eat*.

   ____

3. Although the enemy **had joined** all their soldiers **together**, they decided that they *would* not *make* the attack that night.

4. **Let** us **be** mindful that our opinions <u>are</u> not always just, lest we **speak ill** of others excessively.

5. Why *must* your companions *swear* oaths and *make* such immense shouts?

6. These children, *coming back* from the neighboring city, were asking my mother what kind of cookies she **was accustomed** to make.

7. The haughty king hates how messengers **look back** at him when they bring him gifts from the ambassador.

8. It is necessary that the wicked soothsayers <u>turn back</u> from their sins and <u>confess</u> the one true God.

9. The dragon is eating so many sheep that **he will burst** [asunder] and **die**.

10. We marvel at how the priests *will climb* the very high hill in the snow and not *fall*.

E. Latin to English:

The Conversion of St. Augustine (from his *Confessions*, 8.12.28-30)

Ubī vērō ā *fundō* occultātō alta cōgitātiō tōtam *miseriam* meam trāxit et congregāvit in conspectū cordis mei, orta est tempestās ingēns ferēns ingentem *imbrem lācrimārum*. Et ut tōtum imbrem *effunderem* cum vōcibus suīs, surrēxī ab *Alypiō—sōlitūdō* mihi ad *negōtium* flendī *aptior* vīdēbatur—et *sēcessī* longē nē etiam eius *praesentia* posset mihi onus esse.

Sīc tunc eram, et ille sensit: nōn putō enim aliquid dīxisse in quō apparēbat vōx mea iam *flētū* gravis, et sīc surrēxeram. Mansit ergō ille ubī sedēbāmus nimis mīrāns. Ego sub quādam *fīcī** arbore strāvī mē, nesciō quōmodo, et dedī *habēnās* lācrimīs, et *prōrūperunt* flūmina oculōrum meōrum, *acceptābile* sacrificium Tuum, et nōn quidem hīs verbīs, sed in sermōne huius modī multa dīxī Tibi: "Et Tū, Domine, quamdiu? Quamdiu, Domine, *īrascēris* in fīnem? Nē memor fueris iniquitātum nostrārum antiquārum."* Sentiēbam enim eīs mē tenērī. Loquēbar verba misera: "Quamdiu, quamdiu? Crās et crās? Quārē nōn nunc? Quārē non hāc horā finis turpitūdinis meae?"

Dicēbam haec et flēbam *amārissimā contrītiōne* cordis meī. Et ecce, audiō* vōcem dē vīcīnā domō cum cantū dicentis et crēbrō* *repetentis*, quasi puerī an puellae, nesciō: "Tolle, lege; tolle, lege." Statimque mutātō vultū *intentissimus* cogitāre coepī ūtrum *solērent* puerī in aliquō genere ludendī *cantitāre* tāle aliquid; nec vidēbātur omnīnō audīvisse mē usquam, *repressōque* impetū lācrimārum surrēxī, intellegēns nihil aliud *dīvīnitus* mihi iubērī, *nisi* ut aperīrem* *cōdicem* et legerem prīmum caput* quod invēnissem. Audīveram enim dē *Antōniō*, quod ex *ēvangelicā lectiōne* quam forte invēnerat *admonitus* fuisset*, quasi quod legēbātur sibī dicerētur*: "Vāde, *vende* omnia quae habēs, et dā *pauperibus* et habēbis *thesaurum* in caelīs; et venī, sequere mē,"* et tālī fātō continuō ad Tē *esse conversum*.

Itaque valde mōtus rediī in eum locum ubī sedēbat *Alypius*: ibī enim posueram cōdicem apostolī cum inde surrēxeram. *Arripuī*, aperuī, et legī in *silentiō capitulum* quō prīmum *iectī sunt* oculī meī: "Nōn in *comessatiōnibus* et *ēbrietātibus*, non in *cubīlibus* et *impudīcitiīs*, nōn in *contentiōne* et *aemulatiōne*, sed induite Dominum Iēsum Christum et carnis *prōvidentiam* nē fēcerītis in *concupiscentiīs*."* Nec ultrā voluī legere nec opus erat. Statim quidem cum fīne huius sententiae est quasi lūce salūtātis *infūsā* cordī meō omnēs *dubitātiōnis* tenēbrae strātae sunt.

Tum *cōdicem* sūmpsī et *tranquillō* iam vultū ostendī *Alypiō*. At ille quid in sē agerētur—quod egō nesciēbam—sīc ostendit. Petit vidēre quid legissem: ostendī, et attendit mē etiam ultrā quam egō lēgeram. Et ignōrābam quid sequerētur. Hoc sequēbātur vērō: "*Īnfirmum* autem in fidē *recipīte*"*—quod ille ad sē *rettulit* mihique aperuit. Sed tālī *admonitiōne confirmātus est*; placitōque ac propositō bonō et congruentissimō* suīs moribus, in quibus ā mē in* melius iam olim valdē *distābat*, sine ūllā *turbulentā cunctātiōne* mihi coniunctus est.

Inde ad mātrem ingredimur, *indicāmus*: gaudet. Narrāmus quemadmodum factum sit: *exultat* et *triumphat* et benedicēbat Tibi, quī potēns ēs facere ultrā quam petimus et intellegimus*; quia tantō amplius hōc sibi ā tē *concessum esse* dē mē vidēbat quam petere solēbat miserīs flēbilibusque gemitibus. Convertistī enim mē ad Tē, ut nec uxōrem quaererem nec aliquam spem saeculī* huius, stāns in eā *regulā* fīdeī in quā mē ante tot annōs eī *revelāverās*, et convertistī luctum eius in gaudium* multō* ūberius quam voluerat, et in gaudium multō carius atque castius quam dē nepōtibus carnis meae quaerēbat.*

Notes:

* *fīcī:* appositional genitive; using two nouns (literally, "a tree of fig") instead of an adjective and a noun ("a fig tree")
* *Et Tū...antiquārum:* In these questions Augustine quotes from Ps. 6:4 and Ps. 78:5, 8.
* *audiō:* Historical present; conveys that vivid moment preceding his conversion.
* *crēbrō:* adverb from *crēber*; "frequently, often"
* *aperīrem:* Subjunctive in indirect command (see the next lesson; it's fairly straightforward to translate)
* *caput:* in the context of books, can also mean "chapter, division, section, etc."
* *admonitus fuisset:* subjunctive because....?
* *dicerētur:* subjunctive in a Conditional Clause of Comparison with the protasis left off—basically, this is a type of future condition (see Lesson 10).
* *Vāde, vende...:* from Matt. 19:21
* *Nōn in comessatiōnibus... concupiscentis:* Rom. 13:13-14
* *īnfirmum...recipīte:* Rom. 14:1
* *bonō* and *congruentissimō* go with both *placitō* and *propositō*, which are in turn both ablatives of means with *coniunctus est* at the end of the sentence
* *in:* translate here with sense of purpose, "for"
* *quī...intelligimus:* Allusion to Eph. 3:20, *Ei autem, quī potēns est omnia facere superabundanter quam petimus aut intellegimus....*
* *saeculī: saeculum* can also mean "world, age"
* *convertistī...gaudium:* Reference to Ps. 29:12
* *multō:* adverb, "much, by much, far"
* Line 38: Before Augustine's conversion when he was living with various women outside of wedlock, his mother Monica had encouraged him to get married (as a step toward conversion, in her mind)—but he never did go through with a marriage. His coming to Christ brought her even more joy than children born out of such a marriage would have.

Glossary:

acceptābilis, -e: acceptable
admoneō, -ēre, -uī, -itum: I admonish, warn, advise
admonitiō, -ōnis (f): admonition, reminding
aemulātiō, -ōnis (f): envy, jealousy
Alypius, -iī (m): Alypius of Thagaste, longtime friend of Augustine who also heard the preaching of St. Ambrose; Alypius and Augustine were baptized by Ambrose in 387.
Antōnius, -iī (m): Anthony of Egypt (c. 251-356), one of the Desert Fathers and considered the father of monasticism
amārus, -a, -um: bitter
aptus, -a, -um: suitable, appropriate, fitted
arripiō, -ere, -ripuī, -reptum: I seize, snatch (up), lay hold of
attendō, -ere, -ndī, -ntum: I turn toward, direct (the attention) toward
cantitō (1): I sing often, sing frequently [this is called the frequentative form of *cantō*]
capitulum, -ī (n): chapter, section
cārius: neuter comparative adjective from *cārus, -a, -um*, "dear, beloved" (*KL1*, Lesson 13)
castus, -a, -um: pure, chaste
cōdex, -dicis (m): book, writing [originally made of wooden tablets fastened together]
cōmessātiō, -ōnis (f): rioting, reveling (lit., a Bacchanalian revel with procession and music)
concēdō, -ere, -cessī, -cessum: I grant, allow, concede
concupīscentia, -ae (f): longing, concupiscence, lust
confirmō (1): I make firm, strengthen, confirm
congruēns, -ntis: suitable, appropriate
contentiō, -ōnis (f): contention, strife
contrītiō, -ōnis (f): contrition, grief
cubīle, -is (n): (marriage) bed; pl., fornication
cunctātiō, -ōnis (f): delay, doubt, hesitation
distō (1): I stand apart, differ
dīvīnitus (adv.): from heaven, by divine providence/will
dubitātiō, -ōnis (f): doubt, uncertainty
ēbrietās, -tātis (f): drunkenness, carousing
ēvangelicus, -a, -um: evangelical, of the gospel
exultō/exsultō (1): I leap up, exult, rejoice exceedingly
fīcus, -ī (f): fig (tree)
flēbilis, -e: tearful, lamentable
flētus, -ūs (m): weeping, wailing
fundus, -ī (m): farm, estate; foundation, lowest part
gemitus, -ūs (m): groan, sigh, sorrow
habēna, -ae (f): rein, strap
imber, -bris (m): (heavy) rain-storm
impudīcitia, -ae (f): sexual immorality
indīcō (1): I declare, show, make known
īnfirmus, -a, -um: weak, feeble, infirm
infundō, -ere, -fūdī, -fūsum (+dat.): I pour in(to)
intentus, -a, -um: intent, eager
īrāscor, -scī, īrātus sum: I am angry, am in a rage
lectiō, -ōnis (f): a reading, text
luctus, -ūs (m): sorrow, grief, mourning
miseria, -ae (f): misery, distress, suffering
negōtium, -iī (n): business, occupation
nisi: if not, unless, except
placitum, -ī (n): principle, agreement
praesentia, -ae (f): presence
prōpositum, -ī (n): resolution, purpose
prōrumpō, -ere, -rūpī, -ruptum: I break forth, burst forth
prōvidentia, -ae (f): providence, provision, forethought
quasi: as if, just as; almost, nearly, about
recipiō, -ere, -cēpī, -ceptum: I take back/again, receive
referō, -ferre, -(t)tulī, -(l)lātum: I bring/take back, apply
rēgula, -ae (f): rule, example, pattern
repetō, -ere, -īvī/-iī, -ītum: I repeat, seek again
reprīmō, -ere, -pressī, -pressum: I hold/keep back, restrain
revēlō (1): I unveil, reveal, disclose
sēcēdō, -ere, -cessī, -cessum: I go apart/away, withdraw, separate
silentium, -iī (n): silence, stillness
sōlitūdō, -dinis (f): solitude, loneliness
thēsaurus, -ī (m): a hoard, treasure
tranquillus, -a, -um: quiet, calm
triumphō (1): I triumph, exult, rejoice exceedingly
turbulentus, -a, -um: restless, stormy, turbulent
turpitūdō, -dinis (f): ugliness, shame, dishonor
ūber, -beris: abundant, fruitful, plentiful
vendō, -ere, -didī, -ditum: I sell

Lesson 10

Verbs: Indirect Command; Syncopated Perfects

Word List 26

Nouns

1. ancilla, -ae (f) *maidservant, female slave*
2. ātrium, -iī (n) *hall, court, entryway*
3. cinis, -neris (m) *ashes*
4. convīvium, -iī (n) *banquet, social feast*
5. mensis, -is (m) *month*
6. minister, -strī (m) *attendant, servant, minister*
7. scrība, -ae (m) *scribe, clerk, secretary*
8. virga, -ae (f) *branch, rod, staff*

Adjectives

9. crūdēlis, -e *cruel, savage*
10. dīmidius, -a, -um *half (of)*

Verbs

11. accidō, -ere, -cīdī, —— *I fall upon/out, happen, come to pass*
12. auferō, -ferre, abstulī, ablātum *I carry off/away, remove;* auferō mē, *I remove myself, withdraw*
13. dēprecor, -ārī, -ātus sum *I pray (for), intercede, beseech*
14. imperō (1) *I command, order* (alicuī aliquid)
15. mandō (1) *I order, command; commit, entrust* (alicuī aliquid)
16. pendō, -ere, pependī, pensum *I weigh, suspend, ponder*
17. persuādeō, -ere, -suāsī, -suāsum (+dat.) *I persuade*
18. postulō (1) *I ask, demand, desire* (aliquid ab/dē aliquō; aliquem aliquid)
19. regredior, -gredī, -gressus sum *I go back, return*
20. scindō, -ere, scidī, scissum *I cut, tear, rend*

Memorization

Aeneid 1.1-4

Arma virumque canō, Troiae quī prīmus ab ōrīs
Ītaliam, fātō profugus, Lāvīnaque vēnit
lītora. Multum ille et terrīs iactātus et altō
vī superum saevae memorem Iūnōnis ob īram.

coasts. He was also buffeted much on land and on the sea
by violence of the gods, on account of the remembered anger of cruel Juno.

Grammar

Indirect Command

Another usage of our serviceable subjunctive friend is indirect command. Remember that the subjunctive portrays hypothetical or indirect action, so this fits right in. We have of course studied a few different kinds of direct command—the straight-up imperative (for 2nd person), or the jussive/hortatory subjunctive (for 1st/3rd persons).

Necā dracōnem! Kill the dragon!

Necēmus dracōnem! Let's kill the dragon!

Necet dracōnem! Let him kill the dragon!

Direct commands are useful, but sometimes we need report such commands indirectly—and to do so, we will need the subjunctive.

Rēx Oswaldō imperāvit ut dracōnem necāret. The king commanded Oswald to kill the dragon.

Rēx nōbīs mandābit ut dracōnem necēmus. The king will order us to kill the dragon.

Note that an indirect command is introduced by *ut* (or *nē* if negative), and that it usually sounds better to translate it with a simple English infinitive. (Take the first sentence, for example—translating with an English clause would be a touch awkward: "The king commanded Oswald that he kill the dragon.")

How can we tell the difference between a purpose clause and an indirect command?

Again, context is king. When you are asking this question, look at the meaning of the sentence to narrow your options down. Does the subjunctive have anything to do with commanding or not? Another important thing to remember is that an indirect command can also be called a "jussive noun clause." The entire clause functions as a noun, the direct object of the main verb, because it is what is being commanded. Looking at our first example above, we could ask, "What did the king command?" and the answer would be *ut dracōnem necāret*, "to kill the dragon." A purpose clause, however, is adverbial and describes why the action of the main verb is taking place: *Rēx Oswaldō mandāta dedit ut ea faceret*, "The king gave Oswald commands in order that he might do them." There could possibly be a situation where the clause could be either a purpose clause or an indirect command, and in such a rare event, either answer is acceptable. When translating stories with context, however, make sure you are careful to try the different subjunctives out.

Generally indirect commands refer to the same time or the future of the main verb, and thus you will usually see either the present subjunctive (with a present or future main verb) or the imperfect (with past tenses).

Thus far indirect commands are fairly straightforward. However, things can get a bit exciting depending on the verb of commanding used in the main clause. Some of these verbs will take the dative, some the accusative, and some will use the ablative with a preposition. As you learn new verbs having to do with commanding, you should make note of which cases those verbs take. And honestly, when translating from the Latin, you won't have any problem with this. However, to make things easier with a few of these verbs, long ago my brother and I made a song to help remember them. It is sung to the tune of the theme song from "Gilligan's Island."

The verbs that take the dative case
With indirect command
Are *imperō, mandō,*
And *persuādeō,*
And *persuādeō.*
The verbs that take accusative
With indirect command
Just happen to be these verbs three
Moneō, ōrō, rogō
Moneō, ōrō, rogō.
At last we come to *postulō,*
Quaerō and *petō*—
These are the verbs that choose to take
Ablative with the prep
Ablative with the prep.

Some of these verbs are from way back in *KL1*: *moneō* (*KL1*, Lesson 9), *ōrō* (*KL1*, Lesson 6), and *rogō* (*KL1*, Lesson 6)—remember that *ōrō* and *rogō* take a double accusative, so that both the person asked and the thing asked for are in the accusative. *Petō* (*KL2*, Lesson 12) and *quaerō* (*KL2*, Lesson 3) should look familiar. In the last verse of the song, "ablative with the prep" refers to the verb appearing with a preposition like *ab* or *dē* plus the ablative, just as in English we can say, "Ask of me, and I will give it to you, up to half my kingdom." Simply "Ask me" would also work, but not sound as poetic in this context. **This is not an exhaustive list of all the verbs of commanding**; simply a fun way to remember nine of them. Here are examples of each of these verbs to illustrate how they work with their particular cases.

Rēx Oswaldō imperāvit ut dracōnem necāret. The king commanded Oswald to kill the dragon.

Rēx Oswaldō mandāvit ut dracōnem necāret. The king ordered Oswald to kill the dragon.

Rēx Oswaldō persuāsit ut dracōnem necāret. The king persuaded Oswald to kill the dragon.

Rēx Oswaldum monuit ut dracōnem necāret. The king warned/admonished Oswald to kill the dragon.

Rēx Oswaldum ōrāvit ut dracōnem necāret. The king prayed/begged Oswald to kill the dragon.

Rēx Oswaldum rogāvit ut dracōnem necāret. The king asked Oswald to kill the dragon.

Rēx ab/dē Oswaldō postulāvit ut dracōnem necāret. The king demanded [of] Oswald to kill the dragon.

Rēx ab/dē/ex Oswaldō quaesīvit ut dracōnem necāret. The king asked [of] Oswald to kill the dragon.

Rēx ab/dē/ex Oswaldō petīvit ut dracōnem necāret. The king asked [of] Oswald to kill the dragon.

Keep in mind that these guidelines are generally true, but as happens with language, there will be exceptions to the rule! You might see *petō* used without any preposition at all, for example. Or *imperō* can followed by an accusative and infinitive construction rather than *ut* + subjunctive in indirect command. And by the way, *iubeō*, "I order, command" (Lesson 2) is **usually** followed by accusative and infinitive, and not by indirect command. (Notice I said "usually," not "always"!) Just embrace the variety!

Syncopated Perfects

Sometimes verbs in the perfect system (perfect, pluperfect, and future perfect tenses) ending in *-āvī*, *-ēvī*, or *-īvī* will drop the "v" of their stem before *-s-* or *-r-*, allowing the remaining vowels to contract (Note: verbs in *-īvī* only contract the vowels before *-s-*; these are marked with an * below). These forms are called "syncopated," from a Greek word meaning "to cut," because the letter(s) are cut out of the word. I will not require you to create syncopated Latin verbs; you simply need to know that this occurs and be able to recognize a syncopated verb. Here are some examples from *necō*, *creō*, and *serviō*:

		-ĀVĪ	-ĒVĪ	-ĪVĪ
PERF.	INDICATIVE	necāvistī → necāstī	crēvistī → crēstī	servīvistī → servīstī
		necāvistis → necāstis	crēvistis → crēstis	servīvistis → servīstis
		necāvērunt → necārunt	crēvērunt → crērunt	servīvērunt → servīerunt*
	SUBJUNCTIVE	necāverim → necārim; necāverīs → necārīs, etc.	crēverim → crērim; crēverīs → crērīs, etc.	servīverim → servierim*; servīverīs → servierīs*, etc.
	INFINITIVE	necāvisse → necāsse	crēvisse → crēsse	servīvisse → servīsse
PLUPERF.	INDICATIVE	necāveram → necāram; necāverās → necārās, etc.	crēveram → crēram; creēverās → crērās, etc.	servīveram → servieram; servīverās → servierās, etc.
	SUBJUNCTIVE	necāvissem → necāssem; necāvissēs → necāssēs, etc.	crēvissem → crēssem; crēvissēs → crēssēs, etc.	servīvissem → servīssem; servīvissēs → servīssēs, etc.
FUT. PERF.	INDICATIVE	necāverō → necārō; necāveris → necāris, etc.	crēverō → crērō; crēveris → crēris, etc.	servīverō → servierō; servīveris → servieris, etc.

This frequently happens with *noscō* and its compounds; the syncopated forms look a little strange—so be aware of them!

		NOSCO AND ITS COMPOUNDS
PERF.	INDICATIVE	nōvistī → nōstī
		nōvistis → nōstis
		nōvērunt → nōrunt
	SUBJUNCTIVE	nōverim → nōrim; nōverīs → nōrīs, etc.
	INFINITIVE	nōvisse → nōsse
PLUPERF.	INDICATIVE	nōveram → nōram; nōverās → nōrās, etc.
	SUBJUNCTIVE	nōvissem → nōssem; nōvissēs → nōssēs, etc.
FUT. PERF.	INDICATIVE	nōverō → -nōrō; nōveris → -nōris, etc. (syncopated only in compounds)

Review

Add *indirect command* to your list of subjunctives, and be sure to review the sequence of tenses. Also, review the words *eō, ferō, volō, nōlō,* and *mālō* in the subjunctive. They may not seem important, but they are very common words. Think about how often you go somewhere or want something or tell someone not to do something. You need these words.

Worksheet 10

A. Vocabulary

1. scribe: ____________________
2. __________, ____________, pependī, pensum: ____________________
3. I persuade: ____________________
4. accidō, accidere, accīdī, ——: ____________________
5. twin: ____________________
6. ashes: ____________________
7. virga: ____________________
8. month: ____________________
9. mandō (1): ____________________
10. exeō, exīre, exiī (exīvī), exitum: ____________________
11. ātrium: ____________________
12. dēprecor, dēprecārī, dēprecātus sum: ____________________
13. regredior, regredī, regressus sum: ____________________
14. maidservant: ____________________
15. banquet: ____________________
16. half: ____________________
17. foedus: ____________________
18. unde: ____________________
19. I command: ____________________
20. minister: ____________________
21. quīdam, quaedam, quiddam (pron.): ____________________
22. cruel: ____________________
23. postulō (1): ____________________
24. scindō, scindere, scidī, scissum: ____________________
25. auferō, __________, abstulī, ablātum: ____________________

B. Grammar

1. Turn these direct commands into sentences with indirect commands (in English).

   Eat more pie! ______________________________

   ____

   Let's go home now. ______________________________

   Clean up this mess. ______________________________

   Be quiet. ______________________________

   Let them eat cake. ______________________________

   Don't touch that. ______________________________

   Run faster. ______________________________

2. Do a synopsis of *scindō* in the 1st person singular, first giving principal parts:

   ____

		LATIN ACTIVE	ENGLISH ACTIVE	LATIN PASSIVE	ENGLISH PASSIVE
INDICATIVE	PRES.				
	IMPF.				
	FUT.				
	PF.				
	PLPF.				
	FT. PF.				
SUBJUNCTIVE	PRES.				
	IMPF.				
	PF.				
	PLPF.				

PARTICIPLE	PRES.				
	PF.				
	FUT.				
INFINITIVE	PRES.				
	PF.				
	FUT.				
IMP.	SG.				
	PL.				

C. Memorization

Fill in in the blanks in *Aeneid* 1.1-4 in Latin.

__________ ______________ _________, ___________ _____ ___________ ____ _________

____________, ________ _____________, ________________ _________

____________. Multum ______ ____ _________ iactātus ____ ________

vī _____________ __________ memorem ____________ ob _________.

D. English to Latin

Translate these sentences into Latin.

1. Order your maidservants to remove with their staffs all the sheep on my farm.

____

____

____

2. And it came to pass that the savage kraken had followed the ship in order to devour the pirates.

3. Once the attendants had returned, our Greek neighbors were able to change their garments.

4. Why did the king demand us to make a banquet for two whole months?

5. We will persuade the witness to make known the man who had killed my father.

6. Half the scribes were so sad about the poor man's death that they tore their clothes and sat in the ashes.

7. Do not shed tears for me, for now you must make an attack against the cruel dragon and shed its blood.

8. The ambassor is asking why the army withdrew into the woods and began to eat cookies.

9. I don't know which prophet lied to us for the sake of joining himself to our companions.

10. The righteous priest rushed down from the hill to destroy the foul idols.

E. Latin to English

Adapted from Esther 3:12-5:4

Vocātīque sunt scrībae rēgis mense prīmō *Nisan* tertiādecimā* diē eius, et scriptum est ut iūsserat *Aman* ad omnēs *satrapās* rēgis et iūdicēs *prōvinciārum* dissimiliumque gentium ex nōmine rēgis *Asuerī*. Et litterae ipsius *sīgnātae* ānulō missae sunt per nuntiōs rēgis ad ūniversās prōvinciās ut occiderent atque delērent omnes *Iudaeōs* ā puerō usque ad senem, līberōs et mulierēs, ūnō diē—hōc est tertiōdecimō mensis duodecimī quī vocātur *Adar*, et bona eōrum *dīriperent*. *Summa* autem epistulārum haec fuit, ut omnēs prōvinciae scīrent et parārent sē ad pactam diem. Festinābant nuntiī quī missī erant sequī rēgis imperium, statimque *ēdictum* in *Susīs* positum est, rēge et *Aman celebrante convīvium* et cunctīs quī in urbe erant flentibus.

Quae* cum audīsset *Mardocheus*, scidit vestīmenta sua et indūtus est *saccō spargēns* cinerem capitī et in plateā mediae cīvitātis vōce magnā clamābat, ostendēns *amāritūdinem* animī suī, et hōc clamōre usque ad ōstia rēgiae vadēns—nōn enim erat licitum aliquem indūtum saccō *aulam* rēgis intrāre. In omnibus quoque provinciīs, oppidīs ac locīs ad quae* crūdēle rēgis mandātum pervēnerat, *planctus* ingēns erat apud *Iudaeōs, iēiūnium, ululātus* et *flētus*; *saccō* et cinere multīs prō *strātō* ūtentibus. Ingressae sunt autem puellae* ad *Hester* et *eunuchī* nuntiāvēruntque eī; quod audiēns *cōnsternāta est* et mīsit vestīmentum *Mardocheō* ut ablātō saccō induerent eum—quod accipere nōluit. Vocātōque *Athac* eunūchō quem rēx ministrum eī dederat, praecēpit ut īret ad *Mardocheum* et disceret ab eō cur hoc faceret.

Ēgressusque *Athac* īvit ad *Mardocheum* stantem in plateā cīvitātis ante ōstium rēgiae, quī indicāvit eī omnia quae accīderant, quōmodo *Aman promīsisset* ut in *thēsaurōs* rēgis prō *Iudaeōrum nece* inferret argentum; *exemplar*que *edictī* quod pendēbat in *Susīs* dedit eī, ut rēgīnae ostenderet et monēret eam ut intrāret ad rēgem et deprecāretur eum prō populō suō. Regressus *Athac* nuntiāvit *Hester* omnia quae *Mardocheus* dīxerat.

Quae respondit eī et iūssit ut dīceret *Mardocheō*: "Omnēs servī rēgis et cunctae quae sub *diciōne* eius provinciae sunt nōrunt* quod* quīcumque, sīve vir sīve mulier, nōn *vocātus in ātrium* rēgis intrāverit* statim interficiātur* nisi forte rēx auream *virgam* ad eum tetenderit* prō sīgnō *clementiae*, atque ita possit* vīvere. Ego igitur quōmodo ad rēgem intrāre poterō, quae trīginta iam diēbus nōn sum vocāta ad eum?"

Quod cum audisset* Mardocheus, rursum mandāvit Hester, dīcēns, "Nē putēs quod animam tuam tantum magis quam cunctīs Iudaeīs servāres, quia in domō rēgis es? Sī enim nunc *silueris* per aliam *occāsiōnem* servābuntur Iudaeī, et tū et domus patris tuī perībitis. Et quis nōvit utrum *ideo* ad rēgnum vēneris ut in tālī tempōre parāreris?"

Rursumque *Hester* haec *Mardocheō* verba mandāvit: "Vāde et congregā omnēs Iudaeōs quōs in *Susīs* invēneris et orāte prō mē; *nōn* edātis et *non* bibātis trībus diēbus ac noctibus et egō cum ancillīs meīs similiter* iēiūnābō et tunc ingrediar ad rēgem contrā lēgem faciēns, nōn vōcāta, tradēnsque mē mortī et perīculō." Īvit itaque *Mardocheus* et fēcit omnia quae eī Hester mandāverat.

Diē autem tertiō indūta est Hester *regālibus* vestīmentīs et stetit in ātriō domūs rēgī; at ille sedēbat super *solium* in *consistōriō* rēgiae contrā ōstium domūs. Cumque vīdisset Hester rēgīnam stantem, placuit oculiīs eius et tendit ad eam virgam auream quam tenēbat manū; quae appropinquāns ōsculāta est *summitātem* virgae eius. Dīxitque ad eam rēx, "Quid vīs, Hester Rēgīna? Quae est *petītiō* tua? Etiam sī dīmidiam rēgnī partem petīeris* dābitur tibi." At illa respondit, "Sī rēgī placet, *obsecrō* ut veniās ad mē hōdiē et Aman tēcum ad *convivium* quod parāvī."

Notes:

* *tertiādecimā* = *tertiā* + *decimā*; in other words, "thirteenth"

* *Quae*: When a relative pronoun begins a clause or sentence (such as this one), it can mean "*et* + demonstrative." Thus, here *quae* = *et ea*.

* *quae*: Neuter because all its antecedents—*provinciīs* (f), *oppidīs* (n), and *locīs* (m)—refer to inanimate things, even though their grammatical genders vary.

* *puellae*: Here it probably means "servant girls" or "maids" (just as in English the word "maid" can refer to either a servant or a young woman). Also, the participle in the verb *ingressae sunt* is feminine because the *puellae* is closer to it, but both *puellae* and *eunūchī* are the subjects.

* *nōrunt*: syncopated perfect! Short for *nōverunt*.

* *quod*: Classical Latin would require accusative and infinitive construction for indirect statement; the later Latin of the Vulgate (imitating the original Greek construction it is translating) sometimes uses *quod* or *quia* or a similar word plus an indicative verb.

* *intrāverit, interficiātur, tetenderit, possit*: These verbs are all subjunctive in what is called "informal indirect discourse," because they are reporting the content of a command of someone (the king) other than the speaker (Esther). Translate the perfect subjunctives as English present tense verbs and the present subjuntives as futures.

* *audīsset*: syncopated!

* *similiter*: adverb from *similis*

* *petīeris*: syncopated future perfect! Also it's a future mixed condition, future perfect in the "if" clause with a future verb in the main clause (more on conditions in Lesson 10).

Glossary:

Adar (indecl.): Adar, the twelfth month of the Hebrew ecclesiastical year
Aman (indecl.): Haman the Agagite, one of King Ahasuerus's officials
amāritūdō, -dinis (f): bitterness, sorrow, sadness
ānulus, -ī (m): ring, signet ring
Asuerus, -ī (m): Ahasuerus, traditionally identified as Xerxes I of Persia
Athac (indecl., m): Hathach, one of Esther's attendants/servants
aula, -ae (f): (royal) hall, (royal) court, palace
celēbrō (1): I celebrate
clēmentia, -ae (f): mercy, clemency, kindness
consistōrium, -iī (n): assembly room, hall [where the ruler's cabinet meets]
cōnsternō (1): I dismay, alarm, bring to confusion
convivium, -iī (n): feast, banquet
cunctātiō, -ōnis (f): delay, doubt, hesitation
diciō, -ōnis (f): authority, rule, sway
dīripiō, -ere, -uī, -reptum: I tear asunder, spoil, plunder
ēdictum, -ī (n): edict, proclamation, command
eunūchus, -ī (m): eunuch
exemplar, -āris (n): copy, example, exemplar
flētus, -ūs (m): weeping, wailing
Hester (indecl.) (f): Esther
iēiūnium, -iī (n): a fast, fasting, fast-day
iēiūnō (1): I fast, abstain from
indīcō (1): I declare, show, make known [not to be confused with *indīcō, -ere, -dīxī, indīctum*, I declare, proclaim, announce]
Iudaeus, -a, -um: Jewish; as noun, a Jew
Mardocheus, -ī (m): Mordecai
Nisan (indecl.): Nisan, the first month of the Hebrew ecclesiastical year; the celebration of Passover begins on its fifteenth day
nex, necis (f): (violent) death, slaughter, murder
obsecrō (1): I beseech, implore
occāsiō, -ōnis (f): occasion, opportunity
ōsculor, -ārī, -ātus sum: I kiss
petītiō, -ōnis (f): petition, request
planctus, -ūs (m): lamentation, wailing
prōmittō, -ere, -mīsī, -missum: I send forth, promise
prōvincia, -ae (f): province, territory
rēgālis, -e: royal, regal, kingly
saccus, -ī (m): sack, bag; sackcloth
satrapa, -ae (m): satrap, governor [of a province]
sīgnō (1): I mark (with a seal), seal (up)
sileō, -ēre, -uī, ——: I am silent, keep silent
solium, -iī (n): throne, seat
spargō, -ere, -rsī, -rsum: I scatter, sprinkle
strātum, -ī (n): covering, blanket [noun from *sternō*, *KL2*, Lesson 13]
summa, -ae (f): top, main point, sum(mary)
summitās, -tātis (f): top, tip, summit, height
Susae, -ārum (f, pl): Susa, a city of Persia (modern Shush in Iran)
thēsaurus, -ī (m): treasure, hoard
ululātus, -ūs (m): howling, shrieking, wailing [of mourning]

Questions about the Translation:

Lines 3-5 : What kind of subjunctives are *occiderent, delērent,* and *dīriperent?* ______________________

____

Line 5–6: What kind of subjunctives are *scīrent* and *parārent*? ______________________

Line 8: What kind of subjunctive is *audīsset*? ______________________

____

Line 14: What kind of subjunctive is *induerent*? ______________________

Line 15: What kind of subjunctives are *īret* and *disceret*? ______________________

Line 15: What kind of subjunctive is *faceret*? ______________________

Line 17: What kind of subjunctive is *promīsisset*? ______________________

Line 15: What kind of subjunctives are *ostenderet* and *monēret*? ______________________

Line 18–19: What kind of subjunctives are *intrāret* and *deprecāretur*? ______________________

Line 20: What kind of subjunctive is *dīceret*? ______________________

Line 24: What kind of subjunctive is *audīsset*?______________________

Line 24: What kind of subjunctive is *putēs*? ______________________

Line 27: What kind of subjunctive is *vēneris*? ______________________

Line 27: What kind of subjunctive is *parāreris*?______________________

Line 29: What kind of subjunctives are *edātis* and *bibātis*? ______________________

Line 37: What kind of subjunctive is *vīdisset*? ______________________

Line 36: What kind of subjunctive is *veniās*? ______________________

LESSON 11

Verbs: Conditions

Word List

Nouns

1. cāritās, -tātis (f) *love, esteem*
2. lūmen, -minis (n) *light, lamp*
3. peccātum, -ī (n) *sin, fault, offense*
4. thēsaurus, -ī (m) *treasure, hoard*

Verbs

5. indīcō (1) *I declare, show, make known*
6. recipiō, -ere, -cēpī, -ceptum *I take back/again, receive*
7. remittō, -ere, -mīsī, -missum *I send back, remove, forgive*
8. peccō (1) *I sin, offend, transgress*

Adverbs

9. nisi *if not, unless, except*
10. quasi *as if, just as; almost, nearly, about*

Memorization

Aeneid 1.1-6

Arma virumque canō, Troiae quī prīmus ab ōrīs
Ītaliam, fātō profugus, Lāvīnaque vēnit
lītora. Multum ille et terrīs iactātus et altō
vī superum saevae memorem Iūnōnis ob īram.
Multa quoque et bellō passus, dum conderet urbem,
īnferretque deōs Latiō, genus unde Latīnum,

And he suffered many things also in war, until he would found [his] city
and bring [his] gods to Latium—whence [comes] the Latin race

Grammar

The manifold and wondrous uses of the subjunctive just keep coming. In this lesson we will learn about conditional sentences (also called simply "conditions"). A complete conditional is a sentence with two clauses: the dependent clause that states a stipulation or hypothetical situation, and the main clause that lays out the consequence(s) of that stipulation or situation. In grammatical terminology, the dependent clause is called the ***protasis***, and the main clause is the ***apodosis***.

In Latin, conditionals can refer to the present, past, or future, and can come in both the indicative and subjunctive (making six basic types total). The indicative is used when the consequence or outcome of the stipulation seems more likely; the subjunctive (as we might suspect) appears when the situation is hypothetical or counter-factual. Take these two English examples:

If I am tired, I go to bed. (Indicative verbs are used; going to bed is the likely consequence of being tired.)

If I had been tired, I would have gone to bed. (Subjunctive verbs used; implied is "I wasn't tired, so I didn't go to bed"—thus, here is a situation contrary to actual events.)

Indicative Conditions

There are three basic types of conditionals using the indicative, referring to present, past, and future time:

- The **Simple Fact Present** describes a situation in the present where the result naturally follows. In Latin this condition uses a present indicative in both the protasis and the apodosis: *Sī laeta est, rīdet.* "If she is happy, she laughs."

- The **Simple Fact Past** similarly relates a situation that has its logical result, but both occurring in the past. The Latin will use imperfect or perfect indicatives in both clauses: *Sī laeta erat, rīsit.* "If she was happy, she laughed."

- The **Simple Fact Future** conditional, also known as **Future More Vivid**, describes a likely future event resulting from a future situation. This conditional in Latin will use either a future or future perfect indicative in both the protasis and apodosis: *Sī laeta erit, rīdēbit.* "If she will be happy, she will laugh." Now this one is a little trickier to recognize than the others, because often in English, we use a present tense verb (referring to the future) in the protasis: "If she's happy, she'll laugh." English frequently employs this present-pointing-to-the-future, as in: "My flight leaves tomorrow at 8:00." We can also say, "My flight will leave tomorrow at 8:00," but everyone understands that in the first statement, the present verb is referring to a future event.

With these indicative conditions, you can usually substitute a "when" for the "if" (this might help you confirm that yes, you are dealing with the indicative and not the subjunctive): "When she is happy, she laughs"; "When she was happy, she laughed"; and "When she is happy, she will laugh."

Subjunctive Conditions

And now with subjunctive conditionals we enter the world of hypotheticals and counterfactuals. These also fall into present, past, and future categories:

- The **Contrary to Fact Present** refers to a present situation (with its consequence) that isn't actually happening. The Latin conditional will use imperfect (NOT present) subjunctives for the Contrary to Fact Present: *Sī laeta esset, rīdēret.* "If she were happy, she would be laughing." It's easy to see that this is referring to present time if we look at what is implied: "But she's not happy, so she's not laughing."
- The **Contrary to Fact Past** conditional describes a past stipulation with result that did not happen. Both protasis and apodosis of this Latin conditional are in the pluperfect subjunctive: *Sī laeta fuisset, rīsisset.* "If she had been happy, she would have laughed." (Implied: "But she wasn't happy, so she didn't laugh.")
- Finally we come to the **Future Less Vivid** (compare to the Future More Vivid above), which relates a future situation with a consequence that could happen, but is not as likely to happen as in a Future More Vivid conditional. Both Latin clauses have a present subjunctive: *Sī laeta sit, rīdeat.* "If she should be happy, she would laugh."

Here are two handy charts summarizing these usages, with examples.

	TYPE OF CONDITIONAL	PROTASIS (CONDITION)	APODOSIS (CONCLUSION)
INDICATIVE	1. Simple Fact Present	Present Indicative *(translate as English present indicative)*	Present Indicative *(translate as English present indicative)*
INDICATIVE	2. Simple Fact Past	Imperfect or Perfect Indicative *(translate as English past indicative)*	Imperfect or Perfect Indicative *(translate as English past indicative)*
INDICATIVE	3. Simple Fact Future (Future More Vivid)	Future or Future Perfect Indicative *(translate as English present indicative)*	Future or Future Perfect Indicative *(translate as English future or future perfect indicative)*
SUBJUNCTIVE	1. Contrary to Fact Present	Imperfect Subjunctive *(translate as "were [Xing]")*	Imperfect Subjunctive *(translate as "would [be]")*
SUBJUNCTIVE	2. Contrary to Fact Past	Pluperfect Subjunctive *(translate as "had Xed")*	Pluperfect Subjunctive *(translate as "would have Xed")*
SUBJUNCTIVE	3. Future Less Vivid ("Should-Would")	Present Subjunctive *(translate with "should X")*	Present Subjunctive *(translate as "would X")*

Examples

	TYPE OF CONDITION	LATIN	ENGLISH
INDICATIVE	1. Simple Fact Present	Sī Oswaldus dracōnem pugnat, eum vincit.	If Oswald fights a dragon, he conquers it.
	2. Simple Fact Past	Sī Oswaldus dracōnem pugnāvit, eum vīcit.	If Oswald fought a dragon, he conquered it.
	3. Simple Fact Future (Future More Vivid)	Sī Oswaldus dracōnem pugnābit/ pugnāverit, eum vincet.	If Oswald fights a dragon, he will conquer it.
SUBJUNCTIVE	1. Contrary to Fact Present	Sī Oswaldus dracōnem pugnāret, eum vinceret.	If Oswald were fighting a dragon, he would conquer (would be conquering) it.
	2. Contrary to Fact Past	Sī Oswaldus dracōnem pugnāvisset, eum vīcisset.	If Oswald had fought a dragon, he would have conquered it.
	3. Future Less Vivid ("Should-Would")	Sī Oswaldus dracōnem pugnet, eum vincat.	If Oswald should fight a dragon, he would conquer it.

Now, these are the six basic types of conditionals. However, when you are translating Latin conditionals in their natural habitat, they are often mixed. Thus you might see a protasis of a Future More Vivid combined with the apodosis of a Simple Fact Present, as in our translation in this lesson: *Sī dīxerimus quoniam peccātum nōn habēmus, ipsī nōs sēdūcimus . . .*, "If we say [lit., 'will have said'] that we do not have sin, we deceive ourselves . . . " (1 John 1:8). Or perhaps you could have a Future Less Vivid mixed with a Simple Fact Present: *Sī in hoc scīmus quoniam cognōvimus eum sī mandāta eius observēmus*, "And in this we know that we know Him, if we should keep His commandments" (1 John 2:3). Or, as in English, you could have a protasis with an imperative or an interrogative following: "If you are hungry, eat something!" "If you didn't want to go, why did you?" Therefore, I ask you for a conditional, you can list one of the six above, or you can say "Mixed Condition" and then describe what types the protasis and apodosis each belong to. This is merely an exercise for the present to yourself to recognize verbs (in other words, parse them on the spot) and translate them more accurately.

One final thing you must know about conditionals. Whenever the indefinite pronoun *aliquis, aliquid* appears in the protasis, it drops the *ali-* and becomes *quis, quid* for short. A handy jingle (attributed to a fellow named Tom McCreight) for this is "After *sī, nisi, num*, or *nē, ali-* takes a holiday." Thus you might see this sentence: *Sī quis laeta est, rīdet.* "If anyone is happy, she laughs." And don't forget that you will see this phenomenon also following *num* in questions, and after *nē* with certain subjunctive usages!

Review

Add the *conditionals* to your list of subjunctives. Also, be sure to review the word *possum* in the subjunctive; it's a very important word. You might review it by practicing the sequence of tenses.

Worksheet 11

A. Vocabulary

1. unless: ______________________________
2. invicem: ______________________________
3. lūmen: ______________________________
4. cāritās: ______________________________
5. recipiō, recipere, __________, ____________: ______________________________
6. peccātum: ______________________________
7. treasure: ______________________________
8. mōs: ______________________________
9. indīcō (1): ______________________________
10. petō, -ere, -īvī (-iī), -ītum: ______________________________
11. grātia: ______________________________
12. remittō, remittere, remīsī, remissum: ______________________________
13. comes: ______________________________
14. I sin: ______________________________
15. quasi: ______________________________

B. Grammar

1. Give five examples of different English conditionals (feel free to use book or movie quotations or song lyrics). Describe the kind of conditional, even if it is mixed.

____

____

____

____

____

____

____

____

2. Do a synopsis of *recipiō* in the 3rd person singular, first giving principal parts:

		LATIN ACTIVE	ENGLISH ACTIVE	LATIN PASSIVE	ENGLISH PASSIVE
INDICATIVE	PRES.				
	IMPF.				
	FUT.				
	PF.				
	PLPF.				
	FT. PF.				
SUBJUNCTIVE	PRES.				
	IMPF.				
	PF.				
	PLPF.				

PARTICIPLE	PRES.				
	PF.				
	FUT.				
INFINITIVE	PRES.				
	PF.				
	FUT.				
IMP.	SG.				
	PL.				

C. Memorization

Fill in in the blanks in *Aeneid* 1.1-6 in Latin.

__________ ______________ __________, ___________ ______ ___________ _____ _______

___________, _________ _____________, ______________ _________

___________. M_________ ______ _____ ________ i_________ _____ _________

v__ ___________ __________ m___________ ____________ o___ ________.

Multa ___________ _____ _________ passus, _______ _____________ ___________,

______________ _________ Latiō, _________ unde _____________,

D. English to Latin

1. Translate these sets of conditionals into Latin.

   a) Unless the dragon receives treasure, he is angry.

   ____

b) Unless the dragon received treasure, he was angry.

c) Unless the dragon receives [*lit.*, "will have received"] treasure, he will be angry.

d) If I were there, I would not approach the dragon.

e) If I had been there, I would not have approached the dragon.

f) If I should be there, I would not approach the dragon.

2. Translate this set of indirect statements into Latin.

a) The minister declares that your sins are forgiven in Christ.

b) The minister declares that your sins have been forgiven in Christ.

c) The minister declares that Christ will forgive your sins.

d) The minister has declared that your sins were forgiven in Christ.

e) The minister has declared that your sins had been forgiven in Christ.

f) The minister has declared that Christ would forgive your sins.

3. Translate this set of indirect questions into Latin.

a) I myself wanted to know how they would carry off this idol.

b) I myself want to know how they carried off this idol.

c) I myself wanted to know how they had carried off this idol.

d) I myself want to know how they are carrying off this idol.

e) I myself want to know how they will carry off this idol.

f) I myself wanted to know how they carried off this idol.

4. Do not bring too much light into the banquet; the queen prefers to eat in darkness. [Give at least two ways to express prohibition in Latin.]

5. My father announces that there are so many neighbors here that he is returning to the country.

6. With our weapons let's persuade this Greek to give us half his herd.

7. In the seventh month the poor farmer will set out to the castle to declare his love and esteem to the princess. [Give at least three ways to express purpose in Latin.]

8. The scribe with tears will ask the dying king where he wants his ashes to be scattered.

9. After the branches had been removed, the woman demanded that her filthy nephews bathe in the fountain one at a time.

10. Although the priest wants to weigh the sacrifice, the sheep is constantly rushing down from the altar.

E. Latin to English

1 John 1:1-2:8

[1] 1 Quod* fuit ab initiō, quod audīvimus, quod vīdimus oculīs nostrīs, quod *perspēximus,* et manūs nostrae
temptāvērunt dē verbō vītae—2 et vīta *manifestāta est,* et vīdimus et *testāmur* et adnuntiāmus vōbīs vītam
aeternam quae erat apud Patrem et apparuit nōbīs. 3 Quod vīdimus et audīvimus adnuntiāmus et vōbīs ut
et vōs *societātem* habeātis nōbīscum. Et societās nostra sit cum Patre et cum Fīliō eius Iēsū Christō. 4 Et
haec scrībimus vōbīs ut gaudium nostrum sit plēnum. 5 Et haec est *adnuntiātiō* quam audīvimus ab eō et
adnuntiāmus vōbīs quoniam* Deus lūx est et tenēbrae in eō nōn sunt ūllae.
6 Sī dīxerimus quoniam *societātem* habēmus cum eō et in tenēbrīs ambulāmus mentīmur et nōn facimus
vēritātem. 7 Sī autem in lūce ambulēmus sīcut et ipse est in lūce societātem habēmus ad invicem et sanguis Iēsū Fīliī eius mundat nōs ab omnī peccātō. 8 Sī dīxerimus quoniam peccātum non habēmus ipsī nōs
sēdūcimus et vēritās in nōbīs nōn est. 9 Sī cōnfiteāmur peccāta nostra fidēlis est et iūstus ut *remittat* nōbīs
peccāta et *emundet* nōs ab omnī inīquitāte. 10 Sī dīxerimus quoniam nōn peccāvimus mendācem facimus
eum et verbum eius nōn est in nōbīs.

[2] 1 *Fīliōlī* meī, haec scrībō vōbīs ut nōn *peccētis,* sed et sī quis peccāverit *advocātum* habēmus apud Patrem
Iēsum Christum iūstum. 2 Et ipse est *propitiātiō* prō peccātīs nostrīs, nōn prō nostrīs autem tantum, sed
etiam prō tōtius mundī.
3 Et in hōc scīmus quoniam cognōvimus eum, sī mandāta eius *observēmus.* 4 Quī dīcit se nōsse* eum et
mandāta eius nōn custōdit, mendāx est et in hōc vēritās nōn est. 5 Quī autem servat* verbum eius vērē,* in
hōc *caritās* Deī *perfecta est.* In hōc scīmus quoniam in ipsō sumus. 6 Quī dīcit sē in ipsō manēre debet sīcut
ille ambulāvit et ipse ambulāre*.
7 Cārissimī,* non mandātum novum scrībō vōbīs sed mandātum vetus quod habuistis ab initiō:
mandātum vetus est verbum quod audistis*. 8 Iterum mandātum novum scribō vōbīs quod est vērum et in
ipsō et in vōbīs, quoniam tenēbrae trānseunt et *lūmen* vērum iam lūcet.

Notes:

* *Quod*: Translate this initial *quod* (and the ones that follow) as "that which"

* v. 5: *quoniam*—"that" introduces indirect discourse using an indicative (not accusative and infinitive, as in more "formal" Latin). See also 1:6, 8, 10; 2:3, 5, 8.

* *nōsse*: syncopated!

* *servat*: *servō* can also mean "I preserve, watch, observe, guard"

* *vērē*: adverb from *vērus, -a, -um*

* Reordering the words this way might make translation easier: … *ipse debet ambulāre sīcut et ille ambulāvit.*

* *cārissimī*: superlative of *cārus, -a, -um,* "dear, beloved" (*KL1*, Lesson 13); so, "most beloved" or "dearest" would be the most literal; "dearly beloved" sounds nice and ecclesiastical.

* *audīstis*: syncopated!

Glossary:

adnuntiātiō, -ōnis (f): announcement, message, declaration
advocātus, -ī (m): advocate, legal assistant/counselor
emundō, -āre, ——, -ātum: I cleanse, purify
fīliōlus, -ī (m): little son/child
manifestō (1): I (make) manifest, show clearly
observō (1): I observe, watch, keep, guard
perficiō, -ere, -fēcī, -fectum: I finish, complete, perfect
perspiciō, -ere, -spēxī, -spectum: I look through/at/into
propitiātiō, -ōnis (f): propitiation, atonement
sēdūcō, -ere, -dūxī, -ductum: I lead aside/astray, seduce, deceive
societās, -tātis (f): society, fellowship, community
testor, -ārī, -ātus sum: I testify, bear witness

Questions about Translation

Parse the following verbs (For Indicative and Subjunctive, give Person Number Tense Voice Mood of what verb; for Infinitive, give Tense Voice Mood of what verb)

1:1—*audīvimus*: ______________________________

____

1:2—*manifestāta est*: ______________________________

____

1:2—*testāmur*: ______________________________

____

1:3—*habeātis*: ______________________________

____

1:4—*sit*: ______________________________

____

1:6—*dīxerimus*: ______________________________

____

1:7—*mundat*: ______________________________

____

1:9—*cōnfiteāmur*: ______________________________

____

2:1—*peccētis*: ______________________________

____

2:4—*nōsse*: ______________________________

____

Identify the following subjunctive usages:

1:3—*habeātis*: ______________________________

1:3—*sit*: ______________________________

1:4—*sit*: ______________________________

1:7—*ambulēmus*: ______

1:9—*cōnfiteāmur*: ______

1:9—*remittat*: ______

1:9—*emundet*: ______

2:1—*peccētis*: ______

2:3—*observēmus*: ______

Answer the following questions about conditions:

1:6—*Sī dīxerimus...vēritātem:* What kind of condition? ______

______

1:7—*Sī autem...peccātō:* What kind of condition? ______

______

1:8—*Sī dīxerimus...est:* What kind of condition? ______

______

1:9—*Sī cōnfiteāmur...iūstus:* What kind of condition? ______

______

1:10—*Sī dīxerimus...nōbīs:* What kind of condition? ______

______

2:1—... *et sī quis peccāverit...iūstum:* What kind of condition? ______

______

2:3—*Et in hoc...sī mandāta eius observēmus:* What kind of condition? ______

______

F. For Fun: Crossword Puzzle

Answer the clues on the following page, which feature subjunctives (among other words), and then enter the answers in the crossword grid. Two things to note: Macrons have been left off, and compound verbs are written as one word with no spaces (e.g., NECATAEST for *necāta est*).

ACROSS

2. 1st Person Singuar Present Passive Subjunctive of *ferō*
4. 1st Person Plural Perfect Deponent Subjuctive of *loquor*
8. Feminine Singular Ablative of *quī, quae, quod*
9. 3rd Person Plural Imperfect Active Subjunctive of *eō*
10. 2nd Person Plural Perfect Active Subjunctive of *convertō*
12. 2nd Person Plural Present Active Subjunctive of word for "I sin"
16. Masculine Genitive Plural of *impetus*
18. Present Deponent Infinitive of *regredior*
19. Word for "how"
21. 1st Person Plural Imperfect Active Subjunctive of *sum*
24. Feminine Plural Accusative of *virga*
25. Genitive Plural of word for "idol"
29. 2nd Person Singular Imperfect Active Subjunctive of *auferō*
30. 3rd Person Plural Imperfect Passive Subjunctive of *peccō*
32. 1st Person Singular Present Active Indicative of word for "I order"
33. 1st Person Plural Pluperfect Active Subjunctive of *recipiō*
35. 1st Person Plural Imperfect Passive Subjunctive of *scindō*
38. Word for "I learn"
41. Word for "I have eaten"
42. Word for "so many"
43. 3rd Person Plural Perfect Active Subjunctive of *accidō*
44. Plural Ablative of word for "light"
46. 3rd Person Singular Present Active Subjunctive of *ruō*
47. Word for "so much"
49. Present Active Infinitive of word for "it is proper"
51. 1st Person Plural Present Active Subjunctive of *sum*
53. 1st Person Plural Pluperfect Passive Subjunctive of word for "I remove"
54. 3rd Person Singular Future Active Indicative of word for "I loose"
55. Word for "jewel"
56. 1st Person Singular Present Active Indicative of word for "I throw out"
57. 3rd Person Plural Present Active Subjunctive of *tradō*
58. 3rd Person Plural Imperfect Active Subjunctive of *mandō*

DOWN

1. 2nd Person Singular Present Active Subjunctive of *ferō*
2. Feminine Singular Ablative of a word for "faith"
3. 3rd Person Singular Present Active Subjunctive of *absum*
4. Feminine Singular Accusative of *lacrima*
5. Word for "ear" in the Ablative Singular
6. 3rd Person Singular Present Active Subjunctive of *sciō*
7. 1st Person Singular Present Passive Subjunctive of *indīcō*
8. Word for "as if"
11. Masculine Singular Nominative of word for "neighboring"
12. 2nd Person Singular Present Active Subjunctive of *pendō*
13. 1st Person Singular Imperfect Active Subjunctive of *effundō*
14. Word for "certainly"
15. Word for "by what means?"
17. 1st Person Singular Perfect Active Subjunctive of *eō*
20. "you (sg.) will prefer"
22. Masculine Nominative Singular of word for "holy"
23. Word for "anywhere"
26. Locative of word for "Rome"
27. Genitive Singular of word for "month"
28. 3rd Person Singular Present Active Subjunctive of *incolō*
29. 1st Person Plural Present Active Indicative of *appareō*
30. 3rd Person Plural Pluperfect Passive Subjunctive of *postulō*

31. Dative Plural of word for "banquet"

33. 2nd Person Plural Present Active Subjunctive of *remittō*

34. 3rd Person Plural Pluperfect Passive Subjunctive of *convertō*

36. 3rd Person Plural Present Active Subjunctive of *coniungō*

37. 2nd Person Plural Present Deponent Subjunctive of *regredior*

39. 1st Person Singular Present Passive Subjunctive of *scindō*

40. 2nd Person Plural Pluperfect Active Subjunctive of *offerō*

45. 2nd Person Singular Present Active Subjunctive of word for "I command"

48. 3rd Person Plural Imperfect Active Subjunctive of *volō*

50. Word for "I go out"

52. 1st Person Present Active Subjunctive of *mālō*

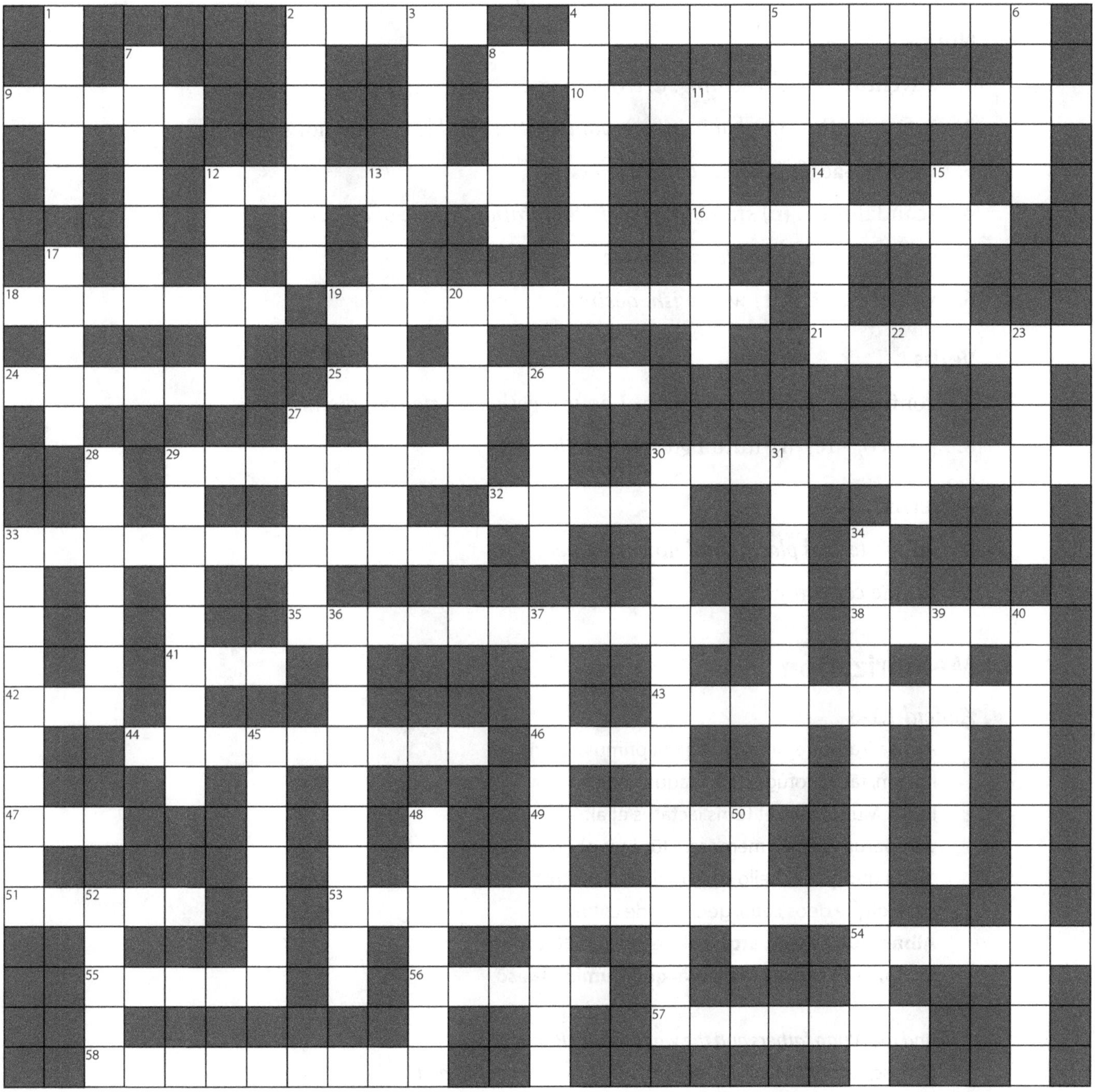

Lesson 12

Verbs: Subjunctive (Relative Clause of Characteristic); 1 John 2:9-29

Word List

Nouns

1. adventus, -ūs (m) *coming, arrival, advent*
2. īnfāns, -ntis (m/f) *baby, infant, young/little child* [lit., "one not speaking"]
3. iūstitia, -ae (f) *justice, righteousness*
4. scandalum, -ī (n) *stumbling block, temptation, cause of offense*
5. superbia, -ae (f) *pride, arrogance*
6. voluntās, -tātis (f) *will, wish, desire*

Verbs

7. confundō, -ere, -fūdī, -fūsum *I pour together, confound, disturb*
8. prōdeō, -īre, -iī, -itum *I go/come forth*

Adverbs

9. adhūc *to this place, until now, still, yet*
10. utique *certainly, surely*

Memorization

Aeneid 1.1-8

Arma virumque canō, Troiae quī prīmus ab ōrīs
Ītaliam, fātō profugus, Lāvīnaque vēnit
lītora. Multum ille et terrīs iactātus et altō
vī superum saevae memorem Iūnōnis ob īram.
Multa quoque et bellō passus, dum conderet urbem,
īnferretque deōs Latiō, genus unde Latīnum,
Albānīque patrēs, atque altae moenia Rōmae.
Mūsa, mihī causās memorā, quō nūmine laesō,

and the Alban fathers and the walls of lofty Rome.
O Muse, recount to me the reasons: which deity was offended,

Grammar

Relative Clause of Characteristic

Way back in *KL2*, Lesson 3 we learned the relative pronoun *quī, quae, quod* and how it introduces relative clauses. The relative pronoun refers back to an antecedent, and then the relative clause describes something about that antecedent. Relative clauses employing the indicative (the ones we have been dealing with thus far) refer to a factual, specific antecedent: *Oswaldus, quī dracōnem necāvit, rēx factus est*—"Oswald, who killed the dragon, became king." However, if we want to describe a non-factual or generic antecedent, we can swap out the indicative verb in the relative clause for a subjunctive, and voilà!—the Relative Clause of Characteristic: *Oswaldus erat vir quī dracōnēs necāret*—"Oswald was a man who [the kind of man who] killed [or, would kill] dragons." Thus, the Relative Clause of Characteristic describes a general characteristic of its antecedent, and that antecedent is also unspecified, negative, or interrogative. Basically, think of the differences between these two clauses like those between an indicative verb and a subjunctive—if it's more hypothetical, vague, or non-factual (because it's negative, for instance), then it's a subjunctive and it'll be a relative clause of characteristic rather than a regular indicative relative clause. Here are some examples comparing the two:

RELATIVE CLAUSE (INDICATIVE)	RELATIVE CLAUSE OF CHARACTERISTIC (SUBJUNCTIVE)
Oswaldus, quī dracōnem necāvit, rēx factus est. Oswald, who killed the dragon, became king.	*Oswaldus erat vir quī dracōnēs necāret.* Oswald was a man who [*or*, the kind of man who] killed [***or***, would kill] dragons.
Illī sunt virī quī dracōnēs necant. Those are the men who kill dragons.	*Sunt aliquī quī dracōnēs necent.* There are some (men) who kill dragons.
Sciēbam virum quī dracōnem necābat. I knew the man who killed the dragon.	*Erat nēmō quī dracōnem necāret.* There was no one who (would) kill [*or* killed] the dragon.
Est dracō quem Oswaldum necāvit. This is a dragon that Oswald killed.	*Est dracō quem Oswaldus necet.* This is the type of dragon that Oswald would kill.
Vidistīne virum quī dracōnem necāvit? Did you see the man who killed the dragon?	*Eratne aliquis ibī quī dracōnem necāret?* Was there anyone there who would kill the dragon?

Review

Be sure to add the *Relative Clause of Characteristic* to your list of subjunctives, and perhaps try making different sentences based on the sequence of tenses. Review the words *eō, ferō, volō, nōlō,* and *mālō* in the subjunctive.

Worksheet 12

A. Vocabulary

1. voluntās: ______
2. mālō, mālle, māluī, —: ______
3. parcō, -ere, pepercī, parsūrum (+dat.): ______
4. confundō, ______ confūdī, confūsum: ______
5. superbia: ______
6. passim: ______
7. prōdeō, prodīre, prodiī, proditum: ______
8. baby: ______
9. adventus: ______
10. adhūc: ______
11. scandalum: ______
12. mūnus: ______
13. I do not wish: ______
14. iūstitia: ______
15. utique: ______

B. Grammar

1. Identify whether these sentences contain a relative clause or a relative clause of characteristic.

   She knows a guy who can fix this. ______

   There are those who say I am wrong, but they are wrong. ______

   The skunk that lived in our alley finally departed. ______

   Do you know the woman who made this chocolate peanut butter pie? ______

   Nobody who is in his right mind would ever attempt that. ______

   ______

   Is there anybody here who speaks German? ______

   ______

2. Review: It's been a while. Time to decline a noun-adjective combo, *voluntās crūdēlis.*

	LATIN SINGULAR	LATIN PLURAL
NOM.		
GEN.		
DAT.		
ACC.		
ABL.		
VOC.		

3. Do a synopsis of *prōdeō* in the 1st person plural, first giving principal parts:

____

		LATIN ACTIVE	ENGLISH ACTIVE	LATIN PASSIVE	ENGLISH PASSIVE
INDICATIVE	PRES.				
	IMPF.				
	FUT.				
	PF.				
	PLPF.				
	FT. PF.				
SUBJUNCTIVE	PRES.				
	IMPF.				
	PF.				
	PLPF.				

PARTICIPLE	PRES.				
	PF.				
	FUT.				
INFINITIVE	PRES.				
	PF.				
	FUT.				
IMP.	SG.				
	PL.				

C. Memorization

Fill in the blanks in *Aeneid* 1.1-8 in Latin.

____

____

__________ ______ ____ __________ ____________ ____ _________

____ ____________ ___________ _____________ ____________ _____ _________.

M________ ____________ ____ ________ p________, _______ ____________ ____________,

_____________ _______ L________, ________ u________ ___________

Albānīque __________, ________ ________ moenia __________.

________, mihī __________ ____________, ______ nūmine ________,

D. Translation

English to Latin

Translate these sentences into Latin; then convert each relative clause into a relative clause of characteristic and translate again.

1. This was the sin that no one was able to forgive.

____

____

____

____

2. A man is here who will save the baby from the dragon.

____

____

____

3. Those were the women who preferred banquets rather than work.

____

____

____

____

Now simply translate these remaining sentences into Latin. It's up to you to figure out which mood each verb should go in.

4. At that time we did not understand how the coming of this infant would be a stumbling block for many.

____

____

5. The rather old prophet warned the servants not to disturb the ancient idol, but filled with pride, they carried it off.

____

____

6. Her maidservants were not accustomed to go forth without lamps into the Cave of Darkness to seek treasure.

7. Don't shed so many tears that you compel the little children to howl too.

8. These cookies will be a cruel temptation for my will; I must throw them out into the sea, or I will withdraw from here immediately.

9. If the poor woman had not returned home when she did [return], she wouldn't have found the golden sheep waiting for her.

10. Is it proper that I remain in the entryway while the servants enter in before me?

E. Latin to English

1 John 2:9-29

9 Quī* dicit sē in lūce esse et frātrem suum ōdit in tenēbrīs est usque adhūc.
10 Quī dīligit frātrem suum in lūmine manet et scandalum in eō nōn est;
11 quī autem ōdit frātrem suum
in tenēbrīs est et in tenēbrīs ambulat et nescit quō **eat** quoniam tenēbrae *obcaecāvērunt* oculōs eius.
12 Scrībō vōbīs, fīliolī, quoniam remittuntur vōbīs peccāta propter nōmen eius.
13 Scrībō vōbīs, patrēs,
quoniam cognōvistis eum quī ab initiō est. Scrībō vōbīs, adulescentēs, quoniam vīcistis *malignum.*
14 Scrīpsī
vōbīs, īnfantēs, quoniam cognōvistis Patrem. Scrīpsī vōbīs, patrēs, quia cognōvistis eum quī ab initiō. Scrīpsī
vōbīs, adulescentēs, quia fortēs estis et verbum Deī in vōbīs manet, et vīcistis *malignum.*

15 Nōlīte dīligere mundum nēque ea quae in mundō sunt. Sī quis* dīligit mundum, nōn est cāritās Patris
in eō; 16 quoniam omne quod est in mundō *concupiscentia* carnis et *concupiscentia* oculōrum est et superbia
vītae, quae nōn est ex Patre sed ex mundō est. 17 Et mundus transit et *concupiscentia* eius; quī autem facit
voluntātem Deī manet in aeternum*.

18 Fīliolī, nōvissima* hōra est, et sīcut audīstis* quia *antichristus* venit, nunc *antichristī* multī factī sunt,
unde scīmus quoniam nōvissima hōra est. 19 Ex nōbīs prodierunt sed nōn erant ex nōbīs, nam sī **fuissent**
ex nōbīs permansissent utique nōbīscum; sed ut manifestī sint quoniam nōn sunt omnēs ex nōbīs. 20 Sed
vōs *unctiōnem* habētis ā Sanctō et nōstis* omnia.

21 Nōn scrīpsī vōbīs quasi ignorantibus vēritātem sed quasi scīentibus eam et quoniam omne mendācium ex
vēritāte nōn est. 22 Quis est mendāx, nisi is quī negat quoniam Iēsus nōn* est Christus? Hic est antīchristus—quī
negat Patrem et Fīlium. 23 Omnis quī negat Fīlium nec Patrem habet; quī cōnfitētur Fīlium et Patrem habet.

24 Vōs quod audīstis* ab initiō in vōbīs permaneat; sī in vōbīs permanserit quod ab initiō audīstis*, et
vōs in Fīliō et Patre manēbitis. 25 Et haec est *reprōmissiō* quam ipse pollicitus est nōbīs, vītam aeternam.
26 Haec scrīpsī vōbīs dē eīs quī *sēdūcunt* vōs. 27 Et vōs *ūnctiōnem* quam accēpistis ab eō manet in vōbīs et
nōn necesse habētis ut aliquis doceat* vōs; sed sīcut *ūnctiō* eius docet vōs dē omnibus et vērum est, et nōn
est mendācium, et sīcut docuit vōs, manēte in eō.

28 Et nunc, fīliolī, manēte in eō, ut cum appāruerit habeāmus fīdūciam et nōn confundāmur ab eō in
adventū eius. 29 Sī scītis quoniam iūstus est, scītōte* quoniam et omnis quī facit iūstitiam ex ipsō nātus est.

Notes:

* *Quī*: Remember that when the relative pronoun begins a clause, it can be equivalent to a demonstrative plus a relative pronoun; here, *Quī=Is quī*, "He who…"

* *quis*: "After *sī, nisi, num,* or *nē*…."

* *in aeternum:* idiomatic adverbial phrase, "forever, eternally"

* *nōvissima*: *Nōvus, -a, -um*, "new" (*KL1*, Lesson 26) has a special meaning in the superlative—"last, latest."

* *audīstis*: syncopated!

* *nōstis*: syncopated!

* *nōn*: Usually in Latin, a double negative will make a positive (as in English: "Nor did he not fight"= "he did fight"). However, with forms of *negō*, the *nōn* is reinforcing its meaning, "I did NOT say." Additionally, the Latin here could simply be imitating the Greek original, which has the two negatives; in Greek, two negatives are emphatic and don't cancel each other out.

* *audīstis*: syncopated!

* *doceat*: In addition to indirect statement, *necesse* can also be followed by *ut* + subjunctive.

* *scītōte*: This is a future imperative form (singular ending *-tō*; plural *-tōte*). Although in a sense all imperatives refer to a future time, the future imperative specifically refers to a future contingent fulfillment (it is often used in legal documents, receipes, and colloquial language). Similar usage in English would be "Congress shall make no law…" (this is not a prediction, but a command); or "Young man, you will clean your room" (again, the mom is not prophesying that her son will clean his room but rather commanding him to do so).

Glossary:

antīchristus, -ī (m): antichrist, the Antichrist

concupiscentia, -ae (f): desire, longing, lust

malignus, -a, -um: evil, wicked, malicious, malignant

manifestus, -a, -um: manifest, apparent, clear

obcaecō (1): I (make) blind, darken, conceal

reprōmissiō, -ōnis (f): (formal) promise, guarantee, counter-promise [business language]

sēdūcō, -ere, -dūxī, -ductum: I lead aside/astray, seduce, deceive

ūnctiō, -ōnis (f): anointing, ointment

Questions about Translation

Parse the following verbs (For Indicative and Subjunctive, give Person, Number, Tense, Voice, and Mood of what verb; for Infinitive and Imperative, give Tense, Voice, and Mood of what verb). Then identify the usage of that verb (e.g., purpose clause, accusative and infinitive, present simple fact condition, etc.).

2:9—*esse:*

a) Parse: ____________________

b) Usage: ____________________

2:11—*eat:*

a) Parse: ____________________

b) Usage: ____________________

2:15—*nōlīte:*

a) Parse: ____________________

b) Usage: ____________________

2:19—*fuissent:*

a) Parse: ____________________

b) Usage: ____________________

2:19—*sint:*

a) Parse: ____________________

b) Usage: ____________________

2:24—*permaneat:*

a) Parse: ____________________

b) Usage: ____________________

2:24—*permanserit:*

a) Parse: ____________________

b) Usage: ____________________

2:28—*habeāmus:*

a) Parse: ____________________

b) Usage: ____________________

2:29—*confundāmur:*

a) Parse: ____________________

b) Usage: ____________________

Other Questions

2:15—*Sī quis dīligit…eō:* What kind of condition? ____________________

2:29—*Sī scītis…nātus est:* What kind of condition? ____________________

____

LESSON 13

Verbs—Optative, Potential, and Deliberative Subjunctives

Word List

Nouns

1. diabolus, -ī (m) *devil*
2. substantia, -ae (f) *substance, essence; property, fortune, worldly goods*
3. vīscus, -eris (n) *internal organs, entrails, inward parts; (metaphorically) heart*

Adjective

4. malignus, -a, -um *evil, wicked, malicious, malignant*

Verbs

5. obsecrō (1) *I beseech, beg, implore;* [tē/vōs] obsecrō *please, pray*
6. pariō, -ere, peperī, par(i)tum *I bring forth, give birth to, beget*
7. trānsferō, -ferre, -tulī, -lātum *I carry/bear/bring across/over, transfer, translate*

Conjunction/Adverbs

8. forsitan *perhaps, peradventure, maybe*
9. vērumtamen *however, nevertheless*
10. utinam *would/oh that! if only! I wish that!*

Memorization

Aeneid 1.1-9

Arma virumque canō, Troiae quī prīmus ab ōrīs
Ītaliam, fātō profugus, Lāvīnaque vēnit
lītora. Multum ille et terrīs iactātus et altō
vī superum saevae memorem Iūnōnis ob īram.
Multa quoque et bellō passus, dum conderet urbem,
īnferretque deōs Latiō, genus unde Latīnum,
Albānīque patrēs, atque altae moenia Rōmae.
Mūsa, mihī causās memorā, quō nūmine laesō,
quidve dolēns, rēgīna deum tot volvere cāsūs

or grieving at what did the queen of the gods force [this] man,

Grammar

In this lesson we will be wrapping up a few final independent subjunctives. Independent subjunctives, as you doubtless will recall, serve as the main verb of the sentence, while dependent subjunctives appear in subordinate clauses. Here is a summary chart of the different subjunctive usages thus far.

INDEPENDENT SUBJUNCTIVE USAGES	DEPENDENT SUBJUNCTIVE USAGES
Hortatory/Jussive (Lesson 4) Prohibitive (Lesson 6) Optative (Lesson 13) Deliberative (Lesson 13) Potential (Lesson 13)	Purpose Clause (Lesson 5) Result Clause (Lesson 5) Cum Clause (Lesson 7) Indirect Question (Lesson 9) Indirect Command (Lesson 10) Present Contrary to Fact Condition (Lesson 11) Past Contrary to Fact Condition (Lesson 11) Future Less Vivid Condition (Lesson 11) Relative Clause of Characteristic (Lesson 12) Fear Clause (Lesson 14) Miscellaneous Clauses (Lesson 15)

Optative Subjunctive

The optative subjunctive derives its name from the Latin verb *optō (1)*, "I choose, wish (for)," and thus expresses a wish, desire, or prayer. It appears most commonly in the present, imperfect, and pluperfect tenses. An optative subjunctive in the present tense (once in a while in the perfect) states a wish for a future event. In the imperfect, it is stating a wish for present event, and in the pluperfect, a wish that an event had occurred in the past. The optative subjunctive regularly is introduced by *utinam*, "would that! oh that! if only! I wish that!"; *nē* is used in negative optative subjunctive sentences. These subjunctives will of course depend on context for the best translation, but since they are expressing a wish or desire, you can translate accordingly using the meanings of *utinam* above, or a "may," or whatever gets the intention across. You will now be able to say, *Vīs tēcum sit*, "May the force be with you."

Some students have trouble distinguishing the hortatory/jussive from the optative. First, while the hortatory is more like a command (Let the gate open!), while the optative is less commanding and merely expresses a hope that the world may be that way. Second, we usually translate hortatory/jussive subjunctives with "let," while we translate optatives with "may it be" or even "I wish that . . . " Again, context is key.

TENSE OF SUBJUNCTIVE	DESCRIPTION	LATIN EXAMPLE	ENGLISH TRANSLATION
PRESENT	states a wish for the future	*[Utinam] dracōnem necēs!*	May you slay the dragon! [future emphasis] Would that you may slay the dragon! I wish that you may slay the dragon!
		[Utinam] nē ā dracōne necēris!	May you not be slain by the dragon! Would that you not be slain by the dragon! [future emphasis] I wish that you may not be slain by the dragon!

IMPERFECT	states a wish for the present	*[Utinam] dracōnem necāres!*	May you slay the dragon! [present emphasis] Would that you may slay the dragon! I wish that you may slay the dragon!
		[Utinam] nē ā dracōne necārēris!	May you not be slain by the dragon! Would that you not be slain by the dragon! [present emphasis] I wish that you may not be slain by the dragon!
PLUPERFECT	states a wish for the past	*[Utinam] dracōnem necāvissēs!*	Would that you had slain the dragon! I wish that you had slain the dragon!
		[Utinam] nē ā dracōne necātus essēs!	Would that you had not been slain by the dragon! I wish that you had not been slain by the dragon!

Finally, here are a few examples I have gathered a few from the Vulgate:

Dixitque ad Deum, "Utinam Ismael vivat coram te!" And he said to God, "O that Ishmael would live before You!" (Gen. 17:18)

Utinam saperent, et intelligerent, ac novissima providerent! O that they were wise and understood, and would provide for their latter end! (Dt. 32:29)

Et murmurati sunt contra Moysen et Aaron cuncti filii Israel, dicentes, "Utinam mortui essemus in Aegypto! Et in hac vasta solitudine utinam pereamus, et non inducat nos Dominus in terram istam…." And all the sons of Israel murmured against Moses and Aaron, saying, "Would that we had died in Egypt! And would that we may perish in this vast wilderness, and that the Lord not lead us into that land…." (Num. 14:2-2)

Cumque indigeret aqua populus, convenerunt adversum Moysen et Aaron. Et versi in seditionem, dixerunt, "Utinam periissemus inter fratres nostros coram Domino." And when the people lacked water, they gathered against Moses and Aaron. And having turned to rebellion, they said, "Would that we had perished with our brothers before the Lord!" (Num. 20:2-3)

Atque utinam taceretis ut putaremini esse sapientes. And I wish that you would be silent so that you may be thought to be wise. (Job 13:5)

Atque utinam sic iudicaretur vir cum Deo, quomodo iudicatur filius hominis cum collega suo! And O that a man would be thus judged with God, how a son of man is judged with his companion! (Job 16:22)

Utinam dirigantur viae meae ad custodiendas iustificationes tuas! O that my ways would be directed toward keeping Your justifications! (Ps. 119:5)

Utinam adtendisses mandata mea! Oh that you had heeded My commandments! (Is. 48:18)

Potential Subjunctive

Way back in *Kraken Latin 1*, the subjunctive mood was defined as portraying "hypothetical, potential, or indirect action." And now, much later on our Latin journey, we come to the Potential Subjunctive, which expresses an action that possibly could happen or that one can imagine would happen. This is in contrast to the indicative, which describes real, actual action. It is also different from a hortatory or jussive subjunctive, which expresses action that is wished for or commanded. Not surprisingly, context will help you determine whether you are dealing with a hortatory subjunctive or a 1st person potential subjunctive, or a jussive versus a 3rd person potential subjunctive. Happily, the negative of a potential subjunctive uses *nōn* rather than *nē*, so that can help identify it as well. The new vocabulary word *forsitan*, "perhaps, peradventure, maybe," is often accompanied by a potential subjunctive (but can also appear with an indicative). *Fortasse*, the other word you have learned for "perhaps" (*KL2*, Lesson 12), will more commonly take the indicative, but can also show up with the subjunctive. Language is so helpful, isn't it?

To express present or future potential action, we will use a present or perfect subjunctive, and the potential of the past will use an imperfect subjunctive. There isn't one simple way to translate the potential subjunctive. Depending on the context, you can select from a wide variety of options, including (but not limited to) *can*, *could*, *may*, *might*, *must*, *should*, and *would*. And this would probably be a good time to review the trickiness of English modals (also known as helping verbs). For example, we have already used "can" as an alternate translation of *possum*, "I am able." So if we say, "I can lift 100 pounds easily," we are simply saying "I am able to lift 100 pounds easily." In this type of sentence, "could" is just the past of "can": "When I was young, I could lift 100 pounds easily." However, we also use "could" to make a polite request, "Could you please pass the salt?" or here to translate a potential subjunctive. Use context and common sense to distinguish the different usages of these English modals so that you can appropriately translate into and from Latin! Here are some examples of ways we could translate a potential subjunctive into English:

I **can** probably eat this whole cake. Yesterday I **could** probably **have** eaten the whole cake.

I **may** just eat this whole cake. Yesterday I **might have** just eaten the whole cake.

I **would** perhaps eat this whole cake. Yesterday I **would have** perhaps eaten this whole cake.

This **should** work.

I **must have** lost my keys at the park.

The potential subjunctive can also function as basically half of a condition: *Amārēs sermōnem eius*, "You would have loved his speech" (implied: "if you had heard it"). Here are a few summary examples of this versatile if slippery subjunctive.

TENSE OF SUBJUNCTIVE	DESCRIPTION	LATIN EXAMPLE	ENGLISH TRANSLATION
PRESENT/ PERFECT	states potential of the present or future	*Forsitan dracōnem crūdēlem necet/ necāverit.*	He can/could/may/might should/would perhaps slay the cruel dragon.
		Forsitan ā dracōne crūdēlī nōn necētur/necātus sit.	He can/could/may/might should/would not perhaps be slain by the cruel dragon.
IMPERFECT	states potential of the past (esp. in 2nd person generic "you")	*Dracōnem crūdēlem necārēs.*	You can/could/may/might should/would have slain the cruel dragon.
		Ā dracōne crūdēlī nōn necārēris.	You can/could/may/might should/would have not been slain by the cruel dragon.

Deliberative Subjunctive

The Deliberative Subjunctive is a tad bit easier to spot than the previous two because it appears in questions. The speaker employs this subjunctive to ask advice from either himself or someone else, or to inquire about someone's inclination or wishes. Sometimes these questions are rhetorical (in which case they resemble the potential subjunctive). The deliberative subjunctive uses *nōn* in the negative. The present tense of the subjunctive appears in questions about a future action, while the imperfect (and sometimes the pluperfect) expresses questions about a past action. Note possible ways of translating the deliberative subjunctive in these examples:

Quid agam? *What am I to do? What should/shall I do?*

Quid faciāmus? *What are we to do? What should/shall we do?*

Quid agerem? *What was I to do? What should I have done?*

Quid agerēmus? *What were we to do? What should we have done?*

And here is another handy chart summarizing this particular subjunctive usage.

TENSE OF SUBJUNCTIVE	DESCRIPTION	LATIN EXAMPLE	ENGLISH TRANSLATION
PRESENT	asks a question about future action	*Huncne dracōnem sed nōn hunc caprum necam?*	Am I to slay [Should I slay] this dragon, but not this goat?
IMPERFECT/ PLUPERFECT	asks a question about past action	*Huncne dracōnem sed nōn hunc caprum necārem/ necāvissem?*	Was I to slay [Should I have slain] this dragon, but not this goat?

Review

Be sure to add *Optative, Potential,* and *Deliberative* to your list of subjunctives, and be sure to notice which tenses to use, especially on the deliberative. Review the hortatory/jussive and prohibitive and make sure you can distinguish them from the optative; also review the indirect question and distinguish it from the deliberative

Worksheet 13

A. Vocabulary

1. neuter, -tra, -trum: ______
2. coepī, coepisse, coeptum (defective): ______
3. vērumtamen: ______
4. forsitan: ______
5. trānsferō, trānsferre, trānstulī, ______: ______

   ______
6. oportet, -ēre, oportuit (impers. +acc.): ______
7. obsecrō (1): ______
8. vīscus: ______
9. substantia: ______
10. undique: ______
11. malignus: ______
12. devil: ______
13. it is permitted: ______
14. pariō, parere, peperī, par(i)tum: ______
15. utinam: ______

B. Grammar

1. Indicate whether you would translate the following English phrases using an optative, potential, or deliberative subjunctive.

   Should I stay or should I go? ______

   I wish I could fly! ______

   She might be able to help us. ______

   May you never be unhappy again. ______

   Would that I had not been seasick! ______

   We should have gone to that concert. ______

   What should we have said to them? ______

2. Do a synopsis of *trānsferō* in the 2nd person plural, first giving principal parts:

____

		LATIN ACTIVE	ENGLISH ACTIVE	LATIN PASSIVE	ENGLISH PASSIVE
INDICATIVE	PRES.				
	IMPF.				
	FUT.				
	PF.				
	PLPF.				
	FT. PF.				
SUBJUNCTIVE	PRES.				
	IMPF.				
	PF.				
	PLPF.				
PARTICIPLE	PRES.				
	PF.				
	FUT.				
INFINITIVE	PRES.				
	PF.				
	FUT.				

IMP.	SG.				
	PL.				

C. Memorization

Fill in the blanks in *Aeneid* 1.1-9 in Latin.

____

____

____

____

_______ _________ ___ _______ ________, _______ _________ ________,

_________ ______ _______, _______ _______ _________,

_________ _______, _______ _______ m________ ________.

______, m_____ _______ _________, _____ n_______ ______,

quidve _______, _______ deum _____ volvere ______

D. English to Latin

1. Peradventure I might be able to swim across the river. Should I attempt it? Oh, would that someone would carry me across this huge river!

   ____

   ____

2. Please don't withdraw from me; I must pour out my heart to you with songs of love. [Translate this in two out of three possible ways.]

   ____

   ____

   ____

   ____

   ____

   ____

3. It happened that, after the king's daughter was born, the wicked woman came forth to Rome to curse the infant and not to bless [her]. [Translate this in three out of five possible ways.]

4. He asked whether the devil was a murderer from the beginning or sinned later.

5. The savage pirate will command his servants to weigh his entire hoard and all his fortune, and then to bring him the most marvelous feast possible.

6. If I hadn't brought in my lamp, we wouldn't have been able to see the sheep tearing our clothing.

7. You (pl.) were declaring that you had seen numerous devils in this place, weren't you?

8. Although the temptation of eating too many cookies was very strong, I turned around and ran from my neighbor's house.

9. If we see ghosts on the hill, we will be so afraid that we will rush down immediately.

10. Your neighbors have the kind of servants who join together at night and disturb the peace.

E. Latin to English

1 John 3

1 Vidēte quālem cāritātem dedit nōbīs Pater ut fīliī Deī *nōminēmur*—et sumus. Propter hōc mundus nōn
nōvit nōs quia nōn nōvit eum. 2 Cārissimī,* nunc fīliī Deī sumus, et nōndum appāruit quid erimus, scīmus
quoniam cum appāruerit similēs eī erimus quoniam vidēbimus eum sīcutī* est.
3 Et omnis quī habet spem hanc in eō sanctificat sē sīcut et ille sanctus est. 4 Omnis quī facit peccātum et
inīquitātem facit, et peccātum est inīquitās. 5 Et scītis quoniam ille appāruit ut peccāta tolleret et peccātum
in eō nōn est. 6 Omnis quī in eō manet nōn peccat. Omnis quī peccat nōn vīdit eum nec cognōvit eum.
7 *Fīliolī,* nēmō vōs *sēdūcat.* Quī facit iūstitiam iūstus est sīcut et ille iūstus est; 8 quī facit peccātum ex
diabolō est quoniam ab initiō diabolus peccat. In hoc appāruit Fīlius Deī ut *dissolvat** opera diabolī. 9 Omnis
quī nātus est ex Deō peccātum nōn facit quoniam *sēmen* ipsius in eō manet, et nōn potest peccāre quoniam
ex Deō nātus est. 10 In hōc *manifestī sunt* fīliī Deī et fīliī diabolī: omnis quī nōn est iūstus nōn est dē Deō,
et quī nōn dīligit frātrem suum.
11 Quoniam haec est *adnuntiātiō* quam audīstis* ab initiō, ut dīligāmus* *alterūtrum.* 12 Nōn sīcut *Cain*:
ex malīgnō erat et occīdit frātrem suum, et propter quid occīdit eum? Quoniam opera eius maligna erant,
frātris autem eius iūsta. 13 Nōlīte mirārī, frātrēs, sī ōdit vōs mundus. 14 Nōs scīmus quoniam trānslātī sumus
dē morte in vītam, quoniam dīligimus frātrēs; quī nōn dīligit manet in morte. 15 Omnis quī ōdit frātrem
suum homicīda est, et scītis quoniam omnis homicīda nōn habet vītam aeternam in sē manentem.
16 In hōc cognōvimus cāritātem quoniam ille prō nōbīs animam suam posuit; et nōs debēmus prō
frātribus animās pōnere. 17 Quī habuerit substantiam mundī et vīderit frātrem suum necesse habēre et
clauserit vīscera sua ab eō, quōmodo cāritās Deī manet in eō? 18 Fīliolī, nōn dīligāmus verbō nec linguā
sed opere et vēritāte. 19 In hōc cognōscimus quoniam ex vēritāte sumus et in conspectū eius *suadēmus*
corda nostra, 20 quoniam sī *reprehenderit* nōs cor, māior est Deus corde nostrō* et nōvit omnia.
21 Cārissimī, sī cor nōn* *reprehenderit* nōs, fīdūciam habēmus ad Deum, 22 et quodcumque petīerimus*
accipiēmus ab eō, quoniam mandāta eius custōdīmus et ea quae sunt *placita* coram eō facimus. 23 Et hoc
est mandātum eius ut crēdāmus* in nōmine Fīliī eius Iesū Christī et dīligāmus* alterūtrum sīcut dedit
mandātum nōbīs. 24 Et quī servat mandāta eius in illō manet et ipse in eō; et in hōc scīmus quoniam manet
in nōbīs dē Spīritū quem nōbīs dedit.

Notes:

* *Cārissimī*: superlative of *cārus, -a, -um*, "dear, beloved" (*KL1*, Lesson 13); so, "most beloved" or "dearest" would be the most literal; "dearly beloved" sounds nice and Kings Jamesish.
* *sīcutī*: alternative spelling of *sīcut*
* *dissolvat*: Notice that this verb violates our Sequence of Tenses rule by being in the present rather than imperfect to go with the perfect tense main verb *appāruit*. These sorts of rule violations happen often in "real" Latin texts—language is messy and not mechanical!
* *audīstis*: syncopated!
* *dīligāmus*: This subjunctive is a little strange, because although we could perhaps loosely call it a subjunctive of purpose, this clause seems to be defining or explaining *adnuntiātiō*. Remember that the Latin Vulgate is a translation of the original Greek, and here *dīligāmus* is merely imitating the Greek. In Greek this is a substantival (noun) clause (also called a "content clause") common in John's works, where the subjunctive clause is in apposition to a word or phrase in the main sentence and explains or defines it.
* *alterutrer, alterūtra, alterūtrum* [*both parts decline—gen.* alteriusutrius] one [of two], the one or the other, either, both; adv. *alterūtrum*, one [to] another
* *corde nostrō:* ablative of comparison
* Notice that one can use either *nisi* or *sī nōn* for "if not."
* *petīerimus:* syncopated
* *crēdāmus...dīligāmus:* See note on *dīligāmus* in 3:11 above.

Glossary:

adnuntiātiō, -ōnis (f): announcement, message
Cain (m, indecl.): Cain
claudō, -ere, clausī, clausum: I close, shut (up)
dissolvō, -ere, -solvī, -solūtum: I dissolve, destroy
fīliolus, -ī (m): little son/child
manifestō (1): I (make) manifest, show clearly; adj. *manifestus, -a, -um* manifest, apparent, clear
nōminō (1): I name, give a name to, call
placitus, -a, -um: pleasing, agreeable [adjective from *placeō*]
reprehendō, -ere, -hendī, -hensum: I hold back, rebuke, censure, find fault with
sēdūcō, -ere, -dūxī, -dūctum: I lead aside/astray, seduce, deceive
sēmen, -minis (n): seed, offspring, origin
suādeō, -ēre, suāsī, suāsum: I persuade, exhort

Questions about Translation

Parse the following verbs (For Indicative and Subjunctive, give Person, Number, Tense, Voice, and Mood of what verb; for Infinitive and Imperative, give Tense, Voice, and Mood of what verb; for Participles give Gender, Number, Case, Tense, Voice, and Mood). Then identify or describe the usage of that verb (e.g., purpose clause, accusative and infinitive, present simple fact condition, etc.).

3:1—*vidēte:* ______________________________

3:1—*nominēmur:* ______________________________

3:2—*erimus:* ______________________________

3:5—*tolleret:* ______________________________

3:7—*sēdūcat:* ______________________________

3:8—*dissolvat:* ______________________________

3:9—*peccāre:* ______________________________

3:13—*nōlīte:* ______________________________

3:13—*mīrārī:* ______________________________

3:15—*manentem:* ______________________________

3:18—*dīligāmus:* ______________________________

Other Questions:

3:13—*sī ōdit… mīrārī:* What kind of condition? ______________________________

3:20—*sī reprehenderit…omnia:* What kind of condition? ______________________________

LESSON 14

Verbs—Subjunctives (Fear Clause); Nouns—Additional Usages of the Dative

Word List

Nouns

1. aciēs, -ēī (f) *sharp edge/point, sharpness (esp. of sight); battle line*
2. canticum, -ī (n) *song, solo*; Canticum Canticōrum, *Song of Songs*
3. plāga, -ae (f) *a blow, wound; plague, destruction*
4. timor, -ōris (m) *fear*

Verbs

5. perficiō, -ere, -fēcī, -fectum: *I complete, finish, perfect*
6. metuō, -ere, -uī, -ūtum *I fear, am afraid of, revere*
7. paveō, -ēre, pāvī, —— *I dread, fear, tremble*
8. probō (1) *I try, examine, test, prove, approve (of)*

Adverbs

9. tantum (adv.) *only, merely, but; so, so much/greatly*
10. umquam (adv.) *ever, at any time*

Memorization

Aeneid 1.1-10

Arma virumque canō, Troiae quī prīmus ab ōrīs
Ītaliam, fātō profugus, Lāvīnaque vēnit
lītora. Multum ille et terrīs iactātus et altō
vī superum saevae memorem Iūnōnis ob īram.
Multa quoque et bellō passus, dum conderet urbem,
īnferretque deōs Latiō, genus unde Latīnum,
Albānīque patrēs, atque altae moenia Rōmae.
Mūsa, mihī causās memorā, quō nūmine laesō,
quidve dolēns, rēgīna deum tot volvere cāsūs
īnsignem pietāte virum, tot adīre labōrēs

renowned for his piety, to endure [such] misfortunes [and]

Grammar

Verbs—Subjunctives (Fear Clause)

Hopefully you are not feeling overwhelmed by the sheer usefulness of the subjunctive. We are almost finished with learning its main uses, and although this book does not contain an exhaustive list of subjunctive types, you should be set to handle most of them when you encounter them in any reading. In this lesson we embark upon the Fear Clause, which is only tricky in that the negative is translated as a positive and the positive as a negative.

But maybe we should take a step back. First off, we need to have a verb of fearing as our main verb. The Fear Clause was originally an optative subjunctive explaining this main verb: *Timeō. Nē drācō veniat*! "I'm afraid. May the dragon not come!" (Implied: "But I'm still afraid that the dragon is coming.") When these two sentences got smashed together at some point in the history of Latin, it became *Timeō nē drācō veniat*, but was translated "I'm afraid that the dragon is coming!" Then, since *nē* expresses the positive (that what we are afraid of *is* going to occur), the negative of this thought (that what we are afraid of is something *not* occurring) must be expressed by *ut* or the double negative *nē nōn*: *Timeō ut Oswaldus veniat. Timeō nē nōn Oswaldus veniat.* "I'm afraid that Oswald is not coming."

So there you have the Fear Clause. Strange, but easy. Feel free to make up stories to help you remember that it uses *ut* and *nē* in opposite ways than they usually do. Here is a chart with more examples, showing that the Fear Clause also very helpfully follows our normal sequence of tenses.

MAIN VERB	LATIN	ENGLISH
PRESENT *OR* FUTURE	Fīlia rēgis timet nē dracō ventūrus sit.	*The princess is afraid that the dragon will/may come.*
	Fīlia rēgis timet ut [**or** timet nē nōn] Oswaldus ventūrus sit.	*The princess is afraid that Oswald will/may not come.*
	Fīlia rēgis timet nē dracō veniat.	*The princess is afraid that the dragon is coming/may come.*
	Fīlia rēgis timet ut [**or** timet nē nōn] Oswaldus veniat.	*The princess is afraid that Oswald is not coming/may not come.*
	Fīlia rēgis timet nē dracō vēnerit.	*The princess is afraid that the dragon has come.*
	Fīlia rēgis timet ut [**or** timet nē nōn] Oswaldus vēnerit.	*The princess is afraid that Oswald has not come.*
IMPERFECT, PERFECT, *OR* PLUPERFECT	Fīlia rēgis timuit nē dracō ventūrus esset.	*The princess was afraid that the dragon would/might come.*
	Fīlia rēgis timuit ut [**or** timuit nē nōn] Oswaldus ventūrus esset.	*The princess was afraid that Oswald would/might not come.*
	Fīlia rēgis timuit nē dracō venīret.	*The princess was afraid that the dragon was coming/might come.*
	Fīlia rēgis timuit ut [**or** timuit nē nōn] Oswaldus venīret.	*The princess was afraid that Oswald was not coming/might not come.*
	Fīlia rēgis timuit nē dracō vēnisset.	*The princess was afraid that the dragon had come.*
	Fīlia rēgis timuit ut [**or** timuit nē nōn] Oswaldus vēnisset.	*The princess was afraid that Oswald had not come.*

You have already learned two common verbs of fearing, *timeō* (*KL1*, Lesson 9) and *vereor* (*KL2*, Lesson 6). This chapter introduces two more, *metuō* and *paveō*. And, as a final teensy tiny note, when the fearing verb really means more of "I don't want" (as in *nōlō*), then it can be followed by an infinitive construction (as *nōlō* would be), rather than a subjunctive clause. Some English examples of this type of "fear" would be along these lines: "I'm afraid I'll get my shoes muddy," or, "She's afraid it will rain on the picnic tomorrow." And here is a Latin example: *Timeō nōs sērius pervenīre*, "I'm afraid we'll arrive too late."

Nouns—Additional Usages of the Dative

As we are nearing the end of this book, it seems a good time to wrap up a few additional usages for the noun cases we have been using for the past two years. This lesson will cover the dative, and next lesson the genitive and ablative. Thus far, we have learnd that the dative acts as the **indirect object**, and can be translated by English word order or "to/for": *Oswaldus fēminae dōna dedit*, "Oswald gave the woman many gifts" or "Oswald gave many gifts to the woman."

Usually in this book's example sentences containing indirect objects, a direct object also appears with a transitive verb. However, the dative can also function as an indirect object with certain *intransitive* verbs (i.e., a verb that does not take a direct object): *Dōna fēminae placēbant*, "The gifts were pleasing to the woman." (Notice in English that the verb "please" can be transitive, as in "The gifts pleased her." However, if you retain the original sense in the Latin of "be pleasing to," then it makes sense to have a dative object.) You have learned a few of these types of verbs already (list follows), with a *(+dat.)* in their dictionary entry indicating that they take the dative rather than the accusative. And sometimes a verb will just take the dative rather than the accusative; these must simply be memorized as you go along.

Other datives we have learned include the **Dative of Possession** (Lesson 5), **Dative of Agent** (used with a Passive Periphrastic, Lesson 13), and **Dative of Reference** (Lesson 1). Here are some examples in case anyone needs a refresher:

Dative of Possession: Hoc canticum **mihi** est. *This song is mine. This is my song.*

Dative of Agent: Hoc canticum **mihi** canendum est. *I must sing this song. (Lit., "This song must be sung by me.")*

Dative of Reference: **Mihi** hoc canticum dīligō. *As for me, I love this song.*

Although there are a few other minor uses of the dative, we will only mention two more: **Dative with Compound Verbs** and **Dative with Certain Adjectives.** We have already learned numerous compound verbs, that is, verbs that consist of a root verb plus a prefix. Now, many (but not all) compound verbs will take the dative when they have one of the following prefixes: *ad-*, *ante-*, *con-* (from *cum*), *in-*, *inter-*, *ob-*, *post-*, *prae-*, *prō-*, *sub-*, *super-*, and sometimes *circum-* and *re-* (when it means "against," not "back, again"). This is helpful to keep in mind when you are reading along and suddenly there's a dative but no accusative, and so you can say, "Aha! this must be a dative object with a compound verb!" and keep translating away.

Certain adjectives in Latin are directional (whether actually or metaphorically) or relational, and these will also be followed by the dative. Happily, in English these adjectives are naturally followed by a "to/toward/for," and so this isn't too difficult to grasp:

Nunc sumus propiōrēs **animālibus.** *Now we are nearer **to the animals.***

Vestīmenta eius sunt similia **meīs [vestīmentīs].** *Her clothing is similar **to mine.***

*The king was cruel **to us.*** Rēx crūdēlis **nōbīs** erat.

*You are dear **to him.*** Ēs **eī** cārus.

Here is a chart summarizing the usages of the Dative covered in the two *Kraken Latin* books:

BASIC USAGES	SPECIAL/IDIOMATIC USAGES
1. Indirect Object (with transitive verbs)	1. Dative of Possession
2. Indirect Object (with intransitive verbs)	2. Dative of Agent
	3. Dative of Reference
	4. Dative with Certain Compound Verbs
	5. Dative with Certain Adjectives

And here is a list of the verbs and adjectives you have learned that can take or be followed by the dative (some of the verbs can also take the accusative):

VERBS THAT CAN TAKE DATIVE	ADJECTIVES THAT CAN BE FOLLOWED BY DATIVE
adsum (Lesson 2) appareō (Lesson 3) appropinquō (*KL1*, Lesson 25) benedīcō (Lesson 4) cēdō (*KL1*, Lesson 28) cōnfiteor (*KL2*, Lesson 6) crēdō (*KL1*, Lesson 26) inferō (Lesson 2) licet (Lesson 1) maledīcō (Lesson 3) necesse est (Lesson 1) parcō (*KL2*, Lesson 13) placeō (Lesson 1) serviō (*KL2*, Lesson 10)	cārus (*KL1*, Lesson 13) crūdēlis (Lesson 10) difficilis (*KL2*, Lesson 5) dissimilis (*KL2*, Lesson 5) facilis (*KL2*, Lesson 5) fidēlis (*KL2*, Lesson 4) fīdus (*KL1*, Lesson 7) grātus (*KL1*, Lesson 27) mīrābilis (Lesson 2) propior (*KL2*, Lesson 5) proximus (*KL2*, Lesson 5) similis (*KL2*, Lesson 5) vīcīnus (Lesson 9)

As a final note, if you come across a dative that you're not sure of, simply translate with a "to" or "for" and you'll probably be fine. Keep in mind the big picture of what the dative does, and the details will naturally follow.

Review

Be sure to add the *Fear Clause* to your list of subjunctives. We're coming to the end of the year, so be sure that you are reviewing the sequence of tenses in this lesson. Use it with something that you haven't seen in a while, such as purpose or result subjunctives.

Worksheet 14

A. Vocabulary

1. perficiō, ____________, __________, perfectum: ________________________________
2. plāga: ____
3. ever (adv.): ____
4. paveō, pavēre, pavī, ——: ____
5. crēber, -bra, -brum: ____
6. threshold: ____
7. fear: ____
8. iubeō, iubēre, iūssī, iūssum: ____
9. metuō, metuere, metuī, metūtum: ____
10. ūtor, ūtī, ūsus sum (+abl.): ____
11. aciēs: ____
12. probō (1): ____
13. burden: ____
14. tantum (adv.): ____
15. canticum: ____

B. Grammar

1. Indicate how you would translate into Latin the italicized words in these fear clauses.

   He's afraid *that* these pirates will rob us. ________________________________

   I dread *that* I will *not* be able to fall asleep again tonight. ________________________________

   They had been afraid *that* they did *not* pass the test. ________________________________

   You fear *that* the worst is yet to come. ________________________________

   Why was she afraid *that* spiders had taken over? ________________________________

   We dreaded *that* our favorite dessert would *not* be there. ________________________________

2. Review Noun-Adjective Declension: Decline *aciēs crūdēlis.*

	LATIN SINGULAR	LATIN PLURAL
NOM.		
GEN.		
DAT.		
ACC.		
ABL.		
VOC.		

3. Do a synopsis of *perficiō* in the 1st person singular, first giving principal parts:

____

		LATIN ACTIVE	ENGLISH ACTIVE	LATIN PASSIVE	ENGLISH PASSIVE
INDICATIVE	PRES.				
	IMPF.				
	FUT.				
	PF.				
	PLPF.				
	FT. PF.				
SUBJUNCTIVE	PRES.				
	IMPF.				
	PF.				
	PLPF.				

PARTICIPLE	PRES.				
	PF.				
	FUT.				
INFINITIVE	PRES.				
	PF.				
	FUT.				
IMP.	SG.				
	PL.				

C. Memorization

Fill in the blanks in *Aeneid* 1.1-10 in Latin.

____

____

____

____

____

____

__________ __________, __________ __________ __________ __________

__________, __________ __________ __________, __________ __________ __________,

q__________ __________, __________ d__________ __________ v__________ __________

īnsignem __________ __________, tot __________ __________

D. English to Latin

1. a) We ourselves feared that the enemy's battle line would break through our walls.

   b) We ourselves feared that the enemy's battle line was breaking through our walls.

   c) We ourselves feared that the enemy's battle line had broken through our walls.

   d) We ourselves fear that the enemy's battle line will break through our walls.

   e) We ourselves fear that the enemy's battle line is breaking through our walls.

   f) We ourselves fear that the enemy's battle line has broken through our walls.

2. I was asking the older sailors whether the kraken would return to attack our ship with very great destruction or would descend to his cave in the sea. [Translate with three out of five ways of expressing purpose.]

3. The poet wants to finish his songs so much that he will walk all night singing to the moon.

4. Because you (sg.) had carried off part of the king's treasure yesterday, your mother was beseeching him that he spare your life. [*Note: There are two ways to translate the first clause, and two ways to translate the second. Any combination of first and second clauses will work.*]

5. If anyone eats camel (which is different from sheep) at any time, his internal organs will by no means feel happy early in the morning.

6. It is fitting that the queen love jewels, but should she also love cookies excessively?

7. My sons, do not attempt to examine the dragon—marvelous to see!—after she has given birth. You would probably suffer. [Translate with two out of three ways of expressing prohibition.]

8. Who is a pirate who loves danger and hates mercy? Let him become our companion!

9. If only there weren't goats running everywhere, eating my flowers and clothing!

10. Now the servants must surely approach the wicked king, who rules them by fear of sharp sword and cruel judgment.

E. Latin to English

1 John 4

1 Cārissimī nōlīte omnī spīrituī crēdere sed probāte spīritūs, sī ex Deō sint, quoniam multī *pseudoprophētae*
exiērunt in mundum. 2 In hōc cognōscitur* Spīritus Deī: omnis spīritus quī cōnfitētur Iēsum Christum in
carne vēnisse ex Deō est. 3 Et omnis spīritus quī nōn cōnfitētur Iēsum ex Deō nōn est; et hoc est antīchristī
quod audīstis quoniam venit et nunc iam in mundō est. 4 Vōs ex Deō estis, fīliolī, et vīcistis eōs quoniam
māior est quī in vōbīs est quam quī in mundō. 5 Ipsī dē mundō sunt; ideo dē mundō loquuntur et mundus eōs audit. 6 Nōs ex Deō sumus. Quī nōvit Deum audit nōs; quī nōn est ex Deō nōn audit nōs. In hōc
cognōscimus Spīritum vēritātis et spīritum *errōris*.

7 Cārissimī, dīligāmus invicem quoniam cāritās ex Deō est, et omnis quī dīligit ex Deō nātus est et
cognōscit Deum. 8 Quī nōn dīligit, nōn nōvit Deum quoniam Deus cāritās est. 9 In hōc appāruit cāritās Deī
in nōbīs quoniam Fīlium suum *ūnigenitum* mīsit Deus in mundum ut vīvāmus per eum. 10 In hōc est cāritās
nōn quasi nōs dīlēxerīmus* Deum sed quoniam ipse dīlēxit nōs et mīsit Fīlium suum *propitiātiōnem* prō
peccātīs nostrīs. 11 Cārissimī, sī sīc Deus dīlēxit nōs, et nōs debēmus alterūtrum dīligere.

12 Deum nēmō vīdit umquam; sī dīligāmus invicem Deus in nōbīs manet et cāritās eius in nōbīs perfecta
est. 13 In hōc intellegimus quoniam in eō manēmus et ipse in nōbīs quoniam dē Spīritū suō dedit nōbīs.
14 Et nōs vīdimus et testificāmur quoniam Pater mīsit Fīlium salvātōrem mundī.

15 Quisque* cōnfessus fuerit* quoniam Iēsus est Fīlius Deī Deus in eō manet et ipse in Deō. 16 Et nōs
cognōvimus et crēdidimus cāritāti quam habet Deus in nōbīs. Deus cāritās est, et quī manet in cāritāte
in Deō manet et Deus in eō. 17 In hōc perfecta est cāritās nōbīscum ut fīdūciam habeāmus in diē iūdiciī
quia sīcut ille est et nōs sumus in hōc mundō. 18 *Timor* nōn est in cāritāte, sed perfecta cāritās forās mittit

timōrem quoniam timor poenam habet; quī autem timet nōn *est perfectus* in cāritāte. 19 Nōs ergō dīligāmus quoniam Deus prior* dīlēxit nōs. 20 Sī quis dīxerit quoniam "Dīligō Deum," et frātrem suum ōderit, mendāx est; quī enim nōn dīligit frātrem suum quem vīdit, Deum quem nōn vīdit quōmodo potest dīligere? 21 Et hōc mandātum habēmus ab eō ut quī dīligit Deum dīligat* et frātrem suum.

Notes:

* *cognōscitur*: Although you learned in Lesson 10 that *cognōscō* means "I learn, get to know," and in the perfect tenses it means "I know," this isn't always true in later Latin such as the Vulgate. It is being used to translate a Greek word that simply means, "I know," and so feel free to translate it that way even in the present tenses.
* *dīlēxerīmus*: Note that this is a perfect subjunctive, not a future perfect indicative. This clause introduced by *quasi* is called a Clause of Comparison or Conditional Sentence of Comparison (the apodosis is left out).
* *quisque:* Supply a *quī*, so it reads *Quisque quī confessus...*
* *confessus fuerit*: This is a periphrastic (roundabout expression) future perfect, and would literally mean "will have been about to confess"—but that would be awkward. Just treat it as a normal future perfect.
* *prior*: This is an adjective but functions almost like an adverb in this sentence.
* *dīligat*: Subjunctive in a content clause (see note on 1 John 3:11 in Lesson 13).

Glossary:

error, -ōris (m): error, mistake
propitiātiō, -ōnis (f): propitiation, atonement
pseudoprophēta, -ae (m): false prophet
unigenitus, -a, -um: only-begotten, only

Questions about Translation

Parse the following verbs (for Indicative and Subjunctive, give Person, Number, Tense, Voice, and Mood of what verb; for Infinitive and Imperative, give Tense, Voice, and Mood of what verb; for Participles give Gender, Number, Case, Tense, Voice, and Mood). Then identify or describe the usage of that verb (e.g., purpose clause, accusative and infinitive, present simple fact condition, etc.).

4:1—*probāte:* ______________________________

____

4:1—*sint:* ______________________________

____

4:2—*cognōscitur:* ______________________________

____

4:2—*vēnisse:* ______________________________

____

4:3—*audīstis:* ______________________________

____

4:5—*loquuntur:* ______________________________

____

4:7—*dīligāmus:* ______________________________

____

4:9—*vīvāmus:* ______________________________

____

4:12—*dīligāmus:* ______________________________

____

4:17—*habeāmus:* ______________________________

____

4:19—*dīligāmus:* ______________________________

____

4:20—*dīxerit:* ______________________________

____

4:20—*dīligere:* ______________________________

____

E. For Fun

Plan your very own Roman *cēna*. Fill out the menu card on the next page using words from the list of commonly eaten Roman foods below.

Historical Note: Although their various meals varied throughout history, the Romans during the late Republic and Empire had a light breakfast (*ientāculum*) and lunch (*prandium*), followed by a nap (*merīdiātio*). The *cēna* was the main meal eaten in the afternoon or early evening. Upper classes of course would have larger and fancier meals than the lower classes. The famous Latin phrase *ab ōvō usque māla*, "from egg to apples," refers to a multi-course *cēna*, which began with eggs (among other things) in the appetizer course and concluded with fruit (among other things) for dessert. Now the phrase can be used to describe any process from beginning to end.

acētāria, -ōrum (n, pl): salad (something seasoned with oil and vinegar)

agnīna, -ae (f): lamb [short for agnīna carō]

amygdala, -ae (f): almond

anas, anatis (f): duck

ānser, -eris (m): goose

aper, -prī (m): wild boar

bōlētus, -ī (m): (the best kind of) mushroom

būbula, -ae (f): beef [short for būbula carō]

cancer, -crī (m): crab

carōta, -ae (f): carrot

cāseus, -ī (m): cheese

cōc(h)lea, -ae (f): snail

conchȳlium, -ī (n): shellfish, oyster

crūstulum, -ī (n): (fancy) pastry, cookie

crūstum, -ī (n): pastry

farcīmen, -minis (n): sausage

fīcus, -ī/-ūs (f): fig

fungus, -ī (m): mushroom

garum, -ī (n): fish sauce, rich sauce

glis, glīris (m): dormouse (yes, the Romans considered dormice a delicacy!)

lāc, lactis (n): milk

mel, mellis (n): honey

mēlo, -ōnis or mēlopepō, -ōnis (f): melon

mulsum, -ī (n): honeyed wine

olea, -ae (f) or olīva, -ae (f): olive

olīvum, -ī (n): oil

ostrea, -ae (f): oyster, mussel, sea-snail

ōvum, -ī (n): egg

pānis, -is (m): bread

pīrum, -ī (n): pear

piscis, -is (m): fish

porcīna, -ae (f): pork [short for porcīna carō]

pullus (gallinaceus), -ī (m): chicken

puls, pultis (f): porridge (made of farro, water, salt, and a fat such as olive oil; or with eggs, cheese & honey)

ūva, -ae (f): grape

vīnum, -ī (n): wine

Other Helpful Words:

calix, -licis (f): goblet, cup, drinking vessel

cochlear, -āris (n): spoon (pointed on one end to use as a fork)

crātēra, -ae (f) or crātēr, -eris (m): bowl, vessel for mixing wine with water

furca, -ae (f): two-pronged fork

lāmina, -ae (f): plate

lectus, -ī (m): couch (for reclining on at meals)

ligula, -ae (f): spoon

mappa, -ae (f): napkin

pōculum, -ī (n): cup, bowl, drinking vessel

triclīnium, -iī (n): dining room; three-sided couch surrounding the dining table

Ferculōrum Index (*Menu*)

gustātiō, -ōnis (f) ***appetizer***	prīmae mensae (f, pl) ***main course***	secundae mensae (f, pl) ***dessert***

LESSON 15

Verbs—Miscellaneous Indicative and Subjunctive Clauses; Nouns—Miscellaneous Genitive and Ablative Usages

Word List

Nouns

1. arvum, -ī (n) *(cultivated) field, region*
2. bēlua, -ae (f) *beast (esp. a ferocious or large one), monster*
3. os, ossis (n) *bone*
4. sīdus, sīderis (n) *constellation, star, heavenly body*
5. terminus, -ī (m) *limit, bound(ary), end*

Verb

6. claudō, -ere, clausī, clausum *I close, shut (up)*

Adverb

7. antequam (conj.) *before, sooner than, until*
8. extrā (adv.) *(on the) outside, besides, except*; (prep.+acc.) *outside (of), beyond*
9. priusquam (conj.) *before, sooner, rather, until*
10. tandem (adv.) *finally, at last*

Memorization

Aeneid 1.1-11

Arma virumque canō, Troiae quī prīmus ab ōrīs
Ītaliam, fātō profugus, Lāvīnaque vēnit
lītora. Multum ille et terrīs iactātus et altō
vī superum saevae memorem Iūnōnis ob īram.
Multa quoque et bellō passus, dum conderet urbem,
īnferretque deōs Latiō, genus unde Latīnum,

Albānīque patrēs, atque altae moenia Rōmae.
Mūsa, mihī causās memorā, quō nūmine laesō,
quidve dolēns, rēgīna deum tot volvere cāsūs
īnsignem pietāte virum, *tot adīre labōrēs*
impulerit. Tantaene animīs caelestibus īrae?

to encounter [such] sufferings. Does such wrath belong to the heavenly mind?

Grammar

At long last, you have learned Latin grammar! Way to go for surviving. Now it's time to finish strong. For our final chapter of learning, we will be wrapping up a few more verb clauses, and then a few additional case usages for nouns.

Miscellaneous Indicative and Subjunctive Clauses

The conjunctions *dum* (or its emphatic form *dummodo*), *antequam*, and *priusquam* can all introduce clauses taking either the indicative or subjunctive. The basic rule of thumb here is the same as the general difference between the indicative and subjunctive: The indicative describes actual, factual action, while the subjunctive relates hypothetical, potential, indirect, or subordinate action. (And this rule of thumb, incidentally, can help you in the future if you encounter unknown subjunctive usages—is it hypothetical, potential, indirect, or subordinate action?) Although this general rule is helpful, we still need to fill in a few more details.

Dum/Dummodo

We learned the various meanings of *dum* (I will use *dum* rather than the cumbersome *dum/dummodo*, but what I say applies to both words) way back in *KL3*, Lesson 11, but have not yet realized its full potential. When *dum* means "until" it can take the indicative. This assumes, naturally, that it is expressing simply a relation of time. If any sense of purpose, doubt, anticipation, or other subjunctive-ish feelings creep in, then use the subjunctive. Often the difference between the two is untranslatable; one feels indicativey, and one subjunctivey. Also, if you have a *dum* clause that would normally take indicative, but is in indirect discourse (fancy term: *ōrātiō oblīqua*), it will take the subjunctive to show that it is subordinate.

Dum, "until," + indicative: *Dracō in spēluncā ātrā erat dum Oswaldus adībat.* The dragon was in the dark cave until Oswald approached.

Dum, "until," + subjunctive (in a temporal clause): *Dracō in spēluncā ātrā erat dum Oswaldus adīret ut eum oppugnāret.* The dragon was in the dark cave until Oswald approached to attack it.

Dum, "until," + subjunctive (in indirect discourse): *Ego rēgī indicāvī dracōnem in spēluncā ātrā esse dum Oswaldus adīret.* I made known to the king that the dragon was in the dark cave until Oswald approached.

Dum can also mean "while," and as such can take two sorts of indicative. If the time referred to in the *dum* clause lasts as long as the time frame of the main clause, then simply use whatever tenses you need. However, if the *dum* clause refers to a longer length of time in which a particular event happened, then it will use a historic present indicative (even if it relates an event in the past). Most often you can translate this Latin historic present with an English imperfect.

Dum, "while," + any indicative: *Dum dracō vivēbat, omnēs terrēbat.* While the dragon lived, he frightened everyone.

Dum, "while," + historic present indicative: *Dum dracō mandūcāns ossa in spēluncā ātrā vīvit, Oswaldus extrā adiit.* While the dragon was living in the dark cave chewinzg on bones, Oswald approached outside.

Finally, we come to *dum* appearing in the Proviso Clause. As its name indicates, the Proviso Clause gives a stipulation or contingency for the main clause. Because this is by nature a hypothetical situation, this clause will take a subjunctive (usually a present or imperfect); its negative will be *nē*. One of the most famous Proviso Clauses was a favorite motto of the Emperor Caligula (although originally attributed to the poet Lucius Accius): Ōderint, dum metuant. *Let them hate, provided they fear.* Here are a few more examples of the Proviso Clause:

Dum Oswaldus dracōnem necet, fīliam rēgis servābit. Provided that Oswald kills the dragon, he will save the princess.

Erāmus gavisūrī, dum Oswaldus ab dracōne nē necārētur. We were about to rejoice, provided that Oswald was not killed by the dragon.

Again to translate this properly, you need context. In any given sentence, look at whether or not the *dum* is followed by an indicative or subjunctive. If an indicative, decide whether "while" or "until" works better in the passage. (And be on the lookout for a historic present.) If subjunctive, see if a temporal clause "until" or proviso clause ("provided that") makes more sense. See the chart a bit further down for a handy summary of these usages.

Antequam and *Priusquam*

The two conjunctions *antequam* and *priusquam*, which are roughly synonymous, behave similarly to *dum*—sometimes they take the indicative, and sometimes subjunctive. If they describe a simple matter of time, then they will be followed by the indicative; if the clause is more subjunctivish (implies more than the idea of time), then it will contain the subjunctive. These two conjunctions, however, do have a few little unique oddities that bear discussing more fully.

When *antequam* and *priusquam* take the indicative, the tenses normally used are the present, perfect, and future perfect. The imperfect is rarely used and the pluperfect even more rarely. The future indicative is also rare because the present and future perfect tenses are used to refer to future time instead. The present indicative generally appears when the main clause is positive; the perfect and future perfect can go with either a positive or negative main clause, but more often a negative one. Here are some examples (and remember, since we are dealing with indicative, we are concerned with the mere sequence of events):

With Present Indicative (positive main clause): *Priusquam dracō suprā volat, Oswaldus adībit.* Before the dragon flies over, Oswald will arrive.

With Perfect and Future Perfect Indicative (here with negative main clauses): *Nōn dormīre poterāmus antequam dracō suprā volāvit.* We could not sleep until/before the dragon flew over. *Nōn dormīre poterimus priusquam dracō suprā volāverit.* We won't be able to sleep until/before the dragon flies over.

Also note that in the above examples I used *antequam* and *priusquam* interchangeably, and that when the main clause is negative, that "not . . . before" is often best translated "until." Before moving on, it is also important to note that *antequam* and *priusquam* often divide into their separate parts (*ante* and *quam*; *prius* and *quam*) and scatter themselves throughout the sentence (whether taking an indicative or subjunctive). Sometimes the *ante* or *prius* appears in the main sentence while *quam* introduces the subordinate clause (especially when the main clause is negative); sometimes the *quam* will appear only a word or two after the *ante* or *prius*:

Nōn prius Oswaldus abībit quam dracōnem necāverit. Oswald will not depart before/until he kills the dragon.

Now, when the *antequam/priusquam* clause has a bigger scope than simple an idea of time, it will take the subjunctive. Perhaps the clause describes an ideal action, or is one we've all been waiting for, or perhaps depends on something else. Perhaps the action will never actually happen, or maybe it is simply being planned. Or else we might just be dealing with a normally indicative clause in indirect discourse. In any event, these clauses will all contain the subjunctive. The present and imperfect subjunctive make regular appearances, while the perfect and pluperfect subjunctive are rare.

Ante audīmus dracōnem quam eum videāmus. We hear the dragon before seeing [lit., before we see] him. (Implied: but we might not see him.)

Prius dracō quam fīliam rēgis mandūcāre posset, Oswaldus eum necāvit. Before the dragon could eat the princess, Oswald killed him. (Implied: the dragon's intention/motive, making it a subjunctive clause.)

Scīvimus dracōnem ovēs nostrās iam necāvisse antequam suprā urbe nostrā volāvisset. We knew that the dragon had already killed our sheep before he had flown over our city. (Rare pluperfect subjunctive used in indirect discourse.)

All of these little idiosyncracies may seem a touch intimidating at first, but really, all of these clauses will be easy to translate from the Latin. You won't even flinch or seize up wondering, "Wait! Is this an indicative clause? or what tense is this? is that allowed?" Probably the trickiest thing will be to remember that *antequam* and *priusquam* can split apart and flit through the sentence as separate units.

CONJUNCTION	TRANSLATION	MOOD/TENSE	EXAMPLE
dum/dummodō	*until* (when expressing simple idea of time)	Indicative (Present, Perfect [rare], Future Perfect)	Semper dīcit dum abit. ***He always speaks until he departs.***
	until a. when purpose, doubt, or anticipation is implied b. in indirect discourse	Subjunctive a. in a Temporal Clause b. in indirect discourse	a. Dīcat dum abeat. ***He might speak until he departs.*** b. Dīxistī eum dictūrum esse dum abīret. ***You said he would speak until he departed.***
	while	Indicative	Et dīcit dummodo abit. ***He also speaks while he departs.***
		Special Use: Historic Present	Dum hīc venīrēmus, usque dīcēbat. ***While we were coming here, he spoke continuously.***
	provided that, if only	Subjunctive in a Proviso Clause (Present & Imperfect) —negative is ***nē***	Dummodo nē dicat, laetī erimus. ***Provided that he doesn't speak, we will be happy.***
antequam/ priusquam (or, **ante...quam/ prius...quam**)	*before, until* (referring to a fact or simple idea of time)	Indicative (esp. Present, Perfect & Future Perfect)	Antequam dīxerit, abībimus. ***Before he speaks, we will depart.***
	before, until a. action is anticipated, contingent, intended, subordinate, or unfulfilled b. in indirect discourse	Subjunctive (esp. Present & Imperfect)	a. Priusquam nimis dīcat, abībimus. ***Before he speaks too much, we will depart.*** b. Ante pollicitī sumus nōs abitūrōs esse quam dīceret. ***We promised that we would depart before he spoke.***

Miscellaneous Genitive and Ablative Usages

Since in the last lesson we covered a few more usages of the dative, it seems only fitting to round out the year with a couple of additional genitive and ablative uses. Some of these may have already appeared in translations, but I wanted to take a few moments and officially recognize them. These will be extremely easy to translate into English, trust me.

Genitive of Material; Ablative of Material or Source

As these names indicate, the Genitive or Ablative of Material indicate the substance of which something is made. The Genitive of Material typically follows the noun it goes with, as in *arx lapidis*, "hill of stone." We could also use the Ablative of Material, which is sometimes a plain old ablative, but sometimes comes along with a preposition. In classical Latin, that preposition would have to be *ex*, but other prepositions such as *ab* or *dē* also appear in other eras or genres of Latin: *arx lapide*, "stony hill"; or *arx ex lapide*, "hill of stone." Note that in English it can sometimes sound better to translate these prepositions as "of" rather than "from" ("hill of stone" rather than "hill from stone"). Also be aware that sometimes we can translate a phrase into Latin in at least two legitimate ways. A "crown of gold" could be *corōna aurī* or *corōna ex aurō*, but we could also use the adjective for "golden, of gold": *corōna aurea*.

The Ablative of Source functions similarly, but specifically tells the source from which something originates: *flūmen ab/ex/dē monte*, "river from the mountain." The river is not made out of the mountain, obviously, but comes from the mountain. In English we often will make the source an adjective: "the mountain river." This ablative will also appear in this lesson's translation: someone who "has been born of God," *nātus est ex Deō.*

Genitive of Quality; Ablative of Quality (sometimes called Genitive/Ablative of Description)
Both the Genitive of Quality and the Ablative of Quality describe an attribute of something, and both must be accompanied by an adjective (or some sort of modifier). Thus we can say, *Est fēmina magnae fortitūdinis*, "She is a *woman of great bravery*," but Latin wouldn't use *fēmina fortitūdinis*, "woman of bravery." We'd have to use a plain adjective like *fortis* to get that idea across. We've already seen this Genitive of Quality in phrases like *verba huius modī*, "words of this kind." The Ablative of Quality does not need a preposition, and is just the plain naked ablative: *Vīdimus virum vultū trīstī*, "We saw a man with a sad face." Notice that sometimes we'll translate this using the English "with." Although the Genitive and Ablative of Quality can sometimes be used interchangeably, often the Romans would use the Genitive of Quality to refer to something's foundational or essential characteristics, while the Ablative of Quality described something's external, physical, or particular characteristics. (Thus the difference between my two examples above.) The Genitive of Quality would be used with numerical measurements, for example, since those are essential characteristics of an object: Goliath was *vir novem cubitōrum*, "a man of nine cubits" (English idiom: "a man nine cubits tall").

Here is a chart summarizing these usages:

	GENITIVE	ABLATIVE
MATERIAL OR SOURCE	-indicates the material or stuff of which something is made arx lapidis, ***hill of stone***	-indicates the material of which something is made, or the source from which something comes -often uses a preposition (such as ***ab***, ***ex***, or ***dē***) arx lapide, ***stony hill*** arx ab/ex/dē lapide, ***hill out of stone***
QUALITY (DESCRIPTION)	-indicates/describes a quality of something -must be accompanied by adjective fēmina magnae fortitūdinis, ***woman of great bravery***	-indicates/describes a quality of something -must be accompanied by adjective vir vultū trīstī, ***the man with a sad face***

As you can see, it will not be a problem to translate these from Latin into English, since the construction is somewhat similar to that of English. It may only cause a problem if you are confused and always translate the genitive as a possessive only with an *'s*.

Review

Be sure to add the *dummodo* and *antequam/postquam* subjunctives to your list.

We've done a bunch of subjunctives, and by now you may have forgotten some or might get a few mixed up. Here's a list of all the different types of subjunctives. There are multiple examples of each subjunctive so you can also see the sequence of tenses more clearly. Pay attention to this before you take the test.

Independent Subjunctives:

- Hortatory/Jussive: *Oswaldus necet dracōnēs!* Let Oswald kill the dragons!
- Deliberative: *Oswaldus necet dracōnēs?* Shall Oswald kill the dragons? *Oswaldus necāret/necāvisset dracōnēs?* Did Oswald kill dragons?
- Prohibitive: *Nē Oswaldus necet dracōnēs!* Let Oswald *not* kill dragons! *Oswaldus cavet nē necet dracōnēs.* Oswald is wary lest he kill dragons.
- Optative: *Oswaldus necet dracōnēs.* I hope Oswald will kill dragons. *Oswaldus necāret dracōnēs.* I hope Oswald is killing dragons. *Oswaldus necāvisset dracōnēs.* I hope Oswald had killed dragons.
- Potential: *Oswaldus necet/necāverit dracōnēs.* Oswald would kill dragons. *Oswaldus necāret dracōnēs.* Oswald would have killed dragons.

Dependent Subjunctives:

- **Indirect Statement:** *Rex dicit ut Oswaldus necet dracōnēs.* The king says that Oswald kills dragons.
- **Purpose Clause (Present/Future):** *Oswaldus necat dracōnēs ut fīliam rēgis salvet.* Oswald kills dragons to save the king's daughter. *Oswaldus necābit dracōnēs ut fīliam rēgis salvet.* Oswald will kill dragons to save the king's daughter. *Oswaldus necat/necābit dracōnēs ut fīliam rēgis salvatūrus sit.* Oswald kills/will kill dragons so that he might save the king's daughter.
- **Purpose Clause (Past):** *Oswaldus necābat dracōnēs ut fīliam rēgis salvāret.* Oswald was killing dragons so he could save the king's daughter. *Oswaldus necāvit dracōnēs ut fīliam rēgis salvāret.* Oswald killed dragons so he could save the king's daughter. *Oswaldus necāverat dracōnēs ut fīliam rēgis salvāret.* Oswald had killed dragons so he could save the king's daughter. *Oswaldus necābat/necāvit/necāverat dracōnēs ut fīliam rēgis salvatūrus sit.* Oswald was killing/killed/had killed the king's daughter so that he would save the king's daughter.
- **Negative Purpose Clause:** *Oswaldus necat dracōnēs nē fīliam rēgis salvet!* Oswald kills dragons so that he might not save the king's daughter!
- **Result Clause (Present/Future):** *Oswaldus ita necat dracōnēs ut fīliam rēgis salvet.* Oswald kills dragons in such a way that he saves the king's daughter. *Oswaldus ita necābit dracōnēs ut fīliam rēgis salvet.* Oswald will kill dragons in such a way that he will save the king's daughter. *Oswaldus ita necat/necābit dracōnēs ut fīliam*

rēgis salutūrus sit. Oswald kills/will kill dragons in such a way that he will save the king's daughter.

- **Result Clause (Past):** *Oswaldus ita necābat dracōnēs ut fīliam rēgis salvāret.* Oswald was killing dragons in such a way that he would save the king's daughter. *Oswaldus ita necāvit dracōnēs ut fīliam rēgis salvāret.* Oswald killed dragons in such a way that he would save the king's daughter. *Oswaldus ita necāverat dracōnēs ut fīliam rēgis salvāret.* Oswald had killed dragons in such a way that he would save the king's daughter. *Oswaldus ita necābat/necāvit/necāverat dracōnēs ut fīliam rēgis salvatūrus sit.* Oswald was killing/killed/had killed dragons in such a way that he would save the king's daughter.
- ***Cum* Clause (Present/Future):** *Cum Oswaldus necet dracōnēs, fīliam rēgis salvat.* When/because/although Oswald kills dragons, he saves the king's daughter. *Cum Oswaldus necet dracōnēs, fīliam rēgis salvābit.* When/because/although Oswald will kill dragons, he will save the king's daughter. *Cum Oswaldus necāverit dracōnēs, fīliam rēgis salvat.* When/because/although Oswald has killed/**is killing** dragons, he saves the king's daughter. *Cum Oswaldus necāverit dracōnēs, fīliam rēgis salvābit.* When/because/although Oswald has killed/**is killing** dragons, he will save the king's daughter. *Cum Oswaldus necatūrus sit dracōnēs, fīliam rēgis salvat/salvābit.* When/because/although Oswald will kill dragons, he saves/will save the king's daughter.
- ***Cum* Clause (Past):** *Cum Oswaldus necāret dracōnēs, fīliam rēgis salvābat.* When/because/although Oswald was killing dragons, he was saving the king's daughter. *Cum Oswaldus necāret dracōnēs, fīliam rēgis salvāvit.* When/because/although Oswald killed dragons, he saved the king's daughter. *Cum Oswaldus necāret dracōnēs, fīliam rēgis salvāverat.* When/because/although Oswald had killed dragons, he had saved the king's daughter. *Cum Oswaldus necāvisset dracōnēs, fīliam rēgis salvābat.* When/because/although Oswald had killed dragons, he was saving the king's daughter. *Cum Oswaldus necāvisset dracōnēs, fīliam rēgis salvāvit.* When/because/although Oswald had killed dragons, he had saved the king's daughter. *Cum Oswaldus necāvisset dracōnēs, fīliam rēgis salvāverat.* When/because/although Oswald had killed dragons, he had saved the king's daughter. *Cum Oswaldus necatūrus sit dracōnēs, fīliam rēgis salvābat/salvāvit/salvāverat.* When/because/although Oswald will kill dragons, he had saved the king's daughter.
- **Indirect Question (Present/Future):** *Nesciō quomodo Oswaldus necet dracōnēs.* I do not know how Oswald kills dragons. *Nesciō quomodo Oswaldus necāverit dracōnēs.* I do not know how Oswald killed dragons. *Nesciō quomodo Oswaldus necatūrus sit dracōnēs.* I do not know how Oswald will kill dragons.

- **Indirect Question (Past):** *Nesciēbam/nescīvī/nescīveram quomodo Oswaldus necāret dracōnēs.* I did not know/had not known how Oswald would kill dragons. *Nesciēbam/nescīvī/nescīveram quomodo Oswaldus necāvisset dracōnēs.* I did not know how Oswald had killed dragons. *Nesciēbam/nescīvī/nescīveram quomodo Oswaldus necatūrus sit dracōnēs.* I did not know how Oswald kills dragons/will kill dragons.
- **Indirect Command (Present/Future):** *Rēx imperat ut Oswaldus necet dracōnēs.* The king commands that Oswald kill the dragons. *Rex imperābit ut Oswaldus necet dracōnēs.* The king will command that Oswald kill the dragons. *Rēx imperat/imperābit ut Oswaldus necatūrus sit dracōnēs.* The king commands/will command that Oswald kill the dragons.
- **Indirect Command (Past):** *Rēx imperābat ut Oswaldus necāret dracōnēs.* The king was commanding that Oswald kill/would kill dragons. *Rēx imperāvit ut Oswaldus necāret dracōnēs.* The king commanded that Oswald kill/would kill dragons. *Rēx imperāverat ut Oswaldus necāret dracōnēs.* The king had commanded that Oswald kill/would kill dragons.
- **Conditional (Contrary to Fact):** *Sī Oswaldus necāret dracōnēs, salvāret rēgis fīliam.* If Oswald were killing dragons, he would save the king's daughter. *Sī Oswaldus necāvisset dracōnēs, salvāvisset rēgis fīliam.* If Oswald had killed dragons, he would have saved the king's daughter. Future Less Vivid: *Sī Oswaldus necet dracōnēs, salvet rēgis fīliam.* If Oswald were to kill dragons, he would save the king's daughter.
- **Relative Clause of Characteristic (Present/Future):** *Oswaldus est vir quī necet dracōnēs.* Oswald is the kind of man who kills dragons. *Oswaldus erit vir quī necet dracōnēs.* Oswald will become the kind of man who will kill dragons. *Oswaldus est/erit vir quī necāverit dracōnēs.* Oswald is/will be the kind of man who had killed dragons. *Oswaldus est/erit vir quī necatūrus sit dracōnēs.* Oswald is/will be the kind of man who will kill dragons.
- **Relative Clause of Characteristic (Past):** *Oswaldus erat/fuit/fuerat vir quī necāret dracōnēs.* Oswald was/had been the kind of man who killed dragons. *Oswaldus erat/fuit/fuerat vir quī necāvisset dracōnēs.* Oswald was/had been the kind of man who had killed dragons. *Oswaldus erat/fuit/fuerat vir quī necatūrus sit dracōnēs.* Oswald was/had been the kind of man who kills/would kill dragons.
- **Fear Clause:** *Timeō nē Oswaldus necet dracōnēs.* I fear lest Oswald kill/will kill dragons. *Timeō nē Oswaldus necatūrus sit dracōnēs.* I fear lest Oswald has killed dragons. *Timēbam/timuī/timueram nē Oswaldus necatūrus sit dracōnēs.* I was afraid lest Oswald would kill the dragons. *Timēbam/timuī/timueram nē Oswaldus necāret*

dracōnēs. I was afraid lest Oswald was killing dragons. *Timēbam/timuī/timueram nē Oswaldus necāvisset dracōnēs.* I was afraid lest Oswald had killed dragons.

- **Negative Fear Clause:** *Timeō ut Oswaldus necet dracōnēs.* I fear that Oswald will *not* kill dragons.
- ***Dum/Dummodo* Clause:** *Dum Oswaldus necet/necāret dracōnēs, non salvat fīliam rēgis.* Unless/until/while Oswald kills/was killing dragons, he does not save the king's daughter. *Antequam Oswaldus necet/necāret dracōnēs, salvat fīliam rēgis.* Before Oswald kills/was killing dragons, he saves the king's daughter.

The End

That's it! You have learned all Latin Grammar! You should go out and eat a pizza. If you want to keep up with your Latin, I highly recommend reading from the Latin translation of the Bible, the Vulgate. There is a wealth of Latin literature out there to study.

Worksheet 15

A. Vocabulary

1. bēlua: ______
2. priusquam (conj.): ______
3. tam: ______
4. extrā (adv. or prep. +acc.): ______
5. arvum: ______
6. ruō, ruere, ruī, rutum: ______
7. I close: ______
8. arbitror, -ārī, -ātus sum: ______
9. star: ______
10. nimis (adv.): ______
11. dēsertus: ______
12. antequam (conj.): ______
13. tandem (adv.): ______
14. bone: ______
15. terminus: ______

B. Grammar

1. Indicate whether you'd be *more likely* to translate these phrases with a genitive or ablative (or if either one would work).

   the girl with pink hair: ______

   chair of wood: ______

   man from Rio: ______

   the pirates with tender consciences: ______

   tooth of gold: ______

   the dragon of fiery eyes: ______

   statues out of marble: ______

   a woman of excessive cheerfulness: ______

   a fairy of the forest: ______

   creature of bad habits: ______

2. Do a synopsis of *claudō* in the 3rd person singular, first giving principal parts:

____

		LATIN ACTIVE	ENGLISH ACTIVE	LATIN PASSIVE	ENGLISH PASSIVE
INDICATIVE	PRES.				
	IMPF.				
	FUT.				
	PF.				
	PLPF.				
	FT. PF.				
SUBJUNCTIVE	PRES.				
	IMPF.				
	PF.				
	PLPF.				
PARTICIPLE	PRES.				
	PF.				
	FUT.				
INFINITIVE	PRES.				
	PF.				
	FUT.				
IMP.	SG.				
	PL.				

C. Memorization

Fill in the blanks in *Aeneid* 1.1-11 in Latin.

____

____

____

____

____

____

____

____

_______ _______, _______ _______ _____ _______ _______

ī_______ _______ _______, t__ _______ _______

_______. Tantaene _______ caelestibus _______?

D. Translation

English to Latin

1. *Dum/Dummodo* Clauses: Translate these sentences, using an indicative in the subordinate clause where you have an (I), and subjunctive where there is an (S).
   a. (I) The beast will be in the field until you (sg.) approach.

   ____

   b. (S) The beast will be in the field until you (sg.) approach to fight it.

   ____

   c. (S) I told your mother that the beast was in the field until you (sg.) approached.

   ____

   ____

   d. (I) While the beast lives, he will eat all your (sg.) sheep.

   ____

   ____

   e. (I) While the beast was eating your sheep, you (sg.) attacked it suddenly.

   ____

   ____

f. (S) Provided that the beast doesn't depart soon, all your (sg.) sheep will be eaten.

____

____

2. *Antequam/Priusquam* Clauses: Translate these sentences, using an indicative in the subordinate clause where you have an (I), and subjunctive where there is an (S).

   a. (I) Before the devil tests that man, he will run.

   ____

   ____

   b. (I) That man did not run before the devil tested him.

   ____

   ____

   c. (S) That man is running before the devil perhaps might test him.

   ____

   d. (S) Before the devil came to test him [use purpose clause], that man ran.

   ____

   ____

   e. (S) She thought that that man had not run before the devil tested him.

   ____

   ____

3. If these hills should be made of bones rather than stones, we would be afraid that ghosts would come to snatch us.

   ____

   ____

   ____

   ____

4. "It is not necessary to see the constellations in Rome," he said, "since here in this great city we have so many lights that we have forgotten the stars."

   ____

   ____

   ____

5. By closing the door against the attacking goats, the rather small girl was finally able to guard the cookies.

6. Is this not the boundary of my fields? You must remove your animals at once, since all of my grass has been eaten!

7. Having considered the witnesses' testimony, the judge of righteous judgment ordered the malicious man to be given twenty blows and then to be sent away.

8. If you (pl.) hadn't shown fear, the wild dogs wouldn't have touched you.

9. The small greedy boy will eat so many cookies and drink so much milk that his innards will suffer.

10. Oh that I were king and had the sort of treasure that I could give to my friends!

E. Latin to English

1 John 5

1 Omnis quī crēdit quoniam Iesus est Christus ex Deō nātus est; et omnis, quī dīligit eum quī genuit, dīligit
eum quī nātus est ex eō. 2 In hōc cognoscimus quoniam dīligimus nātōs* Deī, cum Deum dīligāmus et
mandāta eius faciāmus. 3 Haec est enim cāritās Deī ut mandāta eius custōdiāmus*, et mandāta eius gravia
nōn sunt;

4 quoniam omne quod nātum est ex Deō vincit mundum; et haec est vīctōria quae vincit mundum:
fidēs nostra.

5 Quis est quī vincit mundum nisi quī crēdit quoniam Iesus est Fīlius Dei? 6 Hic est quī venit per aquam
et sanguinem, Iesus Christus—nōn in aquā sōlum* sed in aquā et sanguine. Et Spīritus est quī testificātur
quoniam Christus est vēritās. 7 Quia trēs sunt quī testimōnium dant: 8 Spīritus et aqua et sanguis, et trēs
unum sunt.

9 Sī testimōnium hominum accipimus, testimōnium Deī māius est quoniam hoc est testimōnium Deī,
quod māius est—quīa testificātus est dē Fīliō suō. 10 Quī crēdit in Fīliō Deī habet testimōnium Deī in sē;
quī non crēdit Fīliō mendacem facit eum, quoniam nōn crēdidit in testimōniō quod testificātus est Deus dē
Fīliō suō. 11 Et hoc est testimōnium quoniam vītam aeternam dedit nōbīs Deus et haec vīta in Fīliō eius est.

12 Quī habet Fīlium habet vītam; quī nōn habet Fīlium Dei vītam nōn habet.

13 Haec scrīpsī vōbīs ut sciātis quoniam vītam habētis aeternam quī crēditis in nōmine Fīliī Deī. 14 Et haec
est fīdūcia quam habēmus ad eum quīa quodcumque petīerimus secundum voluntātem eius audit nōs. 15 Et
scīmus quoniam audit nōs, quīcquīd petīerimus scīmus quoniam habēmus petitiōnēs quās postulāvimus
ab eō.

16 Quī scit frātrem suum peccāre peccātum nōn ad mortem petet et dābit eī vītam peccantibus nōn
ad mortem. Est peccātum ad mortem; nōn prō illō dīcō ut roget*. 17 Omnis inīquītās peccātum est et est
peccātum nōn ad mortem. 18 Scīmus quoniam omnis quī nātus est ex Deō non peccat sed generātiō Deī
conservat eum et malignus nōn tangit eum. 19 Scīmus quoniam ex Deō sumus et mundus tōtus in malignō
positus est. 20 Et scīmus quoniam Fīlius Deī vēnit et dedit nōbīs sensum ut cognōscāmus vērum Deum, et
simus in vērō Fīliō eius. Hic est vērus Deus et vīta aeterna.

21 Fīliolī, custōdīte vōs ā simulācrīs!

Notes:

* *nātōs:* As a substantive [noun], *nātus, -ī* means literally, "one born"; in other words, "son, daughter, child."
* *custōdiāmus:* This verb is subjunctive because it is imitating the original Greek's content clause. See note on *dīligāmus* in 1 John 3:11 (Lesson 12) for a fuller explanation.
* *sōlum:* adverb, meaning "only" or "alone."
* *roget:* This verb is subjunctive because it is also imitating the original Greek in a clause that basically amounts to an indirect command.

Glossary:

conservō (1): I preserve, save
petītiō, -ōnis (f): petition, request
testificor, -ārī, -ātus sum: I testify, bear witness

Questions about Translation

Parse the following verbs (For Indicative and Subjunctive, give Person, Number, Tense, Voice, and Mood of what verb; for Infinitive and Imperative, give Tense, Voice, and Mood of what verb; for Participles give Gender, Number, Case, Tense, Voice, and Mood). Then identify or describe the usage of that verb (e.g., purpose clause, accusative and infinitive, present simple fact condition, etc.).

5:1—*nātus est:* ______________________________

5:2—*dīligāmus:* ______________________________

____

5:2—*faciāmus:* ______________________________

____

5:6—*testificātur:* ______________________________

____

5:13—*sciātis:* ______________________________

5:13—*habētis:* ______________________________

____

____

5:15—*petīerimus:* ______________________________

5:16—*peccantibus:* ______________________________ ; ______________

____

5:19—*positus est:* ______________________________

____

5:20—*cognōscāmus* and *simus:* ______________________________

____

5:21—*custōdīte:* ______________________________

Other Questions

5:1—Put brackets and parentheses if necessary around the relative clauses in this verse; it will make it easier to translate! ______________________________

______________________________ . ______________________________

5:9—*Sī testimōnium hominum accipimus...:* What kind of condition? ______________________

LESSON 16

Review and Test

Grātulātiōnēs! (Which, you might suspect, is how the Romans would say "Congratulations!") You have come to the end of this phase of your Latinic journey. The logic stage has been conquered, and now it is time to pursue the Kraken through the wild wonderful deeps of Latin translation. We are going to review all the ground we've covered to give you a solid foundation for continuing.

The worksheet has several noun-adjective combinations to decline in order to review the five declensions and how adjectives modify but might not match nouns in their endings. For your reference, I have compiled a list summarizing the various case usages from all three volumes of the *Kraken* books. Turn to the appropriate Lesson to review each more fully if you or your students have need.

Summary of Case Usages

Nominative

Subject (*KL1*, Lesson 2)

Predicate Nominative (*KL1*, Lesson 3)

Genitive

Possession (*KL1*, Lesson 3)

Partitive (*KL1*, Lessons 17 and 21)

Objective (*KL1*, Lesson 17)

Genitive of Material (*KL3*, Lesson 15)

Genitive of Quality (*KL3*, Lesson 15)

Dative

Indirect Object (*KL1*, Lesson 2),

Dative of Possession (*KL2*, Lesson 5)

Dative of Agent (*KL2*, Lesson 13)

Dative of Reference (*KL3*, Lesson 1)

Dative with Certain Verbs and Adjectives (*KL3*, Lesson 14)

Accusative

Direct Object (*KL1*, Lesson 2)

Object of Preposition (*KL1*, Lesson 3)

Accusative of Place to Which (*KL2*, Lesson 14)

Accusative of Duration of Time (*KL1*, Lesson 28)

Ablative

Object of Preposition (*KL1*, Lesson 3)

Ablative of Means/Instrument (*KL1*, Lesson 3)

Ablative of Time When (*KL1*, Lesson 28)

Ablative of Time Within Which (*KL1*, Lesson 28)

Ablative of Place from Which (*KL2*, Lesson 14)

Ablative of Source (*KL3*, Lesson 15)

Ablative of Material (*KL3*, Lesson 15)

Ablative of Quality (*KL3*, Lesson 15)

Vocative

Direct address (*KL1*, Lesson 11)

Locative

Place Where (*KL2*, Lesson 14)

Verb Review

Indicative

Stating facts, etc. (*KL1*, Lessons 1, 3, 6, 9, 10, 11, 14, 15, 20, 22, 26, 27, 29, 31)

Direct Questions (*KL2*, Lesson 7)

Infinitive

Complementary (*KL1*, Lesson 11)

As Verbal Noun (subject) (*KL2*, Lesson 15)

Indirect Statement/Accusative and Infinitive (*KL3*, Lesson 2)

Imperative

Active (*KL1*, Lesson 11)

Passive (*KL2*, Lesson 6)

Participle

Attributive/Substantive (*KL2*, Lesson 10)

Ablative Absolute (*KL2*, Lesson 11)

Passive Periphrastic (*KL2*, Lesson 13)

Gerund and Gerundive (*KL2*, Lesson 15)

Subjunctive (all lesson references are for *KL2*)

Independent Subjunctive Usages

Hortatory/Jussive (*KL3*, Lesson 4)

Prohibitive (*KL3*, Lesson 6)

Optative (*KL3*, Lesson 13)

Deliberative (*KL3*, Lesson 13)

Potential (*KL3*, Lesson 13)

Dependent Subjunctive Usages

Purpose Clause (*KL3*, Lesson 5)

Result Clause (*KL3*, Lesson 5)

Cum Clause (*KL3*, Lesson 7)

Indirect Question (*KL3*, Lesson 9)

Indirect Command (*KL3*, Lesson 10)

Present Contrary to Fact Condition (*KL3*, Lesson 11)

Past Contrary to Fact Condition (*KL3*, Lesson 11)

Future Less Vivid Condition (*KL3*, Lesson 11)

Fear Clause (*KL3*, Lesson 14)

Dum/Proviso Clause (*KL3*, Lesson 15)

Antequam/Priusquam (*KL3*, Lesson 15)

Worksheet 16

A. Vocabulary

Review all Unit 4 words or most of them; esp. all adverbs/conjunctions/preps!

1. sententia: ______________________________
____
2. arvum: ______________________________
3. aciēs: ______________________________
____
4. lūmen: ______________________________
5. obsecrō (1): ______________________________
6. arrival: ______________________________
7. priusquam (conj.): ______________________________
____
8. os: ______________________________
9. accidō: ______________________________
____
10. īnfāns: ______________________________
____
11. mandō (1): ______________________________
____
12. maidservant: ______________________________
13. ātrium: ______________________________
14. bēlua: ______________________________
____
15. canticum: ______________________________
16. justice: ______________________________
17. cāritās: ______________________________
18. lācrima: ______________________________
19. banquet: ______________________________
20. virga: ______________________________
21. devil: ______________________________
22. auferō: ______________________________
23. ashes: ______________________________
24. murderer: ______________________________
25. coniungō: ______________________________
26. impetus: ______________________________
____
27. month: ______________________________
28. minister, ministrī (m): ______________________________
____
29. thēsaurus: ______________________________
30. dēprecor: ______________________________
____
31. claudō: ______________________________
32. peccātum: ______________________________
33. plāga: ______________________________
____
34. metuō: ______________________________
____
35. confundō: ______________________________
____
36. stumbling block: ______________________________
37. scrība: ______________________________
38. pride: ______________________________
39. limit: ______________________________
40. sīdus: ______________________________
____
41. substantia: ______________________________
____

42. fear: ______________________________
43. internal organs: ______________________________
44. antequam (conj.): ______________________________
____
45. quamdiu: ______________________________
____
46. umquam (adv.): ______________________________
47. voluntās: ______________________________
48. convertō: ______________________________
____
49. I pour out: ______________________________
50. imperō (1): ______________________________
51. indīcō (1): ______________________________
____
52. I give birth to: ______________________________
53. paveō: ______________________________
54. recipiō: ______________________________
55. I sin: ______________________________
56. an (conj.): ______________________________
57. pendō: ______________________________
58. perficiō: ______________________________
59. I persuade: ______________________________
60. postulō (1): ______________________________
61. adhūc: ______________________________
____
62. prōdeō: ______________________________
63. amplius: ______________________________
64. neighboring: ______________________________
65. remittō: ______________________________
66. regredior: ______________________________
67. scindō: ______________________________
68. utique: ______________________________
69. I am accustomed to: ______________________________
____
70. pauper, -eris: ______________________________
71. trānsferō: ______________________________
____
72. cruel: ______________________________
73. half of (adj.): ______________________________
74. malignus: ______________________________
____
75. quārē: ______________________________
____
76. memor, -oris: ______________________________
77. forsitan: ______________________________
78. quālis (interrog. adj.): ______________________________
____
79. probō (1): ______________________________
____
80. so many: ______________________________
81. would/oh that!: ______________________________
82. extrā (adv. or prep. +acc.): ______________________________
____
83. nisi: ______________________________
84. quasi: ______________________________
85. quemadmodum (adv.): ______________________________
86. tandem (adv.): ______________________________
87. tantum (adv.): ______________________________
____
88. usquam: ______________________________
89. ūtrum (adv.): ______________________________
90. vērumtamen: ______________________________

B. Grammar

Decline these noun-adjective combinations, including the vocative and locative (even if hypothetical; you can omit both vocative and locative for demonstratives).

1. Decline *illa lācrima memor*, "that mindful tear"

	LATIN SINGULAR	LATIN PLURAL
NOM.		
GEN.		
DAT.		
ACC.		
ABL.		
VOC.		
LOC.		

2. Decline *hoc peccātum crūdēle,* "this cruel sin"

	LATIN SINGULAR	LATIN PLURAL
NOM.		
GEN.		
DAT.		
ACC.		
ABL.		
VOC.		
LOC.		

3. Decline *dīmidius mensis*, "half a month"

	LATIN SINGULAR	LATIN PLURAL
NOM.		
GEN.		
DAT.		
ACC.		
ABL.		
VOC.		
LOC.		

4. Decline *ipse adventus malignus*, "the wicked arrival itself"

	LATIN SINGULAR	LATIN PLURAL
NOM.		
GEN.		
DAT.		
ACC.		
ABL.		
VOC.		
LOC.		

5. Decline *quālis vīcīna aciēs*, "what kind of nearby battleline"

	LATIN SINGULAR	LATIN PLURAL
NOM.		
GEN.		

DAT.		
ACC.		
ABL.		
VOC.		
LOC.		

6. Deponent Synopsis: Do a synopsis of *regredior* in the 1st person plural, first giving principal parts: ______________________________

		LATIN ACTIVE	ENGLISH ACTIVE	LATIN PASSIVE	ENGLISH PASSIVE
INDICATIVE	PRES.				
	IMPF.				
	FUT.				
	PF.				
	PLPF.				
	FT. PF.				
SUBJUNCTIVE	PRES.				
	IMPF.				
	PF.				
	PLPF.				
PARTICIPLE	PRES.				
	PF.				
	FUT.				

INFINITIVE	PRES.				
	PF.				
	FUT.				
IMP.	SG.				
	PL.				

7. Conjugate *prōdeō* in the Present Active Indicative.

	LATIN SINGULAR	ENGLISH SINGULAR	LATIN PLURAL	ENGLISH PLURAL
1ST				
2ND				
3RD				

8. Conjugate *trānsferō* in the Present Passive Indicative.

	LATIN SINGULAR	ENGLISH SINGULAR	LATIN PLURAL	ENGLISH PLURAL
1ST				
2ND				
3RD				

9. Conjugate *mandō* in the Imperfect Active Indicative.

	LATIN SINGULAR	ENGLISH SINGULAR	LATIN PLURAL	ENGLISH PLURAL
1ST				
2ND				
3RD				

10. Conjugate *claudō* in the Imperfect Passive Indicative.

	LATIN SINGULAR	ENGLISH SINGULAR	LATIN PLURAL	ENGLISH PLURAL
1ST				
2ND				
3RD				

11. Conjugate *perficiō* in the Future Active Indicative.

	LATIN SINGULAR	ENGLISH SINGULAR	LATIN PLURAL	ENGLISH PLURAL
1ST				
2ND				
3RD				

12. Conjugate *imperō* in the Future Passive Indicative.

	LATIN SINGULAR	ENGLISH SINGULAR	LATIN PLURAL	ENGLISH PLURAL
1ST				
2ND				
3RD				

13. Conjugate *pariō* in the Perfect Active Indicative.

	LATIN SINGULAR	ENGLISH SINGULAR	LATIN PLURAL	ENGLISH PLURAL
1ST				
2ND				
3RD				

14. Conjugate *pendō* in the Perfect Passive Indicative.

	LATIN SINGULAR	ENGLISH SINGULAR	LATIN PLURAL	ENGLISH PLURAL
1ST				
2ND				
3RD				

15. Conjugate *coniungō* in the Pluperfect Active Indicative.

	LATIN SINGULAR	ENGLISH SINGULAR	LATIN PLURAL	ENGLISH PLURAL
1ST				
2ND				
3RD				

16. Conjugate *persuādeō* in the Pluperfect Passive Indicative.

	LATIN SINGULAR	ENGLISH SINGULAR	LATIN PLURAL	ENGLISH PLURAL
1ST				
2ND				
3RD				

17. Conjugate *paveō* in the Future Perfect Active Indicative.

	LATIN SINGULAR	ENGLISH SINGULAR	LATIN PLURAL	ENGLISH PLURAL
1ST				
2ND				
3RD				

18. Conjugate *scindō* in the Future Perfect Passive Indicative.

	LATIN SINGULAR	ENGLISH SINGULAR	LATIN PLURAL	ENGLISH PLURAL
1ST				
2ND				
3RD				

19. Conjugate *soleō* in the Present Active Subjunctive.

	LATIN SINGULAR	ENGLISH SINGULAR	LATIN PLURAL	ENGLISH PLURAL
1ST				
2ND				
3RD				

20. Conjugate *obsecrō* in the Present Passive Subjunctive.

	LATIN SINGULAR	ENGLISH SINGULAR	LATIN PLURAL	ENGLISH PLURAL
1ST				
2ND				
3RD				

21. Conjugate *accidō* in the Imperfect Active Subjunctive.

	LATIN SINGULAR	ENGLISH SINGULAR	LATIN PLURAL	ENGLISH PLURAL
1ST				
2ND				
3RD				

22. Conjugate *auferō* in the Imperfect Passive Subjunctive.

	LATIN SINGULAR	ENGLISH SINGULAR	LATIN PLURAL	ENGLISH PLURAL
1ST	auferrer			
2ND	auferrēris			
3RD	auferrētur			

23. Conjugate *indīcō* in the Perfect Active Subjunctive.

	LATIN SINGULAR	ENGLISH SINGULAR	LATIN PLURAL	ENGLISH PLURAL
1ST				
2ND				
3RD				

24. Conjugate *confundō* in the Perfect Passive Subjunctive.

	LATIN SINGULAR	ENGLISH SINGULAR	LATIN PLURAL	ENGLISH PLURAL
1ST				
2ND				
3RD				

25. Conjugate *postulō* in the Pluperfect Active Subjunctive.

	LATIN SINGULAR	ENGLISH SINGULAR	LATIN PLURAL	ENGLISH PLURAL
1ST				
2ND				
3RD				

26. Conjugate *convertō* in the Pluperfect Passive Subjunctive.

	LATIN SINGULAR	ENGLISH SINGULAR	LATIN PLURAL	ENGLISH PLURAL
1ST				
2ND				
3RD				

27. Give all the participles of *recipiō*.

	ACTIVE		PASSIVE	
	LATIN	ENGLISH	LATIN	ENGLISH
PRES.				
PF.				
FUT.				

28. Give all the infinitives of *probō*.

	ACTIVE		PASSIVE	
	LATIN	ENGLISH	LATIN	ENGLISH
PRES.				
PF.				
FUT.				

29. Give all the imperatives of *effundō*.

	ACTIVE		PASSIVE	
	LATIN	ENGLISH	LATIN	ENGLISH
SING.				
PL.				

C. Memorization

Fill in the blanks in *Aeneid* 1.1-11 in Latin.

____

____

____

____

____

____

____

____

____

________ ________ ________, _____ _______ ________

________. ________ _______ __________ _____

D. Translation with Parsing and Questions

Translate the following sentences and answer any questions. This will include parsing verbs and identifying nouns/pronouns/adjectives.

Identify nouns/pronouns/adjectives: Give Gender, Number, Case and the entire dictionary entry that the word is from.

Parse: Follow specifics given below, and provide all the principal parts of the verb.

Indicatives and Subjunctives—Person, Number, Tense, Voice, Mood

Infinitives—Tense, Voice, Mood

Imperatives—Tense, Voice, Mood plus Number (Sg. or Pl.)

Participles—Gender, Number, Case, Tense, Voice, Mood

Example: Cētō necātō, Oswaldus fīliam rēgis servāvit. *The kraken having been killed, Oswald saved the princess.*

a. Parse *necātō*: ______________________________

____

b. Why is *necātō* in the mood it's in? ______________________

c. Parse *servāvit*: ______________________________

____

d. Identify *fīliam*: ______________________________

1. Nē effūderīs cinerēs patris tuī ad convīvium; hoc forsitan sit multīs illīc scandalum.

____

____

a. Parse *effūderīs*: ____

____

b. Why is *effūderīs* in the mood it's in? ____

c. Parse *sit*: ____

____

d. Why is *sit* in the mood it's in? ____

e. Identify *multīs*: ____

2. Sī quīs loquātur sē nōn peccātum habēre, ille mendāx sit Deōque nōn placeat.

____

____

a. Parse *loquātur*: ____

____

b. Why is *loquātur* in the mood it's in? ____

c. Identify *mendāx*: ____

____

d. Parse *habēre*: ____

e. Why is *habēre* in the mood it's in? ____

3. Māter rēgis metuēbat nē suus fīlius ancillam adhūc dīligeret, itaque ista eī imperāvit ut in matrimōniō fīliam rēgis vicīnī ductūrus esset.

____

____

____

a. Parse *dīligeret*: ____

____

b. Why is *dīligeret* in the mood it's in? ____

c. Identify *ancillam*: ______

d. Why is *ancilla* in the case it's in? ______

e. Parse *ductūrus*, then *esset*: ______

______

______

f. What are *ductūrus* and *esset* doing in this sentence? ______

______

______

4. Ossa antiqua bēluae crūdēlis nōbīs invenienda sunt, et nōs prīmō indīcābimus quemadmodum hās plāgās recēperit et deinde quārē sē ad hoc arvum abstulerit.

______

______

______

a. Parse *invenienda* and then *sunt*: ______

______

______

b. What are *invenienda* and *sunt* doing together in this sentence? ______

______

c. Identify *arvum*: ______

d. Parse *abstulerit*: ______

______

e. Why is *abstulerit* in the mood it's in? ______

5. Dēprecāminī fēminam īnfantem nōn parere antequam adventus dracōnis hōc mense accidat, cum editum ovēs nostrās et nostrōs liberōs adierit.

______

______

______

a. Parse *deprecāminī*: ______

______

b. Identify *dracōnis*: ______

c. Parse *accidat*: ______________________________

____

d. What is *editum* doing? ______________________________

____

6. Quis est quī meam substantiam thēsaurumque probet? Quō ea trānsferam ut ea custōdiam?

____

____

a. Parse *probet*: ______________________________

____

b. Why is *probet* in the mood it's in? ______________________________

c. Parse *trānsferam*: ______________________________

____

____

d. Why is *trānsferam* in the mood it's in? ______________________________

____

e. Identify *ea* (either one; they're the same) and explain its gender: ______________________________

____

____

7. Prīnceps hostium tantā superbiā rēplētus est ut fortissimam partem aciēī nostrae peteret, sternēns multōs ex suīs militibus.

____

____

____

a. Identify *superbiā*: ______________________________

b. Parse rēplētus est: ______________________________

____

c. Parse peteret: ______________________________

____

d. Why is *peteret* in the mood it's in? ______________________________

e. Parse *sternēns*: ______________________________

____

8. Dummodo rēx memor meōrum canticōrum mīrābilium maneat, is mihi mandābit ut in suum ātrium ineat et homicīdiam meī nōn mālet.

____

____

a. Parse *maneat*: ______________________________

____

b. Why is *maneat* in the mood it's in? ______________________________

c. Parse *mandābit*: ______________________________

____

d. Parse *mālet*: ______________________________

9. Camēlī aliēnī Carthāgine Rōmam trānsierant ut ab sacerdōtibus sapientibus utrum sīdera ex lūmine an igne aedificāta essent quaererent.

____

____

____

a. Identify *Carthāgine* and explain its case: ______________________________

____

b. Parse *trānsierant*: ______________________________

____

c. Parse *aedificāta essent*: ______________________________

____

d. Parse *quaererent*: ______________________________

____

e. Why is *quaererent* in the mood it's in? ______________________________

10. Cum quīdam ministrī voluntātem diabolī usquam umquamque audīre vellent, nōsmet eōs remittāmus et iūstitiam faciāmus.

____

____

____

b. Parse *audīre*: ______________________________

c. Parse *remittāmus*: ______________________________

____

d. Why is *remittāmus* in the mood it's in? ______________________________

11. Utinam pīrātae trīstēs nē quālia cantica trīstissima canant ut tuam īnfantem dormientem confundant!

____

____

a. Parse *canant*: ______________________________

b. Why is *canant* in the mood it's in? ______________________________

c. Identify *cantica*: ______________________________

d. Parse *dormientem*: ______________________________

____

12. Tū mihi tē ad mē crūstula optima—mīrābile vīsū!—in mundō ūniversō allātūrum esse locūtus ēs, nisi dē tē mentītus sum.

____

____

a. Identify *mihi*: ______________________________

b. What is *vīsū*? ______________________________

c. Parse *allātūrum esse*: ______________________________

____

____

d. Parse *locūtus es*: ______________________________

____

Bonus Latin to English Translation

Starting on the next page, you have a passage from Ovid's *Metamorphoses* to translate for extra practice. Use the right-hand pages to translate each section of the text on the left-hand pages. Write your translation in plain prose paragraphs rather than in verse.

Perseus, Andromeda, and the Kraken (Ovid's *Metamorphoses* IV.663-764)

Clauserat *Hippotadēs Aetnaeo* carcere *ventōs*,
*admonitor*que operum caelō *clārissimus* altō
Lūcifer ortus erat. *Pennīs ligat* ille* *resūmptīs*
parte ab utrāque *pedēs* tēlōque *accingitur uncō*
et *līquidum* mōtīs *tālāribus aera findit.*
Gentibus *innumerīs* circumque *īnfrā*que relictīs
Aethiopum populōs *Cēphēa*que *cōnspicit* arva.
Illīc *inmeritam māternae* pendere linguae
Andromedan poenās *iniustus* iūsserat *Ammōn.* *
Quam* simul ad *dūrās religātam bracchia* * *cautes*
vīdit *Abantiadēs*, nisi quod* *levis* aura *capillōs*
mōverat et *tepidō manābant* lūmina* *flētū*,
marmoreum ratus esset opus. Trahit *īnscius* ignēs
et *stupet* et visae *correptus* imāgine *formae*
paene suās *quatere* est oblītus in *aere pennās.*

Notes:

* *ille* = Perseus

* ll. 670-71: Cassiopeia, Andromeda's mother, had arrogantly boasted that she and Andromeda were more beautiful than the Nereids, daughters of Nereus (a sea god). Thus Poseidon sent the sea monster Cetus (the kraken!) to terrorize the kingdom of Ethiopia until the oracle at Jupiter Ammon's temple revealed that the troubles would cease if Andromeda were sacrificed.

* *Quam* = *Et eam*

* *bracchia:* an accusative of respect/specification, which denotes the part affected; lit., "with respect to her arms"

* *quod:* here, "the fact that"

* *lūmina:* in poetry = eyes

Glossary:

Abantiadēs, -ae (m/f): son/descendent of Abas, king of Argos; here = Perseus (great-grandson of Abas)
accingō, -ere, -cinxī, -cinctum: I gird on/about, arm
admonitor, -ōris (m): admonisher, encourager
āēr, āēris (m): air, atmosphere (pl. nom./acc. sometimes *aēra*)
Aethiops, -opis (m/f): Ethiopian
Aetnaeus, -a, -um: of/belonging to Etna (volcano in Sicily)
Ammōn, -ōnis (m): Ammon, a name of Jupiter as worshipped in Africa
Andromeda, -ae (acc. -an) (f): Andromeda, daughter of Cepheus and Cassiopeia
bracchium, -iī (n): arm
capillus, -ī (m): hair
cautēs, -is (f): rough rock, crag
Cēphēus, -a, -um: Cephean, Ethiopian [Cepheus was the king of Ethiopia, husband of Cassiopeia and father of Andromeda]
clārus, -a, -um: clear, bright
cōnspiciō, -ere, -spēxī, -spectum: I observe, perceive, gaze at
corripiō, -ere, -ripuī, -reptus: I seize/snatch up, carry off
dūrus, -a, -um: hard, rough, harsh
findō, -ere, fissum: I split, part, cleave
flētus, -ūs (m): weeping, tears
forma, -ae (f): form, shape, appearance, beauty
Hippotadēs, -ae (m): son of Hippotes; i.e., Aeolus (ruler of the winds)
īnfrā (adv. and prep. +acc.): below, under *iniūstus, -a, -um* unjust, unreasonable
inmeritus (imm-), -a, -um: undeserved, undeserving, innocent
innumerus, -a, -um: innumerable, countless
īnscius, -a, -um: not knowing, ignorant
levis, -e: light
ligō (1): I bind (up/together), tie
līquidus, -a, -um: liquid, flowing, pure
Lūcifer, -ferī (m): Lucifer (the morning star)
mānō (1): I flow, trickle, drop
marmoreus, -a, -um: (made of) marble, marble-like
māternus, -a, -um: of/belonging to a mother, maternal
penna, -ae (f): feather; in pl., wing(s)
pēs, pedis (m): foot
quatiō, -ere, quassī, quassum: I shake, brandish
religō (1): I bind (back/up), fetter
reor, rērī, ——, ratus sum: I think, suppose, imagine
resūmō, -ere, -sūmpsī, -sūmptum: I resume, take up again, take back
stupeō, -ēre, -uī, ——: I am stunned, am astonished, am stupefied
tālāria, -ium (n, pl): winged sandals/shoes; ankles
tepidus, -a, -um: warm, tepid
uncus, -a, -um: hooked, curved
ventus, -ī (m): wind

At stetit, "Ō," dīxit, "nōn istīs* *digna catēnīs*,
sed quibus inter sē *cupidī iunguntur* amantēs*,
pande requīrentī nōmen terraeque tuumque*,
et cur *vincla* gerās." Prīmō *silet* illa nec audet
*adpellāre** virum virgō, manibusque *modestōs*
celāsset vultūs, sī nōn religāta fuisset*;
lūmina, quod potuit, lacrimīs inplēvit* *obortīs.*
Saepius *instantī*, sua nē *dēlicta* fatērī
nōlle vidērētur, nōmen terraeque suumque,
quantaque *māternae* fuerit fīdūcia formae,
indicat.* Et nōndum *memorātīs* omnibus unda
insonuit, veniēnsque *inmensō* bēlua *pontō*
inminet et lātum sub *pectore possidet* aequor.

Notes:

* Imply a *tū* or *fēmina* going with *digna*
* *amantēs*: "those loving" = "lovers"
* *nōmen terraeque tuumque* = *nōmen tuum et nōmen terrae tuae*
* *adpellāre* = *appellāre*
* *inplēvit* = *implēvit*
* *cēlāsset...sī religāta fusset*: Past Contrary to Fact Condition! Also, *celāsset* is syncopated.
* ll. 685-88: *Saepius...indicat:* Reorder the words thus and follow the hints in brackets to translate more easily: [Andromeda] [*Perseī*—dative] *saepius instantī, nē sua dēlicta* [accusative of respect] *fatērī nōlle vidērētur, indicat nōmen terraeque suumque, quantaque fidūcia fuerit formae māternae* [dative of possession; indirect question].

Glossary:

catēna, -ae (f): chain, fetter, shackle
cēlō (1): I hide, conceal
cupidus, -a, -um: desirous, eager
dēlictum, -ī (n): crime, sin, offense
dignus, -a, -um: worthy, deserving
forma, -ae (f): form, shape, appearance, beauty
inmensus, -a, -um: (imm-) immense, vast
inmineō, -ēre, ——, —— (+dat.): I threaten, menace
insonō, -āre, -uī, -itum: I sound, resound
īnstō, -āre, -stitī, -stātum: I insist, urge, pursue
iungō, -ere, iūnxī, iūnctum: I join (together), unite
māternus, -a, -um: of/belonging to a mother, maternal
memorō (1): I bring to remembrance, relate, recount
modestus, -a, -um: modest, virtuous
pandō, -ere, pansī, pansum/passum: I unfold, explain
pectus, -toris (n): chest, breastbone, stomach
pontus, -ī (m): sea, the deep, wave
possideō, -ēre, -sēdī, -sessum: I possess, master
requīrō, -ere, -quīsīvī (-siī), -quīsitum: I seek, ask
religō (1): I bind (back/up), fetter
sileō, -ēre, -uī, -itum: I am/keep silent
vinc(u)lum, -ī (n): fetter, bond, band

Conclāmat virgō: *genitor lūgūbris* et ūnā
māter adest, *ambo* miserī, sed iūstius* illa;
nec sēcum auxilium, sed *dignōs* tempore *flētūs*
*plangorem*que ferunt vinctōque* in corpore *adhaerent*,
cum sīc *hospes* ait: "Lācrimārum longa manēre
tempora vōs poterunt, ad *opem* brevis hora ferendam est.
hanc ego sī peterem *Perseus Iove* nātus et illā*,
quam clausam inplevit *fecundō* Iuppiter aurō;*
Gorgonis anguicomae Perseus *superātor* et ālīs
aeriās ausus *iactātīs* īre per aurās*—
praeferrer cunctīs certe *gener*; *addere* tantīs
dōtibus et *meritum*, *faveant* modo nūmina, temptō:
ut mea sit servāta meā virtūte, *pacīscor*."
Accipiunt lēgem (quis enim *dubitāret*?) et ōrant
*promittunt*que super rēgnum *dōtāle parentēs*.

Notes:

* *iūstius*: Comparative adverb from *iūstus, -a, -um*; the mother is "more justly" wretched because it is her fault that Andromeda is chained up.
* *vinctōque*: Note that this is the fourth principle part of *vinciō*, not *vincō*
* *Iove* and *illā*: Look! Ablatives of Source!
* ll. 697-98, *Iove nātus…aurō*: Reference to the story of Perseus's origin. After an oracle told King Acrisius of Argos that he would be killed by the son of his daughter, he shut up his daughter Danaë in a tower to prevent her from having any children. However, Jupiter came to her as a shower of golden rain and impregnated her. When Perseus was born, Acrisius put mother and child in a wooden box and threw them into the sea. Jupiter ensured that they survived and came to the island of Seriphos. The king there, Polydectes, wanted to marry Danaë but Perseus wasn't excited about it. To get him out of the way, Polydectes demanded that Perseus fetch him the Gorgon's head. Perseus was successful (see next note), and in one version of the myth he returned to Seriphos with Medusa's head and turned Polydectes to stone. And, as must happen in these stories, he unwittingly killed his grandfather Acrisius by accidentally hitting him with a javelin (or some stories say a discus) at some athletic games.
* ll. 699-700: There are a couple of different versions of Medusa's story, but according to Ovid, Medusa was the beautiful daughter of Phorcus. She was raped by Poseidon in Athena's temple, and so Athena punished her for this desecration (a bit harsh on the rape victim, no?) by turning her into the hideous, snaky-haired monster we are familiar with whose glance turned things to stone. In his quest to kill Medusa, Perseus was helped by the gods, receiving a shield from Athena, winged sandals from Mercury, and a sword from Vulcan. She was pregnant by Poseidon at the time, and when Perseus cut off her head, the winged horse Pegasus sprang forth from her blood.

Glossary:

addō, -ere, -didī, -ditum (+dat.): I add to, bring to
adhaereō, -ēre, -haesī, -haesum: I cling to, adhere to
aerius, -a, -um: airy
ambo, -bae, -bo (pl. adj.): both, the two
anguicomus, -a, -um: with/having snaky hair (a fabulous adjective!)
conclāmō (1): I call/cry out
dignus, -a, -um: worthy, deserving
dōs, dōtis (f): dowry, gift
dōtālis, -e: of/belonging to a dowry
dubitō (1): I hesitate, waver, doubt
faveō, -ēre, fāvī, fautum: I am favorable, favor, protect
fēcundus, -a, -um: fruitful, fertile
flētus, -ūs (m): weeping, tears
gener, -erī (m): son-in-law, daughter's husband
genitor, -tōris (m): begetter, father, parent
Gorgō, -onis (f): a Gorgon, Medusa
hospēs, -pitis (m): guest, visitor; host
iactō (1): I throw, toss, beat about
Iuppiter (Iūpp-), Iovis (m): Jupiter, Jove
lūgūbris, -e: mourning, sorrowing
meritum, -ī (n): merit, reward, benefit
ops, opis (f): power, wealth, help
pacīscor, -scī, pactus sum: I covenant, make a bargain/contract
Perseus, -eī (m): Perseus
plangor, -ōris (m): wailing, lamentation
praeferō, -ferre, -tulī, -lātum: I put before, prefer
prōmittō, -ere, -mīsī, -missum: I promise, put forth
superātor, -tōris (m): conqueror

Ecce, velut nāvis *praefīxō concita rōstrō*
sulcat aquās *iuvenum sūdantibus* acta *lacertīs*,*
sīc fera* *dīmōtīs inpulsū pectoris* undīs;
tantum aberat *scopulīs*, quantum* *Baleārica tortō*
funda potest *plumbō* mediī *trānsmittere* caelī,
cum subitō *iuvenis* pedibus tellūre *repulsā*
arduus in nūbēs abiit. Ut in aequore summō*
umbra virī vīsa est, vīsam fera *saevit* in umbram.
Utque *Iovis praepes*, *vacuō* cum vīdit in arvō
praebentem Phoebō līventia terga* dracōnem*,
occupat āversum, *neu saeva retorqueat* ōra*,
squāmigerīs avidōs fīgit cervicibus unguēs*,
sīc* celerī missus *praeceps* per *ināne volātū*
terga ferae pressit dextrōque *frementis* in *armō*
Īnachides ferrum *curvō tenus abdidit hāmō*.*

Notes:

* ll. 706-708, *velut...sīc*: This is called an **epic simile**, a poetic device used frequently by the ancients. A person, thing, or situation (often unfamiliar to the audience) compared to something else more concrete (often in excruciating detail), and usually with these words, "just as X, so Y...."
* l. 708, *fera:* refers to the *bēlua* of line 689
* l. 709, *tantum...quantum:* translate these correlatives (separate words working together), "as far...as"
* l. 712, *summō:* can also mean "on the top of"
* ll. 714-18, *Utque...sīc:* another epic simile
* l. 715, *līventia terga*; l. 716, *saeva ōra;* l. 717, *squamigerīs cervicibus:* these are all poetic plurals; translate as singular
* l. 715, *dracōnem: dracō* can also mean "serpent" (interesting, is it not?)
* ll. 718-20: Reorder the words thus for easier translating: *sīc*
* *Īnachides, missus praeceps celerī volātū per ināne, terga ferae pressit dextrōque in armō frementis ferrum curvō hāmō tenus abdidit.*

Glossary:

abdō, -ere, -didī, -ditum: I hide, conceal
arduus, -a, -um: lofty, tall, steep
armus, -ī (m): shoulder (of animal), flank, side
āvertō, -ere, -tī, -sum: I turn away from, remove
avidus, -a, -um: eager, greedy
Baleāricus, -a, -um (f, pl): of/belonging to the Balearic Islands (off the coast of Spain; the inhabitants were famously skilled with slings)
cervīx, -vīcis (f): neck
concieō, -ēre, -cīvī, -citum: I excite, rouse, stir up
curvus, -a, -um: curved, bent
dīmoveō, -ēre, -mōvī, -mōtum: I move apart, divide
fīgō, -ere, fīxī, fīxum: I fix (in), fasten, drive (in)
fremō, -ere, -uī, -itum: I roar, growl, howl
funda, -ae (f): a sling, sling-shot
hāmus, -ī (m): hook
Īnachides, -ae (m): descendant of Inachus (first king of Argos); i.e., Perseus
ināne, -is (n): empty/open space, void
inpulsus (imp-), -ūs (m): a pushing, surging, striking
Iuppiter (Iūpp-), Iovis (m): Jupiter, Jove
iuvenis, -e: young; *iuvenis, -is (m/f):* a youth
lacertus, -ī (m): upper arm (esp. muscular)
līvēns, -ntis: bluish, lead-colored, livid
neu (nēve): and not, nor, and lest
pectus, -toris (n): chest, breastbone, stomach
Phoebus, -ī (m): Phoebus (Apollo), god of light; the sun
plumbum, -ī (n): lead, lead ball/shot
praebeō, -ēre, -uī, -itum: I show, give, offer
praeceps, -cipitis: headlong, swift, rash
praefīgō, -ere, -fīxī, -fīxum: I fix/fasten before, I set in front of
praepes, -petis (f): prophetic bird; praepes Iovis = eagle
repellō, -ere, reppulī, repulsum: I drive/push back, repel
retorqueō, -ēre, -torsī, -tortum: I twist back, bend back
rōstrum, -strī (n): beak, prow
saeviō, -īre, -iī, -ītum: I rage, rave, am furious
saevus, -a, -um: raging, furious, fierce, cruel
scopulus, -ī (m): rock, cliff, crag
squāmiger, -gera, -gerum: scaly (another great adjective!)
sūdō (1): I sweat, am drenched (with)
sulcō (1): I plow, traverse
tenus (prep. +abl./gen.; follows its object): down/up to, as far as
torqueō, -ēre, torsī, tortum: I twist, bend, hurl
trānsmittō, -ere, -mīsī, -missum: I send across/through, pass through
unguis, -is (m): claw, talon, fingernail
vacuus, -a, -um: empty, vacant
volātus, -ūs (m): flight, swiftness

Vulnere *laesa* gravī modo* sē sublimīs* in aurās
attollit, modo *subdit* aquīs, modo mōre *ferōcis*
versat aprī, quem turba canum *circumsona* terret.
Ille *avidōs morsūs vēlōcibus effūgit* ālīs;
quāque patet, nunc terga *cavīs* super *obsita conchīs*,
nunc laterum *costās*, nunc quā tenuissima *cauda*
dēsinit in piscem, *falcātō verberat ēnse.*
Bēlua *pūniceō mixtōs* cum sanguine *fluctūs*
ōre *vomit*: *maduere** gravēs *adspergine pennae.*
Nec *bibulīs* ultrā *Perseus tālāribus* ausus
crēdere cōnspēxit scopulum, quī *vertice* summō
stantibus *exstat* aquīs, *operītur* ab aequore motō.
*Nīxus eō rūpis*que tenēns *iuga* prīma sinistrā
ter quater exēgit repetīta per īlia ferrum.

Notes:

* l. 721, *modo: Modo* can also mean "now, just now"; note how it is repeated three times—a rhetorical figure called anaphora. In lines 725-26 there is a parallel repetition of nunc.
* *sublīmīs:* In poetry, the nominative and accusative plural of 3rd Declension masculine/feminine nouns can be either *-ēs* or *-īs.*
* l. 729, *maduere = maduērunt*

Glossary:

aper, -prī (m): wild boar
adspergō, -ginis (f): sprinkling, moisture
attollō, -ere, ——, ——: I lift/raise (up)
avidus, -a, -um: desirous, eager, greedy
bibulus, -a, -um: drinking, absorbent, soaked
cauda, -ae (f): tail (of an animal)
cavus, -a, -um: hollow, empty
circumsonus, -a, -um: making a loud noise roundabout, filled with noise/sound
concha, -ae (f): shellfish, mussel (shell)
cōnspiciō, -ere, -spēxī, -spectum: I observe, perceive, gaze at
costa, -ae (f): rib, side
dēsinō, -ere, -siī, -situm: I cease, end, stop
effugiō, -ere, -fūgī, ——: I flee away, escape
ēnsis, -is (m): sword
eō: there, in that place
exigō, -ere, -ēgī, -actum: I drive out, thrust out
exstō, -stāre, ——, ——: I stand out/above, project
īlia, -ium (n, pl): abdomen, belly
iugum, -ī (n): ridge, summit
falcātus, -a, -um: sickle-shaped, curved, hooked
ferōx, -ōcis: wild, fierce, ferocious
fluctus, -ūs (m): wave
laedō, -ere, -sī, -sum: I offend, grieve, injure
madescō, -ere, -uī, ——: I become wet/moist
misceō, -ēre, -uī, mixtum: I mix, mingle
morsus, -ūs (m): bite, biting
nītor, -ī, nīxus sum (+abl.): I lean/press upon
obserō, -ere, -sēvī, -situm: I cover over, plant
operiō, -īre, -uī, -pertum: I cover (over), hide
pateō, -ēre, -uī, ——: I am open/exposed, lie open
penna, -ae (f): feather; in pl., wing(s)
Perseus, -eī (m): Perseus
pūniceus, -a, -um: red(dish), purple, crimson
quā: where, in which place
quāque: where(so)ever, whithersoever
quater: four times
repetō, -ere, -īvī/iī, -ītum: I strike/attack again
rūpēs, -is (f): rock
scopulus, -ī (m): rock, cliff, crag
subdō, -ere, -didī, -ditum: I put/place under
sublīmis, -e: lofty, high, elevated
ter: three times, thrice
tālāria, -ium (n, pl): winged sandals/shoes; ankles
verberō (1): I whip, lash, scourge
versō (1): I turn, bend, twist
vertex, -ticis (m): top, highest point, whirlpool
vēlōx, -lōcis: fast, swift, quick
vomō, -ere, -uī, -itum: I vomit, spew

Lītora cum *plausū* clāmor superāsque deōrum
inplēvere* domōs. Gaudent *generum*que *salutant*
auxiliumque domūs *servatorem*que *fatentur*
*Cassiope Cepheus*que pater*; *resoluta catēnīs*
incēdit virgō, *pretium*que et causa labōris.
Ipse manus *haustā victricēs abluit* undā,
*anguiferum*que caput *dūra* nē *laedat harēna,*
mollit humum *foliīs* nātāsque sub aequore virgās
sternit et *inponit Phorcynidos* ōra* *Mēdusae.*
Virga *recēns bibula*que *etiamnum* vīva *medulla*
vim rapuit *mōnstrī tactū*que *indūruit* huius,
*percēpit*que nōvum *rāmīs* et *fronde rigōrem.*
At *pelagī nymphae factum* mīrābile temptant
plūribus in virgīs et idem *contingere* gaudent;
*sēmina*que ex illīs *iterant iactāta* per undās—
nunc quoque *cūraliīs* eadem *nātūra remansit,*
dūritiam tactō capiant ut ab *āere* quodque
vīmen in aequore erat, fīat super aequora saxum.*

Notes:

* l. 736, *inplēvere = inplēvērunt* [which also = *implēvērunt*]

* ll. 736-38, *Cassiope Cepheusque pater* are the subjects of *gaudent, salutant,* and *fatentur.*

* l. 743, *ōra: ōs* can also mean "head, face"

* ll. 750-52: This is an example of an etiological myth, a story explaining the origin of something (in this case, where coral comes from).

Glossary:

abluō, -ere, -uī, -ūtum: I wash (off/away), cleanse
āēr, āēris (m): air, atmosphere
anguifer, -fera, -ferum: serpent-bearing
bibulus, -a, -um: drinking, absorbent, soaked
Cassiōpē, -ēs (f): Cassiopeia, mother of Andromeda
catēna, -ae (f): chain, fetter, shackle
Cēpheus, -eī (m): Cepheus, king of Ethiopia and father of Andromeda
contingō, -ere, -tigī, -tactum: I touch, take hold of
cūralium, -iī (n): coral
dūritia, -ae (f): hardness
dūrus, -a, -um: hard, rough
etiamnum: even now, till now, yet
factum, -ī (n): deed, act [noun from *faciō*]
fateor, -ērī, fāssus sum: I confess, acknowledge
folium, -iī (n): leaf
frōns, -ndis (f): foliage, leafy branch
gener, -erī (m): son-in-law, daughter's husband
harēna, -ae (f): sand
hauriō, -īre, hausī, haustum: I draw, drink up
iactō (1): I throw/toss (about), scatter
incēdō, -ere, -cessī, -cessum: I come forth/to
indūrescō, -ere, -dūruī, ——: I harden, become hard
inpōnō (imp-), -ere, -posuī, -positum: I put/lay upon
iterō (1): I repeat, do a second time
laedō, -ere, -sī, -sum: I offend, grieve, injure
medulla, -ae (f): marrow, innermost part
Mēdusa, -ae (f): Medusa
molliō, -īre, -īvī/-iī, -ītum: I soften
mōnstrum, -ī (n): monster, monstrosity; omen
nātūra, -ae (f): nature
nympha, -ae (f): nymph, a demigoddess of waters, forests, or mountains
pelagus, -ī (n): the (open) sea
percipiō, -ere, -cēpī, -ceptum: I seize (entirely), occupy, possess
Phorcȳnis, -idis/-idos (f): daughter of Phorcus (i.e., Medusa)
plausus, -ūs (m): clapping, applause
pretium, -iī (n): price, worth, reward
rāmus, -ī (m): branch, twig, bough
recēns, -ntis: recent, fresh, young
remaneō, -ēre, -mansī, -mansum: I stay, remain (behind)
resolvō, -ere, -solvī, -solūtum: I loose(n), untie
rigor, -ōris (m): rigor, stiffness, hardness
salūtō (1): I salute, hail, greet
sēmen, -minis (n): seed
servātor, -tōris (m): savior, deliverer
tactus, -ūs (m): touch, touching, feeling
victrix, -tricis: conquering, victorious
vīmen, -minis (n): pliant/flexible twig

Dīs* tribus ille *focōs totidem* dē *caespite* ponit,
laevum Mercuriō, dextrum tibi, *bellica* virgō*,
āra *Iovis* media est; *mactātur vacca Minervae*,
ālipedī *vitulus*, taurus tibi, summe deōrum.
Prōtinus Andromedan et tantī *praemia factī*
indōtāta rapit. *Taedās Hymenaeus* Amorque*
praecutiunt; *largīs satiantur odōribus* ignēs,
*serta*que *dependent tectīs* et *ubīquē lyrae*que
tībiaque et cantūs, animī fēlīcia laetī
argūmenta, *sonant*. *Reserātīs* aurea *valvīs*
ātria tōta *patent*, pulchrōque *instructa paratū*
Cēphēnī procerēs ineunt convīvia rēgis.

Notes:

* l. 753, *dīs* = *deīs*; these are the three gods who helped Perseus defeat Medusa

* l. 754, *bellica virgō* = Minerva (Roman name for Athena)

* l. 758, *Amorque*: Here amor is personified (and deified) as Love or Cupid.

Glossary:

ālipēs, -pedis: wing-footed, swift
Andromeda, -ae (acc. -an) (f): Andromeda, daughter of Cepheus and Cassiopeia
āra, -ae (f): altar
argūmentum, -ī (n): argument, proof, evidence
bellicus, -a, -um: warlike, of/pertaining to war
caespes, -pitis (m): turf, sod, grass
Cēphēnus, -a, -um: Cephenian, Ethiopian
dēpendeō, -ēre, ——, ——: I hang down/from
factum, -ī (n): deed, act [noun from *faciō*]
focus, -ī (m): fireplace, hearth, altar
Hymenaeus, -ī (m): Hymen, god of marriage
indōtātus, -a, -um: without dowry, portionless
instruō, -ere, -strūxī, -strūctum: I set up, prepare, arrange
Iuppiter (Iūpp-), Iovis (m): Jupiter, Jove
laevus, -a, -um: left
largus, -a, -um: large, plentiful, abundant
lyra, -ae (f): lyre, lute
mactō (1): I offer, sacrifice
Mercurius, -iī (m): Mercury, messenger god
Minerva, -ae (f): Minerva (Athena), goddess of wisdom
odor, -dōris (m): odor, scent, smell
parātus, -ūs (m): preparation, provision
pateō, -ēre, -uī, ——: I am open/exposed, lie open
praecutiō, -ere, ——, ——: I wave/brandish before
praemium, -iī (n): reward, profit
procer, -eris (m, usu. pl.): prince, noble, chief
prōtinus (adv.): immediately, forthwith
reserō (1): I unbolt, open
satiō (1): I satisfy, fill
sertum, -ī (n): garland, flower wreath
sonō, -āre, -uī, -itum: I sound, resound
taeda, -ae (f): a pine torch, nuptial torch
taurus, -ī (m): bull, ox
tectum, -ī (n): roof, dwelling
tībia, -ae (f): pipe, flute; shin(-bone)
totidem (indecl. adj.): just so many, just as many
ubīquē: everywhere
vacca, -ae (f): cow
valva, -ae (f): (folding) door
vitulus, -ī (m): (bull-)calf

APPENDICES

- Appendix A: Chant Charts
- Appendix B: Latin to English Glossary
- Appendix C: English to Latin Glossary
- Appendix D: Sources and Helps
- Appendix E: Verb Formation Chart

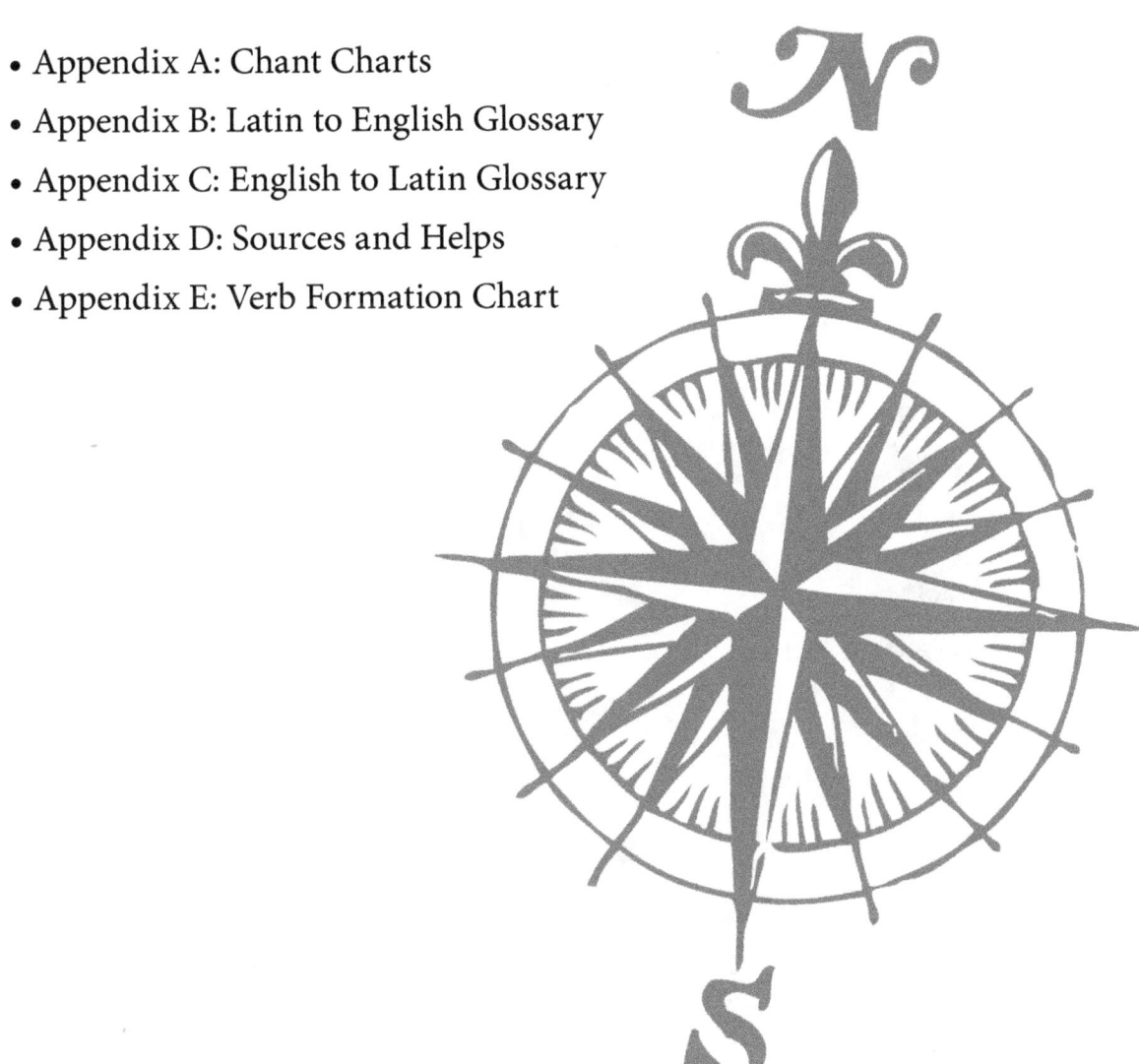

APPENDIX A

Chant Charts

Verbs

Indicative

Present Active Indicative Verb Endings (*KL1,* Lesson 1)

	LATIN SINGULAR	ENGLISH SINGULAR	LATIN PLURAL	LATIN PLURAL
1ST	-ō	I am ***verbing***, I ***verb***	-mus	we are ***verbing***
2ND	-s	you are ***verbing***	-tis	you all are ***verbing***
3RD	-t	he/she/it is ***verbing***	-nt	they are ***verbing***

Present Passive Indicative Verb Endings (*KL1,* Lesson 20)

	LATIN SINGULAR	ENGLISH SINGULAR	LATIN PLURAL	ENGLISH PLURAL
1ST	-r	I am (being) ***verbed***	-mur	we are (being) ***verbed***
2ND	-ris	you are (being) ***verbed***	-minī	you (pl.) are (being) ***verbed***
3RD	-tur	he/she/it is (being) ***verbed***	-ntur	they are being ***verbed***

Imperfect Active Indicative Verb Endings (*KL1,* Lesson 6)

	LATIN SINGULAR	LATIN PLURAL	ENGLISH SINGULAR	ENGLISH PLURAL
1ST	-bam	I was ***verbing***	-bāmus	we were ***verbing***
2ND	-bās	you were ***verbing***	-bātis	you all were ***verbing***
3RD	-bat	he/she/it was ***verbing***	-bant	they were ***verbing***

Imperfect Passive Indicative Verb Endings (*KL1,* Lesson 20)

	LATIN SINGULAR	ENGLISH SINGULAR	LATIN PLURAL	ENGLISH PLURAL
1ST	-ba**r**	I was (being) ***verbed***	-bā**mur**	we were (being) ***verbed***
2ND	-bā**ris**	you were (being) ***verbed***	-bā**minī**	you (pl.) were (being) ***verbed***
3RD	-bā**tur**	he/she/it was (being) ***verbed***	-ban**tur**	they were (being) ***verbed***

Future Active Indicative Verb Endings (*KL1,* Lesson 6)

	LATIN SINGULAR	ENGLISH SINGULAR	LATIN PLURAL	ENGLISH PLURAL
1ST	-bō	I will ***verb***	-bimus	we will ***verb***
2ND	-bis	you will ***verb***	-bitis	you all will ***verb***
3RD	-bit	he/she/it will ***verb***	-bunt	they will ***verb***

Future Passive Indicative Verb Endings (*KL1*, Lesson 20)

	LATIN SINGULAR	ENGLISH SINGULAR	LATIN PLURAL	ENGLISH PLURAL
1ST	-bor	I will be ***verbed***	-bimur	we will be ***verbed***
2ND	-beris	you will be ***verbed***	-biminī	you (pl.) will be ***verbed***
3RD	-bitur	he/she/it will be ***verbed***	-buntur	they will be ***verbed***

Perfect Active Indicative Verb Endings (*KL1*, Lesson 14)

	LATIN SINGULAR	ENGLISH SINGULAR	LATIN PLURAL	ENGLISH PLURAL
1ST	-ī	I ***verbed***, have ***verbed***	-imus	we ***verbed***, have ***verbed***
2ND	-istī	you ***verbed***, have verbed	-istis	you (pl.) ***verbed***, have ***verbed***
3RD	-it	he/she/it ***verbed***, has ***verbed***	-ērunt	they ***verbed***, have ***verbed***

Perfect Passive Indicative (*KL1*, Lesson 22, p. 330)

	LATIN SINGULAR	ENGLISH SINGULAR	LATIN PLURAL	ENGLISH PLURAL
1ST	4th principal part (sg.) + sum	I was/have been ***verbed***	4th p.p. (pl.) + sumus	we were/have been ***verbed***
2ND	4th p.p. (sg.) + ēs	you were/have been ***verbed***	4th p.p. (pl.) + estis	you (pl.) were/have been ***verbed***
3RD	4th p.p. (sg.) + est	he/she/it was/has been ***verbed***	4th p.p. (pl.) + sunt	they were/have been ***verbed***

Pluperfect Active Indicative Verb Endings (*KL1*, Lesson 15)

	LATIN SINGULAR	ENGLISH SINGULAR	LATIN PLURAL	ENGLISH PLURAL
1ST	-eram	I had ***verbed***	-erāmus	we had ***verbed***
2ND	-erās	you had ***verbed***	-erātis	you (pl.) had ***verbed***
3RD	-erat	he/she/it had ***verbed***	-erant	they had ***verbed***

Pluperfect Passive Indicative (*KL1*, Lesson 22)

	LATIN SINGULAR	ENGLISH SINGULAR	LATIN PLURAL	ENGLISH PLURAL
1ST	4th principal part (sg.) + eram	I had been ***verbed***	4th p.p. (pl.) + erāmus	we had been ***verbed***
2ND	4th p.p. (sg.) + erās	you had been ***verbed***	4th p.p. (pl.) + erātis	you (pl.) had been ***verbed***
3RD	4th p.p. (sg.) + erat	he/she/it had been ***verbed***	4th p.p. (pl.) + erant	they had been ***verbed***

Future Perfect Active Indicative Verb Endings (*KL1*, Lesson 15)

	LATIN SINGULAR	ENGLISH SINGULAR	LATIN PLURAL	ENGLISH PLURAL
1ST	-erō	I will have ***verbed***	-erimus	we will have ***verbed***
2ND	-eris	you will have ***verbed***	-eritis	you (pl.) will have ***verbed***
3RD	-erit	he/she/it will have ***verbed***	-erint	they will have ***verbed***

Future Perfect Passive Indicative (*KL1*, Lesson 22)

	LATIN SINGULAR	ENGLISH SINGULAR	LATIN PLURAL	ENGLISH PLURAL
1ST	4th principal part (sg.) + erō	I will have been ***verbed***	4th p.p. (pl.) + erimus	we will have been ***verbed***
2ND	4th p.p. (sg.) + eris	you will have been ***verbed***	4th p.p. (pl.) + eritis	you (pl.) will have been ***verbed***
3RD	4th p.p. (sg.) + erit	he/she/it will have been ***verbed***	4th p.p. (pl.) + erunt	they will have been ***verbed***

Imperative

Present Active and Passive Imperative Endings (*KL1*, Lesson. 11; *KL2*, Lesson 6)

	ACTIVE		PASSIVE	
	LATIN	ENGLISH	LATIN	ENGLISH
SING.	present stem	***verb***!	present stem + ***-re***	Be ***verb***ed!
PLUR.	present stem + ***-te***	***verb***! (pl.)	present stem + ***-minī***	Be ***verb***ed! (pl.)

Participle

(*KL2*, Lesson 10)

	ACTIVE LATIN	ACTIVE ENGLISH	PASSIVE LATIN	PASSIVE ENGLISH
PRES.	-ns, -ntis	*verb*-ing		
PF.			4th principal part	*verb*-ed, having been *verb*-ed
FUT.	4th p. p. stem + -ūrus, -ūra, -ūrum	about to *verb*	pres. stem + -ndus, -nda, -ndum	(about) to be *verbed*-ed

Infinitive

(*KL3*, Lesson 1)

	INFINITIVE			
	LATIN ACTIVE	ENGLISH ACTIVE	LATIN PASSIVE	ENGLISH PASSIVE
PRES.	-re (2nd p.p.)	to ***verb***	-rī/-ī	to be ***verbed***
PF.	perf. stem + -isse	to have ***verbed***	4th p.p. + esse	to have been ***verbed***
FUT.	fut. act. prt. + esse	to be about to ***verb***	(uncommon)	

Subjunctive

Present Active Subjunctive Endings (*KL3*, Lesson 4)

	LATIN SINGULAR	ENGLISH SINGULAR	LATIN PLURAL	ENGLISH PLURAL
1ST	stem vowel change + *-m*	[depends on context]	stem vowel change + ***-mus***	[depends on context]
2ND	stem vowel change + *-s*	[depends on context]	stem vowel change + ***-tis***	[depends on context]
3RD	stem vowel change + *-t*	[depends on context]	stem vowel change + ***-nt***	[depends on context]

Present Passive Subjunctive Endings (*KL1*, Lesson 4)

	LATIN SINGULAR	ENGLISH SINGULAR	LATIN PLURAL	ENGLISH PLURAL
1ST	stem vowel change + *-r*	[depends on context]	stem vowel change + *-mur*	[depends on context]
2ND	stem vowel change + *-ris*	[depends on context]	stem vowel change + *-minī*	[depends on context]
3RD	stem vowel change + *-tur*	[depends on context]	stem vowel change + *-ntur*	[depends on context]

Imperfect Active Subjunctive Endings (*KL1*, Lesson 5)

	LATIN SINGULAR	ENGLISH SINGULAR	LATIN PLURAL	ENGLISH PLURAL
1ST	present active infinitive + *-m*	[depends on context]	present active infinitive + *-mus*	[depends on context]
2ND	present active infinitive + *-s*	[depends on context]	present active infinitive + *-tis*	[depends on context]
3RD	present active infinitive + *-t*	[depends on context]	present active infinitive + *-nt*	[depends on context]

Imperfect Passive Subjunctive Endings (*KL1*, Lesson 5)

	LATIN SINGULAR	ENGLISH SINGULAR	LATIN PLURAL	ENGLISH PLURAL
1ST	present active infinitive + *-r*	[depends on context]	present active infinitive + *-mur*	[depends on context]
2ND	present active infinitive + *-ris*	[depends on context]	present active infinitive + *-minī*	[depends on context]
3RD	present active infinitive + *-tur*	[depends on context]	present active infinitive + *-ntur*	[depends on context]

Perfect Active Subjunctive Endings (*KL1*, Lesson 6)

	LATIN SINGULAR	ENGLISH SINGULAR	LATIN PLURAL	ENGLISH PLURAL
1ST	perfect active stem + *-eri-* + *-m*	[depends on context]	perfect active stem + *-eri-* + *-mus*	[depends on context]
2ND	perfect active stem + *-eri-* + *-s*	[depends on context]	perfect active stem + *-eri-* + *-tis*	[depends on context]
3RD	perfect active stem + *-eri-* + *-t*	[depends on context]	perfect active stem + *-eri-* + *-nt*	[depends on context]

Perfect Passive Subjunctive Endings (*KL1*, Lesson 6)

	LATIN SINGULAR	ENGLISH SINGULAR	LATIN PLURAL	ENGLISH PLURAL
1ST	perfect passive participle + *sim*	[depends on context]	perfect passive participle + *sīmus*	[depends on context]
2ND	perfect passive participle + *sīs*	[depends on context]	perfect passive participle + *sītis*	[depends on context]
3RD	perfect passive participle + *sit*	[depends on context]	perfect passive participle + *sint*	[depends on context]

Pluperfect Active Subjunctive Endings (*KL1*, Lesson 6)

	LATIN SINGULAR	ENGLISH SINGULAR	LATIN PLURAL	ENGLISH PLURAL
1ST	perfect active stem + *-isse-* + *-m*	[depends on context]	perfect active stem + *-isse-* + *-mus*	[depends on context]
2ND	perfect active stem + *-isse-* + *-s*	[depends on context]	perfect active stem + *-isse-* + *-tis*	[depends on context]
3RD	perfect active stem + *-isse-* + *-t*	[depends on context]	perfect active stem + *-isse-* + *-nt*	[depends on context]

Pluperfect Passive Subjunctive Endings (*KL1*, Lesson 6)

	LATIN SINGULAR	ENGLISH SINGULAR	LATIN PLURAL	ENGLISH PLURAL
1ST	perfect passive participle + *essem*	[depends on context]	perfect passive participle + *essēmus*	[depends on context]
2ND	perfect passive participle + *essēs*	[depends on context]	perfect passive participle + *essētis*	[depends on context]
3RD	perfect passive participle + *esset*	[depends on context]	perfect passive participle + *essent*	[depends on context]

Verb Chants, applied to *amō, videō, dūcō, capiō,* and *audiō*

1st Conjugation: *amō, amāre, amāvī, amātum*
2nd Conjugation: *videō, vidēre, vīdī, vīsum*
3rd Conjugation: *dūcō, dūcere, dūxī, ductum*
3rd -iō Conjugation: *capiō, capere, cēpī, captum*
4th Conjugation: *audiō, audīre, audīvī, audītum*

Indicative

	1ST	2ND	3RD	3RD -iō	4TH
PRESENT ACTIVE	am**ō**	vide**ō**	dūc**ō**	capi**ō**	audi**ō**
	amā**s**	vidē**s**	dūci**s**	capi**s**	audī**s**
	ama**t**	vide**t**	dūci**t**	capi**t**	audi**t**
	amā**mus**	vidē**mus**	dūci**mus**	capi**mus**	audī**mus**
	amā**tis**	vidē**tis**	dūci**tis**	capi**tis**	audī**tis**
	ama**nt**	vide**nt**	dūcu**nt**	capiu**nt**	audiu**nt**
IMPERFECT ACTIVE	amā**bam**	vidē**bam**	dūcē**bam**	capiē**bam**	audiē**bam**
	amā**bās**	vidē**bās**	dūcē**bās**	capiē**bās**	audiē**bās**
	amā**bat**	vidē**bat**	dūcē**bat**	capiē**bat**	audiē**bat**
	amā**bāmus**	vidē**bāmus**	dūcē**bāmus**	capiē**bāmus**	audiē**bāmus**
	amā**bātis**	vidē**bātis**	dūcē**bātis**	capiē**bātis**	audiē**bātis**
	amā**bant**	vidē**bant**	dūcē**bant**	capiē**bant**	audiē**bant**
FUTURE ACTIVE	amā**bō**	vidē**bō**	dūca**m**	capia**m**	audia**m**
	amā**bis**	vidē**bis**	dūcē**s**	capiē**s**	audiē**s**
	amā**bit**	vidē**bit**	dūce**t**	capie**t**	audie**t**
	amā**bimus**	vidē**bimus**	dūcē**mus**	capiē**mus**	audiē**mus**
	amā**bitis**	vidē**bitis**	dūcē**tis**	capiē**tis**	audiē**tis**
	amā**bunt**	vidē**bunt**	dūce**nt**	capie**nt**	audie**nt**
PRESENT PASSIVE	am**or**	vide**or**	dūc**or**	capi**or**	audi**or**
	amā**ris**	vidē**ris**	dūce**ris**	cape**ris**	audī**ris**
	amā**tur**	vidē**tur**	dūci**tur**	capi**tur**	audi**tur**
	amā**mur**	vidē**mur**	dūci**mur**	capi**mur**	audī**mur**
	amā**minī**	vidē**minī**	dūci**minī**	capi**minī**	audī**minī**
	ama**ntur**	vide**ntur**	dūcu**ntur**	capiu**ntur**	audiu**ntur**

IMPERFECT PASSIVE	amā**bar**	vidē**bar**	dūcē**bar**	capiē**bar**	audiē**bar**
	amā**bāris**	vidē**bāris**	dūcē**bāris**	capiē**bāris**	audiē**bāris**
	amā**bātur**	vidē**bātur**	dūcē**bātur**	capiē**bātur**	audiē**bātur**
	amā**bāmur**	vidē**bāmur**	dūcē**bāmur**	capiē**bāmur**	audiē**bāmur**
	amā**bāminī**	vidē**bāminī**	dūcē**bāminī**	capiē**bāminī**	audiē**bāminī**
	amā**bantur**	vidē**bantur**	dūcē**bantur**	capiē**bantur**	audiē**bantur**
FUTURE PASSIVE	amā**bor**	vidē**bor**	dūca**r**	capia**r**	audia**r**
	amā**beris**	vidē**beris**	dūcē**ris**	capiē**ris**	audiē**ris**
	amā**bitur**	vidē**bitur**	dūcē**tur**	capiē**tur**	audiē**tur**
	amā**bimur**	vidē**bimur**	dūcē**mur**	capiē**mur**	audiē**mur**
	amā**biminī**	vidē**biminī**	dūcē**minī**	capiē**minī**	audiē**minī**
	amā**buntur**	vidē**buntur**	dūce**ntur**	capie**ntur**	audie**ntur**
PERFECT ACTIVE	amāv**ī**	vīd**ī**	dūx**ī**	cēp**ī**	audīv**ī**
	amāv**istī**	vīd**istī**	dūx**istī**	cēp**istī**	audīv**istī**
	amāv**it**	vīd**it**	dūx**it**	cēp**it**	audīv**it**
	amāv**imus**	vīd**imus**	dūx**imus**	cēp**imus**	audīv**imus**
	amāv**istis**	vīd**istis**	dūx**istis**	cēp**istis**	audīv**istis**
	amāv**ērunt**	vīd**ērunt**	dūx**ērunt**	cēp**ērunt**	audīv**ērunt**
PLUPERFECT ACTIVE	amāv**eram**	vīd**eram**	dūx**eram**	cēp**eram**	audīv**eram**
	amāv**erās**	vīd**erās**	dūx**erās**	cēp**erās**	audīv**erās**
	amāv**erat**	vīd**erat**	dūx**erat**	cēp**erat**	audīv**erat**
	amāv**erāmus**	vīd**erāmus**	dūx**erāmus**	cēp**erāmus**	audīv**erāmus**
	amāv**erātis**	vīd**erātis**	dūx**erātis**	cēp**erātis**	audīv**erātis**
	amāv**erant**	vīd**erant**	dūx**erant**	cēp**erant**	audīv**erant**
FUTURE PERFECT ACTIVE	amāv**erō**	vīd**erō**	dūx**erō**	cēp**erō**	audīv**erō**
	amāv**eris**	vīd**eris**	dūx**eris**	cēp**eris**	audīv**eris**
	amāv**erit**	vīd**erit**	dūx**erit**	cēp**erit**	audīv**erit**
	amāv**erimus**	vīd**erimus**	dūx**erimus**	cēp**erimus**	audīv**erimus**
	amāv**eritis**	vīd**eritis**	dūx**eritis**	cēp**eritis**	audīv**eritis**
	amāv**erint**	vīd**erint**	dūx**erint**	cēp**erint**	audīv**erint**
PERFECT PASSIVE	amāt**us sum**	vīs**us sum**	duct**us sum**	capt**us sum**	audīt**us sum**
	amāt**us ēs**	vīs**us ēs**	duct**us ēs**	capt**us ēs**	audīt**us ēs**
	amāt**us est**	vīs**us est**	duct**us est**	capt**us est**	audīt**us est**
	amāt**ī sumus**	vīs**ī sumus**	duct**ī sumus**	capt**ī sumus**	audīt**ī sumus**
	amāt**ī estis**	vīs**ī estis**	duct**ī estis**	capt**ī estis**	audīt**ī sumus**
	amāt**ī sunt**	vīs**ī sunt**	duct**ī sunt**	capt**ī sunt**	audīt**ī sunt**

PLUPERFECT PASSIVE	amāt**us eram**	vīs**us eram**	duct**us eram**	capt**us eram**	audīt**us eram**
	amāt**us erās**	vīs**us erās**	duct**us erās**	capt**us erās**	audīt**us erās**
	amāt**us erat**	vīs**us erat**	duct**us erat**	capt**us erat**	audīt**us erat**
	amāt**ī erāmus**	vīs**ī erāmus**	duct**ī erāmus**	capt**ī erāmus**	audīt**ī erāmus**
	amāt**ī erātis**	vīs**ī erātis**	duct**ī erātis**	capt**ī erātis**	audīt**ī erātis**
	amāt**ī erant**	vīs**ī erant**	duct**ī erant**	capt**ī erant**	audīt**ī erant**
FUT. PERFECT PASSIVE	amāt**us erō**	vīs**us erō**	duct**us erō**	capt**us erō**	audīt**us erō**
	amāt**us eris**	vīs**us eris**	duct**us eris**	capt**us eris**	audīt**us eris**
	amāt**us erit**	vīs**us erit**	duct**us erit**	capt**us erit**	audīt**us erit**
	amāt**ī erimus**	vīs**ī erimus**	duct**ī erimus**	capt**ī erimus**	audīt**ī erimus**
	amāt**ī eritis**	vīs**ī eritis**	duct**ī eritis**	capt**ī eritis**	audīt**ī eritis**
	amāt**ī erunt**	vīs**ī erunt**	duct**ī erunt**	capt**ī erunt**	audīt**ī erunt**

Imperative

		1ST	2ND	3RD	3RD -iō	4TH
ACT.	SING.	amā!	vidē!	dūc!*	cape!	audī!
	PLUR.	amāte!	vidēte!	dūcite!	capite!	audīte!
PASS.	SING.	amāre!	vidēre!	dūcere!	capere!	audīre!
	PLUR.	amāminī!	vidēminī!	dūciminī!	capiminī!	audīminī!

*The present active imperative of *dūcō* is slightly irregular since it drops the short *-e* that would appear on regular 3rd conjugation verbs (*agō* → *age!*, *mittō* → *mitte!* etc.). Other common verbs that are irregular in this form are *dīcō* → *dīc!* and *faciō* (a 3rd *-iō*) → *fac!*

Participle

		1ST	2ND	3RD	3RD -iō	4TH
ACT.	SING.	amāns	vidēns	dūcēns	capiēns	audiēns
	PLUR.	amātūrus	vīsūrus	ductūrus	captūrus	audītūrus
PASS.	SING.	amātus	vīsus	ductus	captus	audītus
	PLUR.	amandus	videndus	dūcendus	capiendus	audiendus

Infinitive

		1ST	2ND	3RD	3RD -iō	4TH
ACTIVE	PRES.	amāre	vidēre	dūcere	capere	audīre
	PF.	amāvisse	vīdisse	dūxisse	cēpisse	audīvisse
	FUT.	amātūrus esse	vīsūrus esse	ductūrus esse	captūrus esse	audītūrus esse
PASSIVE	PRES.	amārī	vidērī	dūcī	capī	audīrī
	PF.	amātus esse	vīsus esse	ductus esse	captus esse	audītus esse
	FUT.	(uncommon)				

Subjunctive

	1ST	2ND	3RD	3RD -iō	4TH
PRES. ACT. SUBJ.	amem	videam	dūcam	capiam	audiam
	amēs	videās	dūcās	capiās	audiās
	amet	videat	dūcat	capiat	audiat
	amēmus	videāmus	dūcāmus	capiāmus	audiāmus
	amētis	videātis	dūcātis	capiātis	audiātis
	ament	videant	dūcant	capiant	audiant
PRES. PASS. SUBJ.	amer	videar	dūcar	capiar	audiar
	amēris	videāris	dūcāris	capiāris	audiāris
	ametur	videatur	dūcātur	capiātur	audiātur
	amēmur	videāmur	dūcāmur	capiāmur	audiāmur
	amēminī	videāminī	dūcāminī	capiāminī	audiāminī
	amentur	videantur	dūcantur	capiantur	audiantur
IMP. ACT. SUBJ.	amārem	vidērem	dūcerem	caperem	audīrem
	amārēs	vidērēs	dūcerēs	caperēs	audīrēs
	amāret	vidēret	dūceret	caperet	audīret
	amārēmus	vidērēmus	dūcerēmus	caperēmus	audīrēmus
	amārētis	vidērētis	dūcerētis	caperētis	audīrētis
	amārent	vidērent	dūcerent	caperent	audīrent
IMP. PASS. SUBJ.	amārer	vidērer	dūcerer	caperer	audīrer
	amārēris	vidērēris	dūcerēris	caperēris	audīrēris
	amārētur	vidērētur	dūcerētur	caperētur	audīrētur
	amārēmur	vidērēmur	dūcerēmur	caperēmur	audīrēmur
	amārēminī	vidērēminī	dūcerēminī	caperēminī	audīrēminī
	amārentur	vidērentur	dūcerentur	caperentur	audīrentur
PERF. ACT. SUBJ.	amāverim	vīderim	dūxerim	cēperim	audīverim
	amāverīs	vīderīs	dūxerīs	cēperīs	audīverīs
	amāverit	vīderit	dūxerit	cēperit	audīverit
	amāverīmus	vīderīmus	dūxerīmus	cēperīmus	audīverīmus
	amāverītis	vīderītis	dūxerītis	cēperītis	audīverītis
	amāverint	vīderint	dūxerint	cēperint	audīverint
PERF. PASS. SUBJ.	amātus sim	vīsus sim	ductus sim	captus sim	audītus sim
	amātus sīs	vīsus sīs	ductus sīs	captus sīs	audītus sīs
	amātus sit	vīsus sit	ductus sit	captus sit	audītus sit
	amātī sīmus	vīsī sīmus	ductī sīmus	captī sīmus	audītī sīmus
	amātī sītis	vīsī sītis	ductī sītis	captī sītis	audītī sītis
	amātī sint	vīsī sint	ductī sint	captī sint	audītī sint

PLU. ACT. SUBJ.	amāvissem	vīdissem	dūxissem	cēpissem	audīverim
	amāvissēs	vīdissēs	dūxissēs	cēpissēs	audīverīs
	amāvisset	vīdisset	dūxisset	cēpisset	audīverit
	amāvissēmus	vīdissēmus	dūxissēmus	cēpissēmus	audīverīmus
	amāvissētis	vīdissētis	dūxissētis	cēpissētis	audīverītis
	amāvissent	vīdissent	dūxissent	cēpissent	audīverint
PLU. PASS. SUBJ.	amātus essem	vīsus essem	ductus essem	captus essem	audītus essem
	amātus essēs	vīsus essēs	ductus essēs	captus essēs	audītus essēs
	amātus esset	vīsus esset	ductus esset	captus esset	audītus esset
	amātī essēmus	vīsī essēmus	ductī essēmus	captī essēmus	audītī essēmus
	amātī essētis	vīsī essētis	ductī essētis	captī essētis	audītī essētis
	amātī essent	vīsī essent	ductī essent	captī essent	audītī essent

Deponent Verb Chants, applied to *cōnor, misereor, loquor, ēgredior,* and *mētior*

1st Conjugation: *cōnor, cōnārī, cōnātus sum*
2nd Conjugation: *misereor, miserērī, misertus sum*
3rd Conjugation: *loquor, loquī, locūtus sum*
3rd -iō Conjugation: *ēgredior, ēgredī, ēgressus sum*
4th Conjugation: *mētior, mētīrī, mēnsus sum*

Indicative

	1ST	2ND	3RD	3RD -iō	4TH
PRES. PASS. DEP. IND.	cōnor	misereor	loquor	ēgredior	mētior
	cōnāris	miserēris	loqueris	ēgrederis	mētīris
	cōnātur	miserētur	loquitur	ēgreditur	mētītur
	cōnāmur	miserēmur	loquimur	ēgredimur	mētīmur
	cōnāminī	miserēminī	loquiminī	ēgrediminī	mētīminī
	cōnantur	miserentur	loquuntur	ēgrediuntur	mētiuntur
IMP. PASS. DEP. IND.	cōnābar	miserēbar	loquēbar	ēgrediēbar	mētiēbar
	cōnābāris	miserēbāris	loquēbāris	ēgrediēbāris	mētiēbāris
	cōnābātur	miserēbātur	loquēbātur	ēgrediēbātur	mētiēbātur
	cōnābāmur	miserēbāmur	loquēbāmur	ēgrediēbāmur	mētiēbāmur
	cōnābāminī	miserēbāminī	loquēbāminī	ēgrediēbāminī	mētiēbāminī
	cōnābantur	miserēbantur	loquēbantur	ēgrediēbantur	mētiēbantur

FUT. PASS. DEP. IND.	cōnābor	miserēbor	loquar	ēgrediar	mētiar
	cōnāberis	miserēberis	loquēris	ēgrediēris	mētiēris
	cōnābitur	miserēbitur	loquētur	ēgrediētur	mētiētur
	cōnābimur	miserēbimur	loquēmur	ēgrediēmur	mētiēmur
	cōnābiminī	miserēbiminī	loquēminī	ēgrediēminī	mētiēminī
	cōnābuntur	miserēbuntur	loquentur	ēgredientur	mētientur
PERF. PASS. DEP. IND.	cōnātus sum	misertus sum	locūtus sum	ēgressus sum	mēnsus sum
	cōnātus ēs	misertus ēs	locūtus ēs	ēgressus ēs	mēnsus ēs
	cōnātus est	misertus est	locūtus est	ēgressus est	mēnsus est
	cōnātī sumus	misertī sumus	locūtī sumus	ēgressī sumus	mēnsī sumus
	cōnātī estis	misertī estis	locūtī estis	ēgressī estis	mēnsī estis
	cōnātī sunt	misertī sunt	locūtī sunt	ēgressī sunt	mēnsī sunt
PLU. PASS. DEP. IND.	cōnātus eram	misertus eram	locūtus eram	ēgressus eram	mēnsus eram
	cōnātus erās	misertus erās	locūtus erās	ēgressus erās	mēnsus erās
	cōnātus erat	misertus erat	locūtus erat	ēgressus erat	mēnsus erat
	cōnātī erāmus	misertī erāmus	locūtī erāmus	ēgressī erāmus	mēnsī erāmus
	cōnātī erātis	misertī erātis	locūtī erātis	ēgressī erātis	mēnsī erātis
	cōnātī erant	misertī erant	locūtī erant	ēgressī erant	mēnsī erant
FUT. PERF. PASS. DEP. IND.	cōnātus erō	misertus erō	locūtus erō	ēgressus erō	mēnsus erō
	cōnātus eris	misertus eris	locūtus eris	ēgressus eris	mēnsus eris
	cōnātus erit	misertus erit	locūtus erit	ēgressus erit	mēnsus erit
	cōnātī erimus	misertī erimus	locūtī erimus	ēgressī erimus	mēnsī erimus
	cōnātī eritis	misertī eritis	locūtī eritis	ēgressī eritis	mēnsī eritis
	cōnātī erunt	misertī erunt	locūtī erunt	ēgressī erunt	mēnsī erunt

Imperative

		1ST	2ND	3RD	3RD -iō	4TH
PASS.	SING.	cōnāre!	miserēre!	loquere!	ēgredere!	mēnsīre!
	PLUR.	cōnāminī!	miserēminī!	loquiminī!	ēgrediminī!	mēnsīminī!

Participle

		1ST	2ND	3RD	3RD -iō	4TH
ACT.	PRES.	amāns	vidēns	dūcēns	capiēns	audiēns
	FUT.	amātūrus	vīsūrus	ductūrus	captūrus	audītūrus
PASS.	PERF.	amātus	vīsus	ductus	captus	audītus
	FUT.	amandus	videndus	dūcendus	capiendus	audiendus

Infinitive

		1ST	2ND	3RD	3RD -iō	4TH
ACT.	FUT.	cōnātūrus esse	misertūrus esse	locūtūrus esse	ēgressūrus esse	mēnsūrus esse
PASS. DEP.	PRES.	cōnārī	miserērī	loquī	ēgressī	mētīrī
	PERF.	cōnātus esse	misertus esse	locūtus esse	ēgressus esse	mēnsus esse

Subjunctive

	1ST	2ND	3RD	3RD -iō	4TH
PRES. PASS. DEP. SUBJ.	cōner	miserear	loquar	ēgrediar	mētiar
	cōnēris	misereāris	loquāris	ēgrediāris	mētiāris
	cōnētur	misereātur	loquātur	ēgrediātur	mētiātur
	cōnēmur	misereāmur	loquāmur	ēgrediāmur	mētiāmur
	cōnēminī	misereāminī	loquāminī	ēgrediāminī	mētiāminī
	cōnentur	misereantur	loquantur	ēgrediantur	mētiantur
IMP. PASS. DEP. SUBJ.	cōnārer	miserērer	loquerer	ēgrederer	metīrer
	cōnārēris	miserērēris	loquerēris	ēgrederēris	metīrēris
	cōnārētur	miserērētur	loquerētur	ēgrederētur	metīrētur
	cōnārēmur	miserērēmur	loquerēmur	ēgrederēmur	metīrēmur
	cōnārēminī	miserērēminī	loquerēminī	ēgrederēminī	metīrēminī
	cōnārentur	miserērentur	loquerentur	ēgrederentur	metīrentur
PERF. PASS. DEP. SUBJ.	cōnātus sim	misertus sim	locūtus sim	ēgressus sim	mēnsus sim
	cōnātus sīs	misertus sīs	locūtus sīs	ēgressus sīs	mēnsus sīs
	cōnātus sit	misertus sit	locūtus sit	ēgressus sit	mēnsus sit
	cōnātī sīmus	misertī sīmus	locūtī sīmus	ēgressī sīmus	mēnsī sīmus
	cōnātī sītis	misertī sītis	locūtī sītis	ēgressī sītis	mēnsī sītis
	cōnātī sint	misertī sint	locūtī sint	ēgressī sint	mēnsī sint
PLU. PASS. DEP. SUBJ.	cōnātus essem	misertus essem	locūtus essem	ēgressus essem	mēnsus essem
	cōnātus essēs	misertus essēs	locūtus essēs	ēgressus essēs	mēnsus essēs
	cōnātus esset	misertus esset	locūtus esset	ēgressus esset	mēnsus esset
	cōnātī essēmus	misertī essēmus	locūtī essēmus	ēgressī essēmus	mēnsī essēmus
	cōnātī essētis	misertī essētis	locūtī essētis	ēgressī essētis	mēnsī essētis
	cōnātī essent	misertī essent	locūtī essent	ēgressī essent	mēnsī essent

Irregular Verbs *sum, possum, eō, volō, nōlō, mālō*

sum, esse, fuī, futūrum
possum, posse, potuī, ——
eō, īre, iī (īvī), itum
volō, velle, voluī, ——
nōlō, nōlle, nōluī, ——
mālō, mālle, māluī, ——

Indicative

	SUM	POSSUM	EŌ	VOLŌ	NŌLŌ	MĀLŌ
PRES. ACT. IND.	sum	possum	eō	volō	nōlō	mālō
	ēs	potēs	is	vīs	nōn vīs	māvīs
	est	potest	it	vult	nōn vult	māvult
	sumus	possumus	īmus	volumus	nōlumus	mālumus
	estis	potestis	ītis	vultis	nōn vultis	māvultis
	sunt	possunt	eunt	volunt	nōlunt	mālunt
IMP. ACT. IND.	eram	poteram	ībam	volēbam	nōlēbam	mālēbam
	erās	poterās	ībās	volēbās	nōlēbās	mālēbās
	erat	poterat	ībat	volēbat	nōlēbat	mālēbat
	erāmus	poterāmus	ībāmus	volēbāmus	nōlēbāmus	mālēbāmus
	erātis	poterātis	ībātis	volēbātis	nōlēbātis	mālēbātis
	erant	poterant	ībant	volēbant	nōlēbant	mālēbant
FUT. ACT. IND.	erō	poterō	ībō	volam	nōlam	mālam
	eris	poteris	ībis	volēs	nōlēs	mālēs
	erit	poterit	ībit	volet	nōlet	mālet
	erimus	poterimus	ībimus	volēmus	nōlēmus	mālēmus
	eritis	poteritis	ībitis	volētis	nōlētis	mālētis
	erunt	poterint	ībunt	volent	nōlent	mālent
PERF. ACT. IND.	fuī	potuī	iī (īvī)	voluī	nōluī	māluī
	fuistī	potuistī	īstī	voluistī	nōluistī	māluistī
	fuit	potuit	iit	voluit	nōluit	māluit
	fuimus	potuimus	iimus	voluimus	nōluimus	māluimus
	fuistis	potuistis	īstis	voluistis	nōluistis	māluistis
	fuērunt	potuērunt	iērunt	voluērunt	nōluērunt	māluērunt

PLU. ACT. IND.	fueram	potueram	ieram	volueram	nōlueram	mālueram
	fuerās	potuerās	ierās	voluerās	nōluerās	māluerās
	fuerat	potuerat	ierat	voluerat	nōluerat	māluerat
	fuerāmus	potuerāmus	ierāmus	voluerāmus	nōluerāmus	māluerāmus
	fuerātis	potuerātis	ierātis	voluerātis	nōluerātis	māluerātis
	fuerant	potuerant	ierant	voluerant	nōluerant	māluerant
FUT. PERF. ACT. IND.	fuerō	potuerō	ierō	voluerō	nōluerō	māluerō
	fueris	potueris	ieris	volueris	nōlueris	mālueris
	fuerit	potuerit	ierit	voluerit	nōluerit	māluerit
	fuerimus	potuerimus	ierimus	voluerimus	nōluerimus	māluerimus
	fueritis	potueritis	ieritis	volueritis	nōlueritis	mālueritis
	fuerint	potuerint	ierint	voluerint	nōluerint	māluerint

Imperative

		SUM	POSSUM	EŌ	VOLŌ	NŌLŌ	MĀLŌ
ACT.	SING.	es!	——	ī!	——	nōlī!	——
	PL.	este!	——	īte!	——	nōlīte!	——

Participle

		SUM	POSSUM	EŌ	VOLŌ	NŌLŌ	MĀLŌ
ACT.	PRES.	——	potēns	iēns, ***gen.*** euntis	volēns	nōlēns	——
	FUT.	fūtūrus	——	itūrus	——	——	——
PASS.	PERF.	——	——	itum	——	——	——
	FUT.	——	——	eundus	——	——	——

Infinitive

		SUM	POSSUM	EŌ	VOLŌ	NŌLŌ	MĀLŌ
ACT.	PRES.	esse	posse	īre	velle	nōlle	mālle
	PERF.	fuisse	potuisse	īsse	voluisse	nōluisse	māluisse
	FUT.	futūrus esse (*or* fore)	——	itūrus esse	——	——	——

Subjunctive

	SUM	POSSUM	EŌ	VOLŌ	NŌLŌ	MĀLŌ
PRES. ACT. SUBJ.	sim	possim	eam	velim	nōlim	mālim
	sīs	possīs	eās	velīs	nōlīs	mālīs
	sit	possit	eat	velit	nōlit	mālit
	sīmus	possīmus	eāmus	velīmus	nōlīmus	mālīmus
	sītis	possītis	eātis	velītis	nōlītis	mālītis
	sint	possint	eant	velint	nōlint	mālint
IMP. ACT. SUBJ.	essem	possem	īrem	vellem	nōllem	māllem
	essēs	possēs	īrēs	vellēs	nōllēs	māllēs
	esset	posset	īret	vellet	nōllet	māllet
	essēmus	possēmus	īrēmus	vellēmus	nōllēmus	māllēmus
	essētis	possētis	īrētis	vellētis	nōllētis	māllētis
	essent	possent	īrent	vellent	nōllent	māllent
PERF. ACT. SUBJ.	fuerim	potuerim	ierim	voluerim	nōluerim	māluerim
	fuerīs	potuerīs	ierīs	voluerīs	nōluerīs	māluerīs
	fuerit	potuerit	ierit	voluerit	nōluerit	māluerit
	fuerīmus	potuerīmus	ierīmus	voluerīmus	nōluerīmus	māluerīmus
	fuerītis	potuerītis	ierītis	voluerītis	nōluerītis	māluerītis
	fuerint	potuerint	ierint	voluerint	nōluerint	māluerint
PLU. ACT. SUBJ.	fuissem	potuissem	īssem	voluissem	nōluissem	māluissem
	fuissēs	potuissēs	īssēs	voluissēs	nōluissēs	māluissēs
	fuisset	potuisset	īsset	voluisset	nōluisset	māluisset
	fuissēmus	potuissēmus	īssēmus	voluissēmus	nōluissēmus	māluissēmus
	fuissētis	potuissētis	īssētis	voluissētis	nōluissētis	māluissētis
	fuissent	potuissent	īssent	voluissent	nōluissent	māluissent

Irregular Verb *ferō*

ferō, ferre, tulī, lātum

Indicative

	ACTIVE	PASSIVE
PRESENT	ferō	feror
	fers	ferris
	fert	fertur
	ferimus	ferimur
	fertis	feriminī
	ferunt	feruntur
IMPERFECT	ferēbam	ferēbar
	ferēbās	ferēbāris
	ferēbat	ferēbātur
	ferēbāmus	ferēbāmur
	ferēbātis	ferēbāminī
	ferēbant	ferēbantur
FUTURE	feram	ferar
	ferēs	ferēris
	feret	ferētur
	ferēmus	ferēmur
	ferētis	ferēminī
	ferent	ferentur

Imperative

	ACTIVE	PASSIVE
SG.	es!	——
PL.	este!	——

Infinitive

	ACTIVE	PASSIVE
PRES.	ferre	ferrī
PERF.	tulisse	lātus esse
FUT.	lātūrus esse	(uncommon)

Subjunctive

	ACTIVE	PASSIVE
PRESENT	feram	ferar
	ferās	ferāris
	ferat	ferātur
	ferāmus	ferāmur
	ferātis	ferāminī
	ferant	ferantur
IMPERFECT	ferrem	ferrer
	ferrēs	ferrēris
	ferret	ferrētur
	ferrēmus	ferrēmur
	ferrētis	ferrēminī
	ferrent	ferrentur

Nouns

First Declension (*KL1*, Lesson 2)

	ENDINGS		EXAMPLE NOUN	
	SINGULAR	PLURAL	SINGULAR	PLURAL
NOM.	-a	-ae	bēlua	bēluae
GEN.	-ae	-ārum	bēluae	bēluārum
DAT.	-ae	-īs	bēluae	bēluīs
ACC.	-am	-ās	bēluam	bēluās
ABL.	-ā	-īs	bēluā	bēluīs
VOC.	-a	-ae	bēlua	bēluae
LOC.	-ae	īs	[bēluae]*	[bēluīs]*

Second Declension Masculine (*KL1*, Lesson 4)

	ENDINGS		EXAMPLE NOUN	
	SINGULAR	PLURAL	SINGULAR	PLURAL
NOM.	-us/-r/-ius	-ī	mūrus	mūrī
GEN.	-ī	-ōrum	mūrī	mūrōrum
DAT.	-ō	-īs	mūrō	mūrīs
ACC.	-um	-ōs	mūrum	mūrōs
ABL.	-ō	-īs	mūrō	mūrīs
VOC.	-e/-r/-ī	-ī	mūre	mūrī
LOC.	-ī	-īs	[mūrī]*	[mūrīs]*

Second Declension Neuter (*KL1*, Lesson 5)

	ENDINGS		EXAMPLE NOUN	
	SINGULAR	PLURAL	SINGULAR	PLURAL
NOM.	-um	-a	fātum	fāta
GEN.	-ī	-ōrum	fātī	fātōrum
DAT.	-ō	-īs	fātō	fātīs
ACC.	-um	-a	fātum	fāta
ABL.	-ō	-īs	fātō	fātīs
VOC.	-um	-a	fātum	fāta
LOC.	-ī	-īs	[fātī]*	[fātīs]*

Third Declension Masculine/Feminine (*KL1*, Lesson 12)

	ENDINGS		EXAMPLE NOUN	
	SINGULAR	PLURAL	SINGULAR	PLURAL
NOM.	X	-ēs	clāmor	clāmorēs
GEN.	-is	-um	clāmoris	clāmorum
DAT.	-ī	-ibus	clāmorī	clāmoribus
ACC.	-em	-ēs	clāmorem	clāmorēs
ABL.	-e	-ibus	clāmore	clāmoribus
VOC.	X	-ēs	clāmor	clāmorēs
LOC.	-e	-ibus	[clāmore]*	[clāmoribus]*

Third Declension Neuter (*KL1*, Lesson 13)

	ENDINGS		EXAMPLE NOUN	
	SINGULAR	PLURAL	SINGULAR	PLURAL
NOM.	X	-a	genus	genera
GEN.	-is	-um	generis	generum
DAT.	-ī	-ibus	generī	generibus
ACC.	X	-a	genus	genera
ABL.	-e	-ibus	genere	generibus
VOC.	X	-a	genus	genera
LOC.	-e	-ibus	[genere]*	[generibus]*

Third Declension Masculine/Feminine i-Stem (*KL1*, Lesson 18)

	ENDINGS		EXAMPLE NOUN	
	SINGULAR	PLURAL	SINGULAR	PLURAL
NOM.	X	-ēs	collis	collēs
GEN.	-is	-ium	collis	collium
DAT.	-ī	-ibus	collī	collibus
ACC.	-em	-ēs	collem	collēs
ABL.	-e	-ibus	colle	collibus
VOC.	X	-ēs	collis	collēs
LOC.	-e	-ibus	[colle]*	[collibus]*

Third Declension Neuter i-Stem (*KL1*, Lesson 18)

	ENDINGS		EXAMPLE NOUN	
	SINGULAR	PLURAL	SINGULAR	PLURAL
NOM.	X	-ia	altāre	altāria
GEN.	-is	-ium	altāris	altārium
DAT.	-ī	-ibus	altārī	altāribus
ACC.	X	-ia	altāre	altāria
ABL.	-ī	-ibus	altārī	altāribus
VOC.	X	-ia	altāre	altāria
LOC.	-ī	-ibus	[altārī]*	[altāribus]*

Fourth Declension Masculine/Feminine (*KL1*, Lesson 25)

	ENDINGS		EXAMPLE NOUN	
	SINGULAR	PLURAL	SINGULAR	PLURAL
NOM.	-us	-ūs	adventus	adventūs
GEN.	-ūs	-uum	adventūs	adventuum
DAT.	-uī	-ibus	adventuī	adventibus
ACC.	-um	-ūs	adventum	adventūs
ABL.	-ū	-ibus	adventū	adventibus
VOC.	-us	-ūs	adventus	adventūs
LOC.	-ū	-ībus	[adventū]*	[adventibus]*

Fourth Declension Neuter (*KL1*, Lesson 25)

	ENDINGS		EXAMPLE NOUN	
	SINGULAR	PLURAL	SINGULAR	PLURAL
NOM.	-ū	-ua	cornū	cornua
GEN.	-ūs	-uum	cornūs	cornuum
DAT.	-ū	-ibus	cornū	cornibus
ACC.	-ū	-ua	cornū	cornua
ABL.	-ū	-ibus	cornū	cornibus
VOC.	-ū	-ua	cornū	cornua
LOC.	-ū	-ibus	[cornū]*	[cornibus]*

Fifth Declension (*KL1*, Lesson 28)

	ENDINGS		EXAMPLE NOUN	
	SINGULAR	PLURAL	SINGULAR	PLURAL
NOM.	-ēs	-ēs	aciēs	aciēs
GEN.	-eī/-ēī	-ērum	aciēī	aciērum
DAT.	-eī/-ēī	-ēbus	aciēī	aciēbus
ACC.	-em	-ēs	aciem	aciēs
ABL.	-ē	-ēbus	aciē	aciēbus
VOC.	-ēs	-ēs	aciēs	aciēs
LOC.	-ē	-ēbus	[aciē]*	[aciēbus]*

*Recall that the Locative case (*KL2*, Lesson 14) is used to indicate place, so it wouldn't necessarily work with these example nouns (thus they are in brackets). Normally you'd see names of cities, towns, and small islands, along with a few ordinary nouns, such as ***domus***, ***rūs***, and ***humus***.

Irregular Nouns

nēmō (*KL2*, Lesson 4)

NOM.	nēmō
GEN.	nēminis [*or* nūllīus]
DAT.	nēminī
ACC.	nēminem
ABL.	nēmine [*or* nūllō]

vīs, vīs (f) (*KL3*, Lesson 5)

	SG.	PL.
NOM.	vīs	vīrēs
GEN.	vīs	vīrium
DAT.	vī	vīribus
ACC.	vim	vīrēs (-īs)
ABL.	vī	vīribus

Pronouns

Personal Pronouns *(KL1, Lesson 17)*

First Person

	LATIN SINGULAR	ENGLISH SINGULAR	LATIN PLURAL	ENGLISH PLURAL
NOM.	ego	I [subject]	nōs	we [subject]
GEN.	meī	of me	nostrum	of us
DAT.	mihi	to/for me	nōbīs	to/for us
ACC.	mē	me [direct object]	nōs	us [direct object]
ABL.	mē	by/with/from me	nōbīs	by/with/from us

Second Person

	LATIN SINGULAR	ENGLISH SINGULAR	LATIN PLURAL	ENGLISH PLURAL
NOM.	tū	you [subject]	vōs	you (pl.) [subject]
GEN.	tuī	of you	vestrum	of you (pl.)
DAT.	tibi	to/for you	vōbīs	to/for you (pl.)
ACC.	tē	you [direct object]	vōs	you (pl.) [direct object]
ABL.	tē	by/with/from you	vōbīs	by/with/from you (pl.)

Third Person Singular

	MASCULINE	FEMININE	NEUTER	ENGLISH
	HE/HIS/HIM	SHE/HERS/HER	IT/ITS	
NOM.	is	ea	id	he/she/it (this/that, etc.) [subject]
GEN.	eius	eius	eius	of him/his, of her/hers, of it/its
DAT.	eī	eī	eī	to/for him, to/for her, to/for it
ACC.	eum	eam	id	him/her/it [direct object]
ABL.	eō	eā	eō	by/with/from him/her/it

Third Person Plural

	MASCULINE	FEMININE	NEUTER	ENGLISH
	HE/HIS/HIM	SHE/HERS/HER	IT/ITS	
NOM.	eī	eae	ea	they (these/those, etc.) [subject]
GEN.	eōrum	eārum	eōrum	of them, their
DAT.	eīs	eīs	eīs	to/for them
ACC.	eōs	eās	ea	them [direct object]
ABL.	eīs	eīs	eīs	by/with/from them

Demonstrative Pronouns (*KL1*, Lesson 17)

Hic, haec, hoc—this; (pl.) these

	SINGULAR			PLURAL		
	MASCULINE	FEMININE	NEUTER	MASCULINE	FEMININE	NEUTER
NOM.	hic	haec	hoc	hī	hae	haec
GEN.	huius	huius	huius	hōrum	hārum	hōrum
DAT.	huic	huic	huic	hīs	hīs	hīs
ACC.	hunc	hanc	hoc	hōs	hās	haec
ABL.	hōc	hāc	hōc	hīs	hīs	hīs

Ille, illa, illud—that; (pl.) those; that famous

	SINGULAR			PLURAL		
	MASCULINE	FEMININE	NEUTER	MASCULINE	FEMININE	NEUTER
NOM.	ille	illa	illud	illī	illae	illa
GEN.	illīus	illīus	illīus	illōrum	illārum	illōrum
DAT.	illī	illī	illī	illīs	illīs	illīs
ACC.	illum	illam	illud	illōs	illās	illa
ABL.	illō	illā	illō	illīs	illīs	illīs

Iste, ista, istud—that (of yours); such

	SINGULAR			PLURAL		
	MASCULINE	FEMININE	NEUTER	MASCULINE	FEMININE	NEUTER
NOM.	iste	ista	istud	istī	istae	ista
GEN.	istīus	istīus	istīus	istōrum	istārum	istōrum
DAT.	istī	istī	istī	istīs	istīs	istīs
ACC.	istum	istam	istud	istōs	istās	ista
ABL.	istō	istā	istō	istīs	istīs	istīs

Intensive Pronouns

ipse, ipsa, ipsum (*KL2*, Lesson 3)

	SINGULAR			PLURAL		
	MASC.	FEM.	NEUT.	MASC.	FEM.	NEUT.
NOM.	ipse	ipsa	ipsum	ipsī	ipsae	ipsa
GEN.	ipsīus	ipsīus	ipsīus	ipsōrum	ipsārum	ipsōrum
DAT.	ipsī	ipsī	ipsī	ipsīs	ipsīs	ipsīs
ACC.	ipsum	ipsam	ipsum	ipsōs	ipsās	ipsa
ABL.	ipsō	ipsā	ipsō	ipsīs	ipsīs	ipsīs

quī, quae, quod (*KL2*, Lesson 3)

	SINGULAR			PLURAL		
	MASC.	FEM.	NEUT.	MASC.	FEM.	NEUT.
NOM.	quī	quae	quod	qu**ī**	qu**ae**	quae
GEN.	cuius	cuius	cuius	qu**ōrum**	qu**ārum**	qu**ōrum**
DAT.	cui	cui	cui	quibus	quibus	quibus
ACC.	quem	qu**am**	quod	qu**ōs**	qu**ās**	quae
ABL.	qu**ō**	qu**ā**	qu**ō**	quibus	quibus	quibus

aliquis, aliquid (*KL2*, Lesson 12)

	SINGULAR			PLURAL		
	MASC.	FEM.	NEUT.	MASC.	FEM.	NEUT.
NOM.	aliquis	aliquis	aliquid	aliquī	aliquae	aliqua
GEN.	alicuius	alicuius	alicuius	aliquōrum	aliquārum	aliquōrum
DAT.	alicui	alicui	alicui	aliquibus	aliquibus	aliquibus
ACC.	aliquem	aliquem	aliquid	aliquōs	aliquās	aliqua
ABL.	aliquō	aliquō	aliquō	aliquibus	aliquibus	aliquibus

quīdam, quaedam, quiddam (*KL2*, Lesson 12)

	SINGULAR			PLURAL		
	MASC.	FEM.	NEUT.	MASC.	FEM.	NEUT.
NOM.	quīdam	quaedam	**quiddam**/ quoddam*	quīdam	quaedam	quaedam
GEN.	cuiusdam	cuiusdam	cuiusdam	quōrundam	quārundam	quōrundam
DAT.	cuidam	cuidam	cuidam	quibusdam	quibusdam	quibusdam
ACC.	quendam	quandam	**quiddam**/ quoddam*	quōsdam	quāsdam	quaedam
ABL.	quōdam	quādam	quōdam	quibusdam	quibusdam	quibusdam

**quiddam* is the pronoun form, *quoddam* is the adjective

Indefinite Relative Pronoun

quīcumque, quaecumque, quodcumque (*KL2*, Lesson 12)

	SINGULAR			PLURAL		
	MASC.	FEM.	NEUT.	MASC.	FEM.	NEUT.
NOM.	quīcumque	quaecumque	quodcumque	quīcumque	quaecumque	quaecumque
GEN.	cuiuscumque	cuiuscumque	cuiuscumque	quōrumcumque	quārumcumque	quōrumcumque
DAT.	cuicumque	cuicumque	cuicumque	quibuscumque	quibuscumque	quibuscumque
ACC.	quemcumque	quamcumque	quodcumque	quōscumque	quāscumque	quaecumque
ABL.	quōcumque	quācumque	quōcumque	quibuscumque	quibuscumque	quibuscumque

Interrogative Pronoun

quis, quid (*KL2*, Lesson 9)

	SINGULAR			PLURAL		
	MASC.	FEM.	NEUT.	MASC.	FEM.	NEUT.
NOM.	quis?	quis?	quid?	quī?	quae?	quae?
GEN.	cuius?	cuius?	cuius?	quōrum?	quārum?	quōrum?
DAT.	cui?	cui?	cui?	quibus?	quibus?	quibus?
ACC.	quem?	quem?	quid?	quōs?	quās?	quae?
ABL.	quō?	quō?	quō?	quibus?	quibus?	quibus?

Reflexive Pronoun (*KL3*, Lesson 2)

	MEĪ, TUĪ				SUĪ
	1ST PERSON		2ND PERSON		
	SING.	PL.	SING.	PL.	SING. OR PL.
NOM.	——	——	——	——	——
GEN.	meī	nostrī	tuī	vestrī	suī
DAT.	mihi	nōbīs	tibi	vōbīs	sibi
ACC.	mē	nōs	tē	vōs	sē
ABL.	mē	nōbīs	tē	vōbīs	sē

Adjectives

First and Second Declension Adjectives

Endings (*KL1*, Lesson 7)

	SINGULAR			PLURAL		
	MASC.	FEM.	NEUT.	MASC.	FEM.	NEUT.
NOM.	-us / -r	-a	-um	-ī	-ae	-a
GEN.	-ī	-ae	-ī	-ōrum	-ārum	-ōrum
DAT.	-ō	-ae	-ō	-īs	-īs	-īs
ACC.	-um	-am	-um	-ōs	-ās	-a
ABL.	-ō	-ā	-ō	-īs	-īs	-īs
VOC.	-e/ -r	-a	-um	-ī	-ae	-a

Example

	SINGULAR			PLURAL		
	MASC.	FEM.	NEUT.	MASC.	FEM.	NEUT.
NOM.	vastus	vasta	vastum	vastī	vastae	vasta
GEN.	vastī	vastae	vastī	vastōrum	vastārum	vastōrum
DAT.	vastō	vastae	vastō	vastīs	vastīs	vastīs
ACC.	vastum	vastam	vastum	vastōs	vastās	vasta
ABL.	vastō	vastā	vastō	vastīs	vastīs	vastīs
VOC.	vaste	vasta	vastum	vastī	vastae	vasta

Third Declension Adjectives

Endings (*KL1*, Lesson 19)

	SINGULAR		PLURAL	
	MASC./FEM.	NEUTER	MASC./FEM.	NEUTER
NOM.	X	X	-ēs	-ia
GEN.	-is	-is	-ium	-ium
DAT.	-ī	-ī	-ibus	-ibus
ACC.	-em	X	-ēs	-ia
ABL.	**-ī**	-ī	-ibus	-ibus
VOC.	X	X	-ēs	-ia

Example

	SINGULAR		PLURAL	
	MASC./FEM.	NEUTER	MASC./FEM.	NEUTER
NOM.	trīstis	trīste	trīstēs	trīstia
GEN.	trīstis	trīstis	trīstium	trīstium
DAT.	trīstī	trīstī	trīstibus	trīstibus
ACC.	trīstem	trīste	trīstēs	trīstia
ABL.	trīstī	trīstī	trīstibus	trīstibus
VOC.	trīstis	trīste	trīstēs	trīstia

Irregular Adjectives

-ius Adjectives (*KL2,* Lesson 4)

alius, alter, neuter, nūllus, sōlus, tōtus, ūllus, unus, uter are all declined like *sōlus* below:

	SINGULAR			PLURAL		
	MASC.	FEM.	NEUT.	MASC.	FEM.	NEUT.
NOM.	sōlus	sōla	sōlum	sōlī	sōlae	sōla
GEN.	sōlīus	sōlīus	sōlīus	sōlōrum	sōlārum	sōlōrum
DAT.	sōlī	sōlī	sōlī	sōlīs	sōlīs	sōlīs
ACC.	sōlum	sōlam	sōlum	sōlōs	sōlās	sōla
ABL.	sōlō	sōlā	sōlō	sōlīs	sōlīs	sōlīs

plūs (*KL2,* Lesson 5)

	MASC./FEM. SG.	NEUT. SG.	MASC./FEM. PL.	NEUT. PL.
NOM.	—	plūs	plūrēs	plūra
GEN.	—	plūris	plūrium	plūrium
DAT.	—	—	plūribus	plūribus
ACC.	—	plūs	plūrēs	plūra
ABL.	—	plūrē	plūribus	plūribus
VOC.	—	plūs	plūrēs	plūra

Comparison of Adjectives

Regular Comparison of Adjectives (*KL2,* Lesson 4)

	POSITIVE	COMPARATIVE	SUPERLATIVE
3-TERMINATION	superbus, -a, -um *proud*	superbior, -ius *prouder*	superbissimus, -a, -um *proudest*
2-TERMINATION	fortis, -e *brave*	fortior, -ius *braver*	fortissimus, -a, -um *bravest*
SINGLE TERMINATION	sapiēns, -entis *wise*	sapientior, -ius *wiser*	sapientissimus, -a, -um *wisest*

Slightly Irregular Comparison of Adjectives (*KL2,* Lesson 5)

	POSITIVE	COMPARATIVE	SUPERLATIVE
ENDING IN -ER	miser, -era, -erum *wretched*	miserior, -ius *more wretched*	miserrimus, -a, -um *most wretched*
	pulcher, -chra, -chrum *beautiful*	pulchrior, -ius *more beautiful*	pulcherrimus, -a, -um *most beautiful*
	celer, -eris, -e *swift*	celerior, -ius *swifter*	celerrimus, -a, -um *swiftest*

	POSITIVE	COMPARATIVE	SUPERLATIVE
6 ENDING IN -LIS	similis, -e *similar, like*	similior, -ius *more similar*	simillimus, -a, -um most similar
	dissimilis, -e *dissimilar, unlike, different*	dissimilior, -ius *more dissimilar*	dissimillimus, -a, -um *most dissimilar*
	facilis, -e *easy*	facilior, -ius *easier*	facillimus, -a, -um *easiest*
	difficilis *difficult*	difficilior, -ius *more difficult*	difficillimus, -a, -um *most difficult*
	gracilis, -e *slender, thin*	gracilior, -ius *thinner*	gracillimus, -a, -um *thinnest*
	humilis, -e *humble, low(ly)*	humilior, -ius *more humble*	humillimus, -a, -um *most humble*

Irregular Comparison of Adjectives (*KL2*, Lesson 5)

	POSITIVE	COMPARATIVE	SUPERLATIVE
JUST PLAIN IRREGULAR	magnus, -a, -um *big, great*	māior, māius *bigger, greater*	māximus, -a, -um *biggest, greatest*
	parvus, -a, -um *small*	minor, minus *smaller*	minimus, -a, -um *smallest*
	bonus, -a, -um *good*	melior, melius *better*	optimus, -a, -um *best*
	malus, -a, -um *bad, evil*	pēior, pēius *worse, more evil*	pessimus, -a, -um *worst, most evil*
	īnferus, -a, -um *below*	īnferior, -ius *lower*	īnfimus, -a, -um *or* īmus, -a, -um* *lowest, deepest*
	superus, -a, -um *above, high*	superior, -ius *higher*	suprēmus, -a, -um *or* summus, -a, -um* *highest, greatest*
	multus, -a, -um *much*	——, plūs *more*	plūrimus, -a, -um *most*
	—— [prō or prae (adv. & prep. +abl., *below*]	prior, prius *former*	prīmus, -a, -um *first*
	—— [prope (adv.) *near*]	propior, -ius *nearer*	proximus, -a, -um *next, nearest*
	—— [ultrā (adv.) *beyond*]	ulterior, -ius *farther*	ultimus, -a, -um *farthest*

**īmus* and *summus* are often regarded as alternate superlatives of *īnferus* and *superus* respectively, even though they are technically not from these positive forms.

Indefinite Adjective *aliquī, aliquae, aliquod* (*KL2*, Lesson 12)

	SINGULAR			PLURAL		
	MASC.	FEM.	NEUT.	MASC.	FEM.	NEUT.
NOM.	aliquis	aliquis	aliquid	aliquī	aliquae	aliqua
GEN.	alicuius	alicuius	alicuius	aliquōrum	aliquārum	aliquōrum
DAT.	alicui	alicui	alicui	aliquibus	aliquibus	aliquibus
ACC.	aliquem	aliquem	aliquid	aliquōs	aliquās	aliqua
ABL.	aliquō	aliquō	aliquō	aliquibus	aliquibus	aliquibus

	SINGULAR			PLURAL		
	MASC.	FEM.	NEUT.	MASC.	FEM.	NEUT.
NOM.	aliquī	aliqua	aliquod	aliquī	aliquae	aliqua
GEN.	alicuius	alicuius	alicuius	aliquōrum	aliquārum	aliquōrum
DAT.	alicui	alicui	alicui	aliquibus	aliquibus	aliquibus
ACC.	aliquem	aliquam	aliquod	aliquōs	aliquās	aliqua
ABL.	aliquō	aliquā	aliquō	aliquibus	aliquibus	aliquibus

Indefinite Adjective *quīdam, quaedam, quoddam* (*KL2*, Lesson 12)

	SINGULAR			PLURAL		
	MASC.	FEM.	NEUT.	MASC.	FEM.	NEUT.
NOM.	quīdam	quaedam	quiddam	quīdam	quaedam	quaedam
GEN.	cuiusdam	cuiusdam	cuiusdam	quōrundam	quārundam	quōrundam
DAT.	cuidam	cuidam	cuidam	quibusdam	quibusdam	quibusdam
ACC.	quendam	quandam	quiddam	quōsdam	quāsdam	quaedam
ABL.	quōdam	quādam	quōdam	quibusdam	quibusdam	quibusdam

Interrogative Adjective *quī? quae? quod?* (*KL2*, Lesson 9)

	SINGULAR			PLURAL		
	MASC.	FEM.	NEUT.	MASC.	FEM.	NEUT.
NOM.	quī?	quae?	quod?	quī?	quae?	quae?
GEN.	cuius?	cuius?	cuius?	quōrum?	quārum?	quōrum?
DAT.	cui?	cui?	cui?	quibus?	quibus?	quibus?
ACC.	quem?	quam?	quod?	quōs?	quās?	quae?
ABL.	quō?	quā?	quō?	quibus?	quibus?	quibus?

Adverbs

Regular and Irregular Comparison of Adverbs

	ORIGINAL ADJECTIVE	POSITIVE ADVERB	COMPARATIVE ADVERB	SUPERLATIVE ADVERB
REGULAR	superbus, -a, -um *proud*	superbē *proudly*	superbius *more proudly*	superbissimē *most proudly*
	miser, -era, -erum *wretched*	miserē *wretchedly*	miserius *more wretchedly*	miserrimē *most wretchedly*
	pulcher, -chra, -chrum *beautiful*	pulchrē *beautifully*	pulchrius *more beautifully*	pulcherrimē *most beautifully*
	celer, -eris, -ere *swift*	celeriter *swiftly*	celerius *more swiftly*	celerrimē *most swiftly*
	potēns, -entis *powerful*	potenter *powerfully*	potentius *more powerfully*	potentissimē *most powerfully*
IRREGULAR	facilis, -e *easy*	facile *easily*	facilius *more easily*	facillimē *most easily*
	magnus, -a, -um *large, great*	magnoperē *greatly*	magis *more, rather*	māximē *most, especially, very*
	parvus, -a, -um *small, little*	parum *(too) little, not enough*	minus *less*	minimē *least, not at all*
	bonus, -a, -um *good*	bene *well*	melius *better*	optimē *best*
	malus, -a, -um *bad*	male *badly*	pēius *worst*	pessimē *worst*
	multus, -a, -um *much*	multum *much*	plūs *more*	plūrimum most
	——	[prō]	prius *before, earlier*	prīmō/prīmum *(at) first*
	——	diū *for a long time*	diūtius *longer*	diūtissimē *very long*

APPENDIX B

English-Latin Glossary

Here you will find the words for the English-Latin sections of your worksheets. When using any glossary, always keep in mind that two languages don't always mesh perfectly. For example, if you look up "land" you will find *patria, tellūs,* and *terra.* They all can mean "land," but you'll have to use good judgment to decide which is correct in a given context! In brackets you will find the volume of the text (KL1, 2, or 3) and the number of the lesson (L) or worksheet (W) where each word is introduced.

A

a long way off *longē* [KL3, L3]

abandon *relinquō, -ere, -līquī, -lictum* [KL1, L28]

abduction *raptus, -ūs (m)* [KL1, W31]

abide (in) *permaneō, -ēre, -mansī, -mansum* [KL3, L7]

able (am able) *possum, posse, potuī, ——* [KL1, L11]

above *super (+acc. & +abl.)* [KL1, L6]; *suprā (adv. & prep. +acc.)* [KL1, L14]

about (adv.) *quasi* [KL3, L11]

about (prep.) *circā* [KL2, L13]

above (adj.) *superus, -a, -um* [KL2, L5]

absent (I am absent) *absum, -esse, āfuī, āfutūrum* [KL3, L3]

abundance *cōpia, -ae (f)* [KL1, L15]

abundant *plēnus, -a, -um* [KL2, L4]; *ūber, -eris* [KL2, W11]

accept *accipiō, -ere, -cēpī, -ceptum* [KL1, L31]

accomplish *pātrō* [KL3, W4]

according to *secundum (adv. & prep. +acc.)* [KL1, L28]

accordingly *ergo (adv.)* [KL1, L18]

accuse *arguō, -ere, arguī, argutus* [KL2, W9]; *accūsō* [KL3, W1]

accustomed (am accustomed to) *soleō, -ēre, ——, solītus sum (semi-deponent)* [KL3, L9]

across *trāns* [KL1, L11]

agreement *foedus, -deris (n)* [KL2, L12]; *placitum, -ī (n)* [KL3, W9]

aid *auxilium, -ī (n)* [KL1, L5]

aim *tendō, -ere, tetendī, tentum* [KL2, L4]

air *aura, -ae (f)* [KL3, L3]

alas! *heu (ēheu)* [KL1, L22]

alchemy *alchemia, -ae (f)* [KL1, W27]

alder *alnus, -ī (f)* [KL1, L4]

alien (adj.) *aliēnus, -a, -um* [KL2, L12]

all *omnis, -e* [KL1, L19]; *tōtus, -a, -um* [KL2, L3]; **(all of)** *cunctus, -a, -um* [KL2, L9]; **(all together)** *ūniversus, -a, -um* [KL3, L4]

all the way up to *usque* [KL3, L4]

allow *permittō, -ere, -mīsī, -missum* [KL1, W30]; *sinō, -ere, sīvī, situs* [KL2, W13]; *concēdō, -ere, -cessī, -cessum* [KL3, W9]

allowed (it is allowed) *licet, licuit, - (impers. +dat./acc.)* [KL1, W26; KL3, L1]

ally *socius, -iī (m)* [KL2, L13]

almighty *omnipotēns, -tentis* [KL3, W2]

almost *paene (adv.)* [KL1, L19]; *quasi* [KL3, L11]; *ferē* [KL3, L3]

alone (adv.) *sōlum* [KL3, L7]

alone (adj.) *sōlus, -a, -um* [KL1, W12; KL2, L4]

already *iam* [KL1, L15]

also *et* [KL1, L1]; *etiam* [KL1, L22]; *quoque* [KL1, L29]

altar *altāre, -tāris (n)* [KL2, L9]

although *cum* [KL3, L7]; *etsi* [KL3, W2]

altogether *omnīno* [KL3, L5]

always *semper* [KL1, L5]

am a slave to *serviō, -īre, -īvī, -ītum (+dat.)* [KL2, L10]

am absent *absum, -esse, āfuī, āfutūrum* [KL3, L3]

am accustomed (to) *soleō, -ēre, ——, solītus sum (semi-deponent)* [KL3, L9]

am afraid of *metuō, -ere, -uī, -ūtum* [KL3, L15]

am amazed at *mīror, -ārī, ——, mīrātus sum* [KL2, L6]

am away (from) *absum, -esse, āfuī, āfutūrum* [KL3, L3]

am begotten *nāscor, -scī, ——, nātus sum* [KL2, L12]

am born *gignō, -ere, genuī, genitum (in pass.)* [KL2, L9]; *nāscor, -scī, ——, nātus sum* [KL2, L12]; *orior, -īrī, ——, ortus sum* [KL2, L6]

am busy *operor, -ārī, ——, operātus sum* [KL2, L6]

am created *orior, -īrī, ——, ortus sum* [KL2, L6]

am (I am) *sum, esse, fuī, futūrum* [KL1, L3]

am ignorant (of) *nesciō, -īre, -īvī, -ītum* [KL1, L30; KL3, L3]; *ignōrō* [KL2, L15]

am in the habit of *soleō, -ēre, ——, solītus sum (semi-deponent)* [KL3, L9]

am pleasing *placeō, -ēre, -cuī, -citum* [KL3, L1]

am unwilling *nōlō, nōlle, nōluī, ——* [KL2, L14]

am visible *appareō, -ēre, -uī, -itum (+dat.)* [KL3, L4]

am without *careō, -ēre, -uī, -itum (+abl.)* [KL3, L6]

amazement *stupor, -ōris (m)* [KL1, W28]

ambassador *lēgātus, -ī (m)* [KL2, L15]

ambush *īnsidiae, -ārum (f, pl)* [KL2, L15]

among *inter (+acc.)* [KL1, L19]; *apud (+acc.)* [KL2, L4]

ancestor *avus, -ī (m)* [KL1, L22]

anchor *ancora, -ae* [KL2, W12]

ancient *antīquus, -a, -um* [KL1, L7]

and *ac (atque)* [KL1, L27]; *et* [KL1, L1]; *-que (enclitic)* [KL1, L10]

and also *ac (atque)* [KL1, L27]

and not *nec (neque)* [KL1, L14]

and so *itaque* [KL1, L2]

angel *angelus, -ī (m)* [KL3, W5]

anger *fūror, -ōris (m)* [KL3, W6]

be angry *furō, -ere, -uī, ——* [KL2, W13]; *īrāscor, -scī, ——, īrātus sum* [KL3, W9]

anger *īra, -ae (f)* [KL1, L2]

angry *īrātus,-a, -um* [KL1, L15]; *īnfēnsus, -a, -um* [KL2, W15]

animal *animal, -ālis (n)* [KL1, L18]

ankle *tālāria, -ium (n, pl)* [KL3, W16]

announce *nuntiō (1)* [KL1, L14]; *adnūntiō* [KL3, L7]

annoy *vexō (1)* [KL1, L19]

Anointed One *Messīā(s), -ae (m)* [KL2, W12]

anointing *ūnctiō, -ōnis (f)* [KL3, W12]

another *alius, -a, -um* [KL1, W21; KL2, L4]; *aliēnus, -a, -um* [KL2, L12]

answer *respondeō, -ēre, -spondī, -sponsum* [KL1, L9]

anticipate *praecipiō, -ere, -cēpī, -ceptum* [KL3, W5]

any *ūllus, -a, -um* [KL1, W27; KL2, L4]; *aliquī, aliquae, aliquod (adj.)* [KL2, L12]

anyhow *saltem* [KL3, W5]

anyone *ūllus, -a, -um* [KL1, W27]; *aliquis, aliquid (pron.)* [KL2, L12]; *quisquam, quidquam/quicquam* [KL3, L1]

anything *ūllus, -a, -um* [KL1, W27]; *aliquis, aliquid (pron.)* [KL2, L12]; *quisquam, quidquam/quicquam* [KL3, L1]

anywhere *usquam* [KL3, L9]

anxious *sollicitus, -a, -um* [KL2, W14]

Apollo *Apollō, -inis (m)* [KL1, W20]

apostle *apostolus, -ī (m)* [KL1, L11]

apparent (it is apparent) *apparet* [KL3, L4]

appear *appareō, -ēre, -uī, -itum (+dat.)* [KL3, L4]

appearance *cōnspectus, -ūs (m)* [KL2, L9]; *speciēs, -ēi (f)* [KL3, W4]

apple *pōmum, -ī (n)* [KL3, W11]

apply *referō, -ferre, -(t)tulī, -(l)lātum* [KL3, W9]

appointed *pactus, -a, -um* [KL2, L13]

apprentice *discipulus, -ī (m)* [KL1, L5]

approach *appropinquō (1)* [KL1, L25]; *adeō, -īre, -iī, -itum* [KL2, L10]; *propinquō (+dat./acc.)* [KL2, W3]; *aggredior, -ī, ——, -gressus sum* [KL3, W7]

approve (of) *probō* [KL3, L14]

arch *arcus, -ūs (m)* [KL1, L27]

Ares *Mars, Martis (m)* [KL2, W13]

Argus *Argus, -ī (m)* [KL1, W21]

Ariadne *Ariadna, -ae (f)* [KL1, W30]

arise *nāscor, -scī, ——, nātus sum* [KL2, L12]; *orior, -īrī, ——, ortus sum* [KL2, L6]

arise *surgō, -ere, surrēxī, surrēctum* [KL1, L28]

arm *bracchium, -ī (n)* [KL1, W13; KL3, W3]

armor *arma, -ōrum (n, pl)* [KL1, W32]

arms *arma, -ōrum (n, pl)* [KL1, W32; KL2, L3]

army (on the march) *exercitus, -ūs (m)* [KL1, L25]; *āgmen, -minis (n)* [KL3, L6]; *cohors, -hortis (f)* [KL3, W2]

around *circā* [KL2, L13]

arrange *collocō (1)* [KL1, W21]

arrival *adventus, -ūs (m)* [KL3, L12]

arrive *perveniō, -īre, -vēnī, -ventum* [KL2, L11]

arrogance *superbia, -ae (f)* [KL2, L12]

arrow *sagitta, -ae (f)* [KL1, L3]

as far as *usque* [KL3, L4]

as *quam* [KL1, L28]; *sīcut* [KL1, L20]; *ut (+indic.)* [KL3, L5]

as if *quasi* [KL3, L11]

as long as *quamdiu* [KL3, L9]

as (rel. adj.) *quālis* [KL3, L9]

as soon as *simul atque* [KL2, L9]

ascend *ascendō, -ere, -scendī, -scensum* [KL2, L9]

ascertain *perspiciō, -ere, -spēxī, -spectum* [KL3, W2]

ashes *cinis, -neris (m)* [KL3, L10]

ask *rogō (1)* [KL1, L6]; *interrogō* [KL2, W8]; *postulō* [KL3, L10]; *quaerō, -ere, quaesīvī, quaesītum (-situm)* [KL2, L3]

ask for *petō, -ere, -īvī, -ītum* [KL2, L12]

assemble *congregō* [KL2, L14]

assemble (trans. verb) *convocō* [KL3, W5]

assert *āiō* [KL1, L14]

assume *sūmō, -ere, sūmpsī, sūmptum* [KL2, L10]

astonished (be) *stupeō, -ēre, -uī, ——* [KL3, W16]

astonishment *stupor, -ōris (m)* [KL1, W28]

at *ad (+acc.)* [KL1, L3]

at a distance *procul* [KL2, L11]

at all *omnīno* [KL3, L5]

at any time *umquam* [KL3, L14]

at first *prīmum/prīmō* [KL2, L7]

at last *tandem* [KL3, L15]

at least *saltem* [KL3, W5]

at once *continuō* [KL2, L12]

at that place *ibī* [KL1, L5]

at that time *tum* [KL1, L15]; *tunc* [KL2, L4]

at the foot of *sub (+abl.)* [KL1, L14]

at the house of *apud (+acc.)* [KL2, L4]

at the same time *simul* [KL2, L9]

at/in any place *usquam* [KL3, L9]

Athena *Minerva, -ae (f)* [KL3, W6]; *Pallas, -adis (f)* [KL3, W6]

Athenian *Athēniensis, -is (m/f)* [KL1, W30]

Athens *Athēnae, -ārum (f, pl)* [KL1, W30; KL2, L14]

atonement *propitiātiō, -ōnis (f)* [KL2, W11]

attack (noun) *impetus, -ūs (m)* [KL3, L9]

attack (verb) *oppugnō (1)* [KL1, L4]; *petō, -ere, -īvī, -ītum* [KL2, L12]; *aggredior, -ī, ——, -gressus sum* [KL3, W7]

attempt *cōnor, -ārī, ——, cōnātus sum* [KL2, L6]; *temptō* [KL1, W27; KL3, L7]

attendant *minister, -strī (m)* [KL3, L10]

aunt *amita, -ae (f)* [KL1, L22]

authority *imperium, -iī (n)* [KL2, L3]; *diciō, -ōnis (f)* [KL3, W10]

avoid *vītō (1)* [KL1, L30]

away from *ā, ab (+abl.)* [KL1, L3]

awaken *suscitō* [KL3, W5]

away (I am away [from]) *absum, -esse, āfuī, āfutūrum* [KL3, L3]

awful *horrendus, -a, -um* [KL1, L13]

B

baby *īnfāns, -fantis (adj. & noun, m/f)* [KL1, W31; KL3, L12]

Bacchus *Bacchus, -ī (m)* [KL1, W27]

back (adv.) *retrō* [KL1, W23; KL3, W3]; *rursum/rursus* [KL3, L3];

back (noun) *tergum, -ī (n)* [KL3, L6]

back(ward) *retrō* [KL1, W23]

backwards *rursum/rursus* [KL3, L3]; *resupīnus, -a, -um* [KL3, W7]

bad *malus, -a, -um* [KL1, L7]

badly *male* [KL1, L1]

bag *pēra, -ae (f)* [KL1, W32]; *saccus, -ī (m)* [KL2, W6]

ball *pila, -ae (f)* [KL1, W30]

banquet *convīvium, -iī (n)* [KL3, L10]

barbarian *barbarus, -ī (m)* [KL1, L31]

barber *tonsor, -ōris (m)* [KL1, W28]

bare *nūdus, -a, -um* [KL3, W7]

barn *horreum, -ī (n)* [KL2, W14]

barrier *spīna, -ae (f)* [KL1, W23]

bathe *lavō, -āre, lāvī, lōtum/lavātum* [KL1, W27; KL2, L11]

batter (verb) *quassō* [KL3, W1]

battle *proelium, -ī (n)* [KL1, L15]; *pugna, -ae (f)* [KL2, W9]

battle line *aciēs, -ēī (f)* [KL3, L14]

be *sum, esse, fuī, futūrum* [KL1, L3]

be silent *taceō, -ēre, -uī, -itum* [KL1, W26]

be strong *valeō, -ēre, -uī, valitūrum* [KL1, L9]

be well *salveō, -ēre, ——, ——* [KL1, L9]; *valeō, -ēre, -uī, valitūrum* [KL1, L9]

beach *harēna, -ae (f)* [KL1, L3]

beam *trabēs, -is (m)* [KL2, W14]

bear (noun) *ursus, -ī (m)* [KL1, W32]

bear (verb) *gerō, -ere, gessī, gestum* [KL1, L28]; *ferō, ferre, tulī, lātum (irreg. 3rd conj.)* [KL1, W32] *ferō, ferre, tulī, lātum* [KL1, W32; KL2, W11]; **bear across** *trānsferō, -ferre, -tūlī, -lātum* [KL3, L13]; **bear over** *trānsferō, -ferre, -tūlī, -lātum* [KL3, L13]

beast *bēstia, -ae (f)* [KL1, L2]; *bēlua, -ae (f)* [KL3, L15]; **(of burden)** *iūmentum, -ī (n)* [KL3, W4]

beat *percutiō, -ere, -cussī, -cussum* [KL1, W32; KL2, L3]

beautiful *pulcher, -chra, -chrum* [KL1, L7]

beauty *forma, -ae (f)* [KL3, W16]

because (conj.) *quandō* [KL1, L12]; *quia* [KL1, L18]; *quod* [KL1, L10]; *quoniam* [KL1, L26]

because of *propter (+acc.)* [KL1, L25]

become *fiō, fierī, ——, factus sum* [KL1, L31]

bed *cubīle, -is (n)* [KL3, W9]; *lectulus, -ī (m)* [KL3, W5]

before (adj.) *prior, prius* [KL2, L5]

before (conj.) *ante (+acc.)* [KL1, L17]; *cōram (+abl.)* [KL1, L27]; *pro (+abl.)* [KL1, L18]; *antequam* [KL3, L15]; *priusquam* [KL3, L15]

beg *mendicō* [KL2, W8]; *obsecrō* [KL3, L13]

began *coepī, coepisse, ——, coeptum (defective)* [KL3, L1]

beget *gignō, -ere, genuī, genitum* [KL2, L9]; *pariō, -ere, peperī, par(i)tum* [KL3, L13]

begetting *generātiō, -ōnis (f)* [KL3, L7]

beggar *mendicus, -ī (m)* [KL2, W8]

begin *incipiō, -ere, -cēpī, -ceptum* [KL1, L31]; *ineō, -īre, -iī (-īvī), -ītum* [KL3, L4]

beginning *initium, -iī (n)* [KL3, L7]; *prīncipium, -iī (n)* [KL3, L4]

begotten (am begotten) *nāscor, -scī, ——, nātus sum* [KL2, L12]

behind *retrō* [KL1, W23; KL3, W3]; *post (+acc.)* [KL1, L17]

behold! *ecce* [KL1, L17]

believe *crēdō, -ere, -didi, -ditum* [KL1, L26]

belly *uterus, -ī (m)* [KL2, W9]

beloved *cārus, -a, -um* [KL1, L13]; *dīlēctus, -a, -um* [KL3, L1]

below (adj.) *īnferus, -a, -um* [KL2, L5]

below (adv./prep.) *sub (+abl.)* [KL1, L14]; *īnfrā* [KL3, W16]; *prae* [KL2, L5]

bereft *orbus, -a, -um* [KL1, L22]

beseech *dēprecor, -ārī, ——, -ātus sum* [KL3, L10]; *obsecrō* [KL3, L13]

beseige *obsideō, -ēre, -sēdī, -sessum* [KL1, L10]

beside (prep.) *praeter* [KL2, L13]

besides (adv.) *etiam* [KL1, L22]; *amplius* [KL3, L9]; *extrā* [KL3, L15]

best (adj.) *optimus, -a, -um* [KL2, L5]

best (adv.) *optimē* [KL2, L7]

Bethlehem *Bethleem (indecl.)* [KL1, W32]

better (adj.) *melior, -ius* [KL1, W28; KL2, L5]

better (adv.) *melius, -ius* [KL2, L7]

between *inter (+acc.)* [KL1, L19]

beware (of) *caveō, -ēre, cāvī, cautum* [KL1, L12]

beyond *super (+acc./+abl.)* [KL1, L26]; *extrā* [KL3, L15]; *praeter* [KL2, L13]; *ultrā* [KL2, L5]

Bible (Holy Bible) *Biblia Sacra, Bibliae Sacrae (f)* [KL1, L11]

big *magnus, -a, -um* [KL1, L7]

bigger *māior, -ius* [KL1, W31; KL2, L5]

biggest *māximus, -a, -um* [KL1, W31; KL2, L5]

billy goat *caper, -prī (m)* [KL1, L4]

bind *vinciō, -īre, vīnxī, vīnctum* [KL1, L30]

bird *avis, avis (f)* [KL1, L18]

birth *genus, -neris (n)* [KL2, L13]; *nātīvitās, -tātis (f)* [KL2, W8]

bit by bit *minūtātim* [KL1, L20]

bite *mordeō, -ēre, momordī, morsum* [KL1, L9]

black (dead black) *āter, -tra, -trum* [KL1, L17]; **(shining black)** *niger, -gra, -grum* [KL1, L17]

blanket *strātum, -ī (n)* [KL2, L13]

blasphemy *blasphēmia, -ae (f)* [KL3, W1]

blaze *ardeō, ardēre, arsī, ——* [KL1, L20]

bless *benedīcō, -ere, -dīxī, -dictum (+dat.)* [KL3, L4]

blessed *beātus, -a, -um* [KL1, L7]

blind *caecus, -a, -um* [KL1, L27]

blind *obcaecō* [KL3, W12]

blockade *obsidiō, -ōnis (f)* [KL2, W15]

blood *sanguis, -guinis (m)* [KL2, L3]

to make **bloody** *cruentō* [KL2, W11]

bloody *cruentus, -a, -um* [KL2, W15]

blow (noun) *plāga, -ae (f)* [KL3, L14]; *ictus, -ūs (m)* [KL3, W5]

blow (verb) *spīrō* [KL2, W3]

blue *caeruleus, -a, -um* [KL1, L17]; *hyacinthinus, -a, -um* [KL1, L17]

boat *nāvicula, -ae (f)* [KL1, W31]

body *corpus, corporis (n)* [KL1, L13]; **(dead body)** *cadaver, -veris (n)* [KL1, W32]

bold *magnanimus, -a, -um* [KL1, W9]

bone *os, ossis (n)* [KL3, L15]

book *liber, librī (m)* [KL1, L11]; *cōdex, -dicis (m)* [KL3, W9]

booty *praeda, -ae (f)* [KL2, L15]

born (am born) *gignō, -ere, genuī, genitum (in pass.)* [KL2, L9]; *nāscor, -scī, ——, nātus sum* [KL2, L12]

both...and *et...et* [KL1, L1]

bottom (lowest part) *fundus, -ī (m)* [KL2, W10]

bound(ary) *fīnis, -is (m)* [KL1, W4]; *regiō, -ōnis (f)* [KL3, W2]; *terminus, -ī (m)* [KL3, L15]

boundless *infīnītus, -a, -um* [KL3, W2]

bow *arcus, -ūs (m)* [KL1, L27]

box *arca, -ae (f)* [KL2, W6]

boy *puer, puerī (m)* [KL1, L5]

branch *virga, -ae (f)* [KL3, L10]

brandish *quatiō, -ere, quassī, quassus* [KL3, W5]

bravery *fortitūdō, -tudinis (f)* [KL2, L12]

brave *fortis, -e* [KL1, L19]; *magnanimus, -a, -um* [KL1, W9]; *audāx, -ācis* [KL2, W11]

braver *fortior, -tius (gen. fortioris)* [KL1, W31]

bravest *fortissimus, -a, -um* [KL1, W32]

bread *pānis, -is (m)* [KL1, L29]

break *frangō, -ere, frēgī, fractum* [KL1, L27]; *rumpō, -ere, rūpī, ruptum* [KL2, L12]

break (forth) *prōrumpō, -ere, -rūpī, -ruptum* [KL2, W9]

breath *spīritus, -ūs (m)* [KL1, L25]; *anima, -ae (f)* [KL2, L4]

breathe *spīrō* [KL2, W3]

breeze *aura, -ae (f)* [KL3, L3]

bridge *pōns, pontis (m)* [KL1, W19]

brief *brevis, -e* [KL1, L19]

bright (adj.; very bright) *clārus, -a, -um* [KL3, W3]; *limpidissimus, -a, -um* [KL1, W32]

bright (verb; am bright) *lūceō, lūcēre, lūxī, ——* [KL1, L11]

bring—(to) *afferō (adf-), -ferre (adf-), attulī (adt-), allātum (adl-)* [KL3, L5]; **(across)** *trānsferō, -ferre, -tūlī, -lātum* [KL3, L13]; **(back)** *referō, -ferre, -(t)tulī, -(l)lātum* [KL3, W9]; **(forth)** *ferō, ferre, tulī, lātum (irreg. 3rd conj.)* [KL1, W32]; *pariō, -ere, peperī, par(i)tum* [KL3, L13]; **(in)** *inferō, -ferre, intulī, illātum (+dat. or + ad/ in +acc.)* [KL3, L2]; **(out)** *ēdūcō, -ere, -dūxī, -ductum* [KL3, L5]; **(over)** *trānsferō, -ferre, -tūlī, -lātum* [KL3, L13]; **(to)** *offerō, offerre, obtulī, oblātum* [KL2, L11]

broad *lātus, -a, -um* [KL1, L20]

broad way *platēa, -ae (f)* [KL3, L1]

bronze *aēneus, -a, -um* [KL2, W6]

brother *frāter, frātris (m)* [KL1, L12]; *germānus, -ī (m)* [KL1, L4]

brown (dark-brown) *purpureus, -a, -um* [KL1, L17]

build *aedificō* [KL2, L4]; *mōlior, -īrī, ——, mōlītus sum* [KL2, L6]

bull *bōs, bovis (m)* [KL1, L19]

business (mind one's own business) *suum negōtium agere* [KL1, W29]

burden *onus, oneris n.* [KL1, L13; KL3, L3]

burdensome *gravis, -e* [KL3, L6]

burn (intransit.) *ardeō, ardēre, arsī, ——* [KL1, L20]; *torreō, -ēre, torruī, tostum* [KL1, L17]

burn (transit.) *cremō (1)* [KL1, L2]

burnt offering *altāre, -tāris (n)* [KL2, L9]

burst *rumpō, -ere, rūpī, ruptum* [KL2, L12]

burst (forth) *prōrumpō, -ere, -rūpī, -ruptum* [KL2, W9]

business *negōtium, -iī (n)* [KL3, W9]

but *modo* [KL1, L27]; *sed* [KL1, L1]; *at* [KL3, L1]; *tantum* [KL3, L14]

buy *emō, -ere, ēmī, ēmptum* [KL2, L10]

by *iūxta (adv. & prep. +acc.)* [KL1, L28]

by chance *forte* [KL2, L3]; *temere* [KL2, W15]

by no means *haud* [KL3, L1]; *nequaquam* [KL2, W8]

by turns *invicem* [KL2, L12]

by what means? *quārē* [KL3, L9]

C

cabin (of a ship) *diaeta, -ae (f)* [KL1, W18]

call *appellō (1)* [KL1, L15]; *vocō (1)* [KL1, L1]

call (back/again) *revocō* [KL3, W2]

calm (verb) *mītigō* [KL3, W7]

calm (adj.) *placidus, -a, -um* [KL1, W29]; *tranquillus, -a, -um* [KL3, W9]

camel *camēlus, -ī (m/f)* [KL1, L4]

camp *castra, -ōrum (n, pl)* [KL1, L15]

can *possum, posse, potuī, ——* [KL1, L11]

capture *capiō, -ere, cēpī, captum* [KL1, L31]

carcass *cadaver, -veris (n)* [KL1, W32]

care for *cūrō (1)* [KL1, L15]

careless *immemor, -oris* [KL2, W6]

carpenter *faber, -brī (m)* [KL3, W2]

carry on *gerō, -ere, gessī, gestum* [KL1, L28]

carry *ferō, ferre, tulī, lātum* [KL1, W32; KL2, W11]; *portō (1)* [KL1, L4]; *vehō, -ere, vexī, vectum* [KL1, L27]; **(to)** *afferō (adf-), -ferre (adf-), attulī (adt-), allātum (adl-)* [KL3, L5]; *offerō, offerre, obtulī, oblātum* [KL2, L11]; **(across)** *trānsferō, -ferre, -tūlī, -lātum* [KL3, L13]; **(in)** *inferō, -ferre, intulī, illātum (+dat. or + ad/in +acc.)* [KL3, L5]; *importō* [KL3, W2]; **(off/away)** *rapiō, -ere, rapuī, raptum* [KL1, L31]; *auferō, -ferre, abstulī, ablatum* [KL1, W32; KL3, L10]; **(over)** *trānsferō, -ferre, -tūlī, -lātum* [KL3, L13]

Carthage *Carthāgo, -ginis (f)* [KL2, L14]

cast *iaciō, -ere, iēcī, iactum* [KL1, L31]

cast down *dēiciō, -icere, -iēcī, iectum* [KL1, W23]

cast out *ēiciō, -ere, -iēcī, -iectum* [KL2, L14]

castle *castellum, -ī (n)* [KL1, L5]

cattle *plural of bōs, bovis (m/f)* [KL1, L19]; *pecus, -coris (n)* [KL3, L2]

cause (verb) *efficiō, -ere, -fēcī, -fectum* [KL3, W10]

cause (noun) *causa, -ae (f)* [KL2, L15]

cause of offense *scandalum, -ī (n)* [KL3, L12]

cavalry *equitātus, -ūs (m)* [KL3, W2]

cavalryman *eques, -quitis (m)* [KL1, L20]

cave *spēlunca, -ae (f)* [KL1, L3]; *caverna, -ae (f)* [KL2, W6]

censure *reprehendō, -ere, -hendī, -hensum* [KL3, W13]

centaur *centaurus, -ī (m)* [KL1, L10]

certain (adj.) *quīdam, quaedam, quiddam* [KL2, L12]; *certus, -a, -um* [KL3, L6]

certain one *quīdam, quaedam, quiddam* [KL2, L12]

certain thing *quīdam, quaedam, quiddam* [KL2, L12]

certainly *enim (postpositive conj.)* [KL1, L17]; *certē* [KL3, L6]; *nam* [KL1, W32; KL2, L9]; *quidem* [KL2, L3]; *vērō* [KL2, L15]; *utique* [KL3, L12]

chair *sella, -ae (f)* [KL1, L31]

challenge *provocō (1)*

chance (by chance) *forte* [KL2, L3]

chance *sors, -rtis (f)* [KL3, L6]

change *mūtō (1)* [KL1, L20]; *vertō, -ere, vertī, versum* [KL1, L28]; *convertō, -ere, -vertī, -versum* [KL3, L9]

chant *carmen, -inis (n)* [KL1, L13]

chapter *capitulum, -ī (n)* [KL3, W9]

character *faciēs, -ēī (f)* [KL1, L28]; *mōs, mōris (m) (pl.)* [KL2, L13]

chariot (four-horse chariot) *quadrīgae, -ārum (f)* [KL1, W23]

charioteer *aurīga, -ae (m/f)* [KL1, W23]

chasm *profundum, -ī (n)* [KL3, W9]

cheap *vīlis, -e* [KL2, W15]

cheese *caseus, -a, -um* [KL2, W4]

cherish *foveō, -ēre, fōvī, fōtum* [KL1, L25]

chew *mandūcō (1)* [KL1, L6]

chief *prīnceps, -cipis (m)* [KL2, L3]

children *līberī, -ōrum (m, pl)* [KL1, L10]

choice *optio, optiōnis (f)* [KL1, W12]

choose *dēligō, -ere, lēgī, -lēctum* [KL1, L28]; *legō, -ere, lēgī, lēctum* [KL1, L28]; *ēligō, -ere, -lēgī, -lectum* [KL3, L1]

choose out *dīligō, -ere, -lēxī, -lēctum* [KL3, L1]

Christ *Christus, -ī (m)* [KL1, L4]

church *ecclēsia, -ae (f)* [KL1, L11]

Circus Maximus *Circus Maximus, Circī Maximī (m)* [KL1, W23]

citadel *arx, arcis (f)* [KL2, L7]

citizen *cīvis, -is (m/f)* [KL2, L7]

citizenship *cīvitās, -tātis (f)* [KL2, L7]

city *urbs, urbis (f)* [KL1, L18]; *cīvitās, -tātis (f)* [KL2, L7]

city walls *moenia, -ium (n, pl)* [KL1, L18]

clan *gens, -ntis (f)* [KL1, L31]

class *classis, -is (f)* [KL1, L30]

clay *lutum, -ī (n)* [KL3, W8]

clean (verb) *mundō* [KL3, L5]

clean (adj.) *mundus, -a, -um* [KL3, L5]

cleanse *mundō* [KL3, L5]; *emundō, -āre, ——, -ātum* [KL3, W11]

clear (make) *manifestō* [KL2, W8]

clear (it is clear) *scīlicet* [KL3, L6]

clear (very clear) *limpidissimus, -a, -um* [KL1, W32]

clemency *clēmentia, -ae (f)* [KL1, W21]

clerk *scrība, -ae (f)* [KL3, L10]

cliff *cautēs, -is (f)* [KL3, W16]; *scopulus, -ī (m)* [KL1, W30]

climb *ascendō, -ere, -scendī, -scensum* [KL2, L9]

cloak *pallium, -ī (n)* [KL3, W7]

close (adv. & prep. +acc.) *iūxta* [KL1, L28]

close (verb) *claudō, -ere, clausī, clausum* [KL3, W15]; *conclūdō, -ere, -clūsī, -clūsum* [KL2, W9]

close to *sub (+acc.)* [KL1, L14]

clothe *induō, -ere, -duī, dūtum* [KL2, L14]

clothing *vestis, vestis (f)* [KL1, L18]; *vestīmentum, -ī (n)* [KL2, L14]

cloud *nūbēs, nūbis (f)* [KL1, L18]

coil *spīra, -ae (f)* [KL3, W6]

coin *nummus, -ī (m)* [KL1, W22]

cold *gelidus, -a, -um* [KL1, L31]

collect (into a flock/herd) *congregō* [KL2, L14]

colonnade *porticus, -ūs (f)* [KL3, W5]

color *color, -ōris (m)* [KL2, W11]

come *veniō, -īre, vēnī, ventum* [KL1, L29]

come—(back) *redeō, -īre, -iī, -itum* [KL3, L2]; **(down)** *dēscendō, -ere, -scendī, -scensum* [KL3, L7]; **(forth)** *prōdeō, -īre, -iī, -itum* [KL3, L12]; **(through to)** *perveniō, -īre, -vēnī, -ventum* [KL2, L11]; **(near)** *propinquō (+dat./acc.)* [KL2, W3]; **(to pass)** *accidō, -ere, -cīdī, ——* [KL3, L10]; **(upon)** *inveniō, -īre, -vēnī, -ventum* [KL1, L29]

coming *adventus, -ūs (m)* [KL3, L12]

command (noun) *imperium, -iī (n)* [KL2, L3]; *mandātum, -ī (n)* [KL2, L10]

command (verb) *iubeō, -ēre, iūssī, iūssum* [KL3, L2]; *imperō* [KL3, L10]; *mandō* [KL3, L10]; *praecipiō, -ere, -cēpī, -ceptum* [KL3, W5]

commandment *mandātum, -ī (n)* [KL2, L10]

commence *incipiō, -ere, -cēpī, -ceptum* [KL1, L31]

commencement *initium, -iī (n)* [KL3, L7]

commit *mandō* [KL3, L10]

common *commūnis, -e* [KL3, W2]

community *societās, -tātis* (f) [KL3, W11]

companion *comes, -mitis (m)* [KL2, L13]; *socius, -iī (m)* [KL2, L13]

compel *cōgō, -ere, -ēgī, -āctum* [KL1, L28]

complete *perficiō, -ere, -fēcī, -fectum* [KL1, W23]; *contendō, -ere, -tendī, -tentum* [KL2, W9]

complaint *gemitus, -ūs (m)* [KL3, W6]

complete *impleō, -ēre, -plēvī, -plētum* [KL2, L7]; *rēpleō, -ēre, -plēvī, -plētum* [KL3, L5]; *perficiō, -ere, -fēcī, -fectum* [KL1, W23; KL3, L14]

comrade *comes, -mitis (m)* [KL2, L13]

conceal *occultō (1)* [KL1, L22]; *obcaecō* [KL3, W12]

concerning *dē (+abl.)* [KL1, L4]

confess *cōnfiteor, -ērī, ——, -fessus sum (+dat./acc.)* [KL2, L6]

confidence *fīdūcia, -ae (f)* [KL3, L7]

confound *confundō, -ere, -fūdī, -fūsum* [KL3, L12]

confuse *cōnsternō* [KL3, W7]

conquer *superō (1)* [KL1, L2]; *vincō, -ere, vīcī, victum* [KL1, L26]

conqueror *victor, -toris (m)* [KL2, L13]

consecrated *sanctus, -a, -um* [KL1, L25]

consequently *ergo* (adv.) [KL1, L18]

consider *putō* [KL3, L3]

constantly *usque* [KL3, L4]

constellation *sīdus, sīderis (n)* [KL3, L15]

consume *consūmō, -ere, -sūmpsī, -sūmptum* [KL3, L2]

consume by fire *cremō (1)* [KL1, L2]

contest *certāmen, -minis (n)* [KL1, W23]

continent *continēns, -entis (f)* [KL3, W2]

continue *permaneō, -ēre, -mansī, -mansum* [KL3, L7]

continuously *usque* [KL3, L4]

on the **contrary** *immō* [KL3, W7]

conversation *sermō, -ōnis (m)* [KL2, L9]

convert *convertō, -ere, -vertī, -versum* [KL3, L9]

convey *vehō, -ere, vexī, vectum* [KL1, L27]

cookie *crustulum, -ī (n)* [KL1, L5]

corner *angularis, -e* [KL2, W9]

couch (pallet) *grabātus, -ī (m)* [KL3, W5]

council *concilium, -iī (n)* [KL3, L5]

counsel *cōnsilium, -iī (n)* [KL1, L30]

counterfeit *mendācium, -iī (n)* [KL3, L6]

countless *innumerus, -a, -um* [KL3, W16]

country house *villa, -ae (f)* [KL1, L2]

country(side) *rūs, rūris (n)* [KL2, L14]

countryside (adj.) *rusticus, -a, -um* [KL3, W7]

courage *virtūs, virtūtis (f)* [KL1, L12]

course *curriculum, -ī (n)* [KL1, W23]; *āgmen, -minis (n)* [KL3, L6]

court *ātrium, -iī (n)* [KL3, L10]

cousin (on the father's side) *patruēlis, -is (m/f)* [KL1, L22]; **(on the mother's side)** *consōbrīna, -ae (f)* & *consōbrīnus, -ī (m)* [KL1, L22]

covenant *foedus, -deris (n)* [KL2, L12]; *lēx, lēgis (f)* [KL2, L10]

covenanted *pactus, -a, -um* [KL2, L13]

cover (verb) *obumbrō* [KL3, W4]

covering *strātum, -ī (n)* [KL2, L13]; *vēlāmen, -minis (n)* [KL2, W11]

cow *bōs, bovis (m/f)* [KL1, L19]

crack *rīma, -ae (f)* [KL2, W11]

crash *naufragium, -ī (n)* [KL1, W23]

crawl *reptō (1)* [KL1, L14]

crazy (adj.) *insānus, -a, -um* [KL3, W3]

be **crazy (verb)** *furō, -ere, -uī, ——* [KL2, W13]

create *creō (1)* [KL1, L6]

creep *reptō (1)* [KL1, L14]

creeping *reptilis, -e* [KL3, W4]

create *gignō, -ere, genuī, genitum* [KL2, L9]

Crete *Crēta, -ae (f)* [KL1, W30]

crime *nefās (n, indecl.)* [KL3, W2]; *scelus, -leris (n)* [KL3, L6]; *crīmen, -minis (n)* [KL3, W1]

crops *plural of frūmentum, -ī (n)* [KL1, L15]

cross *crux, crucis (f)* [KL1, L15]

cross (over) *trānseō, -īre, -iī, -itum* [KL2, L15]

crowd *turba, -ae (f)* [KL1, L2]; *multitūdō, -tudinis (f)* [KL2, L12]; *congregātiō, -ōnis (f)* [KL3, W4]

crowded *confertus, -a, -um* [KL2, W15]

crown *corōna, -ae (f)* [KL1, L2]

cruel *crūdēlis, -e* [KL3, L10]; *saevus, -a, -um* [KL2, W11]

crush *premō, -ere, pressī, pressum* [KL2, L10]

cry (noun) *clāmor, -oris (m)* [KL1, W20]; *clāmor, -oris (m)* [KL1, W20; KL2, L13]; *gemitus, -ūs (m)* [KL3, W6]; *planctus, -ūs (m)* [KL3, W8]

cubit *cubitum, -ī (n)* [KL2, L14]

cultivate *colō, -ere, coluī, cultum* [KL1, L29]; *incolō, -ere, -coluī, -cultum* [KL3, L2]

cultivated field *arvum, -ī (n)* [KL3, L15]

Cupid *Cupīdo, -dinis (m)* [KL1, W20]

curse *maledīcō, -ere, -dīxī, -dictum (+dat.)* [KL1, W30; KL3, L4]

curved *uncus, -a, -um* [KL3, W16]

custom *mōs, mōris (m)* [KL2, L13]

cut *scindō, -ere, scidī, scissum* [KL3, L10]; *dissecō* [KL2, W5]; **cut (down)** *occīdō, -ere, -cīdī, -cīsum* [KL1, L30]; *percutiō, -ere, -cussī, -cussum* [KL1, W32]; *caedō, -ere, cecīdī, caesum* [KL2, L12]; **(off)** *praecīdō, -ere, -cīdī, -cīsum* [KL1, W32; KL2, W6]

cyclops *Cȳclōps, Cȳclōpis (m)* [KL2, W4]

D

Daedalus *Daedalus, -ī (m)* [KL1, W30]

dagger *sīca, -ae (f)* [KL1, L3]

danger *perīculum, -ī (n)* [KL1, L5]

Daphne *Daphne, -ēs (f)* [KL1, W20]

dare *audeō, -ēre, ——, ausus sum* [KL1, L11]

dark *āter, -tra, -trum* [KL1, L17]; *tenēbrōsus, -a, -um* [KL2, W15]

dark-colored *niger, -gra, -grum* [KL1, L17]

darken *obcaecō* [KL3, W12]

darkness *tenēbrae, -ārum (f, pl)* [KL1, L11]

daughter *fīlia, -ae (f)* [KL1, L6]

David *David (indecl.)* [KL1, W32]

day *diēs, diēī (m/f)* [KL1, L28]

dead *mortuus, -a, -um* [KL2, L3]

dead body *cadaver, -veris (n)* [KL1, W32]

deadly *fātālis, -e* [KL3, W6]

dear *cārus, -a, -um* [KL1, L13]

death *mors, mortis (f)* [KL1, L18]; *nex, necis (f)* [KL3, W10]

deceit *dolus, -ī (m)* [KL3, L6]

deceitful *falsus, -a, -um* [KL2, W13]

deceive *mentior, -īrī, ——, -ītus sum* [KL3, L6]; *sēdūcō, -ere, -dūxī, -ductum* [KL3, W11]

decide *cōnstituō, -ere, -stituī, -stitūtum* [KL2, L15]; *iūdicō* [KL2, L14]

decision *iūdicium, -ī (n)* [KL2, L9]

declare *dēclārō (1)* [KL1, L10]; *nuntiō (1)* [KL1, L14]; *indīcō* [KL3, L11]; *ostendō, -ere, -dī, -sum/tum* [KL3, L5]; *praedīcō* [KL3, W7]; *polliceor, -ērī, ——, pollicitus sum* [KL3, L7]

declaration *ēdictum, -ī (n)* [KL3, W10]

dedicate *dēdicō* [KL3, W7]

deed *opus, operis (n)* [KL2, L3]

deep *altus, -a, -um* [KL1, L19]

deepest *īmus, -a, -um* [KL2, L5]; *īnfimus, -a, -um* [KL2, L5]

deer *cervus, -ī (m)* [KL1, L10]

defeat *superō (1)* [KL1, L2]; *vincō, -ere, vīcī, victum* [KL1, L26]

defend *dēfendō, -ere, -fendī, -fēnsum* [KL1, L28]; *custōdiō, -īre, -iī/-īvī, -ītum* [KL3, L3]

defender *custōs, -ōdis (m/f)* [KL3, L3]

delay *cunctātiō, -ōnis (f)* [KL3, W9]

delay (verb) *cunctor, -ārī, ——, -ātus sum* [KL3, W9]

deliverance *salūs, -ūtis (f)* [KL3, W7]

demand (verb) *postulō* [KL3, L10]

demand (noun) *condiciō, -ōnis (f)* [KL2, W15]

demon *daemonium, -iī (n)* [KL3, L1]

deny *negō* [KL3, L3]

depart *abeō, -īre, -iī, -itum* [KL1, W32; KL2, L9]

deprive of *viduō (1)* [KL1, W19]

deprived of parents/children *orbus, -a, -um* [KL1, L22]

depth *profundum, -ī (n)* [KL3, W9]

descend *dēscendō, -ere, -scendī, -scensum* [KL3, L7]

descendant *nepōs, -pōtis (m/f)* [KL2, L13]

desert places *dēserta, -ōrum (n, pl)* [KL3, L4]

deserted *dēsertus, -a, -um* [KL3, L4]

deserve *mereō, -ēre, -uī, -itum* [KL1, L15; KL3, W6]

desire (noun) *voluntās, -tātis (f)* [KL3, L12]

desire (verb) *cupiō, -ere, cupīvī, cupītum* [KL1, L31]; *postulō* [KL3, L10]

desolate *vastus, -a, -um* [KL2, L6]

despise *despiciō, -ere, -spexī, -spectum* [KL1, W32]

destiny *sors, -rtis (f)* [KL3, L6]

destroy *dēleō, -ēre, -lēvī, -lētum* [KL1, L9]; *interficiō, -ere, -fēcī, -fectum* [KL1, L31]; *perdō, -ere, perdidī, perditum* [KL1, L27]; *dissolvō, -ere, -solvī, -solūtum* [KL3, W5]; *ēvertō, -ere, -tī, -sum* [KL3, W7]; *tollō, -ere, sustulī, sublātum* [KL1, W25; KL2, L13]

destruction *plāga, -ae (f)* [KL3, L14]; *clādēs, -is (f)* [KL2, W15]

devastate *vastō (1)* [KL1, L14]

device *māchina, -ae (f)* [KL3, W6]

devil *diabolus, -ī (m)* [KL3, W13]; *Satanās, -ae (m)* [KL3, W1]

devour *edō, -ere, ēdī, ēsum* [KL3, L1]

dew *rōs, rōris (m)* [KL2, W9]

Diana *Diāna, -ae (f)* [KL1, W20]

die *morior, morī, ——, mortuus sum* [KL2, L6]

different *dissimilis, -e* [KL2, L5]

difficult *difficilis, -e* [KL1, L20; KL2, L5]

dig *fodiō, -ere, fōdī, fossum* [KL1, W28]

dinner *cēna, -ae (f)* [KL1, L20]

direct *gubernō (1)* [KL1, L25]

direction *pars, partis (f)* [KL2, L3]

dirty *immundus, -a, -um* [KL3, L5]

disciple *discipula, -ae (f); discipulus, -ī (m)* [KL1, L5]

discus *discus, -ī (m)* [KL2, W6]

disgust *odium, -iī (n)* [KL3, L4]

dishonor (verb) *violō* [KL3, W1]

dishonor (noun) *turpitūdō, -dinis (f)* [KL3, W9]

dislike *ōdī, ōdisse, [fut. prt.] ōsūrum* [KL3, L6]

dismal *trīstis, -e* [KL1, L20]

dismiss *dīmittō, -ere, -mīsī, -missum* [KL1, L30]

dissimilar *dissimilis, -e* [KL2, L5]

distance *intervāllum, -ī (n)* [KL3, W2]

distant *longinquus, -a, -um* [KL1, L7]

distress *miseria, -ae (f)* [KL3, W9]

disturb *confundō, -ere, -fūdī, -fūsum* [KL3, L12]; *turbō* [KL2, W13]

diverse *dīversus, -a, -um* [KL3, W7]

divine *dīvīnus, -a, -um* [KL3, W7]

divine law *fās (n, indecl.)* [KL3, L2]

divine will *nūmen, -minis (n)* [KL2, L7]

divinity *nūmen, -minis (n)* [KL2, L7]

division *schisma, -ae (f)* [KL2, W8]

do *agō, -ere, ēgī, actum* [KL1, L26]; *faciō, -ere, fēcī, factum* [KL1, L31]

do not know *ignōrō* [KL2, L15]; *nesciō, -īre, -īvī, -ītum* [KL1, L30; KL3, L3]

dog *canis, canis (m/f)* [KL1, L18]

done (be done) *fīō, fierī, ——, factus sum* [KL1, L31]

donkey *asinus, -ī (m)* [KL1, L27]

door *porta, -ae (f)* [KL1, L31]; *ōstium, -iī (n)* [KL2, L4]

doorway *līmen, -minis (n)* [KL3, L3]

doubt (verb) *dubitō* [KL3, W7]

doubt (noun) *dubitātiō, -ōnis (f)* [KL3, W9]

doubtful *dubius, -a, -um* [KL3, W7]

down from *dē (+abl.)* [KL1, L4]

downfall *cāsus, -ūs (m)* [KL1, L28]

drag *trahō, -ere, trāxī, trāctum* [KL1, L30]

dragon *dracō, dracōnis (m)* [KL1, L12]

draw *trahō, -ere, trāxī, trāctum* [KL1, L30]

draw near *appropinquō (1)* [KL1, L25]

draw (up) *hauriō, -īre, hausī, haustum* [KL2, W12]; *subdūcō, -ere, -dūxī, -ductum* [KL2, W2]; **(out)** *stringō, -ere, strinxī, strictum* [KL3, W7]

dread (noun) *metus, -ūs (m)* [KL1, L26]

dread (verb) *paveō, -ēre, pavī, ——* [KL3, L15]

dreadful *horrendus, -a, -um* [KL1, L13]

dream (noun) *īnsōmnium, -iī (n)* [KL2, W13]

dream (verb) *somniō (1)* [KL1, W18]

drench *perfundō, -ere, -fūdī, -fūsus* [KL3, W6]

drink (verb) *bibō, -ere, bibī, potum* [KL2, L10]; *hauriō, -īre, hausī, haustum* [KL2, W12]

drink (heavily), *pōtō, -āre, -āvī, pōtātum* or *pōtum* [KL1, L6]

drip *mānō* [KL3, W16]

drive *agō, -ere, ēgī, actum* [KL1, L26]

drive (out) *ēiciō, -ere, -iēcī, -iectum* [KL2, L14]; **(back)** *repellō, -ere, reppulī, repulsum* [KL3, W2]

drive together *cōgō, -ere, -ēgī, -āctum* [KL1, L28]

driver *aurīga, -ae (m/f)* [KL1, W23]

drop *cadō, -ere, cecidī, casūrum* [KL1, L27]

drunk *ēbrius, -a, -um* [KL1, W13; KL2, W4]

dry *āridus, -a, -um* [KL1, L27]

dry up *torreō, -ēre, torruī, tostum* [KL1, L17]

dryness *ārida, -ae (f)* [KL3, W1]

duty *iūs, iūris (n)* [KL2, L15]; *mūnus, -neris (n)* [KL2, L15]; *pietās, -tātis (f)* [KL2, W13]

dye (verb) *inficiō, -ere, -fēcī, -fectum* [KL3, W2]

dwell *habitō (1)* [KL1, L3]

dwell in *incolō, -ere, -coluī, -cultum* [KL3, L2]

E

each (one) *quisque, quaeque, quidque* [KL3, L2]

each other *invicem* [KL2, L12]

eager *ācer, ācris, ācre* [KL1, L20]; *cupidus, -a, -um* [KL3, W2]

eagerly *certātim* [KL1, L20]

ear *auris, -is (f)* [KL1, W28]

ear of corn *spīca, -ae (f)* [KL3, W1]

early (in the morning) *māne* [KL1, W19; KL2, L6]; *mātūtīnus, -a, -um* [KL3, W9]

earn *mereō, -ēre, -uī, -itum* [KL1, L15; KL3, W6]

earth *tellūs, tellūris (f)* [KL1, L14]; *terra, -ae (f)* [KL1, L4]; *humus, -ī (f)* [KL2, L14]

easily *facile* [KL2, L7]

easy *facilis, -e* [KL1, L20; KL2, L5]

eat *mandūcō (1)* [KL1, L6]; *edō, -ere, ēdī, ēsum* [KL3, L1]; *comedō, -ere, -ēdī, -ēsus* [KL3, W1]

echo *īnsonō, -āre, -uī, -ītum* [KL2, W6]

eight *octō* [KL1, L21]

eighteen *duodēvīgintī* [KL1, L21]

eighteenth *duodēvīcēsimus, -a, -um* [KL1, L23]

eighth *octāvus, -a, -um* [KL1, L23]

either *uter, utra (ūtra), utrum (ūtrum) (interrog.)* [KL2, L15]

elbow *cubitum, -ī (n)* [KL2, L14]

elder (adj.) *senior, -ōris* [KL3, L5]

elder (noun) *senior, -ōris* [KL3, L5]

elect *ēligō, -ere, -lēgī, -lectum* [KL3, L1]

elegant *mundus, -a, -um* [KL3, L5]

elephant *elephantus, -ī (m)* [KL1, L19]

eleven *ūndecim* [KL1, L21]

eleventh *ūndecimus, -a, -um* [KL1, L23]

empire *imperium, -iī (n)* [KL2, L3]

empty *inānis, -e* [KL3, W4]; *vacuus, -a, -um* [KL3, W4]

end *fīnis, -is (m)* [KL1, W4]; *terminus, -ī (m)* [KL3, L15]

endure *patior, -ī, ——, passus sum* [KL2, L6]

enemy (of the state) *hostis, -is (m)* [KL1, L18]; **(personal enemy)** *inimīcus, -ī (m)* [KL1, L10]

enjoy *ūtor, ūtī, ——, ūsus sum (+abl.)* [KL3, L2]

enjoyment *voluptās, -tātis (f)* [KL3, W2]

enormous *ingēns, (gen.) -entis* [KL1, L19]; *immānis, -e* [KL3, L7]; *vastus, -a, -um* [KL2, L6]

enough *satis (adv./indecl., adj./noun)* [KL1, L30]

engine (military) *māchina, -ae (f)* [KL3, W6]

enraged *īnfēnsus, -a, -um* [KL2, W15]

entangle *implicō* [KL3, W5]

enter *intrō (1)* [KL1, L9]; *ineō, -īre, -iī (-īvī), -ītum* [KL3, L4]

entire *ūniversus, -a, -um* [KL3, L4]

entrails *vīscus, -eris (n)* [KL3, L13]

entrance *initium, -iī (n)* [KL3, L7]; *ōstium, -iī (n)* [KL2, L4]

entrust *mandō* [KL3, L10]

entryway *ātrium, -iī (n)* [KL3, L10]

envious *invidus, -a, -um* [KL2, W11]

envoy *lēgātus, -ī (m)* [KL2, L15]

envy (noun) *aemulātiō, -ōnis (f)* [KL3, W7]

envy (verb) *invideō, -ēre, -vīdī, -vīsum* [KL1, W29]

Ephramite *Ephratheus, -ī (m)* [KL1, W32]

epistle *plural of littera, -ae (f)* [KL1, L26]

equally *pariter* [KL3, L1]

equipment (kit) *vās, vāsis (n)* [KL3, W1]

err *errō (1)* [KL1, L14]

error *error, -ōris (m)* [KL3, W7]

escape *effugiō, -ere, -fūgī, -fugitum* [KL1, W10]; *ēlābor, -lābī, ——, -lapsus sum* [KL2, L6]; *ēvādō, -ere, -vāsī, -vāsum* [KL3, L7]

especially *māximē* [KL2, L7]

essence *substantia, -ae (f)* [KL3, L13]

establish *cōnstituō, -ere, -stituī, -stitūtum* [KL2, L15]

esteem (noun) *cāritās, -tātis (f)* [KL3, L11]

esteem (verb) *foveō, -ēre, fōvī, fōtum* [KL1, L25]

eternal *aeternus, -a, -um* [KL1, L15]

evangelical *ēvangelicus, -a, -um* [KL3, W9]

even *et* [KL1, L1]; *etiam* [KL1, L22]; *quidem* [KL2, L3]

evening star *vesper, vesperis (m)* [KL1, L14]

evening *vesper, vesperis (m)* [KL1, L14]

event *cāsus, -ūs (m)* [KL1, L28]

ever *quandō* [KL1, L12]; *quondam* [KL2, L13]; *umquam* [KL3, L14]

every *omnis, -e* [KL1, L19]; *cunctus, -a, -um* [KL2, L9]; *tōtus, -a, -um* [KL2, L3]

every(one) *quisque, quaeque, quidque* [KL3, L2]

everywhere *ubīque* [KL1, W29]; *passim* [KL2, L13]; *undique* [KL1, L30; KL2, L15]

evidence *testimōnium, -ī (n)* [KL2, L10]

evident (verb, it is evident) *apparet* [KL3, L4]

evident (adj.) *manifestus, -a, -um* [KL3, W1]

evil *malus, -a, -um* [KL1, L7]; *malignus, -a, -um* [KL3, L13]

evil spirit *daemonium, -iī (n)* [KL3, L1]

exalt *exaltō* [KL3, W5]

examine *probō* [KL3, L14]

example *exemplum, -ī (n)* [KL3, W7]; *rēgula, -ae (f)* [KL3, W9]

exceedingly *nimium* [KL2, W13]; *valde* [KL2, L10]

excellent *ēgregius, -a, -um* [KL1, L29]

except *extrā* [KL3, L15]; *nisi* [KL3, L11]

excessively *nimis* [KL3, L4]; *nimium* [KL2, W13]

exercise *exerceō, -ēre, -uī, -itum* [KL1, L14]

exile *exsilium, -iī (n)* [KL3, W3]

exit *exitus, -ūs (m)* [KL2, W13]

expect *exspectō (1)* [KL1, L3]; *spērō* [KL3, L1]

expects a no answer *num* [KL2, L7]

expects a yes answer *nōnne* [KL2, L7]

expensive *pretiōsus, -a, -um* [KL2, W2]

explain *dēclārō (1)* [KL1, L10]

expose *aperiō, -īre, aperuī, apertum* [KL1, L29]

exposed *nūdus, -a, -um* [KL3, W7]

expression *vultus, -ūs (m)* [KL1, L25]

exstinguish *exstinguō, -ere, -stinxī, -stinctum* [KL3, W1]; *rēstinguō, -ere, -stinxī, -stinctum* [KL3, W3]

extend *extendō, -ere, -tendī, -tensum* [KL1, W26; KL3, W1]; *sternō, -ere, strāvī, strātum* [KL2, L13]

exult *exultō* [KL3, W9]; *triumphō* [KL3, W9]

eye *oculus, -ī (m)* [KL2, L3]

F

Fabius *Fabius, -iī (m)* [KL1, W19]

face *faciēs, -ēī (f)* [KL1, L28]; *vultus, -ūs (m)* [KL1, L25]

fair *iūstus, -a, -um* [KL1, L7]

faith *fidēs, -eī (f)* [KL1, L28]; *fīdūcia, -ae (f)* [KL3, L7]

faithful *fīdus, -a, -um* [KL1, L7]; *fidēlis, -e* [KL2, L4]

fall *cadō, -ere, cecidī, cāsūrum* [KL1, L27]; *lābor, -ī, ——, lapsus sum* [KL2, L6]; **fall (down)** *dēscendō, -ere, -scendī, -scensum* [KL3, L7]; **fall down (violently)** *ruō, -ere, ruī, rutum* [KL3, L4]; **fall upon/out** *accidō, -ere, -cīdī, ——* [KL3, L10]

false *falsus, -a, -um* [KL2, W13]

falsehood *mendācium, -iī (n)* [KL3, L6]

fame *fāma, -ae (f)* [KL2, L13]

fame *glōria, -ae* [KL1, L15]; *fāma, -ae* [KL1, W23]

family *familia, -ae* [KL1, L22]

famous *nōbilis, -e* [KL2, W15]

famous (that famous) *ille, illa, illud* [KL1, L30]

far away *longinquus, -a, -um* [KL1, L7]

far and wide *passim* [KL2, L13]

far off *longē* [KL3, L3]

far *procul* [KL2, L11]

farm *rūs, rūris (n)* [KL2, L14]; *fundus, -ī (m)* [KL2, W10]

farmer *agricola, -ae (m)* [KL1, L3]

farmhouse *villa, -ae (f)* [KL1, L2]

farther *ulterior, -ius* [KL2, L5]

farthest *ultimus, -a, -um* [KL2, L5]

fast (verb) *iēiūnō* [KL3, W10]

fast (noun) *iēiūnium, -iī (n)* [KL3, W10]

fast (adv) *cito* [KL1, L27]

fasten in *infīgō, -ere, -fīxī, -fīxum* [KL1, W32]

fat *pinguis, -e* [KL1, W25]

fatal *fātālis, -e* [KL3, W6]

fate *fātum, -ī (n)* [KL1, L5; KL2, 13]

father *pater, patris (m)* [KL1, L12]; *parēns, -entis (m/f)* [KL1, W11; KL2, W8]

fault *peccātum, -ī (n)* [KL3, L11]

favor *grātia, -ae (f)* [KL1, L27]

favorable *dexter, -tra, -trum (or -tera, -terum)* [KL1, L30]

fear (noun) *metus, -ūs (m)* [KL1, L26]; *timor, -ōris (m)* [KL3, L14]

fear (verb) *timeō, -ēre, -uī, ——* [KL1, L9]; *paveō, -ēre, pavī, ——* [KL3, L15]; *metuō, -ere, -uī, -ūtum* [KL3, L15]; *vereor, -ērī, ——, veritus sum* [KL2, L6]

fearful *horrendus, -a, -um* [KL1, L13]

feast *epulae, -ārum (f, pl)* [KL1, L20]

feather *penna, -ae (f)* [KL3, W16]

feeble *īnfirmus, -a, -um* [KL3, W5]

feed *pascō, -ere, pāvī, pastum* [KL1, W32; KL2, W14]; *alō, alere, aluī, altum/alītum* [KL3, W2]

feel *sentiō, -īre, sēnsī, sēnsum* [KL3, L3]

feeling *sensus, -ūs (m)* [KL2, L15]

fellowship *societās, -tātis (f)* [KL3, W11]

female *fēmīnus, -a, -um* [KL3, W4]

female slave *ancilla, -ae (f)* [KL3, L10]

few *paucī, -ae, -a* [KL1, L7]

field *ager, agrī (m)* [KL1, L4]; *arvum, -ī (n)* [KL3, L15]

fierce *ācer, ācris, ācre* [KL1, L20]; *ferus, -a, -um* [KL1, L7]; *asper, -era, -erum* [KL2, W12]; *saevus, -a, -um* [KL2, W11]

fiery *caldus, -a, -um* [KL1, L7]

fifteen *quīndecim* [KL1, L21]

fifteenth *quīntus, -a, -um decimus, -a, -um* [KL1, L23]

fifth *quīntus, -a, -um* [KL1, L23]

fiftieth *quīnquāgēsimus, -a, -um* [KL1, L23]

fifty *quīnquāgintā* [KL1, L21]

fight (verb) *pugna, -ae (f)* [KL2, W9]

fight (noun) *pugnō (1)* [KL1, L1]

fill *rēpleō, -ēre, -plēvī, -plētum* [KL3, L5]

fill up *rēpleō, -ēre, -plēvī, -plētum* [KL3, L5]; *impleō, -ēre, -plēvī, -plētum* [KL2, L7]; *compleō, -ēre, -plēvī, -plētum* [KL2, W6]

fill again *rēpleō, -ēre, -plēvī, -plētum* [KL3, L5]

finally *dēnique* [KL1, L10]; *tandem* [KL3, L15]

find *inveniō, -īre, -vēnī, -ventum* [KL1, L29]

finish *perficiō, -ere, -fēcī, -fectum* [KL1, W23; KL3, L14]

fire *ignis, ignis* [KL1, L18]; *aestus, -ūs (m)* [KL2, W9]

fire-pan *foculus, -ī (m)* [KL2, W15]

set on **fire** *accendō, -ere, -censī, -censum* [KL2, W15]; *incendō, -ere, -cendī, -censum* [KL2, W13]

first (adj.) *prīmus, -a, -um* [KL1, L23]

first (adv.) *prīmum/prīmō* [KL2, L7]

fish (noun) *piscis, -is (m)* [KL1, L19]

fish (verb) *piscor, -ārī, ——, -ātus sum* (deponent) [KL1, W29]

fisherman *piscātor, -ōris (m)* [KL3, W6]

fissure *rīma, -ae (f)* [KL2, W11]

fitting (it is fitting) *decet, -ēre, ——, decuit (impers. +acc.)* [KL3, L1]

five hundred *quīngentī* [KL1, L21]

five hundredth *quīngentēsimus, -a, -um* [KL1, L23]

five *quīnque* [KL1, L21]

fix in *infīgo, -ere, -fixī, -fixum* [KL1, W32]

flag (starting flag) *mappa, -ae (f)* [KL1, W23]

flank *latus, lateris (n)* [KL3, L6]

flash (verb) *micō, -āre, -uī, ——* [KL3, W3]

flee *fugiō, -ere, fūgī, fugitum* [KL1, L31]

fleet (of ships) *classis, -is (f)* [KL1, L30]

flicker *vibrō* [KL3, W6]

flesh *caro, carnis (f)* [KL1, L31]

flock *grex, gregis (m)* [KL1, L31]

flourish *flōreō, -ēre, -uī, ——* [KL1, L17]

flow *mānō* [KL3, W16]

flower *flōs, flōris (m)* [KL1, L15]

fly *volō (1)* [KL1, L10]; *circumvolō* [KL2, W12]

flying *volātilis, -e* [KL3, W4]

foam (verb) *spūmō* [KL3, W6]

fold *spīra, -ae (f)* [KL3, W6]

follow *sequor, sequī, ——, secūtus sum (deponent)* [KL1, W30; KL2, L6]

folly *stultitia, -ae (f)* [KL1, W27]

food *cibus, -ī (m)* [KL1, L4]; *esca, -ae (f)* [KL2, W14]

foolish *stultus, -a, -um* [KL1, L7]

foolishness *stultitia, -ae (f)* [KL1, W27]

foot *pēs, pedis (m)* [KL3, W3]

foot (at the foot of) *sub (+abl.)* [KL1, L14]

footprint *vestīgium, -iī (n)* [KL2, W11]

for (conj.) *enim (postpositive conj.)* [KL1, L17]; *nam* [KL1, W32; KL2, L9]

for (prep.) *ob (+acc.)* [KL2, L3]

for a long time *diū* [KL1, L13]

for that reason *ideo* [KL2, L14]

for (the sake of) *pro (+abl.)* [KL1, L18]; *causā (+ gen.)* [KL2, L15]

forbid *vetō, -āre, vetuī, vetitum* [KL3, W11]

forbidden *nefās (n, indecl.)* [KL3, W2]

force (noun) *vīs, vīs (f)* [KL3, L5]

force (verb) *cōgō, -ere, -ēgī, -āctum* [KL1, L28]

forehead *frōns, -ntis (f)* [KL1, W32]

foreign *barbarus, -a, -um* [KL1, L31]; *aliēnus, -a, -um* [KL2, L12]

foreigner *aliēnus, -a, -um* [KL2, L12]; *barbarus, -ī (m)* [KL1, L31]

forever *perpetuō* [KL2, W2]

forest *silva, -ae (f)* [KL1, L3]

forethought *prōvidentia, -ae (f)* [KL2, W9]

forget *oblīvīscor, -vīscī, ——, oblītus sum (+gen.)* [KL2, L7]

forgive *dīmittō, -ere, -mīsī, -missum* [KL1, L30]; *remittō, -ere, -mīsī, -missum* [KL3, L11]

forgiveness *remissiō, -ōnis (f)* [KL3, W5]; *venia, -ae (f)* [KL3, W12]

form *faciēs, -ēī (f)* [KL1, L28]; *īdōlum, -ī (n)* [KL3, L7]

former *prior, prius* [KL2, L5]

formerly *ōlim* [KL1, L6]; *quondam* [KL2, L13]

forsaken *dēsertus, -a, -um* [KL3, L4]

fort *arx, arcis (f)* [KL2, L7]

fortification *mūnītiō, -ōnis (f)* [KL3, W2]

fortifications *moenia, -ium (n, pl)* [KL1, L18]

forth *forās* [KL3, L6]

fortunate *fēlix, (gen.) -līcis* [KL1, L19]

fortune *substantia, -ae (f)* [KL3, L13]

foul *immundus, -a, -um* [KL3, L5]

fountain *fōns, fontis (m)* [KL2, L11]

foundation *basis, -is (f)* [KL2, W9]; *fundamentum, -ī (n)* [KL2, W9]

four *quattuor* [KL1, L21]

four times *quater* [KL3, W6]

four-horse chariot *quadrīgae, -ārum (f)* [KL1, W23]

fourteen *quattuordecim* [KL1, L21]

fourteenth *quārtus, -a, -um decimus, -a, -um* [KL1, L23]

fourth *quārtus, -a, -um* [KL1, L23]

fraud *dolus, -ī (m)* [KL3, L6]

free *līberō (1)* [KL1, L1]

frequent *crēber, -bra, -brum* [KL3, L2]

fresh *vīridis, -e* [KL1, L17]; *recēns, -centis* [KL2, W11]

friend *amīca, -ae (f)* [KL1, L15]; *amīcus, -ī (m)* [KL1, L15]; *comes, -mitis (m)* [KL2, L13]

frighten *terreō, -ēre, -uī, -itum* [KL1, L9]

from a distance *procul* [KL2, L11]

from all sides *undique* [KL1, L30; KL2, L15]

from *ā, ab (+abl.)* [KL1, L3]; *dē (+abl.)* [KL1, L4]; *ē, ex (+abl.)* [KL1, L3]

from all sides *undique* [KL1, L30]

from every direction *undique* [KL1, L30]

from here *hinc* [KL2, L11]

from that place *deinde* [KL1, L24]

from that side *illinc* [KL2, L11]

from there *illinc* [KL2, L11]; *inde* [KL2, L10]

from this side *hinc* [KL2, L11]

from where (?) *unde* [KL2, L11]

frost *gelū, -ūs (n)* [KL2, W9]

fruit *frūctus, -ūs (m)* [KL1, L25]; *pōmum, -ī (n)* [KL3, W11]

fruit-bearing *pōmifer, -era, -erum* [KL3, W6]

fruitful *ūber, -eris* [KL2, W11]

full *plēnus, -a, -um* [KL2, L4]

funeral *fūnus, -neris (n)* [KL2, W13]

funeral pyre *pyra, -ae (f)* [KL1, W8]

furrow *versus, -ūs (m)* [KL1, L27]

further *amplius* [KL3, L9]; *ultrā* [KL2, L5]

future (adj.) *futūrus, -a, -um* [KL2, W10]

G

garden *hortus, -ī (m)* [KL2, W6]

garment *vestis, vestis (f)* [KL1, L18]; *vestīmentum, -ī (n)* [KL2, L14]

gate *porta, -ae (f)* [KL1, L31]; *ōstium, -iī (n)* [KL2, L4]

gates (starting gates of a horse race) *plural of carcer, -eris (m)* [KL1, W23]

general *dux, ducis (m)* [KL1, L14]

generally *plērumque* [KL3, W7]

generation *saeculum, -ī (n)* [KL1, L6]; *generātiō, -ōnis (f)* [KL3, L7]

get to know *cognoscō, -ere, -nōvī, -nitum* [KL2, L10]; *noscō, -ere, nōvī, nōtum* [KL2, L9]

ghost *umbra, -ae (f)* [KL3, L3]

giant *gigās, gigantis (m)* [KL1, L15]

gift *dōnum, -ī (n)* [KL1, L5]; *mūnus, -neris (n)* [KL2, L15]

girl *puella, -ae (f)* [KL1, L3]

give *dō, dare, dedī, datum* [KL1, L1]; *praebeō, -ēre, -uī, -ītum* [KL3, W7]

give birth to *pariō, -ere, peperī, par(i)tum* [KL3, L13]

give over *trādō, -ere, -didī, -ditum* [KL1, W13; KL2, L4]

give thanks *grātiās agō (+dat.)* [KL1, L27]

gladiator (in a chariot) *essedarius, -ī (m)* [KL3, W2]

gladness *laetitia, -ae (f)* [KL3, L7]

glide *lābor, -ī, ——, lapsus sum* [KL2, L6]

glitter *fulgeō, -ēre, fulsī, ——* [KL2, W13]; *micō, -āre, -uī, ——* [KL3, W3]

glad *laetus, -a, -um* [KL1, L7]

gloom *nūbēs, nūbis (f)* [KL1, L18]

gloomy *trīstis, -e* [KL1, L20; KL2, L3]; *tenēbrōsus, -a, -um* [KL2, W15]

gloomy place *tenēbrae, -ārum (f, pl)* [KL1, L11]

glory *glōria, -ae* [KL1, L15]

go *cēdō, -ere, cessī, cessum* [KL1, L28]; *eō, īre, iī (īvī), itum* [KL1, L29]; *vādō, -ere, vāsī, ——* [KL2, L9]; **(across)** *trānseō, -īre, -iī, -itum* [KL2, L15]; **(apart)** *sēcēdō, -ere -cessī, -cessum* [KL3, W1]; **(away [from])** *abeō, -īre, -iī, -itum* [KL1, W32; KL2, L9]; **(away)** *exeō, -īre, -iī (-īvī), -itum* [KL2, L12]; **(back)** *redeō, -īre, -iī, -itum* [KL3, L2]; *regredior, -gredī, ——, -gressus sum* [KL3, L10]; *revertor, -vertī, ——, reversus sum* [KL2, L6]; **(forth)** *prōdeō, -īre, -iī, -itum* [KL3, L12]; **(in)** *ingredior, -gredī, ——, -gressus sum* [KL2, L6]; **(in[to])** *ineō, -īre, -iī (-īvī), -ītum* [KL3, L4]; **(out)** *ēgredior, -gredī, ——, -gressus sum* [KL2, L6]; *exeō, -īre, -iī (-īvī), -itum* [KL2, L12]; **(over)** *trānseō, -īre, -iī, -itum* [KL2, L15]; **(to[ward])** *adeō, -īre, -iī, -itum* [KL2, L10]; **(up)** *ascendō, -ere, -scendī, -scensum* [KL2, L9]

goal *mēta, -ae (f)* [KL1, W23]

goat *caper, -prī (m)* [KL1, L4]

goblet *calix, calicis (m)* [KL1, W13]

god *deus, -ī (m)* [KL1, L4]; *nūmen, -minis (n)* [KL2, L7]

God *Deus, -ī (m)* [KL1, L4]

goddess *dea, -ae (f)* [KL1, L6]

gold (noun) *aurum, -ī (n)* [KL1, L5]

gold(en) *aureus, -a, -um* [KL1, L17]

good *bonus, -a, -um* [KL1, L7]

Good day! *salvē(te)* [KL1, L9]

good news *ēvangelium, -ī* [KL1, L5]

Goodbye! *valē(te)* [KL1, L9]

goose *ānser, -eris (m)* [KL3, W2]

Gorgon *Gorgō, -onis (f)* [KL2, L6]

gospel *ēvangelium, -ī* [KL1, L5]

govern *gubernō (1)* [KL1, L25]; *regnō (1)* [KL1, L6]

governor *satrapa, -ae (f)* [KL3, W10]

grace *grātia, -ae (f)* [KL1, L27]

gradually *minūtātim* [KL1, L20]; *paulātim* [KL3, W7]

grain (head) *frūmentum, -ī (n)* [KL1, L15]; *spīca, -ae (f)* [KL3, W1]

granddaughter *nepōs, -pōtis (m/f)* [KL2, L13]

grandfather *avus, -ī (m)* [KL1, L22]

grandmother *avia, -ae (f)* [KL1, L22]

grandson *nepōs, -pōtis (m/f)* [KL2, L13]

grass *grāmen, grāminis (n)* [KL1, L13]

grateful *grātus, -a, -um* [KL1, L27]

grave *sepulcrum, -ī (n)* [KL2, L13]; *tumulus, -ī (m)* [KL2, W11]

great (so/such great) *tantus, -a, -um* [KL3, L5]

greater *māior, -ius* [KL1, W31; KL2, L5]

greatest *māximus, -a, -um* [KL1, W31; KL2, L5]; *summus, -a, -um* [KL2, L5]; *suprēmus, -a, -um* [KL2, L5]

greatly *magnopere* [KL1, L29]

greedy *avārus, -a, -um* [KL1, L7]

Greek (adj.) *Graecus, -a, -um* [KL3, L6]

Greek (noun) *Graecus, -ī* [KL3, L6]

green *vīridis, -e* [KL1, L17]

greenery *grāmen, grāminis (n)* [KL1, L13]

grief *lūctus, -ūs (m)* [KL3, W13]

grim *trīstis, -e* [KL1, L20; KL2, L3]

groan *gemitus, -ūs (m)* [KL3, W6]

ground *tellūs, tellūris (f)* [KL1, L14]; *humus, -ī (f)* [KL2, L14]

group *classis, -is (f)* [KL1, L30]

grow *crēscō, -ere, crēvī, crētum* [KL2, L11]

guarantee *reprōmissiō, -ōnis (f)* [KL3, W12]

guard (noun) *custōs, -ōdis (m/f)* [KL3, L3]

guard (verb) *custōdiō, -īre, -iī/-īvī, -ītum* [KL3, L3]; *observō* [KL3, W11]

guard against *caveō, -ēre, cāvī, cautum* [KL1, L12]

guest *hospes, -pitis (m)* [KL2, W6]

guide (verb) *dūcō, -ere, duxī, ductum* [KL1, L26]

guide (noun) *dux, ducis (m)* [KL1, L14]

H

habit (am in the habit of) *soleō, -ēre, ——, solitus sum (semi-deponent)* [KL3, L9]

Hades *Plūto, -tōnis (m)* [KL2, W6]

hail *grandō, -dinis (f)* [KL2, W9]

hair *capillus, -ī (m)* [KL2, W6]; *coma, -ae (f)* [KL3, W3]

half (of) *dīmidius, -a, -um* [KL3, L10]

hall *ātrium, -iī (n)* [KL3, L10]; *aula, -ae (f)* [KL1, W13; KL3, W10]; *consistōrium, -iī (n)* [KL3, W10]

halt *resistō, -ere, -stitī, ——* [KL3, W2]; *subsistō, -ere, -stitī, ——* [KL3, W6]

hand *manus, -ūs (f)* [KL1, L25]; *palma, -ae (f)* [KL1, W13]

hand down *trādō, -ere, -didī, -ditum* [KL1, W13; KL2, L4]

hand over *trādō, -ere, -didī, -ditum* [KL1, W13; KL2, L4]

handle *temptō* [KL1, W27; KL3, L7]

handsome *pulcher, -chra, -chrum* [KL1, L7]

hang *suspendō, -ere, -pendī, -pensum* [KL3, W5]

happen *fīō, fierī, ——, factus sum* [KL1, L31]; *accidō, -ere, -cīdī, ——* [KL3, L10]; *ēveniō, -īre, -vēnī, -ventum* [KL3, W3]

happily ever after *fēlīciter in aeternum* [KL1, W6; KL2, W2]

happiness *gaudium, -ī (n)* [KL1, L5]

happy *beātus, -a, -um* [KL1, L7]; *fēlix, (gen.) -līcis* [KL1, L19]; *laetus, -a, -um* [KL1, L7]; *fēstus, -a, -um* [KL3, W6]

harbor *portus, -ūs (m)* [KL1, L25]

hard *dūrus, -a, -um* [KL3, W16]

hardship *labor, labōris (m)* [KL1, L12]

hare *lepus, -oris (m)* [KL3, W2]

hardly *vix* [KL3, L3]

harmful *nocēns, -ntis* [KL2, W11]

harmless *innoxius, -a, -um* [KL3, W3]

harp *citara, -ae (f)* [KL2, W2]

harvest *metō, -ere, messuī, messum* [KL2, W14]

hasten *festīnō (1)* [KL1, L9]; *tendō, -ere, tetendī, tentum* [KL2, L4]

hate (verb) *ōdī, ōdisse, [fut. prt.] ōsūrum* [KL3, L6]

hatred *odium, -iī (n)* [KL3, L4]

haughty *superbus, -a, -um* [KL1, W18; KL2, L4]

haul up *subdūcō, -ere, -dūxī, -ductum* [KL2, W2]

have *habeō, -ēre, -uī, -itum* [KL1, L9]

have mercy on *misereor, -ērī, ——, misertus sum (+gen.)* [KL2, L6]

hay *fēnum, -ī (n)* [KL2, W14]; **(straw)** *festūca, -ae (f)* [KL2, W14]

he *is, ea, id* [KL1, L17]

head *caput, -itis (n)* [KL1, L13]

heal *curō* [KL1, L15]

health *salūs, -ūtis (f)* [KL3, W7]

healthy *sānus, -a, -um* [KL3, W1]

hear *audiō, -īre, -īvī, -ītum* [KL1, L29]

heart *cor, cordis (n)* [KL1, L13]

heart (metaphorically) *vīscus, -eris (n)* [KL3, L13]

heathen *gentīlis, -is (m/f)* [KL3, W7]

heaven *caelum, -ī (n)* [KL1, L5]; *aura, -ae (f)* [KL3, L3]

heavenly body *sīdus, sīderis (n)* [KL3, L15]

heaviness *gravitās, -tātis (f)* [KL3, W2]

heavy *gravis, -e* [KL3, L6]

heedless *immemor, -oris* [KL2, W6]

height *summitās, -tātis (f)* [KL2, W10]

Hello! *salvē(te)* [KL1, L9]

helmet *galea, -ae (f)* [KL2, W6]

help (noun) *auxilium, -ī (n)* [KL1, L5]

help (verb) *iuvō, -āre, iūvī, iūtum* [KL1, L22]

hen *gallīna, -ae (f)* [KL3, W2]

hence *hinc* [KL2, L11]

her (own) *suus, -a, -um* [KL1, W31; KL3, L2]

herd *grex, gregis (m)* [KL1, L31]; *pecus, -coris (n)* [KL3, L2]

here *hīc* [KL2, L11]

Hermes *Mercurius, -ī (m)* [KL1, W21; KL2, W6]

herself (pron./adj.) *ipse, ipsa, ipsum* [KL2, L3]; **(reflex. pron.)** *suī* [KL3, L2]

hide (noun) *pellis, -is (f)* [KL3, W2]

hide (verb) *occultō (1)* [KL1, L22]; *celō* [KL1, W28]

high *altus, -a, -um* [KL1, L19]; *excelsus, -a, -um* [KL2, L4]; *superus, -a, -um* [KL2, L5]

higher *superior, -ius* [KL2, L5]

highest *summus, -a, -um* [KL2, L5]; *suprēmus, -a, -um* [KL2, L5]

hill *arx, arcis* [KL2, L7]; *collis, collis (m)* [KL3, L2]

himself (pron./adj.) *ipse, ipsa, ipsum* [KL2, L3]; **(reflex. pron.)** *suī* [KL3, L2]

himself *sē (acc. reflexive pronoun)* [KL1, W8]

hinder *impediō, -īre, -īvī, -ītum* [KL1, L29]; *obstō, -stāre, -stitī, -stātūrum (+dat.)* [KL2, W11]

hinge *cardō, -dinis (m)* [KL2, W11]

his (own) *suus, -a, -um* [KL1, W31; KL3, L2]

hissing *sībilus, -a, -um* [KL3, W6]

hit *pulsō* [K2L, W14]

hither *hūc* [KL2, L11]

hoard *thēsaurus, -ī (m)* [KL3, L11]

hold *habeō, -ēre, -uī, -itum* [KL1, L9]; *teneō, -ēre, tenuī, tentum* [KL1, L9]

hold back *reprehendō, -ere, -hendī, -hensum* [KL3, W13]; *reprimō, -ere, -pressī, -pressum* [KL3, W9]

hollow *lacus, -ūs (m)* [KL1, L27]

holy *sanctus, -a, -um* [KL1, L25]; *sacer, -cra, -crum* [KL2, L3]

Holy Bible *Biblia Sacra, Bibliae Sacrae (f)* [KL1, L11]

home *domus, -ūs (f)* [KL1, L25]

homicide *homicīda, -ae (m/f)* [KL3, L13]

hooked *uncus, -a, -um* [KL3, W16]

hope (noun) *spēs, speī (f)* [KL1, L28]

hope (verb) *spērō* [KL3, L1]

horn *cornū, -ūs (n)* [KL1, L25]

horrible *foedus, -a, -um* [KL1, L7]

horse *equus, -ī (m)* [KL1, L4]

horseman *eques, -quitis (m)* [KL1, L20]

hostile *īnfēnsus, -a, -um* [KL2, W15]

hot *caldus, -a, -um* [KL1, L7]

hour *hōra, -ae (f)* [KL1, L31]

house *domus, -ūs (f)* [KL1, L25]; *(country house) villa, -ae (f)* [KL1, L2]; *līmen, -minis (n)* [KL3, L3]

household *familia, -ae* [KL1, L22]

how (adv.) *quemadmodum* [KL3, L9]; **(conj.)** *ut (+indic.)* [KL3, L5]

how (?) *quam* [KL1, L28]; *quōmodo* [KL1, L25]; *quārē* [KL3, L9]

how great *quantus, -a, -um* [KL2, W13]

how long? *quamdiu* [KL3, L9]

how many *quantus, -a, -um* [KL2, W13]

how much (adj.) *quantus, -a, -um* [KL2, W13]; **(by)** *quantō* [KL2, W14]

however *autem (postposit. conj.)* [KL1, L12] *vērumtamen* [KL3, L13]

howl *ululō (1)* [KL1, L6]

howling *ululātus, -ūs (m)* [KL3, W10]

hug *amplector, amplectī, ——, amplexus sum* [KL2, W11]; *complector, -plectī, ——, -plexus sum* [KL3, W3]

huge *ingēns, (gen.) -entis* [KL1, L19]

human *hūmānus, -a, -um* [KL3, W2]

human being *homō, hominis (m)* [KL1, L12]

humble *humilis, -e* [KL2, L5]

hungry *famēlicus, -a, -um* [KL1, L29]

be **hungry** *ēsuriō, -īre, -iī, -ītum* [KL3, W1]

hurl down *ruō, -ere, ruī, rutum* [KL3, L4]

hunt *captō (1)* [KL1, L10]

hunt down *persequor, -sequī, ——, -secutus sum (deponent)* [KL1, W32]

hurl down *dēicio, -icere, -iēcī, -iectum* [KL1, W23]

hurl *iaciō, -ere, iēcī, iactum* [KL1, L31]

hurry *festīnō (1)* [KL1, L9]; *properō (1)* [KL1, L20]

husband *coniunx, -iugis (m)* [KL1, L22]

hypocrite *hypocrita, -ae (m)* [KL2, W14]

I

I *ego (sg)* [KL1, L17]

I wish that! *utinam* [KL3, L13]

ice: *gelū, -ūs (n)* [KL2, W9]

icy *gelidus, -a, -um* [KL1, L31]

idol *īdōlum, -ī (n)* [KL3, L7]; *simulācrum, -ī (n)* [KL3, L6]

if *sī (conj.)* [KL1, L16]

if not *nisi* [KL3, L11]

if only *dum, dummodo* [KL2, L11]

if only! *utinam* [KL3, L13]

ignorant (adj.) *inperitus* [KL2, W9]; *īnscius, -a, -um* [KL3, W16]

ignorant (am ignorant of) *ignōrō* [KL2, L15]; *nesciō, -īre, -īvī, -ītum* [KL1, L30; KL3, L3]

ill *male* [KL1, L1]

image *īdōlum, -ī (n)* [KL3, L7]; *imāgō, -ginis (f)* [KL3, L4]; *simulācrum, -ī (n)* [KL3, L6]

imagine *reor, rērī, ——, ratus sum* [KL3, W16]

immediately *statim* [KL1, L13]; *continuō* [KL2, L12]; *subitō/subitum* [KL3, L3]

immense *immānis, -e* [KL3, L7]

immorality *impudīcitia, -ae (f)* [KL3, W9]

immortal *immortālis, -e* [KL2, W6]

impartial *iūstus, -a, -um* [KL1, L7]

impetus *impetus, -ūs (m)* [KL3, L9]

impious *impius, -a, -um* [KL3, L1]

implore *obsecrō* [KL3, L13]

imprison *incarcerō* [KL2, W4]

in *in (+abl.)* [KL1, L3]

in error *frustrā* [KL3, L3]

in front of *pro (+abl.)* [KL1, L18]; *ob (+acc.)* [KL2, L3]

in one *ūnā* [KL1, L29]

in order that/to *quō* [KL2, L11]; *ut (+subj.)* [KL3, L5]

in that place *illīc* [KL2, L11]

in the presence of *cōram (+abl.)* [KL1, L27]

in the meantime *intereā* [KL2, L12]

in the morning (early in the morning) *māne* [KL1, W19; KL2, L6]

in the same place *eōdem* [KL3, L2]

in this place *hīc* [KL2, L11]

in turn *invicem* [KL2, L12]

in vain *frustrā* [KL3, L3]

in what manner *quemadmodum* [KL3, L9]

in what way *quōmodo* [KL1, L25]

in which place *quō(?)* [KL2, L11]

in/to what/which place (?) *quō* [KL2, L11]

Inachus *Īnachus, -ī (m)* [KL1, W21]

inauspicious *sinister, -stra, -strum* [KL1, L30]

incident *cāsus, -ūs (m)* [KL1, L28]

increase *augeō -ēre, auxī, auctum* [KL1, L19]; *crēscō, -ere, crēvī, crētum* [KL2, L11]; *multiplicō* [KL3, W20]

indeed *enim (postpositive conj.)* [KL1, L17]; *quidem* [KL2, L3]

indicates a simple yes/no question *-ne* [KL2, L7]

indignity *indīgnitās, -tātis (f)* [KL2, W15]

inexperienced *inperitus, -a, -um* [KL2, W9]

infant *īnfāns, -fantis (adj. & noun, m/f)* [KL1, W31; KL3, L12]

infinite *infīnītus, -a, -um* [KL3, W2]

inhabit *colō, -ere, coluī, cultum* [KL1, L29]; *habitō (1)* [KL1, L3]; *incolō, -ere, -coluī, -cultum* [KL3, L2]

iniquity *inīquitās, -tātis (f)* [KL2, L10]

injury *nocēns, -ntis* [KL2, W11]

injustice *inīquitās, -tātis (f)* [KL2, L10]

inner *interior, -ius (gen. -teriōris)* [KL3, W2]

inner court *aula, -ae (f)* [KL1, W13]

innocent *inmeritus, -a, -um* [KL3, W16]

inquire *quaerō, -ere, quaesīvī, quaesītum (-situm)* [KL2, L3]

insane *insānus, -a, -um* [KL3, W3]

insanity *insānia, -ae (f)* [KL3, W6]

inside *intrā (prep. +acc.; adv.)* [KL2, L15]

instead of *prō (+abl.)* [KL1, L18]

instruction *doctrīna, -ae (f)* [KL3, L5]

insult *contumēlia, -ae (f)* [KL3, W5]

intercede *dēprecor, -ārī, ——, -ātus sum* [KL3, L10]

interior *interior, -ius (gen. -teriōris)* [KL3, W2]

internal organs *vīscus, -eris (n)* [KL3, L13]

into *in (+acc.)* [KL1, L3]

intoxicated *ēbrius, -a, -um* [KL1, W13]

invest *consūmō, -ere, -sūmpsī, -sūmptum* [KL3, L2]

invincible *invīctus, -a, -um* [KL3, W13]

invite *vocō (1)* [KL1, L1]

inward parts *vīscus, -eris (n)* [KL3, L13]

inwardly *intrā (prep. +acc.; adv.)* [KL2, L15]

Io *Īō, -ōnis (f)* [KL1, W21]

iron *ferrum, -ī (n)* [KL2, L15]

irreverent *impius, -a, -um* [KL3, L1]

island *īnsula, -ae (f)* [KL1, L3]

Israel *Israhel (indecl.) or Israhel, -is* [KL1, W32; KL2, W3]

Israelite *Israhelita, -ae (m)* [KL1, W32]

is it really possible that...? *numquid* [KL2, L9]

it *is, ea, id* [KL1, L17]

it is allowed *licet, licuit, - (impers. +dat./acc.)* [KL1, W26; KL3, L1]

it is apparent *apparet* [KL3, L4]

it is clear *scīlicet* [KL3, L6]

it is evident *apparet* [KL3, L4]

it is fitting *decet, decuit* [KL3, L1]

it is lawful *licet, licuit, —— (impers. +dat./acc.)* [KL1, W26; KL3, L1]

it is necessary *necesse est* [KL3, L1]; *oportet, -ēre, -tuit, -tuitum (impers. +acc.)* [KL3, L1]

it is permitted *licet, licuit, - (impers. +dat./acc.)* [KL1, W26; KL3, L1]

it is proper *decet, -ēre, ——, decuit (impers. +acc.)* [KL3, L1]; *oportet, -ēre, -tuit, -tuitum (impers. +acc.)* [KL3, L1]

it is right *decet, -ēre, ——, decuit (impers. +acc.)* [KL3, L1]

it is suitable *decet, -ēre, ——, decuit (impers. +acc.)* [KL3, L1]

Italy *Ītalia, -ae (f)* [KL1, W8; KL2, W5]

its (own) *suus, -a, -um* [KL1, W31; KL3, L2]

itself (acc. reflexive pronoun) *sē* [KL1, W8]

itself (pron./adj.) *ipse, ipsa, ipsum* [KL2, L3]

itself (reflex. pron.) *suī* [KL3, L2]

Iulia *Iūlia, -ae (f)* [KL1, W11]

Iulius *Iūlius, -iī (m)* [KL1, W19]

Iunia *Iūnia, -ae (f)* [KL1, W11]

J

jail *carcer, -eris (m)* [KL1, W23; KL3, L5]

jar *vās, vāsis (n)* [KL3, W1]

jealousy *zēlus, -ī (m)* [KL3, W7]

Jerusalem *Hierusalem (indecl.)* [KL1, W32]

Jesse *Isai (indecl.)* [KL1, W32]

Jesus *Iēsus, -ūs (m)* [KL1, L25]

jewel *lapis, -idis (m)* [KL1, W27; KL2, L14]

Jew (Jewish) *Iudaeus, -a, -um* [KL2, W3]

job *negōtium, -iī (n)* [KL3, W9]

join (together) *coniungō, -ere, -iūnxī, -iūnctum* [KL3, L9]

joint *artus, -ūs (m)* [KL2, L6]

join *iungō, -ere, iūnxī, iunctum* [KL1, L27]

journey *iter, itineris (n)* [KL1, L13]

Jove *Iuppiter, Iovis (m)* [KL1, W21]

joy *gaudium, -ī (n)* [KL1, L5]; *laetitia, -ae (f)* [KL3, L7]

joyful *laetus, -a, -um* [KL1, L7]

judge (noun) *iūdex, -dicis (m)* [KL1, W28; KL3, L1]

judge (verb) *arbitror, -ārī, ——, -ātus sum* [KL3, L4]; *iūdicō* [KL2, L14]

judgment *iūdicium, -ī (n)* [KL2, L9]

judgment seat *tribūnal, -ālis (n)* [KL2, W15]

jug *hydria, -ae (f)* [KL2, W12]

Julia *Iūlia, -ae (f)* [KL1, W11]

Julius *Iūlius, -iī (m)* [KL1, W19]

jump *saliō, -īre, -uī, saltum* [KL1, W29; KL2, W12]

jump *saliō, -īre, saluī, saltum* [KL1, W29]

Junia *Iūnia, -ae (f)* [KL1, W11]

Juno *Iūno, -ōnis (f)* [KL1, W21; KL3, W3]

Jupiter *Iuppiter, Iovis (dat. Iovī, acc. Iovem, abl. Iove) (m)* [KL1, W21; KL2, W6]

just (adj.) *iūstus, -a, -um* [KL1, L7]

just (adv.) *modo* [KL1, L27]

just as *sīcut* [KL1, L20]; *quasi* [KL3, L11]

justice *iūs, iūris (n)* [KL2, L15]; *iūstitia, -ae (f)* [KL3, L12]

K

keep *custōdiō, -īre, -iī/-īvī, -ītum* [KL3, L3]; *observō* [KL3, W11]

kidnapping *raptus, -ūs (m)* [KL1, W31]

kill *interficiō, -ere, -fēcī, -fectum* [KL1, L31]; *necō (1)* [KL1, L1]; *occīdō, -ere, -cīdī, -cīsum* [KL1, L30]; *caedō, -ere, cecīdī, caesum* [KL2, L12]

kind (noun) *genus, -neris (n)* [KL2, L13]

kindle (verb) *accendō, -ere, -censī, -censum* [KL2, W15]; *incendō* [KL2, W13]

kindness *clēmentia, -ae (f)* [KL1, W21; KL3, W10]; *grātia, -ae (f)* [KL1, L27]

king *rēx, rēgis (m)* [KL1, L12]

kingdom *regnum, -ī (n)* [KL1, L5]

kingly *rēgālis, -e* [KL3, W10]

kiss *ōsculum, -ī (n)* [KL2, W11]

knee *genū, -ūs (n)* [KL1, L25]

knight *eques, -quitis (m)* [KL1, L20]

knock *pulsō* [K2L, W14]

know *sciō, -īre, sciī (scīvī), scītum* [KL1, L29]; *cognoscō (pf. tense)* [KL2, L10]; *noscō, -ere, nōvī, nōtum (pf. tense)* [KL2, L9]

kraken *cētus, -ī (m)* [KL1, L10]

L

labor (noun) *labor, labōris (m)* [KL1, L12]

labor (verb) *mōlior, -īrī, ——, mōlītus sum* [KL2, L6]; *operor, -ārī, ——, operātus sum* [KL2, L6]

labyrinth *labyrinthus, -ī (m)* [KL1, W30]

lack *careō, -ēre, -uī, -itum (+abl.)* [KL3, L6]; *indigeō, -ēre, -diguī, —— (+ gen./abl.)* [KL2, W14]

lake *lacus, -ūs (m)* [KL1, L27]

lamp *lūmen, -minis (n)* [KL3, L11]

land *tellūs, tellūris (f)* [KL1, L14]; *terra, -ae (f)* [KL1, L4]; **(native land)** *patria, -ae (f)* [KL1, L3]

language *lingua, -ae* [KL1, L26]

lap (of a race) *curriculum, -ī (n)* [KL1, W23]

large *magnus, -a, -um* [KL1, L7]

late (adv.) *sērō, sērius, sērissimē (adv.)* [KL2, L11]

Latin (adj.) *Latīnus, -a, -um* [KL2, W13]

laugh *rīdeō, -ēre, rīsī, rīsum* [KL1, L9]

laurel (tree) *laurus, -ī (f)* [KL1, W20]

lay waste *vastō (1)* [KL1, L14]

laying on *impositiō, -ōnis (f)* [KL3, W7]

law *lēx, lēgis (f)* [KL2, L10]

lawful *fās (n, indecl.)* [KL3, L2]; **(it is lawful)** *licet, licuit, - (impers. +dat./acc.)* [KL1, W26; KL3, L1]

lead (adj) *plumbeus, -a, -um* [KL1, W20]

lead (verb) *dūcō, -ere, duxī, ductum* [KL1, L26]

lead (out) *ēdūcō, -ere, -dūxī, -ductum* [KL3, L5]; **(to)** *addūcō* [KL2, L8]; **(forth)** *prōdūcō, -ere, -dūxī, -ductum* [KL3, W4]; **(aside/astray)** *sēdūcō, -ere, -dūxī, -ductum* [KL3, W11]

lead (metal) *plumbum, -ī (n)* [KL3, W2]

leaden *plumbeus, -a, -um* [KL1, W20]

leader *dux, ducis (m)* [KL1, L14]; *prīnceps, -cipis (m)* [KL2, L3]

leaf *folium, -ī (n)* [KL1, W20]; *frōns, -ontis (f)* [KL1, W32]

leaky *pertūsus, -a, -um* [KL1, W29]

leap *saliō, -īre, -uī, saltum* [KL1, W29; KL2, W12]

learn *cognoscō, -ere, -nōvī, -nitum* [KL2, L10]; *noscō, -ere, nōvī, nōtum* [KL2, L9]

learned *doctus, -a, -um* [KL1, L13]

least (adj.) *minimus, -a, -um* [KL1, W31]

least (adv.) *minimē* [KL2, L7]

leave *discēdō, -ere, -cessī, -cessum* [KL3, W5]

leave alone *dēsōlō* [KL3, W7]

leave behind *relinquō, -ere, -līquī, -lictum* [KL1, L28]

left(-handed) *sinister, -stra, -strum* [KL1, L30]

leg *crūs, crūris (n)* [KL1, W19]

legend *fābula, -ae (f)* [KL1, L2]

legion *legiō, -ōnis (f)* [KL3, W2]

less *minus* [KL2, L7]

lest *nē* [KL3, L4]

let *sinō, -ere, sīvī, situs* [KL2, W13]

let go *mittō, -ere, mīsī, missum* [KL1, L26]

letter (of the alphabet) *littera, -ae (f)* [KL1, L26]

letter *plural of littera, -ae (f)* [KL1, L26]

level surface *aequor, -oris (n)* [KL3, L6]

liar *mendāx, -dacis (m/f)* [KL3, L6]

lick *lambō, -ere, lambī, lambitum* [KL3, W3]

lie (noun) *mendācium, -iī (n)* [KL3, L6]

lie (verb) *mentior, -īrī, ——, -ītus sum* [KL3, L6]

lie down *iaceō, -ēre, -uī, ——* [KL1, L9]

lie flat *iaceō, -ēre, -uī, ——* [KL1, L9]

lieutenant *lēgātus, -ī (m)* [KL2, L15]

life *vīta, -ae* [KL1, L11]; *aetās, -tātis (f)* [KL2, L14]; *anima, -ae (f)* [KL2, L4]

lift (up) *levō* [KL3, W1]; *tollō, -ere, sustulī, sublātum* [KL1, W25; KL2, L13]

light (adj.) *levis, -e* [KL2, W6]

light (noun) *lux, lūcis (f)* [KL1, L12]; *lūmen, -minis (n)* [KL3, L11]; *lūmināre, -āris (n)* [KL3, W4]

light (up) *illūminō* [KL3, W4]

lightly *leviter* [KL2, W6]

lightning *fulgur, -uris (n)* [KL1, W25]

like (adj.) *similis, -e* [KL2, L5]

like (adv.) *sīcut* [KL1, L20]

likeness *imāgō, -ginis (f)* [KL3, L4]; *īnstar (indecl.)* [KL2, L13]; *simulācrum, -ī (n)* [KL3, L6]; *speciēs, -ēi (f)* [KL3, W4]

lily *līlium, -iī (n)* [KL3, W13]

limit *fīnis, -is (m)* [KL1, W4]; *terminus, -ī (m)* [KL3, L15]

lion *leō, leōnis (m)* [KL1, L12]

lioness *lea, -ae (f)* [KL2, W11]

line *ōrdō, -dinis (m)* [KL2, L15]

line (of poetry) *versus, -ūs (m)* [KL1, L27]

lion *leō, leōnis (m)* [KL1, L12]

lip *lābrum, -ī (n)* [KL3, W2]

listen to *audiō, -īre, -īvī, -ītum* [KL1, L29]

little (adj.) *parvus, -a, -um* [KL1, L7]; *modicus, -a, -um* [KL2, L14]

little (adv.) *parum* [KL2, L7]

little by little *paulātim* [KL3, W7]

little child *īnfāns, -fantis (adj. & noun, m/f)* [KL1, W31; KL3, L12]

live *habitō (1)* [KL1, L3]; *vīvō, -ere, vīxī, victum* [KL1, L27]

live in *incolō, -ere, -coluī, -cultum* [KL3, L2]

living *vīvus, -a, -um* [KL1, L20]

load *onus, oneris (n)* [KL1, L13; KL3, L3]

lofty *altus, -a, -um* [KL1, L19]; *excelsus, -a, -um* [KL2, L4]

loin *lumbus, -ī (m)* [KL2, W9]

loneliness *sōlitūdō, -dinis (f)* [KL3, W9]

long (adj.) *longus, -a, -um* [KL1, L20]

long (for) (verb) *cupiō, -ere, cupīvī, cupītum* [KL1, L31]

long way off (a long way off) *longē* [KL3, L3]

longer *amplius* [KL3, L9]

look at *spectō (1)* [KL1, L1]; *cōnspiciō, -ere, -spēxī, -spectum* [KL3, W16]

look back *rēspiciō, -ere, -spēxī, -spectum* [KL2, L14]

look down on *despiciō, -ere, -spexī, -spectum* [KL1, W32]

loose *solvō, -ere, solvī, solūtum* [KL2, L10]

lop *praecīdō, -ere, -cīdī, -cīsum* [KL1, W32]

lop off *praecīdō, -ere, -cīdī, -cīsum* [KL1, W32; KL2, W6]

lord *dominus, -ī (m)* [KL1, L4]

lose *perdō, -ere, perdidī, perditum* [KL1, L27]

lot *sors, -rtis (f)* [KL3, L6]

love (noun) *amor, amōris (m)* [KL1, L14]; *cāritās, -tātis (f)* [KL3, L11]

love (verb) *amō (1)* [KL1, L1]; *foveō, -ēre, fōvī, fōtum* [KL1, L25]; *dīligō, -ere, -lēxī, -lēctum* [KL3, L1]

low(ly) (adj.) *humilis, -e* [KL2, L5]

lower *īnferior, -ius* [KL2, L5]

lowest *īmus, -a, -um* [KL2, L5]; *īnfimus, -a, -um* [KL2, L5]

loyalty *pietās, -tātis (f)* [KL2, W13]

lucky *fēlix, (gen.) -līcis* [KL1, L19]

lust *concupiscentia, -ae (f)* [KL3, W9]

lying on one's back *resupīnus, -a, -um* [KL3, W7]

lyre *lyra, -ae (f)* [KL1, W28]

M

machine *māchina, -ae (f)* [KL3, W6]

made (am made) *fīō, fierī, ——, factus sum* [KL1, L31]

magic (adj.) *magicus, -a, -um* [KL2, W2]

maiden *virgō, virginis (f)* [KL1, L12]

maidservant *ancilla, -ae (f)* [KL3, L10]

magistrate *magistrātus, -ūs (m)* [KL3, W5]

make *faciō, -ere, fēcī, factum* [KL1, L31]; *aedificō* [KL2, L4]

make clear *dēclārō (1)* [KL1, L10]

make firm *solidō* [KL2, W9]

make holy *sanctificō* [KL3, L4]

make known *adnūntiō* [KL3, L7]; *indīcō* [KL3, L11]

male *masculus, -a, -um* [KL3, W4]

malice *malitia, -ae (f)* [KL2, L14]

malicious *malignus, -a, -um* [KL3, L13]

malignant *malignus, -a, -um* [KL3, L13]

man (as opposed to animal) *homō, hominis (m)* [KL1, L12]; **(as opposed to woman)** *vir, virī (m)* [KL1, L4]

manifest (verb) *manifestō* [KL2, W8]

manifest (adj.) *manifestus, -a, -um* [KL3, W1]

manliness *virtūs, virtūtis (f)* [KL1, L12]

manslayer *homicīda, -ae (m/f)* [KL3, L13]

manner *modus, -ī (m)* [KL3, L7]; *mōs, mōris (m)* [KL2, L13]

many *multus, -a, -um* [KL1, L7]

marble *marmoreus, -a, -um* [KL3, W16]

march out *ēgredior, -gredī, ——, -gressus sum* [KL2, L6]

maritime *maritimus, -a, -um* [KL3, W2]

marriage (adj.) *nūptiālis, -e* [KL2, W2]

marriage (noun) *mātrimōnium, -ī (n)* [KL1, L20]

marry *nūbō, -ere, nūpsī, nūptum* [KL3, W2]

Mars *Mars, Martis (m)* [KL2, W13]

marvel at *mīror, -ārī, ——, mīrātus sum* [KL2, L6]

marvelous *mīrābilis, -e* [KL3, L3]

master *dominus, -ī (m)* [KL1, L4]

mat *grabātus, -ī (m)* [KL3, W9]

material *māteria, -ae (f)* [KL3, W2]

maybe *forsitan* [KL3, L13]

maze *labyrinthus, -ī (m)* [KL1, W30]

meadow *prātum, -ī (n)* [KL2, W15]

meager *exiguus, -a, -um* [KL3, W2]

meal *cēna, -ae (f)* [KL1, L20]

meantime (in the meantime) *interim* [KL1, L9]

meanwhile *interim* [KL1, L9]; *intereā* [KL2, L12]; *propterea* [KL2, L10]

measure (noun) *mēnsūra, -ae (f)* [KL2, L14]; *modus, -ī (m)* [KL3, L7]

measure (verb) *mētior, -īrī, ——, mēnsus sum* [KL2, L14]

measurement *mēnsūra, -ae (f)* [KL2, L14]

meat *caro, carnis (f)* [KL1, L31]

mediterranean *mediterrāneus, -a, -um* [KL3, W2]

meeting *concilium, -iī (n)* [KL3, L5]

memorial *monumentum, -ī (n)* [KL2, W11]

memory *memoria, -ae (f)* [KL3, L2]

menace (verb) *minor, -ārī, ——, -ātus sum* [KL2, W5]

Mercury *Mercurius, -ī (m)* [KL1, W21; KL2, W6]

mercy *clēmentia, -ae (f)* [KL1, W21]; *misericordia, -ae (f)* [KL2, L10]; *venia, -ae (f)* [KL3, W12]

merely *modo* [KL1, L27]; *sōlum* [KL3, L7]; *tantum* [KL3, L14]

merit *mereō, -ēre, -uī, -itum* [KL1, L15; KL3, W6]

messenger *nuntius, -ī (m)* [KL2, L12]

Messiah *Messīā(s), -ae (m)* [KL2, W12]

Midas *Midās, -ae (m)* [KL1, W27]

middle (of) *medius, -a, -um* [KL1, L26]

midst (of) *medius, -a, -um* [KL1, L26]

milk *lac, lactis (n)* [KL1, L13]

mind *animus, -ī (m)* [KL1, L29]

mind one's own business *suum negōtium agere* [KL1, W29]

mindful *memor, -oris* [KL3, L9]

mine *meus, -a, -um* [KL1, L11]

Minerva *Minerva, -ae (f)* [KL3, W6]; *Pallas, -adis (f)* [KL3, W6]

minister *minister, -strī (m)* [KL3, L10]

Minos *Mīnōs, -ōnis (m)* [KL1, W30]

Minotaur *Mīnōtaurus, -ī (m)* [KL1, W30]

miracle *sīgnum, -ī (n)* [KL3, L4]

miserable *infēlix, (gen.) -līcis* [KL1, L19]; *miser, -era, -erum* [KL1, L7]

misery *miseria, -ae (f)* [KL3, W9]

misfortune *cāsus, -ūs (m)* [KL1, L28]

mistaken (am mistaken) *errō (1)* [KL1, L14]

mob *turba, -ae (f)* [KL1, L2]

moderate *modicus, -a, -um* [KL2, L14]

monastery *monastērium, -iī (n)* [KL3, W7]

money *aes, aeris (n)* [KL3, W2]; *argentum, -ī (n)* [KL1, L5]; *pecucnia, -ae (f)* [KL1, L3]

monk *monachus, -ī (m)* [KL3, W7]

monster *mōnstrum, -ī (n)* [KL1, W30]; *bēlua, -ae (f)* [KL3, L15]

monstrous *immānis, -e* [KL3, L7]

month *mensis, -is (m)* [KL3, L10]

monument *monumentum, -ī (n)* [KL2, W11]

moon *lūna, -ae* [KL1, L2]

morals *mōs, mōris (m) (pl.)* [KL2, L13]

more *amplius* [KL3, L9]; *magis* [KL2, L7]; *plūs* [KL2, L5]; *potius* [KL3, L7]

moreover *autem (postposit. conj.)* [KL1, L12]

morning (in the morning) *māne* [KL1, W19; KL2, L6]

mortal *mortālis, -e* [KL2, W6]

most (adj.) *plūrimus, -a, -um* [KL2, L5]

most (adv.) *plūrimum* [KL2, L7]; *māximē* [KL2, L7]

mother (noun) *māter, mātris (f)* [KL1, L12]; *parēns* [KL1, W11; KL2, W8]

mother (adj.) *māternus, -a, -um* [KL3, W16]

mountain *mōns, montis (m)* [KL1, L18]

mourning *lūctus, -ūs (m)* [KL3, W13]

mouth *ōs, ōris (n)* [KL1, L13]

move (intransit.) *cēdō, -ere, cessī, cessum* [KL1, L28]

move (transit.) *moveō, -ēre, mōvī, mōtum* [KL1, L14]

movement *āgmen, -minis (n)* [KL3, L6]

much (adj.) *multus, -a, -um* [KL1, L7]

much (noun) *multum* [KL2, L7]

mud *lutum, -ī (n)* [KL3, W8]

mulberry *mōrus, -ī (f)* [KL2, W11]

multiply *multiplicō* [KL3, W20]

multitude *multitūdō, -tudinis (f)* [KL2, L12]

murder *nex, necis (f)* [KL3, W10]

murderer/-ess *homicīda, -ae (m/f)* [KL3, L13]

musician *musicus, -ī (m)* [KL1, W28]

mute *mūtus, -a, -um* [KL3, W1]

my *meus, -a, -um* [KL1, L11]

N

name (verb) *appellō (1)* [KL1, L15]; *nōminō* [KL3, W13]

name (noun) *nōmen, nōminis (n)* [KL1, L13]; *cognōmen, -minis (n)* [KL2, W15]

napkin *mappa, -ae (f)* [KL1, W23]

naked *nūdus, -a, -um* [KL3, W7]

nation *gens, -ntis (f)* [KL1, L31]; *populus, -ī (m)* [KL1, L11]

native land *patria, -ae (f)* [KL1, L3]

nativity *nātīvitās, -tātis (f)* [KL2, W8]

naturally *scīlicet* [KL3, L6]

near *ad (+acc.)* [KL1, L3]; *prope (adv. & prep. +acc.)* [KL1, L19]; *propter (+acc.)* [KL1, L25]

near(by) *vīcīnus, -a, -um* [KL3, L9]

near (to) *iūxta (adv. & prep. +acc.)* [KL1, L28]

nearer *propior, -ius* [KL2, L5]

nearest *proximus, -a, -um* [KL2, L5]

nearly *ferē* [KL3, L3]; *quasi* [KL3, L11]

neat *mundus, -a, -um* [KL3, L5]

necessary *necesse* [KL3, L1]; **(it is necessary)** *oportet, -ēre, -tuit, -tuitum (impers. +acc.)* [KL3, L1]

need *indigeō, -ēre, -diguī, —— (+gen./abl.)* [KL2, W14]

neighbor(ing) *vīcīnus, -a, -um* [KL3, L9]

neither *neuter, -tra, -trum* [KL2, L15]

neither...nor *nec...nec* [KL1, L14]

nephew *nepōs, -pōtis (m/f)* [KL2, L13]

Neptune *Neptūnus, -ī (m)* [KL2, W7]

never *numquam* [KL1, L5]

nevertheless *tamen* [KL1, L30]; *vērumtamen* [KL3, L13]

new *novus, -a, -um* [KL1, L26]

next (adj.) *proximus, -a, -um* [KL2, L5]

next (adv.) *deinde* [KL1, L22]; *tum* [KL1, L15]

next to *prope (adv. & prep. +acc.)* [KL1, L19]

niece *nepōs, -pōtis (m/f)* [KL2, L13]

night *nox, noctis (f)* [KL1, L18]

nine *novem* [KL1, L21]

nineteen *ūndēvīgintī* [KL1, L21]

nineteenth *ūndēvīcēsimus, -a, -um* [KL1, L23]

ninth *nōnus, -a, -um* [KL1, L23]

no (adj.) *nūllus, -a, -um* [KL2, L4]

no (adv.) *nē* [KL3, L4]

no (expects a no answer) *num* [KL2, L7]; *numquid* [KL2, L9]

no longer *nōn iam* [KL1, L15]

no one *nēmō, neminis (m/f)* [KL2, L4]

noble *magnanimus, -a, -um* [KL1, W9]; *excelsus, -a, -um* [KL2, L4]; *nōbilis, -e* [KL2, W15]

nobody *nēmō, neminis (m/f)* [KL2, L4]

nod *nūtō* [KL3, W7]

noise *clāmor, -oris (m)* [KL1, W20; KL2, L13]; *fragor, -ōris (m)* [KL3, W7]; *sonitus, -ūs (m)* [KL3, W3]

none *nūllus, -a, -um* [KL2, L4]

noon *merīdiēs, -ēī (m)* [KL1, L28]

nor *nec (neque)* [KL1, L14]

not *nōn* [KL1, L1]; *nec (neque)* [KL1, L14]

not any *nūllus, -a, -um* [KL2, L4]

not at all *nihil (n. indecl.)* [KL1, L6]; *haud* [KL3, L1]; *minimē* [KL2, L7]; *nequaquam* [KL2, W8]

not enough *parum* [KL2, L7]

not know *nesciō, -īre, -īvī, -ītum* [KL1, L30]

not *nē* [KL3, L4]

nothing *nihil (n, indecl.)* [KL1, L6]

notice *attendō, -ere, -ndī, -ntum* [KL3, W9]

not want *nōlō, nōlle, nōluī, ——* [KL2, L14]

not wish *nōlō, nōlle, nōluī, ——* [KL2, L14]

not yet *nōndum* [KL3, L7]

now *iam* [KL1, L15]; *nunc* [KL1, L1]

number *numerus, -ī (m)* [KL3, L2]

numerous *crēber, -bra, -brum* [KL3, L2]

nymph *nympha, -ae (f)* [KL1, W20; KL2, W6]

O

oar *rēmus, -ī (m)* [KL2, W5]

oath *iūs iūrandum* [KL2, L15]; *iūsiūrandum* [KL2, L15]

obey *oboediō [obediō], -īre, -īvī, -ītum (+dat.)* [KL3, L5]

observe *observō* [KL3, W11]

obstruct *obstō, -stāre, -stitī, -stātūrum (+dat.)* [KL2, W11]

occasion *occāsiō, -ōnis (f)* [KL3, W10]

occupation *negōtium, -iī (n)* [KL3, W9]

ocean *ōceanus, -ī (m)* [KL1, L4]

Odysseus *Ulixēs, -is (m)* [KL2, W5]

of course *scīlicet* [KL3, L6]

of such a sort (rel. adj.) *quālis* [KL3, L9]

of such size *tantus, -a, -um* [KL3, L5]

of what sort (interrog. adj.) *quālis* [KL3, L9]

offend *laedō, -ere, laesī, laesus* [KL3, W6]; *peccō* [KL3, L11]

offense *peccātum, -ī (n)* [KL3, L11]

offer (verb) *offerō, offerre, obtulī, oblātum* [KL2, L11]; *polliceor, -ērī, ——, pollicitus sum* [KL3, L7]

offering *sacrificium, -iī (n)* [KL2, L4]

office *mūnus, -neris (n)* [KL2, L15]

often *saepe* [KL1, L6]

oh! *heu (ēheu)* [KL1, L22]

oh that! *utinam* [KL3, L13]

ointment *ūnctiō, -ōnis (f)* [KL3, W12]

old man *senex, senis (m)* [KL1, L14]

old *vetus, -teris* [KL1, L30]

older *māior, māius (gen. māioris)* [KL1, W31]; *senior, -ōris* [KL3, L5]

oldest (son) *postnatus, -ī (m)* [KL1, W19]

oldest *māximus, -a, -um* [KL1, W31]

omen *mōnstrum, -ī (n)* [KL1, W13]; *prōdigium, -iī (n)* [KL3, W5]

omnipotent *omnipotēns, -tentis* [KL3, W2]

on *in (+abl.)* [KL1, L3]

on account of *propter (+acc.)* [KL1, L25]; *causā (+gen.)* [KL2, L15]; *ob (+acc.)* [KL2, L3]

on all sides *undique* [KL1, L30; KL2, L15]

on that side *illinc* [KL2, L11]

on the outside *extrā* [KL3, L15]

on this side *hinc* [KL2, L11]

once *quondam* [KL2, L13]

once upon a time *ōlim* [KL1, L6]

one *ūnicus, -a, -um* [KL1, W22]; *ūnus, -a, -um* [KL1, L21]

one another *invicem* [KL2, L12]

one at a time *singulī, -ae, -a* [KL2, L13]

one (in one) *ūnā* [KL1, L29]

one hundred *centum* [KL1, L21]

one hundredth *centēsimus* [KL1, L23]

one (of two) *uter, utra (ūtra), utrum (ūtrum) (interrog.)* [KL2, L15]

one which *uter, utra (ūtra), utrum (ūtrum) (interrog.)* [KL2, L15]

only (adj.) *sōlus, -a, -um* [KL1, W12; KL2, L4]; *ūnicus, -a, -um* [KL1, W22]

only (adv.) *modo* [KL1, L27]; *sōlum* [KL3, L7]; *tantum* [KL3, L14];

only-begotten *unigenitus, -a, -um* [KL2, W3]

onset *impetus, -ūs (m)* [KL3, L9]

open *aperiō, -īre, -uī, apertum* [KL1, L29]

openly *cōram* [KL1, L27]

opinion *cōgitātiō, -tiōnis (f)* [KL3, L1]; *sententia, -ae (f)* [KL3, L9]

opportunity *occāsiō, -ōnis (f)* [KL3, W10]

oppose *obsistō, -ere, -stitī, -stitum* [KL3, W7]

opposite *dīversus, -a, -um* [KL3, W7]

or *aut* [KL1, L1]; *sīve (sēū)* [KL1, L30]; *an* [KL3, L9]; *vel* [KL2, L9]

or rather *vel* [KL2, L9]

or whether *an* [KL3, L9]

oracle *ōrāculum, -ī (n)* [KL1, W31]; *fātum, -ī (n)* [KL1, L5; KL2, 13]; *sors, -rtis (f)* [KL3, L6]

order (verb) *imperō* [KL3, L10]; *iubeō, -ēre, iūssī, iūssum* [KL3, L2]; *mandō* [KL3, L10]

order (noun) *mandātum, -ī (n)* [KL2, L10]; *ōrdō, -dinis (m)* [KL2, L15]

ordinary *mediōcris, -e* [KL1, L19]; *modicus, -a, -um* [KL2, L14]

origin *genus, -neris (n)* [KL2, L13]; *prīncipium, -iī (n)* [KL3, L4]

ornament *ornātus, -ūs (m)* [KL3, W6]

orphan *orba, -ae (f)/orbus, -ī (m)* [KL1, L22]

Oswald *Oswaldus, -ī (m)* [KL1, W19]

other *alius, -a, -um* [KL1, W21; KL2, L4]; *cēterus, -a, -um* [KL2, L15]; **the other (of two)** *alter, -era, -erum* [KL2, L4]

ought *dēbeō, -ēre, -uī, -itum* [KL1, L11]

our(s) *noster, -stra, -strum* [KL1, L11]

out of *ē, ex (+abl.)* [KL1, L3]

out(side) *forās* [KL3, L6]

outside (of) *extrā* [KL3, L15]

outstanding *ēgregius, -a, -um* [KL1, L29]

over *super (+acc./+abl.)* [KL1, L26]; *suprā (adv./prep. +acc.)* [KL1, L14]

overpower *premō, -ere, pressī, pressum* [KL2, L10]

overshadow *obumbrō* [KL3, W4]

overturn *ēvertō, -ere, -tī, -sum* [KL3, W7]; *subvertō, -ere, -vertī, -versus* [KL3, W7]

owe *dēbeō, -ēre, -uī, -itum* [KL1, L11]

ox *bōs, bovis (m/f)* [KL1, L19]

P

pacify *mītigō* [KL3, W7]

Pactolus *Pactōlus, -ī (m)* [KL1, W27]

palace *rēgia, -ae (f)* [KL1, L2]

pale (verb) *palleō, -ēre, -uī, ——* [KL3, W7]

pale (adj.) *exsanguis, -e* [KL3, W6]

Pan *Pān, Pānos (acc. Pāna) (m)* [KL1, W28]

pan pipe *avēna, -ae (f)* [KL1, W21]

parch *torreō, -ēre, torruī, tostum* [KL1, L17]

pardon *venia, -ae (f)* [KL3, W12]

parent *parēns, -entis (m/f)* [KL1, W11; KL2, W8]

part *pars, partis (f)* [KL2, L3]

pass (by/over) *trānseō, -īre, -iī, -itum* [KL2, L15]

passages [in a book] *loca (n, pl)*

past (prep.) *praeter* [KL2, L13]

pastoral *pastoralis, -e* [KL1, W32]

pasture *pascō, -ere, pāvī, pastum* [KL1, W32; KL2, W14]

pattern *rēgula, -ae (f)* [KL3, W9]

pause *subsistō, -ere, -stitī, ——* [KL3, W6]

pay (noun) *stīpendium, -iī (n)* [KL2, W15]

pay (verb) *solvō, -ere, solvī, solūtum* [KL2, L10]

pay the penalty *poenās dō* [KL1, L27]

peace *pāx, pācis (f)* [KL1, L15]

peacock *pāvo, -ōnis (m)* [KL1, W21]

penalty *poena, -ae (f)* [KL1, L27]

people *populus, -ī (m)* [KL1, L11]

peradventure *forsitan* [KL3, L13]

perceive *intellegō, -ere, -lēxī, -lēctum* [KL3, L2]; *perspiciō, -ere, -spēxī, -spectum* [KL3, W2]; *sentiō, -īre, sēnsī, sēnsum* [KL3, L3]

perchance *forte* [KL2, L3]

perfect *perficiō, -ere, -fēcī, -fectum* [KL1, W23; KL3, L14]

perhaps *fortasse* [KL1, L26]; *forte* [KL2, L3]; *forsitan* [KL3, L13]

period of time *diēs, diēī (m/f)* [KL1, L28]

permit *permittō, -ere, -mīsī, -missum* [KL1, W30]

permitted *fās (n, indecl.)* [KL3, L2]; **(it is permitted)** *licet, licuit, - (impers. +dat./acc.)* [KL1, W26; KL3, L1]

personally *cōram* [KL1, L27]

persuade *persuādeō, -ēre, -suāsī, -suāsum (+dat.)* [KL1, W15; KL3, L10]

petition *petītiō, -ōnis (f)* [KL3, W16]

Pharisee *Pharisaeus, -ī (m)* [KL2, W3]

Philistine *Philistheus, -ī (m)*

phoenix *phoenīx, -nīcis (m)* [KL3, W3]

Phrygia *Phrygia, -ae (f)* [KL1, W27]

pick *dēligō, -ere, lēgī, -lēctum* [KL1, L28]

pick out *ēligō, -ere, -lēgī, -lectum* [KL3, L1]

pierce *percutiō, -ere, -cussī, -cussum* [KL1, W32; KL2, L3]

piety *pietās, -tātis (f)* [KL2, W13]

pig *porcus, -ī (m)* [KL1, L10]

pig-sty *hara, -ae (f)* [KL1, W25]

pine *pīnus, -ī (f)* [KL3, W7]

pipe (reed-pipe) *calamus, -ī (m)* [KL1, W28]

pirate *pīrāta, -ae (m)* [KL1, L2]

pit *abyssus, -ī (f)* [KL3, W9]; *fovea, -ae (f)* [KL3, W1]; *puteus, -ī (m)* [KL2, L12]

pity (verb) *misereor, -ērī, ——, misertus sum (+gen.)* [KL2, L6]

pity (noun) *misericordia, -ae (f)* [KL2, L10]

place (noun) *locus, -ī (m)* [KL2, L7]

place (verb) *collocō (1)* [KL1, W21]; *pōnō, -ere, posuī, positum* [KL1, L26]

places [geographic] *locī (m, pl)*; **[in a book]** *loca (n, pl)* [KL2, L7]

plague *plāga, -ae (f)* [KL3, L14]

plain (noun) *prātum, -ī (n)* [KL2, W15]

planet *lūmināre, -āris (n)* [KL3, W4]

plan *cōnsilium, -iī (n)* [KL1, L30]

plant (verb) *serō, -ere, sēvī, satum* [KL2, W11]

play (music) *cantō (1)* [KL1, L1]; *canō, -ere, cecinī, cāntum* [KL2, L10]

play *lūdō, lūdere, lūsī, lūsum* [KL1, L26]

please (interj.) *obsecrō* [KL3, L13]

please (verb) *placeō, -ēre, -cuī, -citum* [KL3, L1]

pleasing *grātus, -a, -um* [KL1, L27]; *placitus, -a, -um* [KL3, W12]

pleasure *voluptās, -tātis (f)* [KL3, W2]

plenty *cōpia, -ae (f)* [KL1, L15]

plot *īnsidiae, -ārum (f, pl)* [KL2, L15]

pluck *vellō, -ere, vulsī/vellī, vulsum* [KL3, W1]

plump *plēnus, -a, -um* [KL2, L4]

plunder (noun) *praeda, -ae (f)* [KL2, L15]

plunder (verb) *dīripiō, -ere, -ripuī, -reptum* [KL3, W1]

Pluto *Plūto, -tōnis (m)* [KL2, W6]

poem *carmen, -inis (n)* [KL1, L13]

poet *poēta, -ae* [KL1, L2]

point out *ostendō, -ere, -dī, -sum/tum* [KL3, L5]; *sīgnō* [KL3, W3]

poison *venēnum, -ī (n)* [KL1, L10; KL3, W6]

polite *urbānus, -a, -um* [KL1, W29]

Polyphemus *Polyphēmus, -ī (m)* [KL2, W4]

ponder *pendō, -ere, pependī, pensum* [KL3, L10]

pool *natātōria, -ae (f)* [KL2, W8]

poor *pauper, -eris* [KL3, L9]

porch *porticus, -ūs (f)* [KL3, W5]

port *portus, -ūs (m)* [KL1, L25]

portent *mōnstrum, -ī (n)* [KL1, W13]; *prōdigium, -iī (n)* [KL3, W5]

Poseidon *Neptūnus, -ī (m)* [KL2, W7]

possess *teneō, -ēre, tenuī, tentum* [KL1, L9]

possible *fās (n, indecl.)* [KL3, L2]

pour *fundō, -ere, fūdī, fūsum* [KL3, W3]; **(out/forth)** *effundō, -ere, -fūdī, -fūsum* [KL3, L9]; **(together)** *confundō, -ere, -fūdī, -fūsum* [KL3, L12]; **(in)** *infundō, -ere, -fūdī, -fūsum (+dat.)* [KL3, W9]; **(over)** *perfundō, -ere, -fūdī, -fūsus* [KL3, W6]

power *vīs, vīs (f)* [KL3, L5]

powerful *potēns, (gen.) -entis* [KL1, L19]

praise (noun) *laus, laudis (f)* [KL1, L15]

praise (verb) *laudō (1)* [KL1, L1]; *benedīcō, -ere, -dīxī, -dictum (+dat.)* [KL3, L4]

pray *ōrō (1) (takes double acc.)* [KL1, L6]; *obsecrō* [KL3, L13]; **(for)** *dēprecor, -ārī, ——, -ātus sum* [KL3, L10]

preach *ēvangelīzō* [KL3, W5]; *praedīcō* [KL3, W7]

predict *cantō (1)* [KL1, L1]; *praedīcō, -ere, -dīxī, -dictum* [KL1, W31]

prefer *mālō, mālle, māluī, ——* [KL2, L14]; *praeferō, -ferre, -tuli, -lātum* [KL2, W11]

pregnant *fētus, -a, -um* [KL3, W6]

preparation *ornātus, -ūs (m)* [KL3, W6]

prepare *parō (1)* [KL1, L14]; *accingō, -ere, -cinxī, -cinctum* [KL2, W9]

press *premō, -ere, pressī, pressum* [KL2, L10]

press on *īnstō, -āre, -stitī, -stātum* [KL2, W6]

prevent *vetō, -āre, vetuī, vetitum* [KL3, W11]

presence (in the presence of) *cōram (+abl.)* [KL1, L27]

pride *superbia, -ae (f)* [KL3, L12]

priest *sacerdōs, -dōtis (m)* [KL2, L3]

prince *prīnceps, -cipis (m)* [KL2, L3]

principle *placitum, -ī (n)* [KL3, W9]

prison *carcer, -eris (m)* [KL1, W23; KL3, L5]

proclaim *praedīcō* [KL3, W7]

proceed *vādō, -ere, vāsī, ——* [KL2, L9]

produce (verb) *prōdūcō, -ere, -dūxī, -ductum* [KL3, W4]

profit *frūctus, -ūs (m)* [KL1, L25]

promise (verb) *polliceor, -ērī, ——, pollicitus sum* [KL3, L7]

promise (noun, formal) *reprōmissiō, -ōnis (f)* [KL3, W12]

proper (it is proper) *decet, -ēre, ——, decuit (impers. +acc.)* [KL3, L1]

property *substantia, -ae (f)* [KL3, L13]

prophecy *carmen, -inis (n)* [KL1, L13]; *ōrāculum, -ī (n)* [KL1, W31; KL2, W6]; *fātum, -ī (n)* [KL1, L5; KL2, 13]

prophesy *praedīcō, -ere, -dīxī, -dictum* [KL1, W31]

prophesy *canō, -ere, cecinī, cāntum* [KL2, L10]; *for, fārī, ——, fātus sum* [KL3, L3]

prophet *vātēs, -is (m)* [KL1, W31]; *prophēta, -ae (f)* [KL3, L4]; **(false)** *pseudoprophēta, -ae (f)* [KL3, W14]

prophetess *vātēs, -is (f)* [KL1, W31]

propitiation *propitiātiō, -ōnis (f)* [KL2, W11]

proposition *prōpositiō, -tiōnis (f)* [KL3, W1]

proud *superbus, -a, -um* [KL1, W18; KL2, L4]

prove *probō* [KL3, L14]

provided that *dum, dummodo* [KL2, L11]

providence *prōvidentia, -ae (f)* [KL2, W9]

province *prōvincia, -ae (f)* [KL3, W10]

provision *prōvidentia, -ae (f)* [KL2, W9]

prow *prōra, -ae (f)* [KL2, W13]

pull *stringō, -ere, strinxī, strictum* [KL3, W7]; **(pluck)** *vellō, -ere, vulsī/vellī, vulsum* [KL3, W1]

punishment *poena, -ae (f)* [KL1, L27]

pure *castus, -a, -um* [KL3, W9]

purple *purpureus, -a, -um* [KL1, L17]

purplish-blue *hyacinthinus, -a, -um* [KL1, L17]

pursue *persequor, -sequī, ——, -secutus sum (deponent)* [KL1, W32; KL2, W6]

push (back) *repellō, -ere, reppulī, repulsum* [KL3, W2]

put *pōnō, -ere, posuī, positum* [KL1, L26]

put (in) *inficiō, -ere, -fēcī, -fectum* [KL3, W2]; **(on)** *impōnō, -ere, -posuī, -positum* [KL2, W13]; *induō, -ere, -duī, dūtum* [KL2, L14]; **(out)** *rēstinguō, -ere, -stinxī, -stinctum* [KL3, W3]

putting on *impositiō, -ōnis (f)* [KL3, W7]

pyre *pyra, -ae (f)* [KL1, W8]

Q

quake *tremō, -ere, -uī, ——* [KL1, W25]

queen *rēgīna, -ae (f)* [KL1, L2]

quick *celer, celeris, celere* [KL1, L19]

quickly *cito* [KL1, L27]

quiet *placidus, -a, -um* [KL1, W29]; *tranquillus, -a, -um* [KL3, W9]

R

rabbit (hare) *lepus, -oris (m)* [KL3, W2]

race *certāmen, -minis (n)* [KL1, W23]; *genus, -neris (n)* [KL2, L13]

rain *imber, -bris (m)* [KL2, W9]; *pluvia, -ae (f)* [KL2, L9]

rainbow *arcus, -ūs (m)* [KL1, L27]

raise *tollō, -ere, sustulī, sublātum* [KL1, W25]

raise (up) *levō* [KL3, W1]; *tollō, -ere, sustulī, sublātum* [KL1, W25; KL2, L13]; **(from death)** *suscitō* [KL3, W5]

ram *ariēs, -ietis (m)* [KL1, W32]

randomly *temere* [KL3, W15]

rashly *temere* [KL3, W15]

rather *immō* [KL3, W7]; *magis* [KL2, L7]; *potius* [KL3, L7]; *priusquam* [KL3, L15]

ravage *vexō (1)* [KL1, L19]

rave *furō, -ere, -uī, ——* [KL2, W13]

reach *perveniō, -īre, -vēnī, -ventum* [KL2, L11]

read *legō, -ere, lēgī, lēctum* [KL1, L28]

receive *accipiō, -ere, -cēpī, ceptum* [KL1, L31]

recent *recēns, -centis* [KL2, W11]

reciprocally *invicem* [KL1, W26]

recount *narrō (1)* [KL1, L2]

red *ruber, -bra, -brum* [KL1, L17]; *rūfus, -a, -um* [KL1, W32]; **(dark-red)** *purpureus, -a, -um* [KL1, L17]

reed *calamus, -ī (m)* [KL1, W28]

relieve *excipiō, -ere, -cēpī, -ceptum* [KL3, W2]

reading *lectiō, -ōnis (f)* [KL3, W9]

realize *sentiō, -īre, sēnsī, sēnsum* [KL3, L3]

reap *metō, -ere, messuī, messum* [KL2, W14]

rear *tergum, -ī (n)* [KL3, L6]

reason *causa, -ae (f)* [KL2, L15]

rebuke *reprehendō, -ere, -hendī, -hensum* [KL3, W13]

receive *recipiō, -ere, -cēpī, -ceptum* [KL3, L11]

redeemer *salvātor, -ōris (m)* [KL3, L5]

reed *arundō, -inis (f)* [KL3, W1]

refer *referō, -ferre, -(t)tulī, -(l)lātum* [KL3, W9]

regal *rēgālis, -e* [KL3, W10]

regard *rēspiciō, -ere, -spēxī, -spectum* [KL2, L14]

region *arvum, -ī (n)* [KL3, L15]; *regiō, -ōnis (f)* [KL3, W2]

reign *regnō (1)* [KL1, L6]

rein *habēna, -ae (f)* [KL3, W8]

rejoice *gaudeō, -ēre, ——, gāvīsus sum* [KL1, L22]; *exultō* [KL3, W9]

relate *narrō (1)* [KL1, L2]

religion *religiō, -ōnis (f)* [KL3, W7]

remain *maneō, -ēre, mansī, mansum* [KL1, L10]; *permaneō, -ēre, -mansī, -mansum* [KL3, L7]

remain near *obsideō, -ēre, -sēdī, -sessum* [KL1, L10]

remaining *reliquus, -a, -um* [KL2, L6]

remake *reficiō, -ere, -fēcī, -fectum* [KL1, W29; KL3, W2]

remembering *memor, -oris* [KL3, L9]

remembrance *memoria, -ae (f)* [KL3, L2]

remission *remissiō, -ōnis (f)* [KL3, W5]

remove *auferō, -ferre, abstulī, ablatum (3rd conj. irreg.)* [KL1, W32]; *removeō, -ēre, -mōvī, -mōtum* [KL1, L14]; *excipiō, -ere, -cēpī, -ceptum* [KL3, W2]; *remittō, -ere, -mīsī, -missum* [KL3, L11]; **(myself)** *auferō mē* [KL3, L10]

replace *succedō, -ere, -cessī, -cessum* [KL3, W2]

reptile *reptilis, -e* [KL3, W4]

resist *obsistō, -ere, -stitī, -stitum* [KL3, W7]

rend *scindō, -ere, scidī, scissum* [KL3, L10]

repair *reficiō, -ere, -fēcī, -fectum* [KL1, W29; KL3, W2]

repeat *repetō, -ere, -īvī/-iī, -ītum* [KL3, W9]

repel *repellō, -ere, reppulī, repulsum* [KL3, W2]

repentance *paenitentia, -ae (f)* [KL3, W5]

report *fāma, -ae (f)* [KL2, L13]

reproach *exprobrō (1)* [KL1, W32]

reputation *fāma, -ae (f)* [KL2, L13]

request (verb) *poscō, -ere, pōposcī, ——* [KL3, W12]

request (noun) *petītiō, -ōnis (f)* [KL3, W16]

rescue *ēripiō, -ere, -ripuī, -reptum* [KL2, L3]

resolution *prōpositiō, -tiōnis (f)* [KL3, W1]

respect *vereor, -ērī, ——, veritus sum* [KL2, L6]

respond *respondeō, -ēre, -spondī, -sponsum* [KL1, L9]

rest (adj.) *cēterus, -a, -um* [KL2, L15]; **(of)** *reliquus, -a, -um* [KL2, L6]

rest (verb) *quiēscō, -ere, quiēvī, quiētum* [KL3, W7]; *requiēscō, -ere, -quiēvī, -quiētum* [KL3, L4]

restless *turbulentus, -a, -um* [KL3, W9]

restrain *reprimō, -ere, -pressī, -pressum* [KL3, W9]

restore *restituō, -ere, -stituī, -stitutus* [KL3, W1]

resume *resūmō, -ere, -sūmpsī, -sūmptum* [KL3, W16]

return *redeō, -īre, -iī, -itum* [KL3, L2]; *revertor, -vertī, ——, reversus sum* [KL2, L6]; *regredior, -gredī, ——, -gressus sum* [KL3, L10]

reveal *exprōmō, -ere, -mpsī, -mptum* [KL2, W15]; *manifestō* [KL2, W8]; *revēlō* [KL3, W9]

revere *metuō, -ere, -uī, -ūtum* [KL3, L15]

reverence (verb) *vereor, -ērī, ——, veritus sum* [KL2, L6]

reverence (noun) *religiō, -ōnis (f)* [KL3, W7]

revive *restituō, -ere, -stituī, -stitutus* [KL3, W1]

reward *praemium, -ī (n)* [KL1, W27]

riches *dīvitiae, -ārum (f, pl)* [KL1, L2]

riddle *enigma, -matis (n)* [KL1, W19]

ride *vehō, -ere, vexī, vectum* [KL1, L27]

right (adj.) *iūstus, -a, -um* [KL1, L7]

right (verb, it is right) *decet, -ēre, decuit ——, (impers. +acc.)* [KL3, L1]

right (noun) *iūs, iūris (n)* [KL2, L15]

right(-handed) *dexter, -tra, -trum (or -tera, -terum)* [KL1, L30]

righteous *iūstus, -a, -um* [KL1, L7; KL3, L7]

righteousness *iūstitia, -ae (f)* [KL3, L12]

ring *ānulus, -ī (m)* [KL3, W10]

rise *surgō, -ere, surrēxī, surrēctum* [KL1, L28]; *orior, -īrī, ——, ortus sum* [KL2, L6]

rise again *resurgō, -ere, -surrēxī, -surrēctum* [KL1, L29]

river *flūmen, flūminis (n)* [KL1, L13]

road *iter, itineris (n)* [KL1, L13]; *via, -ae (f)* [KL1, L11]

rock *saxum, -ī (n)* [KL1, L29]

rod *virga, -ae (f)* [KL3, L10]

roll *volvō, -ere, volvī, volūtum* [KL3, W1]

Roman (adj./noun) *Rōmānus, -a, -um* [KL2, L15]

Rome *Rōma, -ae (f)* [KL2, L14]

route *iter, itineris (n)* [KL1, L13]

row *versus, -ūs (m)* [KL1, L27]; *ōrdō, -dinis (m)* [KL2, L15]

royal court *aula, -ae (f)* [KL1, W13]

ruddy *ruber, -bra, -brum* [KL1, L17]; *rūfus, -a, -um* [KL1, W32]

ruin *perdō, -ere, perdidī, perditum* [KL1, L27]

rule (noun) *lēx, lēgis (f)* [KL2, L10]; *rēgula, -ae (f)* [KL3, W9]

rule (verb) *regnō (1)* [KL1, L6]; *regō, -ere, rexī, rectum* [KL1, L26]

ruin *subvertō, -ere, -vertī, -versus* [KL3, W7]

rumor *fāma, -ae (f)* [KL2, L13]

run *currō, -ere, cūcurrī, cursum* [KL1, L26]

run away *fugiō, -ere, fūgī, fugitum* [KL1, L31]

rush *properō (1)* [KL1, L20]

rush (down) *ruō, -ere, ruī, rutum* [KL3, L4]

S

Sabbath *sabbatum, -ī (n)* [KL3, L1]

sack *saccus, -ī (m)* [KL2, W6]

sacred *sanctus, -a, -um* [KL1, L25]; *sacer, -cra, -crum* [KL2, L3]

sacrifice *sacrificium, -iī (n)* [KL2, L4]

sad *amārus, -a, -um* [KL3, W9]; *flēbilis, -e* [KL3, W9]; *trīstis, -e* [KL1, L20; KL2, L3]

sad *trīstis, -e* [KL1, L20]

sadness *contrītio, -ōnis (f)* [KL3, W9]; *dolor, -ōris (m)* [KL3, L3]

safe *salvus, -a, -um* [KL1, L25]; *incolumis* [KL3, W2]; *tūtus, -a, -um* [KL3, L7]

safety *salūs, -ūtis (f)* [KL3, W7]

sail (noun) *vēlum, -ī (n)* [KL1, W30]

sail (verb) *nāvigō (1)* [KL1, L4]

sailor *nauta, -ae (m)* [KL1, L3]

salvation *salūs, -ūtis (f)* [KL3, W7]

same (the same) *īdem, eadem, idem* [KL3, L2]

same place (in the same place, to the same place/purpose) *eōdem* [KL3, L2]

sanctify *sanctificō* [KL3, L4]

sand *harēna, -ae (f)* [KL1, L3]

sandal *solea, -ae (f)* [KL2, W6]; **(winged)** *tālāria, -ium (n, pl)* [KL3, W16]

Satan *Satanās, -ae (f)* [KL3, W1]

satchel *pēra, -ae (f)* [KL1, W32]

satisfy *impleō, -ēre, -plēvī, -plētum* [KL2, L7]

Saul *Saul (indecl.)* [KL1, W32]

savage *barbarus, -a, -um* [KL1, L31]; *crūdēlis, -e* [KL3, L10]; *saevus, -a, -um* [KL2, W11]

save *conservō* [KL3, W15]; *servō (1)* [KL1, L6]

saved *salvus, -a, -um* [KL1, L25]

savior *salvātor, -ōris (m)* [KL3, L5]

say *āiō* [KL1, L14]; *dīcō, -ere, dīxī, dictum* [KL1, L26]; *for, fārī, ——, fātus sum* [KL3, L3]; *loquor, -quī, ——, locūtus sum* [KL2, L6]

say falsely *mentior, -īrī, ——, -ītus sum* [KL3, L6]

say no *negō* [KL3, L3]

scaly *squāmeus, -a, -um* [KL3, W6]

scarcely *vix* [KL3, L3]

scatter *spargō, -ere, sparsī, sparsum* [KL2, W9]; *sternō, -ere, strāvī, strātum* [KL2, L13]

scattered *fūsus, -a, -um* [KL3, W6]; *rārus, -a, -um* [KL3, W2]

schism *schisma, -ae (f)* [KL2, W8]

scream *ululō (1)* [KL1, L6]

scribe *scrība, -ae (f)* [KL3, L10]

sea *aequor, -oris (n)* [KL3, L6]; *sālum, -ī (n)* [KL3, W6]; *mare, maris (n)* [KL1, L18]

sea serpent *hydrus, -ī (m)*

seaside (adj.) *maritimus, -a, -um* [KL3, W2]

seat *sella, -ae (f)* [KL1, L31]; *solium, -iī (n)* [KL3, W10]

second (adj.) *alter, -era, -erum* [KL2, L4]; *secundus, -a, -um* [KL1, L23]

second (adv.; a second time) *iterum* [KL1, L25]

secretary *scrība, -ae (f)* [KL3, L10]

secret *sēcrētum, -ī (n)* [KL1, W28]

secretly *clam* [KL1, L29]

secure *tūtus, -a, -um* [KL3, L7]

see *videō, -ēre, vīdī, vīsum* [KL1, L9]

seek *petō, -ere, -īvī, -ītum* [KL2, L12]; *quaerō, -ere, quaesīvī, quaesītum (-situm)* [KL2, L3]; **(after)** *praeferō, -ferre, -tulī, -lātum* [KL2, L11]; **(again)** *repetō, -ere, -īvī/-iī, -ītum* [KL3, W9]

seize *capiō, -ere, cēpī, captum* [KL1, L31]; *occupō (1)* [KL1, L6]; *rapiō, -ere, rapuī, raptum* [KL1, L31]; *arripiō, -ere, -ripuī, -reptum* [KL3, W9]; *corripiō, -ere, -ripuī, -reptus* [KL3, W16]

-self (intensifying suffix on pers. pron.) *-met* [KL3, L7]

sell *vendō, -ere, -didī, -ditum* [KL3, W9]

senate *senātus, -ūs (m)* [KL3, W15]

send *mittō, -ere, mīsī, missum* [KL1, L26]

send (back) *remittō, -ere, -mīsī, -missum* [KL3, L11]; **(away)** *āmittō, -ere, -misī, -missum* [KL2, W6]; *dīmittō, -ere, -mīsī, -missum* [KL1, L30; KL2, W15]; **(forth)** *prōmittō, -ere, -mīsī, -missum* [KL3, W2]

sense *sensus, -ūs (m)* [KL2, L15]

sentence *sententia, -ae (f)* [KL3, L9]

separate (adj.) *singulī, -ae, -a* [KL2, L13]

separate (verb) *differō, -ferre, distulī, dīlātum* [KL3, W2]; *dīvidō, -ere, -vīsī, -vīsum* [KL2, W9]

serpent *anguis, -is (m)* [KL3, W5]; *serpēns, -pentis (m/f)* [KL2, W4]

servant *serva, -ae (f)* [KL1, L4]; *servus, -ī (m)* [KL1, L4]; *minister, -strī (m)* [KL3, L10]

serve *oboediō [obediō], -īre, -īvī, -ītum (+dat.)* [KL3, W5]; *serviō, -īre, -īvī, -ītum (+dat.)* [KL2, L10]

set *collocō (1)* [KL1, W21]

set free *līberō (1)* [KL1, L1]; *solvō, -ere, solvī, solūtum* [KL2, L10]

set out *proficīscor, -ficīscī, ——, -fectus sum* [KL2, W7]

set up *cōnstituō, -ere, -stituī, -stitūtum* [KL2, L15]; *statuō, -ere, -uī, -ūtum* [KL2, W7]

seven *septem* [KL1, L21]

seventeen *septendecim* [KL1, L21]

seventeenth *septimus, -a, -um decimus, -a, -um* [KL1, L23]

seventh *septimus, -a, -um* [KL1, L23]

shade *umbra, -ae (f)* [KL3, L3]

shadow *umbra, -ae (f)* [KL3, L3]

shadows *tenēbrae, -ārum (f, pl)* [KL1, L11]

shake *nūtō* [KL3, W7]; *quatiō, -ere, quassī, quassus* [KL3, W5]; **(violently)** *quassō* [KL3, W1]; **(off)** *excutiō, -ere, -cussī, -cussum* [KL3, W3]; **(shiver)** *tremō, -ere, -uī, ——* [KL1, W25; KL3, W6]

shame *turpitūdō, -dinis (f)* [KL3, W9]

shape *forma, -ae (f)* [KL3, W16]; *faciēs, -ēī (f)* [KL1, L28]

share *commūnicō* [KL2, W6]

sharp *ācer, ācris, ācre* [KL1, L20]

sharp point *aciēs, -ēī (f)* [KL3, L14]

sharpness (esp. of sight) *aciēs, -ēī (f)* [KL3, L14]

shatter *frangō, -ere, frēgī, fractum* [KL1, L27]

shave *rādō, -ere, rāsī, rāsum* [KL3, W2]

she *is, ea, id* [KL1, L17]

shed *effundō, -ere, -fūdī, -fūsum* [KL3, L9]

sheep *ovis, ovis (f)* [KL2, L3]

shepherd *pastor, pastōris (m)* [KL1, L20]

shepherd (of/belonging to a shepherd) *pastoralis, -e* [KL1, W32]

shepherd's pipe *avēna, -ae (f)* [KL1, W21]

shield *clypeum, -ī (n)* [KL1, W32]; *scūtum, -ī (m)* [KL1, L10]; *clipeus (clypeus), -ī (m)* [KL3, W3]

shine *fulgeō, -ēre, fulsī, ——* [KL3, W13]; *lūceō, lūcēre, lūxī, ——* [KL1, L11]

ship *nāvis, -is (f)* [KL1, L18]; *alnus, -ī (f)* [KL1, L4]

shipwreck *naufragium, -ī (n)* [KL1, W23]

shiver *tremō, -ere, -uī, ——* [KL1, W25; KL3, W6]

shoot *petō, -ere, -īvī, -ītum* [KL1, W20]

shore *lītus, lītoris (n)* [KL1, L13]; *ōra, -ae (f)* [KL1, L13]

shoreline *lītus, lītoris (n)* [KL1, L13]

short *brevis, -e* [KL1, L19]

shortly *breviter* [KL3, W5]

shoulder *umerus, -ī (m)* [KL3, W3]

shout (noun) *clāmor, -oris (m)* [KL1, W20]

shout (verb) *clāmō (1)* [KL1, L1]

show *indīcō* [KL3, L11]; *praebeō, -ēre, -uī, -ītum* [KL3, W7]; *ostendō, -ere, -dī, -sum/tum* [KL3, L5]

shrieking *ululātus, -ūs (m)* [KL3, W10]

shrine *templum, -ī (n)* [KL1, W25]

shun *vītō (1)* [KL1, L30]

shut (in/up) *claudō, -ere, clausī, clausum* [KL3, W15]; *inclūdō, -ere, -clūsī, -clūsum* [KL3, W6]

the **Sibyl** *Sibylla, -ae (f)* [KL2, W13]

Sicily *Sicilia, -ae (f)* [KL2, W5]

sick *aeger, -gra, -grum* [KL3, W5]

sickness *īnfīrmitās, -tātis (f)* [KL3, W5]

side *lātus, -eris (n)* [KL3, L6] *pars, partis (f)* [KL2, L3]

siege *obsidiō, -ōnis (f)* [KL2, W15]

sight *cōnspectus, -ūs (m)* [KL2, L9]

sign *sīgnum, -ī (n)* [KL3, L4]; *prōdigium, -iī (n)* [KL3, W5]

signal *sīgnum, -ī (n)* [KL3, L4]

silence *silentium, -iī (n)* [KL3, W9]

silent (be silent) *taceō, -ēre, -uī, -itum* [KL1, W26]; *conquiēscō, -ere, -quiēvī, -quiētum* [KL2, W9]; *conticescō, -ere, -ticuī, ——* [KL3, W6]; *sileō, -ēre, -uī, ——* [KL3, W10]

Silenus *Sīlēnus, -ī (m)* [KL1, W27]

silver (adj.) *argenteus, -a, -um* [KL1, L17]

silver (noun) *argentum, -ī (n)* [KL1, L5]

similar *similis, -e* [KL2, L5]

sin (noun) *peccātum, -ī (n)*

sin (verb) *peccō* [KL3, L11]

sin *nefās (n, indecl.)* [KL3, W2]; *scelus, -leris (n)* [KL3, L6]

since *quandō* [KL1, L12]; *quia* [KL1, L18]; *quoniam* [KL1, L26]; *cum* [KL3, L7]

sing *cantō (1)* [KL1, L1]; *canō, -ere, cecinī, cāntum* [KL2, L10]; *cantitō* [KL3, W9]

singing *cantus, -ūs (m)* [KL1, L25]

single *sōlus, -a, -um* [KL1, W12]; *singulī, -ae, -a* [KL2, L13]

sinner *peccātor, -ōris (m)* [KL3, L5]; *peccātrix, -trīcis (f)* [KL3, L5]

sink *cadō, -ere, cecidī, cāsūrum* [KL1, L27]

sister *germāna, -ae (f)* [KL1, L4]; *soror, sorōris (f)* [KL1, L12]

sit *sedeō, -ēre, sēdī, sessum* [KL1, L9]

six *sex* [KL1, L21]

sixteen *sēdecim* [KL1, L21]

sixteenth *sextus, -a, -um decimus, -a, -um* [KL1, L23]

sixth *sextus, -a, -um* [KL1, L23]

size (of such size) *tantus, -a, -um* [KL3, L5]

skilled *dexter, -tra, -trum (or -tera, -terum)* [KL1, L30]; *doctus, -a, -um* [KL1, L13]

skin *pellis, -is (f)* [KL3, W2]

sky *firmāmentum, -ī (n)* [KL3, W4]; *caelum, -ī (n)* [KL1, L5]

slander *maledīcō, -ere, -dīxī, -dictum (+dat.)* [KL1, W30; KL3, L4]

slaughter *nex, necis (f)* [KL3, W10]

slave (noun) *serva, -ae (f)* [KL1, L4]; *servus, -ī (m)* [KL1, L4]

slave (verb, am a slave to) *serviō, -īre, -īvī, -ītum (+dat.)* [KL2, L10]

slay *interficiō, -ere, -fēcī, -fectum* [KL1, L31]; *necō (1)* [KL1, L1]; *occīdō, -ere, -cīdī, -cīsum* [KL1, L30]

sleep *dormiō, -īre, -īvī, -ītum* [KL1, L29]; *somnus, -ī (n)* [KL3, W13]; **(deep)** *sopor, -ōris (m)* [KL3, W6]

slender *gracilis, -e* [KL2, L5]; *tenuis, -e* [KL2, L11]

sling *funda, -ae (f)* [KL1, W32]

slip *lābor, -ī, ——, lapsus sum* [KL2, L6]

small *brevis, -e* [KL1, L19]; *parvus, -a, -um* [KL1, L7]

small cake *crustulum, -ī (n)* [KL1, L5]

smaller *minor, -ārī, ——, -ātus sum* [KL2, W5]

smallest *minimus, -a, -um* [KL1, W31; KL2, L5]

smash *frangō, -ere, frēgī, fractum* [KL1, L27]

smile *rīdeō, -ēre, rīsī, rīsum* [KL1, L9]

smoke *fūmigō* [KL3, W1]

snake *anguis, -is (m)* [KL3, W5]; *serpēns, -pentis (m/f)* [KL2, W4]

snatch (away/from) *ēripiō, -ere, -ripuī, -reptum* [KL2, L3]

snare (noun) *fovea, -ae (f)* [KL3, W1]

snatch *rapiō, -ere, rapuī, raptum* [KL1, L31]

snow *nix, nivis (f)* [KL2, L9]

so great a number *tot (indecl. adj.)* [KL3, L9]

so great *tantus, -a, -um* [KL3, L5]

so greatly *tantum* [KL3, L14]

so *īta* [KL2, L6]; *sīc* [KL2, L4]; *tam* [KL3, L5]; *tantum* [KL3, L14]

so many *tot (indecl. adj.)* [KL3, L9]

so much *tam* [KL3, L5]; *tantum* [KL3, L14]

so that *ut (+subj.)* [KL3, L5]

so...as *tam...quam* [KL3, L5]

social feast *convīvium, -iī (n)* [KL3, L10]

society *societās, -tātis (f)* [KL3, W11]

softly *leviter* [KL2, W6]

soil *humus, -ī (f)* [KL2, L14]

soldier *mīles, mīlitis (m)* [KL1, L12]

solitary *dēsertus, -a, -um* [KL3, L4]

solitude *sōlitūdō, -dinis (f)* [KL3, W9]

sole *ūnicus, -a, -um* [KL1, W22]

solo *canticum, -ī (n)* [KL3, L14]

some *aliquī, aliquae, aliquod (adj.)* [KL2, L12]; *quīdam, quaedam, quiddam (adj.)* [KL2, L12]

someone *aliquis, aliquid (pron.)* [KL2, L12]; *quīdam, quaedam, quiddam* [KL2, L12]; *quisquam, quidquam/quicquam* [KL3, L1]

something *aliquis, aliquid (pron.)* [KL2, L12]; *quīdam, quaedam, quiddam* [KL2, L12]; *quisquam, quidquam/quicquam* [KL3, L1]

son *fīlius, -ī (m)* [KL1, L4]

son (little) *fīliolus, -ī (m)* [KL3, W10]

song *cantus, -ūs (m)* [KL1, L25]; *carmen, -inis (n)* [KL1, L13]; *canticum, -ī (n)* [KL3, L14]

Song of Songs *Canticum Canticōrum* [KL3, L14]

soon *mox* [KL1, L15]

sooner *priusquam* [KL3, L15]

sooner than *antequam* [KL3, L15]

soothe (verb) *mītigō* [KL3, W7]

soothsayer *prophēta, -ae* [KL3, L4]

sorrow *lūctus, -ūs (m)* [KL3, W13]

sort (of what sort, of such a sort) *quālis* [KL3, L9]

sort *modus, -ī (m)* [KL3, L7]

soul *anima, -ae (f)* [KL2, L4]

sound (adj.) *salvus, -a, -um* [KL1, L25]

sound (noun) *sonitus, -ūs (m)* [KL3, W3]

source *fōns, fontis (m)* [KL2, L11]

sow (verb) *serō, -ere, sēvī, satum* [KL2, W11]

spare *parcō, -ere, pepercī, parsūrum (+dat.)* [KL2, L13]

speak *dīcō, -ere, dīxī, dictum* [KL1, L26]; *ōrō (1) (takes double acc.)* [KL1, L6]; *for, fārī, ——, fātus sum* [KL3, L3]; *loquor, -quī, ——, locūtus sum* [KL2, L6]

speak ill of *maledīcō, -ere, -dīxī, -dictum (+dat.)* [KL1, W30; KL3, L4]

speak well *benedīcō, -ere, -dīxī, -dictum (+dat.)* [KL3, L4]

spear *hasta, -ae (f)* [KL1, L3]

species *speciēs, -ēī (f)* [KL3, W4]

speech *sermō, -ōnis (m)* [KL2, L9]

speedily *cito* [KL1, L27]

spend *consūmō, -ere, -sūmpsī, -sūmptum* [KL3, L2]

spin (wool) *neō, nēre, nēvī, nētus* [KL2, W14]

spine *spīna, -ae (f)* [KL1, W23]

spirit *spīritus, -ūs (m)* [KL1, L25]; *anima, -ae (f)* [KL2, L4]

spirit of the age *saeculum, -ī (n)* [KL1, L6]

spit out *expuō, -ere, -puī, -putum* [KL2, W8]

split *findō, -ere, fidī, fissum* [KL3, W16]

spoil *praeda, -ae (f)* [KL2, L15]

spray (verb) *spūmō* [KL3, W6]

spread (out) *sternō, -ere, strāvī, strātum* [KL2, L13]

spring (fountain) *fōns, fontis (m)* [KL2, L11]

spring (jump) *saliō, -īre, -uī, saltum* [KL1, W29; KL2, W12]

sprinkle *spargō, -ere, sparsī, sparsum* [KL2, W9]

sprout *germinō* [KL3, W4]

spurious *spurius, -a, -um* [KL1, W32]

staff *virga, -ae (f)* [KL3, L10]; *baculum, -ī (n)* [KL1, W32]

stag *cervus, -ī (m)* [KL1, L10]

stand *stō, stāre, stetī, statum* [KL1, L1]

stand (back/still) *resistō, -ere, -stitī, ——* [KL3, L2]; **(apart)** *distō* [KL3, W9]; **(in the way)** *obstō, -stāre, -stitī, -stātūrum (+dat.)* [KL2, W11]; **(cause to)** *statuō, -ere, -uī, -ūtum* [KL2, W7]

star *stella, -ae* [KL1, L11]; *lūmināre, -āris (n)* [KL3, W4]; *sīdus, sīderis (n)* [KL3, L15]; **(evening)** *vesper, vesperis (m)* [KL1, L14]

start *proficīscor, -ficīscī, ——, -fectus sum* [KL3, W7]

starting gates (of a horse race) *plural of carcer, -eris (m)* [KL1, W23]

state *cīvitās, -tātis (f)* [KL2, L7]; **(USA)** *prōvincia, -ae (f)* [KL3, W10]

statue *simulācrum, -ī (n)* [KL1, W25]

steer *gubernō (1)* [KL1, L25]

step-mother *noverca, -ae (f)* [KL1, W22]

stick to *haereō, -ēre, haesī, haesum* [KL3, W3]

still *etiam* [KL1, L22]; *tamen* [KL1, L30]; *adhūc* [KL3, L12]

stillness *silentium, -iī (n)* [KL3, W9]

sting *mordeō, -ēre, momordī, morsum* [KL1, L9]

stone *lapis, -idis (m)* [KL1, W27; KL2, L14]

storm *tempestās, -tātis (f)* [KL1, L26]

stormy *turbulentus, -a, -um* [KL3, W9]

story *fābula, -ae (f)* [KL1, L2]

strange *barbarus, -a, -um* [KL1, L31]; *mīrus, -a, -um* [KL1, L7]

stranger *aliēnus, -a, -um* [KL2, L12]

stream *torrens, -ntis (m)* [KL1, W32]

strength *virtūs, virtūtis (f)* [KL1, L12]

street *platēa, -ae (f)* [KL3, L1]

stretch out *extendō, -ere, -tendī, -tensum* [KL1, W26]

strength *fortitūdō, -tudinis (f)* [KL2, L12]; *vīs, vīs (f)* [KL3, L5]

strength (verb: to gain strength) *convalēscō, -ere, -valuī, -valitus* [KL3, W9]

strengthen *confirmō* [KL3, W9]; *firmō* [KL3, W3]; *solidō* [KL2, W9]

stretch *tendō, -ere, tetendī, tentum* [KL2, L4]

strife *contentiō, -ōnis (f)* [KL3, W9]

strike *tangō, -ere, tetigī, tactum* [KL1, L27]; *pulsō* [K2L, W14]; **(through)** *percutiō, -ere, -cussī, -cussum* [KL1, W32; KL2, L3]

strike down *percutiō, -ere, -cussī, -cussum* [KL1, W32]

string *fīlum, -ī (n)* [KL1, W30]; *linea, -ae (f)* [KL3, W9]

strive *tendō, -ere, tetendī, tentum* [KL2, L4]

stroke (noun) *ictus, -ūs (m)* [KL3, W5]

strong *fortis, -e* [KL1, L19]

strongest *fortissimus, -a, -um* [KL1, W32]

student (female) *discipula, -ae (f)* & **(male)** *discipulus, -ī (m)* [KL1, L5]

stumbling block *scandalum, -ī (n)* [KL3, L12]

stunned (be) *stupeō, -ēre, -uī, ——* [KL3, W16]

subdue *domō, -āre, domuī, domitum* [KL1, L12]

substance *substantia, -ae (f)* [KL3, L13]

succeed *succedō, -ere, -cessī, -cessum* [KL3, W2]

such (adj.) *iste, ista, istud* [KL1, L30]

such (of such a sort) (rel. adj.) *quālis* [KL3, L9]

such as (rel. adj.) *quālis* [KL3, L9]

such great *tantus, -a, -um* [KL3, L5]

such *tālis, -e* [KL3, L5]

sudden (adj.) *subitus, -a, -um* [KL3, W3]

suddenly *repentē* [KL1, L10]; *subitō/subitum* [KL3, L3]

suffer *expendō, -ere, -dī, -sum* [KL3, W6]; *patior, -ī, ——, passus sum* [KL2, L6]

suffering *miseria, -ae (f)* [KL3, W9]

suffice *sufficiō, -ere, -fēcī, -fectum* [KL2, W14]

sufficient(ly) *satis (adv. & indecl. adj./noun)* [KL1, L30]

suitable (verb: it is suitable) *decet, -ēre, ——, decuit (impers. +acc.)* [KL3, L1]

suitable (adj) *aptus, -a, -um* [KL3, W2]; *commodus, -a, -um* [KL3, W2]; *congruēns, -ntis* [KL3, W9]

sum(mary) *summa, -ae (f)* [KL2, W10]

summon *vocō (1)* [KL1, L1]

sun *sōl, sōlis (m)* [KL1, L12]

supply *cōpia, -ae (f)* [KL1, L15]

suppose *arbitror, -ārī, ——, -ātus sum* [KL3, L4]; *putō* [KL3, L3]; *reor, rērī, ——, ratus sum* [KL3, L16]

supine *resupīnus, -a, -um* [KL3, W7]

sure *certus, -a, -um* [KL3, L6]

surely *utique* [KL3, L12]

surely...not? *numquid* [KL2, L9]

surface (level surface) *aequor, -oris (n)* [KL3, L6]

surrender *trādō, -ere, -didī, -ditum* [KL1, W13; KL2, L4]

suspend *pendō, -ere, pependī, pensum* [KL3, L10]; *suspendō, -ere, -pendī, -pensum* [KL3, W5]

suspicious *suspīciōsus, -a, -um* [KL1, W21]

swamp *palus, palūdis (f)* [KL1, W13]

swear *iūrō* [KL2, L15]

sweet *dulcis, -e* [KL1, L19]

swift *celer, celeris, celere* [KL1, L19]

swim *nō (1)* [KL1, L14]

swimming pool *natātōria, -ae (f)* [KL2, W8]

sword *gladius, -ī (m)* [KL1, L4]; *ferrum, -ī (n)* [KL2, L15]

synagogue *synagōga, -ae (f)* [KL1, W26]

T

table *mensa, -ae (f)* [KL1, L31]

tail *cauda, -ae (f)* [KL1, W21]

take *accipiō, -ere, -cēpī, ceptum* [KL1, L31]; *capiō, -ere, cēpī, captum* [KL1, L31]

take away *removeō, -ēre, -mōvī, -mōtum* [KL1, L14]; *tollō, -ere, sustulī, sublātum* [KL1, W25; KL2, L13]

take an oath *iūrō* [KL2, L15]

take back/again *recipiō, -ere, -cēpī, -ceptum* [KL3, L11]; *referō, -ferre, -(t) tulī, -(l)lātum* [KL3, W9]

take for myself *adsūmō, -ere, -sumpsī, -sumptum* [KL1, W32]

take (up) *sūmō, -ere, sūmpsī, sūmptum* [KL2, L10]; **(again)** *resūmō, -ere, -sūmpsī, -sūmptum* [KL3, W16]

tale *fābula, -ae (f)* [KL1, L2]

talk (noun) *sermō, -ōnis (m)* [KL2, L9]

tame *domō, -āre, domuī, domitum* [KL1, L12]

tax *tribūtum, -ī (n)* [KL1, W30]; *stīpendium, -iī (n)* [KL2, W15]

teach *doceō, -ēre, docuī, doctum* [KL1, L9]; *trādō, -ere, -didī, -ditum* [KL1, W13; KL2, L4]

teacher (female) *magistra, -ae (f)*/**(male)** *magister, -strī (m)* [KL1, L6]

teaching *doctrīna, -ae (f)* [KL3, L5]

tear (noun) *lācrima, -ae (f)* [KL3, L9]

tear (verb) *scindō, -ere, scidī, scissum* [KL3, L10]; *dīripiō, -ere, -ripuī, -reptum* [KL3, W1]; *dirumpō, -ere, -rūpī, -ruptum* [KL2, W14]

tease *lūdō, lūdere, lūsī, lūsum* [KL1, L26]

tell *narrō (1)* [KL1, L2]

temple *templum, -ī (n)* [KL1, W25; KL2, L10]

temptation *scandalum, -ī (n)* [KL3, L12]

ten *decem* [KL1, L21]

ten at a time *dēnī, -ae, -a* [KL3, W2]

tent *tabernāculum, -ī (n)* [KL1, W32]

tenth *decimus, -a, -um* [KL1, L23]

tepid *tepidus, -a, -um* [KL3, W16]

terrify *terreō, -ēre, -uī, -itum* [KL1, L9]

territory *prōvincia, -ae (f)* [KL3, W10]; *regiō, -ōnis (f)* [KL3, W2]

test *probō* [KL3, L14]

testify *testificor, -ārī, ——, -ātus sum* [KL3, W14]; *testor, -ārī, ——, -ātus sum* [KL3, W11]

testimony *testimōnium, -ī (n)* [KL2, L10]

text (noun) *lectiō, -ōnis (f)* [KL3, W9]

than *quam* [KL1, L28]

thank *grātiās agō (+dat.)* [KL1, L27]

thanks *grātia, -ae (f)* [KL1, L27]

that (pron.) *quī*; **(conj.)** *quia* [KL1, L18]; *quoniam* [KL1, L26]; *ut (+subj.)* [KL3, L5]

that (of yours) *iste, ista, istud* [KL1, L30]

that (adj./pron.) *ille, illa, illud* [KL1, L30]; *is, ea, id* [KL1, L17]

that (conj.) *quia* [KL1, L18]; *quod* [KL1, L10]

that not *nē* [KL3, L4]

their (own) *suus, -a, -um* [KL1, W31; KL3, L2]

themselves *suī* [KL3, L2]

then (therefore) *igitur* [KL2, L9]; *tunc* [KL2, L4]; *deinde* [KL1, L22]; *ergo (adv.)* [KL1, L18]; **(of time)** *ibī* [KL1, L5]; *ōlim* [KL1, L6]; *tum* [KL1, L15]

thence *illinc* [KL2, L11]; *inde* [KL2, L10]

there *ibī* [KL1, L5]; *illīc* [KL2, L11]

therefore *ergo (adv.)* [KL1, L18]; *itaque* [KL1, L2]; *ideo* [KL2, L14]; *igitur* [KL2, L9]; *īta* [KL2, L6]

thereupon *deinde* [KL1, L22]; *tum* [KL1, L15]; *tunc* [KL2, L4]

these *plural of hic, haec, hoc* [KL1, L30]

Theseus *Thēsēūs, -eī (m)* [KL1, W30]

they *is, ea, id* [KL1, L9]

thick *crēber, -bra, -brum* [KL3, L2]

thin *gracilis, -e* [KL2, L5]; *rārus, -a, -um* [KL3, W2]; *tenuis, -e* [KL2, L11]

thing *rēs, reī (f)* [KL1, L28]

think *cōgitō (1)* [KL1, L6]; *arbitror, -ārī, ——, -ātus sum* [KL3, L4]; *putō* [KL3, L3]; *reor, rērī, ——, ratus sum* [KL3, L16]

think about *considerō* [KL2, W14]

third *tertius, -a, -um* [KL1, L23]

thirst (verb) *sitiō, -īre, -īvī, ——* [KL2, L12]

thirteen *tredecim* [KL1, L21]

thirteenth *tertius, -a, -um decimus, -a, -um* [KL1, L23]

this *hic, haec, hoc* [KL1, L30]; *is, ea, id* [KL1, L17]

thither *illūc* [KL2, L11]

those *plural of ille, illa, illud* [KL1, L30]

though *etsi* [KL3, W2]

thought *cōgitātiō, -tiōnis (f)* [KL3, L1]; *sententia, -ae (f)* [KL3, L9]

thousand *mīlle* [KL1, L21]

thousandth (one thousandth) *mīllēsimus, -a, -um* [KL1, L23]

thread *fīlum, -ī (n)* [KL1, W30]

threaten *comminor, -ārī, ——, -ātus sum* [KL3, W1]; *minor, -ārī, ——, -ātus sum* [KL2, W5]

three *trēs, tria* [KL1, L21]

three times *ter* [KL3, W5]

threshold *līmen, -minis (n)* [KL3, L3]

throat *faucēs, -ium (f, pl)* [KL3, W3]

throne *solium, -iī (n)* [KL3, W10]

throng *turba, -ae (f)* [KL1, L2]

through *per (+acc.)* [KL1, L3]

throw *iaciō, -ere, iēcī, iactum* [KL1, L31]

throw down *dēiciō, -icere, -iēcī, -iectum* [KL1, W23]

throw (out) *ēiciō, -ere, -iēcī, -iectum* [KL2, L14]; **(to)** *adiciō, -ere, -iēcī, -iectum* [KL2, W14]; **(into/onto)** *iniciō, -ere, -iēcī, -iectum* [KL2, W15]; **(back)** *rēiciō, -ere, -iēcī, -iectum* [KL3, W7]; **(under)** *sūbiciō, -ere, -iēcī, -iectum* [KL3, W4]

thunder (noun) *tonitrus, -ūs (m)* [KL1, L25]

thunder (verb) *intonō, -āre, -uī/-āvī, ——* [KL3, W3]

thus *īta* [KL2, L6]; *sīc* [KL2, L4]

timber *māteria, -ae (f)* [KL3, W2]

tie *vinciō, -īre, vīnxī, vīnctum* [KL1, L30]

tie up *alligō* [KL3, W1]; *implicō* [KL3, W5]; *ligō* [KL3, W16]; **(back/up)** *religō* [KL3, W16]

tiger *tigris, tigridis (m/f)* [KL1, L12]

time *tempus, temporis (n)* [KL1, L13]

time of life *aetās, -tātis (f)* [KL2, L14]

times (the times) *saeculum, -ī (n)* [KL1, L6]

tip *summitās, -tātis (f)* [KL2, W10]

tired *fessus, -a, -um* [KL1, L20; KL3, W6]; *lassus, -a, -um* [KL3, W3]

tire out *dēfatīgō* [KL3, W2]; *fatigō* [KL2, W12]

Tmolus *Tmōlus, -ī (m)* [KL1, W28]

to *ad (+acc.)* [KL1, L3]

to that place *illūc* [KL2, L11]

to the same place *eōdem* [KL3, L2]

to the same purpose *eōdem* [KL3, L2]

to this place *adhūc* [KL3, L12]; *hūc* [KL2, L11]

to *ut (+subj.)* [KL3, L5]

to what/which place (?) *quō (?)* [KL2, L11]

today *hodiē* [KL1, L2]

together (all together) (adj.) *ūniversus, -a, -um* [KL3, L4]; **(adv.)** *simul* [KL2, L9]

together (prep.) *ūnā* [KL1, L29]

toil (noun) *labor, labōris (m)* [KL1, L28]

tomb *sepulcrum, -ī (n)* [KL2, L13]; *tumulus, -ī (m)* [KL2, W11]

tomorrow (adj.) *crastinus, -a, -um* [KL2, W14]; **(adv.)** *crās* [KL1, L6]

tomorrow (adv.) *crās* [KL1, L6]

tongue *lingua, -ae (f)* [KL1, L26]

too (also) *quoque* [KL1, L29]

too (much) *nimis* [KL3, L4]; *nimium* [KL2, W13]

too little *parum* [KL2, L7]

top *summa, -ae (f)* [KL2, W10]; *summitās, -tātis (f)* [KL2, W10]

topics [in a book] *loca (n, pl)* [KL2, L7]

torrent *torrens, -ntis (m)* [KL1, W32]

touch (noun) *tactus, -ūs (m)* [KL1, W28]

touch (verb) *tangō, -ere, tetigī, tactum* [KL1, L27]

toward *ad (+acc.)* [KL1, L3]

tower *turris, turris (f)* [KL1, L18]

town *oppidum, -ī (n)* [KL1, L5]

track *vestīgium, -iī (n)* [KL2, W11]

tragedy *tragoedia, -ae (f)* [KL1, W4]

train *exerceō, -ēre, -uī, -itum* [KL1, L14]

trample *conculcō* [KL2, W14]

transfer *trānsferō, -ferre, -tūlī, -lātum* [KL3, L13]

transgress *peccō* [KL3, L11]

translate *trānsferō, -ferre, -tūlī, -lātum* [KL3, L13]

trap *fovea, -ae (f)* [KL3, W1]

traverse *mētior, -īrī, ——, mēnsus sum* [KL2, L14]

treasure *thēsaurus, -ī (m)* [KL3, L11]

treaty *foedus, -deris (n)* [KL2, L12]

tree *arbor, arboris (f)*; *līgnum, -ī (n)* [KL2, L13]; **(trunk)** *trabēs, -is (m)* [KL2, W14]; **(elm)** *abiēs, -etis (f)* [KL3, W2]; **(beach)** *fāgus, -ī (f)* [KL3, W2]; **(fig)** *fīcus, -ī (f)* [KL3, W8]

trek *iter, itineris (n)* [KL1, L13]

tremble *paveō, -ēre, pavī, ——* [KL3, L15]; *tremō, -ere, -uī, ——* [KL1, W25; KL3, W6]

trial *iūdicium, -ī (n)* [KL2, L9]

tribe *gens, -ntis (f)* [KL1, L31]

tribunal *tribūnal, -ālis (n)* [KL2, W15]

tribute *tribūtum, -ī (n)* [KL1, W30]

trick *lūdō, lūdere, lūsī, lūsum* [KL1, L26]

trickle *mānō* [KL3, W16]

triumph *triumphō* [KL3, W9]

troops *plural of cōpia, -ae (f)* [KL1, L15]

trouble (verb) *turbō* [KL2, W13]

troubled *sollicitus, -a, -um* [KL2, W14]

troy *Troia, -ae (f)* [KL2, W4]

true *vērus, -a, -um* [KL1, L22; KL2, W13]

truly *enim (postpositive conj.)* [KL1, L17]; *vērō* [KL2, L15]

trust (verb) *confīdō, -ere, ——, confīsus sum (+dat.) (semi-deponent)* [KL2, L6]

trust (noun) *fīdūcia, -ae (f)* [KL3, L7]

trustworthy *fīdus, -a, -um* [KL1, L7]

truth *vēritas, -tātis (f)* [KL1, L27]

try *cōnor, -ārī, ——, cōnātus sum* [KL2, L6]; *probō* [KL3, L14]; *temptō* [KL1, W27; KL3, L7]

tub *lacus, -ūs (m)* [KL1, L27]

turban *mītra, -ae (f)* [KL1, W28]

turbulent *turbulentus, -a, -um* [KL3, W9]

turn (around) *vertō, -ere, vertī, versum* [KL1, L28; KL2, L11]; **(around/back)** *convertō, -ere, -vertī, -versum* [KL3, L9]; **(around/over)** *volvō, -ere, volvī, volūtum* [KL3, W1]; **(back)** *revertor, -vertī, ——, reversus sum* [KL2, L6]

turning-post *mēta, -ae (f)* [KL1, W23]

turret *turris, turris (f)* [KL1, L18]

in turn (adv.) *deinceps* [KL3, W2]

twelfth *duodecimus, -a, -um* [KL1, L23]

twelve *duodecim* [KL1, L21]

twelve times *duodēnī, -ae, -a* [KL3, W2]

twentieth *vīcēsimus, -a, -um* [KL1, L23]

twenty *vīgintī* [KL1, L21]

twenty-first *vīcēsimus, -a, -um prīmus, -a, -um* [KL1, L23]

twenty-one *vīgintī ūnus, -a, -um (ūnus et vīgintī)* [KL1, L21]

twice *bis* [KL3, L6]

twin *geminus, -ī (m)* [KL1, L10]

two *duo, duae, duo* [KL1, L21]

twofold *bis* [KL3, L6]

U

ugliness *turpitūdō, -dinis (f)* [KL3, W9]

ugly *foedus, -a, -um* [KL1, L7]

Ulysses *Ulixēs, -is (m)* [KL2, W5]

unavoidable *necesse (n, indecl.)* [KL3, L1]

uncertain *incertus, -a, -um* [KL2, W11]

uncircumcised *incircumcisus, -a, -um* [KL1, W32]

uncle (father's brother) *patruus, -ī (m)* [KL1, L22]; **(mother's brother)** *avunculus, -ī (m)* [KL1, L22]

unclean *immundus, -a, -um* [KL3, L5]

unconquered *invīctus, -a, -um* [KL3, W13]

under *sub (+acc.)* [KL1, L24]; *īnfrā* [KL3, W16]

under(neath) *sub (+abl.)* [KL1, L14]

understand *intellegō, -ere, -lēxī, -lēctum* [KL3, L2]

understanding *sensus, -ūs (m)* [KL2, L15]

undertake *ingredior, -gredī, ——, -gressus sum* [KL2, L6]; *mōlior, -īrī, ——, mōlītus sum* [KL2, L6]

undertook *coepī, coepisse, ——, coeptum (defective)* [KL3, L1]

undeserved *inmeritus, -a, -um* [KL3, W16]

unexpectedly *subitō/subitum* [KL3, L3]

unfairness *inīquitās, -tātis (f)* [KL2, L10]

unfortunate *infēlix, (gen.) -līcis* [KL1, L19]

ungodliness *impietās, -tātis (f)* [KL3, W7]

unhappy *miser, -era, -erum* [KL1, L7]

unhurt *incolumis, -e* [KL3, W2]; *intāctus, -a, -um* [KL2, W15]; *inviolātus, -a, -um* [KL3, W1]

unimportant *parvus, -a, -um* [KL1, L7]

uninjured *incolumis, -e* [KL3, W2]; *intāctus, -a, -um* [KL2, W15]; *inviolātus, -a, -um* [KL3, W1]

unite *iungō, -ere, iūnxī, iunctum* [KL1, L27]; *coniungō, -ere, -iūnxī, -iūnctum* [KL3, L9]

universe *mundus, -ī (m)* [KL1, L6]

unjust *iniūstus, -a, -um* [KL3, W16]

unless *nisi* [KL3, L11]

unlike *dissimilis, -e* [KL2, L5]

unlucky *infēlix, (gen.) -līcis* [KL1, L19]

unsure *incertus, -a, -um* [KL2, W11]

until now *adhūc* [KL3, L12]

until *antequam* [KL3, L15]; *dōnec* [KL3, W3]; *dum/dummodo* [KL2, L11]; *priusquam* [KL3, L15]; *quamdiu* [KL3, L9]; *quoad* [KL2, W15]

untouched *intāctus, -a, -um* [KL2, W15]; *integer, -tēgra, -tēgrum* [KL3, W2]

unveil *revēlō* [KL3, W9]

unwilling (am unwilling) *nōlō, nōlle, nōluī, ——* [KL2, L14]

unworthiness *indīgnitās, -tātis (f)* [KL2, W15]

up under *sub (+acc.)* [KL1, L14]

upper arm *umerus, -ī (m)* [KL3, W3]

upright *iūstus, -a, -um* [KL1, L7; KL3, L7]

urn *urna, -ae (f)* [KL2, W11]

use *ūtor, ūtī, ——, ūsus sum (+abl.)* [KL3, L2]

V

vacant *vacuus, -a, -um* [KL3, W4]

vain (in vain) *frustrā* [KL3, L3]

vale *vallēs, vallis (f)* [KL1, L18]

valley *vallēs, vallis (f)* [KL1, L18]

vast *ingēns, (gen.) -entis* [KL1, L19]; *vastus, -a, -um* [KL2, L6]

vehement *vehemens, -mentis* [KL2, W9]

veil *vēlāmen, -minis (n)* [KL2, W11]

venom *venēnum, -ī (n)* [KL1, L10; KL3, W6]

very (adv.) *māximē* [KL2, L7]; *valde* [KL2, L10]; **(the very, adj.)** *ipse, ipsa, ipsum* [KL2, L3]

very much *magnoperē* [KL1, L29]

vessel *vās, vāsis (n)* [KL3, W1]

vex *vexō (1)* [KL1, L19]

vibrate *vibrō* [KL3, W6]

victor *victor, -toris (m)* [KL2, W13]

victory *victōria, -ae (f)* [KL1, L11]

view *cōnspectus, -ūs (m)* [KL2, L9]

vigorous *vīridis, -e* [KL1, L17]

violate *violō* [KL3, W1]

violence *vīs, vīs (f)* [KL3, L5]

violent *vehemens, -mentis* [KL2, W9]

violet *hyacinthinus, -a, -um* [KL1, L17]; **(dark-violet)** *purpureus, -a, -um* [KL1, L17]

visible (am visible) *appareō, -ēre, -uī, -itum (+dat.)* [KL3, L4]

voice *vōx, vōcis (f)* [KL1, L14]

void *vacuus, -a, -um* [KL3, W4]

vow *iūrō* [KL2, L15]

W

wage war *bellum gerō* [KL1, L28]

wailing *planctus, -ūs (m)* [KL3, W8]; *ululātus, -ūs (m)* [KL3, W10]

wait for *exspectō (1)* [KL1, L3]

walk *ambulō (1)* [KL1, L1]

wall *mūrus, -ī (m)* [KL2, L11]

walls (city walls) *moenia, -ium (n, pl)* [KL1, L18]

wander *errō (1)* [KL1, L14]

want instead *mālō, mālle, māluī, ——* [KL2, L14]

want more *mālō, mālle, māluī, ——* [KL2, L14]

want *volō/velle, voluī, ——, ——* [KL2, L14]

war *bellum, -ī (n)* [KL1, L15]

warm *caldus, -a, -um* [KL1, L7]; *tepidus, -a, -um* [KL3, W16]

warn *moneō, -ēre, -uī, -itum* [KL1, L9]; *admoneō, -ēre, -uī, -itum* [KL3, W9]; *praecipiō, -ere, -cēpī, -ceptum* [KL3, W5]

warrior *bellator, -toris (m)* [KL1, W32]

wash *lavō, -āre, lāvī, lōtum/lavātum* [KL1, W27; KL2, L11]

watch (noun) *custōs, -ōdis (m/f)* [KL3, L3]

watch (verb) *spectō (1)* [KL1, L1]; *custōdiō, -īre, -iī/-īvī, -ītum* [KL3, L3]; *observō* [KL3, W11]

watchman *custōs, -ōdis (m/f)* [KL3, L3]

water *aqua, -ae (f)* [KL1, L2]

wave *unda, -ae (f)* [KL1, L10]

way *via, -ae (f)* [KL1, L11]; *modus, -ī (m)* [KL3, L7]

we *nōs (pl.)* [KL1, L17]

weak *īnfīrmus, -a, -um* [KL3, W5]

weakness *īnfīrmitās, -tātis (f)* [KL3, W5]

wealth *dīvitiae, -ārum (f, pl)* [KL1, L2]

weapon *tēlum, -ī (n)* [KL3, L6]

weapons *arma, -ōrum (n, pl)* [KL1, W32; KL2, L3]

wear *induō, -ere, -duī, -dūtum* [KL2, L14]

weary *fessus, -a, -um* [KL1, L20]

weather *tempestās, -tātis (f)* [KL1, L26]

weave *neō, nēre, nēvī, nētus* [KL2, W14]

wedding *nūptiālis, -e* [KL2, W2]

weep *fleō, -ēre, flēvī, flētum* [KL1, L14]

weeping *flētus, -ūs (m)* [KL3, W9]

weigh *pendō, -ere, pependī, pensum* [KL3, L10]

weight *onus, oneris (n)* [KL1, L13]; *gravitās, -tātis (f)* [KL3, W2]

well (adj.) *salvus, -a, -um* [KL1, L25]

well (adv.) *bene* [KL1, L1]

well (noun) *puteus, -ī (m)* [KL2, L12]

well (verb; be well) *salveō, -ēre, ——, ——* [KL1, L9]; *valeō, -ēre, valuī, valitūrum* [KL1, L9]

west (sunset) *vesper, vesperis (m)* [KL1, L14]

wet (sopping) *aquōsus, -a, -um* [KL1, W29]

what *quī, quae, quod* [KL2, L3]; **(what?)** *quis, quid* [KL2, L9]

what? *quid* [KL1, W19]

what kind of (interrog. adj.) *quālis* [KL3, L9]; **(what kind of?)** *quī? quae? quod?* [KL2, L9]

whatever *quīcumque, quaecumque, quodcumque* [KL2, L12]; *quisquis, quidquid (quicquid) (pron.)* [KL2, L12]

whatsoever *quīcumque, quaecumque, quodcumque* [KL2, L12]

when *cum; ut (+indic.)* [KL3, L5]

when (?) *quandō* [KL1, L12]; *ubi* [KL1, L12]

whence (?) *unde* [KL2, L11]

where (?) *ubi* [KL1, L12]; *quō* [KL2, L11]

wherefore (?) *quārē* [KL3, L9]

whether *ūtrum* [KL2, L15]

whether...or *sīve/sēū... sīve/sēū* [KL1, L30]

which (of two)? *uter, utra (ūtra), utrum (ūtrum) (interrog.)* [KL2, L15]

which *quī, quae, quod* [KL2, L3]; **(which?)** *quī?, quae?, quod?* [KL2, L9]

whichever (of two) *uter, utra (ūtra), utrum (ūtrum) (interrog.)* [KL2, L15]

whichever *quīcumque, quaecumque, quodcumque* [KL2, L12]; *quisquis, quidquid (quicquid) (pron.)* [KL2, L12]

whichsoever *quīcumque, quaecumque, quodcumque* [KL2, L12]

while *cum* [KL3, L7]; *dum, dummodo* [KL2, L11]; *dōnec* [KL3, W3]

whither (?) *quō* [KL2, L11]

whirlwind *turbō* [KL2, W13]

whisper *susurrō (1)* [KL1, W28]

whistling *sībilus, -a, -um* [KL3, W6]

white (dead) *albus, -a, -um* [KL1, L17]; **(glittering)** *candidus, -a, -um* [KL1, L17]

who *quī, quae, quod* [KL3, L6]; **(who?)** *quis* [KL1, W31]

who (?) quis [KL1, W31]

whoever *quīcumque, quaecumque, quodcumque* [KL2, L12]; *quisquis, quidquid (quicquid) (pron.)* [KL2, L12]

whole *tōtus, -a, -um* [KL2, L3]; *ūniversus, -a, -um* [KL3, L4]

wholly *omnīno* [KL3, L5]

whosoever *quīcumque, quaecumque, quodcumque* [KL2, L12]

why *cūr* [KL1, L2]; *quō (?)* [KL2, L11]; *quārē* [KL3, L9]

wicked *improbus, -a, -um* [KL1, L29]; *impius, -a, -um* [KL3, L1]; *malignus, -a, -um* [KL3, L13]

wickedness *malitia, -ae (f)* [KL2, L14]

wide *lātus, -a, -um* [KL1, L20]

widow *vidua, -ae (f)* [KL1, L22]

widowed *viduāta, -ae* [KL1, W19]

width *lātitūdō, -dinis (f)* [KL2, W9]

wife *coniūnx, -iugis (f)* [KL1, L22]; *uxor, -ōris (f)* [KL1, L30]

wild *ferus, -a, -um* [KL1, L7]

wilderness *dēserta, -ōrum (n, pl)* [KL3, L4]

will (noun) *voluntās, -tātis (f)* [KL3, L12]

will (verb) *volō/velle, voluī, ——, ——* [KL2, L14]

wind *ventus, -ī (m)* [KL1, W28; KL3, W16]; **(breath)** *anima, -ae (f)* [KL2, L4]

window *fenestra, -ae (f)* [KL1, L31]

wine *vīnum, -ī (n)* [KL1, L5]

wing *āla, -ae (f)* [KL1, L10]; *penna, -ae (f)* [KL3, W16]

winged *pennātus, -a, -um* [KL2, W6]; *volātilis, -e* [KL3, W4]

wisdom *cōnsilium, -iī (n)* [KL1, L30]; *sapientia, -ae (f)* [KL2, L10]

wise *doctus, -a, -um* [KL1, L13]; *sapiēns, -entis* [KL2, L4]

wish (noun) *voluntās, -tātis (f)* [KL3, L12]

wish (for) *cupiō, -ere, cupīvī, cupītum* [KL1, L31]; *volō/velle, voluī, ——, ——* [KL2, L14]

with *apud* [KL2, L4]; *cum* [KL3, L7]; *cum (+abl.)* [KL1, L9]

withdraw *auferō mē* [KL3, L10]; *sēcēdō, -ere -cessī, -cessum* [KL3, W1]

withered *āridus, -a, -um* [KL1, L27]

within *intrā (prep. +acc.; adv.)* [KL2, L15]

without *sine (+abl.)* [KL1, L9]

without (am without) *careō, -ēre, -uī, -itum (+abl.)* [KL3, L6]

witness (noun) *testimōnium, -ī (n)* [KL2, L10]; *testis, -is (m)* [KL3, L5]

witness (verb) *testificor, -ārī, ——, -ātus sum* [KL3, W14]; *testor, -ārī, ——, -ātus sum* [KL3, W11]

woad *vitrum, -ī (n)* [KL2, W2]

woman *fēmina, -ae* [KL1, L2]; *mulier, mulieris (f)* [KL1, L22]; **(young woman)** *virgō, virginis (f)* [KL1, L12]

womb *uterus, -ī (m)* [KL2, W9]

wonder *prōdigium, -iī (n)* [KL3, W5]

wonderful *mīrus, -a, -um* [KL1, L7]; *mīrābilis, -e* [KL3, L3]

wood *līgnum, -ī (n)* [KL2, L13]

wooden *līgneus, -a, -um* [KL3, W6]

word *verbum, -ī* [KL1, L5]

work (noun) *labor, labōris (m)* [KL1, L12]; *opus, operis (n)* [KL2, L3]

work (verb) *labōrō (1)* [KL1, L22]; *operor, -ārī, ——, operātus sum* [KL2, L6]

worker *faber, -brī (m)* [KL3, W2]

world *mundus, -ī (m)* [KL1, L6]

worldly goods *substantia, -ae (f)* [KL3, L13]

worse (adj.) *pēior* [KL2, L5]

worse (adv.) *pēius* [KL2, L5]

worship *colō, -ere, coluī, cultum* [KL1, L29]; *adorō* [KL2, W8]

worst (adj.) *pessimus, -a, -um* [KL2, L5]

worst (adv.) *pessimē* [KL2, L7]

worthless *vīlis, -e* [KL2, W15]

worthy (adj.) *dignus, -a, -um* [KL3, W5]

worthy (verb, am worthy of) *mereō, -ēre, -uī, -itum* [KL1, L23]

would that! *utinam* [KL3, L13]

wound (noun) *vulnus, vulneris (n)* [KL1, L13]; *plāga, -ae (f)* [KL3, L14]

wound (verb) *vulnerō (1)* [KL1, L1]; *laedō, -ere, laesī, laesus* [KL2, W6]

wrap (verb) *involvō, -ere, -volvī, -volutum* [KL2, W9]

wrathful *īrātus, -a, -um* [KL1, L15]

wreck *naufragium, -ī (n)* [KL1, W23]

wretched *miser, -era, -erum* [KL1, L7]

write *scrībō, -ere, scrīpsī, scriptum* [KL1, L26]

wrongly *male* [KL1, L1]

Y

year *annus, -ī (m)* [KL2, L7]

yes (expects a yes answer) *nōnne* [KL2, L7]

yes *vērō* [KL2, L15]

yesterday *herī* [KL1, L6]

yet *tamen* [KL1, L30]; *adhūc* [KL3, L12]; *at* [KL3, L1]

yield *cēdō, -ere, cessī, cessum* [KL1, L28]

yoke *iungō, -ere, iūnxī, iunctum* [KL1, L27]

you (sg.) *tū* [KL1, L17]; **(pl.)** *vōs* [KL1, L17]

young *vīridis, -e* [KL1, L17]; *iuvenis, -e* [KL2, W2]

young child *īnfāns, -fantis (adj. & noun, m/f)* [KL1, W31; KL3, L12]

young man *adulescens, -entis (m)* [KL1, L30]

young woman *adulescens, -entis (f)* [KL1, L30]; *virgō, virginis (f)* [KL1, L12]

younger *minimus, -a, -um* [KL1, W31]

youngest *iuvenissimus, -a, -um* [KL1, W19]

your (sg.) *tuus, -a, -um* [KL1, L11]; **(pl.)** *vester, -stra, -strum* [KL1, L11]

yours (sg.) *tuus, -a, -um* [KL1, L11]; **(pl.)** *vester, -stra, -strum* [KL1, L11]

youth *adulescentia, -ae (f)* [KL1, W32]; *iuventūs, -tūtis (f)* [KL2, W15]

Z

zeal *zēlus, -ī (m)* [KL3, W7]

Appendix C

Latin-English Glossary

A

ā, ab, (+abl.) *from, away from* [KL1, L3]

abeō, -īre, -iī, -itum *I go away, depart* [KL1, W32; KL2, L9]

abiēs, -etis (f) *fir (tree)* [KL3, W2]

absum, -esse, āfuī, āfutūrum *I am absent, am away (from)* [KL3, L3]

abyssus, -ī (f) *abyss, deep, infernal pit* [KL3, W9]

ac (atque) *and, and also* [KL1, L27]

accendō, -ere, -censī, -censum *I kindle, light, set on fire* [KL2, W15]

accidō, -ere, -cīdī, —— *I fall upon/out, happen, come to pass* [KL3, L10]

accingō, -ere, -cinxī, -cinctum *I gird on/about, equip, prepare* [KL2, W9]

accipiō, -ere, -cēpī, -ceptum *I accept, receive, take* [KL1, L31]

acclīnis, -e *leaning (on), inclined (to/toward)* [KL3, W7]

accūsō (1) *I accuse* [KL3, W1]

ācer, ācris, ācre *sharp, eager; fierce* [KL1, L20]

aciēs, -ēī (f) *sharp edge/point, sharpness (esp. of sight); battle line* [KL3, L14]

ad (+acc.) *to, toward, at, near* [KL1, L3]

adducō, -ere, -dūxī, -ductum *I lead to* [KL2, W8]

adeō, -īre, -iī, -itum *I go to(ward), approach* [KL2, L10]

adhūc *to this place, until now, still, yet* [KL3, L12]

adimpleō, -ēre, -ēvī, -ētum *I fill up, fulfill* [KL3, W1]

admoneō, -ēre, -uī, -itum *I admonish, warn, advise* [KL3, W9]

admonitiō, -ōnis (f) *admonition, reminding* [KL3, W9]

admonitor, -ōris (m) *admonisher, encourager* [KL3, W16]

adnūntiō (1) [annūntiō, etc.] *I announce, make known* [KL3, L7]

adiciō, -ere, -iēcī, -iectum *I throw to, add, increase* [KL2, W14]

adorō (1) *I adore, worship* [KL2, W8]

adsūmō, -ere, -sumpsī, -sumptum *I take for myself* [KL1, W32]

adulescens, -entis (m/f) *young man/woman* [KL1, L30]

adulescentia, -ae (f) *youth* [KL1, W32]

adventus, -ūs (m) *coming, arrival, advent* [KL3, L12]

adversus (+acc.) *against* [KL3, W1]

advocātus, -ī (m) *advocate, legal assistant/ counselor* [KL3, W11]

aedificium, -iī (n) *building, structure* [KL3, W2]

aedificō (1) *I build, make* [KL2, L4]

aeger, -gra, -grum *sick, diseased, ill* [KL3, W5]

Aegeus, -a, -um *Aegean* [KL1, W30]

Aegeus, -eī (m) *Aegeus* [KL1, W30]

aegis, -gidis (f) *an aegis* [KL2, W6]

aemulātiō, -ōnis (f) *envy, jealousy* [KL3, W7]

Aeneas, -ae (m) *Aeneas* [KL2, W13]

aēneus, -a, -um *(made of) bronze, copper* [KL2, W6]

aequor, -oris (n) *sea, level surface* [KL3, L6]

āēr, āēris (m) *air, atmosphere* [KL2, W12]

aes, aeris (n) *copper, bronze; money* [KL3, W2]

aestus, -ūs (m) *heat, fire, passion* [KL2, W9]

aetās, -tātis (f) *age, (time of) life* [KL2, L14]

aeternus, -a, -um *eternal* [KL1, L15]

afferō (adf-), -ferre (adf-), attulī (adt-), allātum (adl-) *I bring (to), carry (to)* [KL3, L5]

ager, agrī (m) *field* [KL1, L4]

aggredior, -ī, ——, -gressus sum *I approach, attack* [KL3, W7]

āgmen, -minis (n) *movement, course; army (on the march)* [KL3, L6]

agō, -ere, ēgī, actum *I do, act, drive* [KL1, L26]

agricola, -ae (m) *farmer* [KL1, L3]

āiō (defective) *I say, assert, affirm* [KL1, L14]

āla, -ae (f) *wing* [KL1, L10]

albus, -a, -um *(dead) white* [KL1, L17]

alchemia, -ae (f) *alchemy* [KL1, W27]

aliēnō (1) *I alienate, estrange* [KL2, W15]

aliēnus, -a, -um *of another, foreign, alien*

aliēnus, -ī (m) *stranger, foreigner* [KL2, L12]

aliquī, aliquae, aliquod (adj.) *some, any* [KL2, L12]

aliquis, aliquid (pron.) *someone, something, anyone, anything* [KL2, L12]

alius, alia, aliud *another, other* [KL1, W21; KL2, L4]

alligō (1) *I bind up, tie up* [KL3, W1]

alnus, -ī (f) *ship, alder (wood)* [KL1, L4]

alō, alere, aluī, altum/alītum *I nourish, feed, cherish* [KL3, W2]

altāre, -tāris (n) *altar, burnt offering (pl. forms often used with sg. meaning)* [KL2, L9]

alter, -era, -erum *the other (of two), second* [KL2, L4]

altus, -a, -um *high, lofty, deep* [KL1, L19]

amāritūdō, -dinis (f) *bitterness, sorrow, sadness* [KL3, W10]

amārus, -a, um *bitter* [KL3, W9]

ambulō (1) *I walk* [KL1, L1]

amīca, -ae (f) *(female) friend* [KL1, L15]

amīcus, -ī (m) *(male) friend* [KL1, L15]

amita, -ae (f) *aunt* [KL1, L22]

amō (1) *I love* [KL1, L1]

amor, amōris (m) *love* [KL1, L14]

amplector, amplectī, ——, amplexus sum *I embrace, hug* [KL2, W11]

āmittō, -ere, -misī, -missum *I send away, lose* [KL2, W6]

amplius *more, longer, further, besides* [KL3, L9]

animal, -ālis (n) *animal* [KL1, L18]

animus, -ī (m) *mind* [KL1, L29]

an (introduces 2nd half of a question, often with ūtrum) *or, or whether* [KL3, L9]

ancilla, -ae (f) *maidservant, female slave* [KL3, L10]

ancora, -ae (f) *anchor* [KL2, W12]

angelus, -ī (m) *angel, messenger* [KL3, W5]

angularis, -e *corner, placed at corners* [KL2, W9]

anguis, -is (m) *serpent, snake* [KL3, W5]

anima, -ae (f) *soul, spirit, life; wind, breath* [KL2, L4]

annus, -ī (m) *year* [KL2, L7]

ānser, -eris (m) goose [KL3, W2]

ante (+acc.) *before* [KL1, L17]

antequam (conj.) *before, sooner than, until* [KL3, L15]

antīchristus, -ī (m) *antichrist, the Antichrist* [KL3, W12]

antīquus, -a, -um *ancient* [KL1, L7]

ānulus, -ī (m) *ring, signet ring* [KL3, W10]

aperiō, -īre, -uī, apertum *I open, expose* [KL1, L29]

Apollo, -inis (m) *Apollo (god of prophesy, music, archery, the sun, etc.)* [KL1, W20]

apostolus, -ī (m) *apostle* [KL1, L11]

appareō, -ēre, -uī, -itum (+dat.) *I appear, am visible (impers.* apparet, *"it is evident/ apparent that")* [KL3, L4]

appellō (1) *I name, call* [KL1, L15]

appropinquō (1) *I approach, draw near* [KL1, L25]

aptus, -a, -um *suitable, suited, fitted* [KL3, W2]

apud (+acc.) *among, at the house of, with* [KL2, L4]

aqua, -ae (f) *water* [KL1, L2]

aquōsus, -a, -um *sopping wet* [KL1, W29]

arbitror, -ārī, ——, -ātus sum *I judge, think, suppose* [KL3, L4]

arbor, arboris (f) *tree* [KL1, L20]

arca, -ae (f) *box, chest* [KL2, W6]

arcus, -ūs (m) *bow, arch, rainbow* [KL1, L27]

ardeō, ardēre, arsī, —— *I burn, blaze* [KL1, L20]

argenteus, -a, -um *silver(y)* [KL1, L17]

argentum, -ī (n) *silver, money* [KL1, L5]

arguō, -ere, arguī, argutus *I accuse* [KL2, W9]

Argus, -ī (m) *Argus, a hundred-eyed giant* [KL1, W21]

Ariadna, -ae (f) *Ariadne* [KL1, W30]

ārida, -ae (f) *dryness, dry place, dry land* [KL3, W1]

āridus, -a, -um *dry, withered* [KL1, L27]

ariēs, -ietis (m) *ram* [KL1, W32]

arma, -ōrum (n, pl) *arms, armor, weapons* [KL1, W32; KL2, L3]

arripiō, -ere, -ripuī, -reptum *I seize, snatch (up), lay hold of* [KL3, W9]

artus, -ūs (m) *joint, limb* [KL2, W6]

arundō, -inis (f) [= harundō, -dinis] *reed* [KL3, W1]

arvum, -ī (n) *(cultivated) field, region* [KL3, L15]

arx, arcis (f) *citadel, fort; hill* [KL2, L7]

ascendō, -ere, -scendī, -scensum *I go up, ascend, climb* [KL2, L9]

asinus, -ī (m) *donkey* [KL1, L19]

asper, -era, -erum *harsh, fierce* [KL2, W12]

at *yet, but* [KL3, L1]

āter, -tra, -trum *(dead) black, dark* [KL1, L17]

Athēnae, -ārum (f, pl) Athens [KL1, W30; KL2, L14]

Athēniensis, -is (m/f) an Athenian [KL1, W30]

atque (ac) *and, and also* [KL1, L27]

ātrium, -iī (n) *hall, court, entryway* [KL3, L10]

attendō, -ere, -ndī, -ntum *I turn toward, direct (the attention) toward* [KL3, W9]

audāx, -ācis *bold, courageous, daring* [KL2, W11]

audeō, -ēre, ——, ausus sum *I dare* [KL1, L11]

audiō, -īre, -īvī, -ītum *I hear, listen to* [KL1, L29]

auferō, -ferre, abstulī, ablatum (3rd conj. irreg.) *I carry away/off, remove;* **auferō mē** *I remove myself, withdraw* [KL1, W32; KL3, L10]

augeō, -ēre, auxī, auctum *I increase* [KL1, L19]

aula, -ae (f) *hall, inner/royal court* [KL1, W13; KL3, W10]

aura, -ae (f) *breeze, air, heaven* [KL3, L3]

auris, -is (f) *ear* [KL3, L4]

aureus, -a, -um *golden, gold* [KL1, L17]

aurīga, -ae (m/f) *charioteer, driver* [KL1, W23]

auris, -is (f) *ear* [KL1, W28]

aurum, -ī (n) *gold* [KL1, L5]

aut *or* [KL1, L1]

autem (postpositive conj.) *however, moreover* [KL1, L12]

auxilium, -ī (n) *help, aid* [KL1, L5]

avārus, -a, -um *greedy* [KL1, L7]

avēna, -ae (f) *pan pipe, shepherd's pipe* [KL1, W21]

avia, -ae (f) *grandmother* [KL1, L22]

avis, avis (f) *bird* [KL1, L18]

avunculus, -ī (m) *uncle (mother's brother)* [KL1, L22]

avus, -ī (m) *grandfather, ancestor* [KL1, L22]

B

Bacchus, -ī (m) *Bacchus, the god of wine* [KL1, W27]

baculum, -ī (n) *staff* [KL1, W32]

barbarus, -a, -um *foreign, strange, savage* [KL1, L31]

barbarus, -ī (m) *foreigner, barbarian* [KL1, L31]

basis, -is (f) *pedestal, base, foundation* [KL2, W9]

beātus, -a, -um *happy, blessed* [KL1, L7]

Beelzebul, -ulis (m) *(sometimes indecl.) Beelzebub* [KL3, W1]

bellator, -toris (m) *warrior* [KL1, W32]

bellum, -ī (n) *war* [KL1, L15]; **bellum gerō** *I wage war* [KL1, L28]

bēlua, -ae (f) *beast (esp. a ferocious or large one), monster* [KL3, L15]

bene *well* [KL1, L1]

benedīcō, -ere, -dīxī, -dictum (+dat.) *I speak well, bless, praise* [KL3, L4]

bēstia, -ae (f) *beast* [KL1, L2]

Bethleem (indecl.) *Bethlehem* [KL1, W32]

Biblia Sacra, Bibliae Sacrae (f) *Holy Bible* [KL1, L11]

bibō, -ere, bibī, potum *I drink* [KL2, L10]

bis *twice, twofold* [KL3, L6]

blasphēmia, -ae (f) *blasphemy, slander* [KL3, W1]

bonus, -a, -um *good* [KL1, L7]

bōs, bovis (m/f) *cow, bull, ox (pl.) cattle* [KL1, L19]

bracchium, -ī (n) *arm* [KL1, W13; KL3, W3]

brevis, -e *short, small, brief* [KL1, L19]

breviter *shortly, for a short time* [KL3, W5]

C

cadaver, -veris (n) *dead body, carcass* [KL1, W32]

cadō, -ere, cecidī, cāsum *I fall, sink, drop* [KL1, L27]

caecus, -a, -um *blind* [KL1, L27]

caedō, -ere, cecīdī, caesum *I cut (down), kill* [KL2, L12]

caelum, -ī (n) *sky, heaven* [KL1, L5]

caeruleus, -a, -um *blue* [KL1, L17]

calamus, -ī (m) *reed, reed-pipe* [KL1, W28]

caldus, -a, -um *warm, hot, fiery* [KL1, L7]

calix, calicis (m) *goblet* [KL1, W13]

camēlus, -ī (m/f) *camel* [KL1, L4; KL2, W4]

candidus, -a, -um *(glittering) white* [KL1, L17]

canis, canis (m/f) *dog* [KL1, L18]

canticum, -ī (n) *song, solo*; Canticum Canticōrum, *Song of Songs* [KL3, L14]

cantitō (1) *I sing often, sing frequently [this is called the frequentative form of* cantō*]* [KL3, W9]

cantō (1) *I sing, play (music), predict* [KL1, L1]

canō, -ere, cecinī, cāntum *I sing, play, prophesy* [KL2, L10]

cantus, -ūs (m) *song, singing* [KL1, L25]

caper, -prī (m) *(billy) goat* [KL1, L4]

capillus, -ī (m) *hair* [KL2, W6]

capiō, -ere, cēpī, captum *I take, capture, seize* [KL1, L31]

capitulum, -ī (n) *chapter, section* [KL3, W9]

captō (1) *I hunt* [KL1, L10]

caput, -itis (n) *head* [KL1, L13]

carcer, -eris (m) *prison; (generally in pl.) starting gates (of a horse race)* [KL1, W23; KL3, L5]

cardō, -dinis (m) *hinge* [KL2, W11]

careō, -ēre, -uī, -itum (+abl.) *I lack, am without* [KL3, L6]

cāritās, -tātis (f) *love, esteem* [KL3, L11]

carmen, -inis (n) *song, chant, poem, prophecy* [KL1, L13]

caro, carnis (f) *flesh, meat* [KL1, L31]

Carthāgo, -ginis (f) *Carthage (city in north Africa, now a suburb of Tunis, Tunisia)* [KL2, L14]

cārus, -a, -um *dear, beloved* [KL1, L13]

caseus, -ī (m) *cheese* [KL2, W4]

castellum, -ī (n) *castle* [KL1, L5]

castra, -ōrum (n, pl) *camp* [KL1, L15]

castus, -a, -um *pure, chaste* [KL3, W9]

cāsus, -ūs (m) *event, incident; misfortune, downfall* [KL1, L28]

cauda, -ae (f) *tail* [KL1, W21]

causa, -ae (f) *cause, reason*; **causā (+ gen.)** *on account of, for the sake of [usually follows its gen. object]* [KL2, L15]

cautēs, -is (f) *rough rock, crag* [KL3, W16]

caveō, -ēre, cāvī, cautum *I guard against, beware (of)* [KL1, L12]

caverna, -ae (f) *cavity, cavern* [KL2, W6]

cavus, -a, -um *hollow, empty* [KL3, W6]

cēdō, -ere, cessī, cessum *I go, move, yield* [KL1, L28]

celēbrō (1) *I celebrate* [KL3, W10]

celer, celeris, celere *swift, quick* [KL1, L19]

celō (1) *I hide* [KL1, W28]

cēna, -ae (f) *dinner, meal* [KL1, L20]

centaurus, -ī (m) *centaur* [KL1, L10]

centēsimus, -a, -um *one hundredth* [KL1, L23]

centum *one hundred* [KL1, L21]

Cerēs, -eris (f) *Ceres* [KL3, W3]

certāmen, -minis (n) *contest, race* [KL1, W23]

certātim *eagerly* [KL1, L20]

certus, -a, -um *certain, sure* [KL3, L6]

certe, *certainly* [KL3, L6]

cervīx, -vīcis (f) *neck* [KL3, W3]

cervus, -ī (m) *stag, deer* [KL1, L10]

cessō (1) *I cease from, stop* [KL3, W4]

cēterus, -a, -um *the other, the rest (usually used in pl.)* [KL2, L15]

cētus, -ī (m) *sea monster, kraken, whale* [KL1, L10; KL2, W7]

Christus, -ī (m) *Christ* [KL1, L4]

cibus, -ī (m) *food* [KL1, L4]

cinis, -neris (m) *ashes* [KL3, L10]

circā (adv. and prep. +acc.) *around, about* [KL2, L13]

circumvolō (1) *I fly around* [KL2, W12]

Circus Maximus, Circī Maximī (m) *the Circus Maximus, a famous racetrack at the foot of the Palatine Hill in Rome* [KL1, W23]

citara, -ae, (f) *harp* [KL2, W2]

cito *quickly, fast, speedily* [KL1, L27]

cīvis, -is (m/f) *citizen* [KL2, L7]

cīvitās, -tātis (f) *city, state, citizenship* [KL2, L7]

clādēs, -is (f) *destruction, ruin, loss* [KL2, W15]

clam *secretly* [KL1, L29]

clāmō (1) *I shout* [KL1, L1]

clāmor, -oris (m) *shout, cry* [KL1, W20; KL2, L13]

clārus, -a, -um *bright, clear* [KL3, W3]

classis, -is (f) *group, class, fleet (of ships)* [KL1, L30]

claudō, -ere, clausī, clausum *I close, shut (up)* [KL3, L15]

clēmentia, -ae (f) *mercy, clemency* [KL1, W21; KL3, W10]

clipeus (clypeus), -ī (m) *shield* [KL3, W3]

clypeum, -ī (n) *shield* [KL1, W32]

cōdex, -dicis (m) *book, writing* [KL3, W9]

coepī, coepisse, ——, coeptum (defective) *I began, undertook* [KL3, L1]

cōgitātiō, -tiōnis (f) *thought, opinion* [KL3, L1]

cōgitō (1) *I think* [KL1, L6]

cognōmen, -minis (n) *surname, family name, cognōmen* [KL2, W15]

cognoscō, -ere, -nōvī, -nitum *I learn, get to know;* pf. tense, *I know* [KL2, L10]

cōgō, -ere, -ēgī, -āctum *I drive together, force, compel* [KL1, L28]

cohors, -hortis (f) *cohort* [KL3, W2]

collis, collis (m) *hill* [KL3, L2]

collocō (1) *I place, set, arrange* [KL1, W21]

cōllum, -ī (n) *neck* [KL3, W6]

colō, -ere, coluī, cultum *I cultivate, inhabit, worship* [KL1, L29]

color, -ōris (m) *color* [KL2, W11]

coma, -ae *hair* [KL3, W3]

comedō, -ere, -ēdī, -ēsus *I eat up, consume* [KL3, W1]

comes, -mitis (m) *companion, comrade* [KL2, L13]

cōmessātio, -ōnis (f) *rioting, reveling* [KL3, W9]

comminor, -ārī, ——, -ātus sum *I threaten* [KL3, W1]

commodus, -a, -um *suitable, convenient* [KL3, W2]

commūnicō (1) *I share* [KL2, W6]

commūnis, -e *common* [KL3, W2]

complector, -plectī, ——, -plexus sum *I embrace, hug* [KL3, W3]

compleō, -ēre, -plēvī, -plētum *I fulfill, fill up* [KL2, W6]

concēdō, -ere, -cessī, -cessum *I grant, allow, concede* [KL3, W9]

concilium, -iī (n) *council, meeting* [KL3, L5]

conclūdō, -ere, -clūsī, -clūsum *I shut up, close* [KL2, W9]

conculcō (1) *I trample, tread underfoot* [KL2, W14]

concupiscentia, -ae (f) *longing, concupiscence, lust* [KL3, W9]

condiciō, -ōnis (f) *condition, demand, agreement* [KL2, W15]

confertus, -a, -um *crowded, thick, dense* [KL2, W15]

confīdō, -ere, ——, confīsus sum (+dat.) (semi-deponent) *I trust, have confidence in* [KL2, W6]

confirmō (1) *I make firm, strengthen, confirm* [KL3, W9]

cōnfiteor, -ērī, ——, -fessus sum (+dat./acc.) *I confess* [KL2, L6]

confundō, -ere, -fūdī, -fūsum *I pour together, confound, disturb* [KL3, L12]

congregō (1) *I collect (into a flock/herd), assemble* [KL2, L14]

congregātiō, -ōnis (f) *assembling, union* [KL3, W4]

congruēns, -ntis *suitable, appropriate* [KL3, W9]

coniungō, -ere, -iūnxī, -iūnctum *I join (together), unite* [KL3, L9]

coniunx, -iugis (m/f) *husband or wife* [KL1, L22]

cōnor, -ārī, ——, cōnātus sum *I try, attempt* [KL2, L6]

conquiēscō, -ere, -quiēvī, -quiētum *I fall silent, am still* [KL2, W9]

cōnsentiō, -īre, -sensī, -sensum (+dat.) *I agree (with), consent (to)* [KL3, W5]

conservō (1) *I preserve, save* [KL3, W15]

considerō (1) *I inspect, examine, consider* [KL2, W14]

cōnsilium, -iī (n) *plan, counsel, advice; wisdom* [KL1, L30]

consistōrium, -iī (n) *assembly room, hall* [KL3, W10]

consōbrīna, -ae (f) *cousin (female, mother's side)* [KL1, L22]

consōbrīnus, -ī (m) *cousin (male, mother's side)* [KL1, L22]

cōnspectus, -ūs (m) *sight, view, appearance* [KL2, L9]

cōnspiciō, -ere, -spēxī, -spectum *I observe, perceive, gaze at* [KL3, W16]

cōnsternō (1) *I bring to confusion, terrify, dismay* [KL3, W7]

cōnstituō, -ere, -stituī, -stitūtum *I set up, establish, decide* [KL2, L15]

consūmō, -ere, -sūmpsī, -sūmptum *I consume, spend, invest* [KL3, L2]

contendō, -ere, -tendī, -tentum *I contend, strive with, stretch out* [KL2, W9]

contentiō, -ōnis (f) *contention, strife* [KL3, W9]

conticescō, -ere, -ticuī, —— *I become silent, fall silent* [KL3, W6]

continuō *immediately, at once* [KL2, L12]

continēns, -entis (f) *continent, mainland* [KL3, W2]

contrā (+acc.) *against* [KL1, L11]

contrītio, -ōnis (f) *contrition, grief* [KL3, W9]

contumēlia, -ae (f) *insult, reproach, abuse* [KL3, W5]

convalēscō, -ere, -valuī, -valitus *I grow strong, gain strength* [KL3, W7]

convertō, -ere, -vertī, -versum *I turn around/ back, change, convert* [KL3, L9]

convīvium, -iī (n) *banquet, social feast* [KL3, L10]

convocō (1) *I call together, assemble* [KL3, W5]

cōpia, -ae (f) *supply, plenty, abundance; (pl.) troops* [KL1, L15]

cor, cordis (n) *heart* [KL1, L13]

cōram (+abl.) *in the presence of, before;* **(adv.)** *personally, openly* [KL1, L27]

cornū, -ūs (n) *horn* [KL1, L25]

corōna, -ae (f) *crown* [KL1, L2]

corpus, corporis (n) *body* [KL1, L13]

corripiō, -ere, -ripuī, -reptus *I seize/ snatch up, carry off* [KL3, W16]

coūtor, -ūtī, ——, —— (+abl.) *I associate with, have dealings with* [KL3, W12]

crās *tomorrow* [KL1, L6]

crastinus, -a, -um *tomorrow's, next* [KL2, W14]

crēber, -bra, -brum *thick, frequent, numerous* [KL3, L2]

crēdō, -ere, -didī, -ditum *I believe* [KL1, L26]

cremō (1) *I burn, consume by fire* [KL1, L2]

creō (1) *I create* [KL1, L6]

crēscō, -ere, crēvī, crētum *I grow, increase* [KL2, L11]

Crēta, -ae (f) *Crete* [KL1, W30]

crīmen, -minis (n) *crime, fault, offence* [KL3, W1]

crūdēlis, -e *cruel, savage* [KL3, L10]

cruentō (1) *I stain with blood, make bloody* [KL2, W11]

cruentus, -a, -um *bloody* [KL2, W15]

crūs, crūris (n) *leg* [KL1, W19]

crustulum, -ī (n) *cookie, small cake* [KL1, L5]

crux, crucis (f) *cross* [KL1, L15]

cubīle, -is (n) *(marriage) bed; pl., fornication* [KL3, W9]

cubitum, -ī (n) *elbow; a cubit (distance from elbow to tip of middle finger; approx. 18 inches)* [KL2, L14]

cum (prep. +abl.) *with* [KL1, L9]; **(conj.)** *when, while, since, after, although* [KL3, L7]

cunctātiō, -ōnis (f) *delay, doubt, hesitation* [KL3, W9]

cunctor, -ārī, ——, -ātus sum *I delay, hesitate* [KL3, W7]

cunctus, -a, -um *all (of), every* [KL2, L9]

Cupīdo, -dinis (m) *Cupid (son of Venus and god of love)* [KL1, W20]

cupidus, -a, -um *eager, zealous* [KL3, W2]

cupiō, -ere, cupīvī, cupītum *I wish (for), desire, long (for)* [KL1, L31]

cūr *why?* [KL1, L2]

cūrō (1) *I care for, take care of, heal, cure* [KL1, L15]

curriculum, -ī (n) *lap (of a race), course* [KL1, W23]

currō, -ere, cūcurrī, cursum *I run* [KL1, L26]

custōdiō, -īre, -iī/-īvī, -ītum *I guard, watch, defend, keep* [KL3, L3]

custōs, -ōdis (m/f) *guard, watch(man), defender* [KL3, L3]

Cȳclōps, Cȳclōpis (m) *Cyclops* [KL2, W4]

D

Daedalus, -ī (m) *Daedalus (a skilled inventor and craftsman)* [KL1, W30]

daemonium, -iī (n) *demon, evil spirit* [KL3, L1]

Daphne, -ēs (f) *Daphne* [KL1, W20]

David (indecl.) *David* [KL1, W32]

dē (+abl.) *from, down from, concerning* [KL1, L4]

dea, -ae (f) *goddess; dat. and abl. pl. usually* **deābus** [KL1, L6]

dēbeō, -ēre, -uī, -itum *I owe, ought* [KL1, L11]

decem *ten* [KL1, L21]

decet, -ēre, ——, decuit (impers. +acc.) *it is fitting, proper, suitable, right* [KL3, L1]

decimus, -a, -um *tenth* [KL1, L23]

dēclārō (1) *I declare, make clear, explain* [KL1, L10]

dēdicō (1) *I dedicate, consecrate* [KL3, W7]

dēfatīgō (1) *I tire (out), exhaust* [KL3, W2]

dēfendō, -ere, -fendī, -fēnsum *I defend* [KL1, L28]

dēiciō, -icere, -iēcī, -iectum *I throw down, cast down, hurl down* [KL1, W23]

deinceps *successively, in turn* [KL3, W2]

deinde *from that place, then, thereupon, next* [KL1, L24]

dēleō, -ēre, -lēvī, -lētum *I destroy* [KL1, L9]

dēligō, -ere, lēgī, -lēctum *I pick, choose* [KL1, L28]

dēnī, -ae, -a *ten at a time, ten each* [KL3, W2]

dēnique *finally* [KL1, L10]

dēprecor, -ārī, ——, -ātus sum *I pray (for), intercede, beseech* [KL3, L10]

dēscendō, -ere, -scendī, -scensum *I come down, descend, fall (down)* [KL3, L7]

dēserta, -ōrum (n, pl) *desert places, wilderness* [KL3, L4]

dēsertus, -a, -um *deserted, solitary, forsaken* [KL3, L4]

dēsōlō (1) I leave alone, forsake [KL3, W7]

dēspiciō, -ere, -spexī, -spectum *I look down on, despise* [KL1, W32]

Deus, -ī (m) *God*; **deus, -ī (m)** *a god* [KL1, L4]

dexter, -tra, -trum (or -tera, -terum) *right(-handed); skilled, favorable* [KL1, L30]

diabolus, -ī (m) *devil* [KL3, L13]

diaeta, -ae (f) *cabin (of a ship)* [KL1, W18]

Diāna, -ae (f) *Diana (virgin goddess of the moon and hunting)* [KL1, W20]

dīcō, -ere, dīxī, dictum *I say, speak* [KL1, L26]

diciō, -ōnis (f) authority, rule, sway [KL3, W10]

diēs, diēī (m/f) *day, period of time* [KL1, L28]

differō, -ferre, distulī, dīlātum *I separate, differ* [KL3, W2]

difficilis, -e *difficult* [KL1, L20; KL2, L5]

dignus, -a, -um *worthy, deserving* [KL3, W5]

dīlēctus, -a, -um (adj.) *beloved* [KL3, L1]

dīligō, -ere, -lēxī, -lēctum *I choose out, love*

dīmidius, -a, -um *half (of)* [KL3, L10]

dīmittō, -ere, -mīsī, -missum *I send away, dismiss, forgive* [KL1, L30; KL2, W15]

dīripiō, -ere, -ripuī, -reptum *I tear apart, plunder* [KL3, W1]

dirumpō, -ere, -rūpī, -ruptum *I burst asunder, tear asunder* [KL2, W14]

discēdō, -ere, -cessī, -cessum *I separate, go away from* [KL3, W5]

discipula, -ae (f) *student (female), disciple* [KL1, L5]

discipulus, -ī (m) *student (male), apprentice, disciple* [KL1, L5]

discus, -ī (m) *discus* [KL2, W6]

dissecō (1) *I cut (to the heart)* [KL2, W5]

dissimilis, -e *dissimilar, unlike, different* [KL2, L5]

dissolvō, -ere, -solvī, -solūtum *I dissolve, destroy* [KL3, W5]

distō (1) *I stand apart, differ* [KL3, W9]

diū *for a long time* [KL1, L13]

dīversus, -a, -um *diverse, opposite* [KL3, W7]

dīvidō, -ere, -vīsī, -vīsum *I divide, separate* [KL2, W9]

dīvīnitus (adv.) *from heaven, by divine providence/will* [KL3, W9]

dīvīnus, -a, -um *divine* [KL3, W7]

dīvitiae, -ārum (f, pl) *riches, wealth* [KL1, L2]

dō, dare, dedī, datum *I give* [KL1, L1]

doceō, -ēre, docuī, doctum *I teach* [KL1, L9]

doctrīna, -ae (f) *teaching, instruction* [KL3, L5]

doctus, -a, -um *learned, wise, skilled* [KL1, L13]

dolor, -ōris (m) *pain, grief* [KL3, W3]

dolus, -ī (m) *deceit, fraud* [KL3, L6]

dominus, -ī (m) *lord, master* [KL1, L4]

dōmō, -āre, domuī, domitum *I tame, subdue* [KL1, L12]

domus, -ūs (f) *house, home* [KL1, L25]

dōnec *until; as long as, while* [KL3, W3]

dōnum, -ī (n) *gift* [KL1, L5]

dormiō, -īre, -īvī, -ītum *I sleep* [KL1, L29]

draco, dracōnis (m) *dragon* [KL1, L12]

dubitātiō, -ōnis (f) *doubt, uncertainty* [KL3, W9]

dubitō (1) *I doubt, am uncertain, question* [KL3, W7]

dubius, -a, -um *doubtful, dubious, uncertain* [KL3, W7]

dūcō, -ere, duxī, ductum *I lead, guide* [KL1, L26]

dulcis, -e *sweet* [KL1, L19]

dum/dummodo (conj.) *while, until; provided that, if only* [KL2, L11]

duo, duae, duo *two* [KL1, L21]

duodecim *twelve* [KL1, L21]

duodecimus, -a, -um *twelfth* [KL1, L23]

duodēnī, -ae, -a *twelve at a time, twelve each* [KL3, W2]

duodēvīcēsimus, -a, -um *eighteenth* [KL1, L23]

duodēvīgintī *eighteen* [KL1, L21]

dūrus, -a, -um *hard, rough, harsh* [KL3, W16]

dux, ducis (m) *leader, guide, general* [KL1, L14]

E

ē *see* **ex**

ēbrietās, -tātis (f) *drunkenness, carousing* [KL3, W9]

ēbrius, -a, -um *drunk, intoxicated* [KL1, W13; KL2, W4]

ecce *behold!* [KL1, L17]

ecclēsia, -ae (f) *church* [KL1, L11]

ēdictum, -ī (n) *edict, proclamation, command* [KL3, W10]

edō, -ere, ēdī, ēsum *I eat, devour* [KL3, L1]

ēdūcō, -ere, -dūxī, -ductum *I lead out/forth, bring out* [KL3, L5]

efficiō, -ere, -fēcī, -fectum *I effect, cause, accomplish* [KL3, W10]

effugiō, -ere, -fūgī, -fugitum *I escape* [KL1, W10]

effundō, -ere, -fūdī, -fūsum *I pour out/forth, shed* [KL3, L9]

ego (sg.) *I* [KL1, L17]

ēgredior, -gredī, —, -gressus sum *I go out, march out* [KL2, L6]

ēgregius, -a, -um *outstanding, excellent* [KL1, L29]

ēheu (heu) *alas! oh! (expressing grief or pain)* [KL1, L22]

ēiciō, -ere, -iēcī, -iectum *I throw out, cast out, drive out* [KL2, L14]

ēlābor, -lābī, —, -lapsus sum *I slip away, escape* [KL2, W6]

elephantus, -ī (m) *elephant* [KL1, L19]

ēligō, -ere, -lēgī, -lectum *I pick out, choose, elect* [KL3, L1]

emō, -ere, ēmī, ēmptum *I buy* [KL2, L10]

emundō, -āre, —, -ātum *I cleanse, purify* [KL3, W11]

enigma, -matis (n) *riddle* [KL1, W19]

enim (postpositive conj.) *indeed, truly, certainly; for* [KL1, L17]

eō, īre, iī (īvī), itum *I go* [KL1, L29]

eōdem (adv.) *in the same place, to the same place/purpose* [KL3, L2]

Ephratheus, -ī (m) *an Ephramite* [KL1, W32]

epulae, -ārum (f, pl) *feast* [KL1, L20]

eques, -quitis (m) *knight, horseman, cavalryman* [KL1, L20]

equitātus, -ūs (m) *cavalry* [KL3, W2]

equus, -ī (m) *horse* [KL1, L4]

ergō *therefore, then, consequently, accordingly* [KL1, L18]

ēripiō, -ere, -ripuī, -reptum *I snatch away/from, rescue* [KL2, L3]

errō (1) *I wander, err, am mistaken* [KL1, L14]

error, -ōris (m) *error, mistake* [KL3, W7]

esca, -ae (f) *food* [KL2, W14]

essedarius, -ī (m) *charioteer (fighter in a war-chariot, not just a driver); gladiator* [KL3, W2]

ēsuriō, -īre, -iī, -ītum *I hunger, desire food* [KL3, W1]

et *and, even, also;* **et…et** *both…and* [KL1, L1]

etiam *even, also, besides, still* [KL1, L22]

etsi *although, though* [KL3, W2]

eunūchus, -ī (m) *eunuch* [KL3, W10]

ēvādō, -ere, -vāsī, -vāsum *I go out/forth, escape* [KL3, W7]

ēvangelicus, -a, -um *evangelical, of the gospel* [KL3, W9]

ēvangelium, -ī (n) *good news, gospel* [KL1, L5]

ēvangelīzō (1) *I preach/proclaim (the Gospel)* [KL3, W5]

ēveniō, -īre, -vēnī, -ventum *I come to pass, happen* [KL3, W3]

ēvertō, -ere, -tī, -sum *I overturn, overthrow, destroy* [KL3, W7]

ex, ē (+abl.) *out of, from* [KL1, L3]

exaltō (1) *I raise, exalt* [KL3, W5]

excelsus, -a, -um *high, lofty, noble* [KL2, L4]

excipiō, -ere, -cēpī, -ceptum *I take out, relieve* [KL3, W2]

excutiō, -ere, -cussī, -cussum *I shake out/off* [KL3, W3]

exemplar, -āris (n) *copy, example, exemplar* [KL3, W10]

exemplum, -ī (n) *example* [KL3, W7]

exeō, -īre, -iī (-īvī), -itum *I go out, go away* [KL2, L12]

exerceō, -ēre, -uī, -itum *I train, exercise* [KL1, L14]

exercitus, -ūs (m) *army* [KL1, L25]

exiguus, -a, -um *meager, scanty* [KL3, W2]

exitus, -ūs (m) *exit* [KL2, W13]

expendō, -ere, -pendī, -pensum *I pay for, suffer* [KL3, W6]

exprobrō (1) *I reproach* [KL1, W32]

exprōmō, -ere, -mpsī, -mptum *I take out, reveal, disclose* [KL2, W15]

expuō, -ere, -puī, -putum *I spit out* [KL2, W8]

exsanguis, -e *bloodless, pale* [KL3, W6]

exsilium, -iī (n) *exile, banishment* [KL3, W3]

exspectō (1) *I wait for, expect* [KL1, L3]

exstinguō, -ere, -stinxī, -stinctum *I put out, quench, exstinguish* [KL3, W1]

extendō, -ere, -tendī, -tensum *I stretch out, extend* [KL1, W26; KL3, W1]

extrā (adv.) *(on the) outside, besides, except;* **(prep. +acc.)** *outside (of), beyond* [KL3, L15]

exultō [exsultō] (1) *I leap up, exult, rejoice exceedingly* [KL3, W9]

F

Fabius, -ī (m) *Fabius* [KL1, W19]

faber, -brī (m) *worker, carpenter, smith* [KL3, W2]

fābula, -ae (f) *story, legend, tale* [KL1, L2]

faciēs, -ēī (f) *shape, form; face; character* [KL1, L28]

facile *easily* [KL2, L7]

facilis, -e *easy* [KL1, L20; KL2, L5]

faciō, -ere, fēcī, factum *I make, do (for present passive system, use* **fīō***)* [KL1, L31]

fāgus, -ī (f) *beech (tree)* [KL3, W2]

falsus, -a, -um *false, deceitful* [KL2, W13]

fāma, -ae *rumor, report, reputation, fame* [KL1, W23; KL2, L13]

famēlicus, -a, -um *hungry* [KL1, L29]

familia, -ae *household, family* [KL1, L22]

fās (n, indecl.) *divine law;* **(usu. transl. as adj.)** *lawful, permitted, possible* [KL3, L2]

fātālis, -e *fatal, fated, deadly* [KL3, W6]

fatigō (1) *I weary, tire* [KL2, W12]

fātum, -ī (n) *fate, prophecy, oracle* [KL1, L5; KL2, 13]

faucēs, -ium (f, pl) *throat, gullet* [KL3, W3]

felīciter in aeternum *happily ever after* [KL1, W6; KL2, W2]

fēlix, (gen.) -līcis *lucky, fortunate, happy* [KL1, L19]

fēmina, -ae (f) *woman* [KL1, L2]

fēmīnus, -a, -um *female* [KL3, W4]

fenestra, -ae (f) *window* [KL1, L31]

fēnum [faenum], -ī (n) *hay* [KL2, W14]

ferē *nearly, almost* [KL3, L3]

ferō, ferre, tulī, lātum (irreg. 3rd conj.) *I carry, bring (forth), bear* [KL1, W32; KL2, W11]

ferrum, -ī (n) *iron, sword* [KL2, L15]

ferus, -a, -um *fierce, wild* [KL1, L7]

fessus, -a, -um *tired, weary, exhausted* [KL1, L20; KL3, W6]

festīnō (1) *I hasten, hurry* [KL1, L9]

festūca, -ae (f) *straw* [KL2, W14]

fēstus, -a -um *festal, festive, joyful, merry* [KL3, W6]

fētus, -a, -um *pregnant, filled* [KL3, W6]

fīcus, -ī (f) *fig (tree)* [KL3, W8]

fidēlis, -e *faithful* [KL2, L4]

fidēs, -eī (f) *faith* [KL1, L28]

fīdūcia, -ae (f) *trust, faith, confidence* [KL3, L7]

fīdus, -a, -um *faithful, trustworthy* [KL1, L7]

fīlia, -ae (f) *daughter (dat. and abl. pl. often* **fīliābus***)* [KL1, L6]

fīliolus, -ī (m) *little son/child* [KL3, W10]

fīlius, -ī (m) *son* [KL1, L4]

fīlum, -ī (n) *thread, string* [KL1, W30]

findō, -ere, fidī, fissum *I split, part, cleave* [KL3, W16]

fīnis, -is (m) *end, boundary, limit* [KL1, W4]

fiō, fierī, ——, factus sum *I am made, am done, become, happen [used as present passive system of* **faciō***]* [KL1, L31]

firmāmentum, -ī (n) *support, prop; the firmament, the sky* [KL3, W4]

firmō (1) *I confirm, strengthen* [KL3, W3]

flēbilis, -e *tearful, lamentable* [KL3, W9]

fleō, -ēre, flēvī, flētum *I weep* [KL1, L14]

flētus, -ūs (m) *weeping, wailing* [KL3, W9]

flōreō, -ēre, -uī, —— *I flourish* [KL1, L17]

flōs, flōris (m) *flower* [KL1, L15]

flūmen, flūminis (n) *river* [KL1, L13]

foculus, -ī (m) *fire-pan, brazier* [KL2, W15]

fodiō, -ere, fōdī, fossum *I dig* [KL1, W28]

foedus, -a, -um *horrible, ugly* [KL1, L7]

foedus, -deris (n) *treaty, covenant, agreement* [KL2, L12]

folium *leaf* [KL1, W20]

fōns, fontis (m) *fountain, spring, source* [KL2, L11]

for, fārī, ——, fātus sum *I say, speak, prophesy* [KL3, L3]

forās *out(side), forth* [KL3, L6]

forma, -ae (f) *form, shape, appearance, beauty* [KL3, W16]

forsitan *perhaps, peradventure, maybe* [KL3, L13]

fortasse *perhaps* [KL1, L26]

forte *by chance, perhaps, perchance* [KL2, L3]

fortior, -tius (gen. fortioris) *braver* [KL1, W31]

fortis, -e *strong, brave* [KL1, L19]

fortissimus, -a, -um *bravest, strongest* [KL1, W32]

fortitūdō, -tudinis (f) *strength, bravery* [KL2, L12]

fovea, -ae (f) *pit, snare* [KL3, W1]

foveō, -ēre, fōvī, fōtum *I cherish, love, esteem* [KL1, L25]

fragor, -ōris (m) *a crashing, crash, noise, din* [KL3, W7]

frangō, -ere, frēgī, fractum *I break, smash, shatter* [KL1, L27]

frāter, frātris (m) *brother* [KL1, L12]

frōns, frondis (f) *foliage, garland, greenery* [KL3, W6]

frōns, frontis (f) *forehead* [KL1, W32]

fructus, -ūs (m) *fruit, profit* [KL1, L25]

frūmentum, -ī (n) *grain; (pl.) crops* [KL1, L15]

frustrā *in vain, in error* [KL3, L3]

fugiō, -ere, fūgī, fugitum *I flee, run away* [KL1, L31]

fulgeō, -ēre, fulsī, —— *I shine, glitter* [KL2, W13]

fulgur, -uris (n) *lightning* [KL1, W25]

fūmigō (1) *I smoke* [KL3, W1]

funda, -ae (f) *sling* [KL1, W32]

fundamentum, -ī (n) *foundation* [KL2, W9]

fundō, -ere, fūdī, fūsum *I pour (out), shed* [KL3, W3]

fundus, -ī (m) *farm, estate; foundation, lowest part* [KL3, W10]

fūnus, -neris (n) *funeral (rites)* [KL2, W13]

furō, -ere, -uī, —— *I rage, rave, am furious* [KL2, W13]

fūror, -ōris (m) *madness, fury, rage* [KL3, W6]

fūsus, -a, -um *spread out, scattered* [KL3, W6]

futūrus, -a, -um *future, about to be* [KL2, W10]

G

galea, -ae (f) *helmet* [KL2, W6]

Gallicus, -a, -um *Gallic, of/belonging to the Gauls* [KL3, W2]

gallīna, -ae (f) *hen* [KL3, W2]

gaudeō, -ēre, ——, gāvīsus sum *I rejoice* [KL1, L22]

gaudium, -ī (n) *joy, happiness* [KL1, L5]

gelidus, -a, -um *cold, icy* [KL1, L31]

gelū, -ūs (n) *frost, ice* [KL2, W9]
geminus, -ī (m) *twin* [KL1, L10]
gemitus, -ūs (m) *groan, complaint* [KL3, W6]
generātiō, -ōnis (f) *generation, begetting* [KL3, L7]
gens, -ntis (f) *clan, tribe, nation* [KL1, L31]
gentīlis, -is (m/f) *Gentile, pagan, heathen* [KL3, W7]
genu, -ūs (n) *knee* [KL1, L25]
genus, -neris (n) *birth, origin, race, kind* [KL2, L13]
germāna, -ae (f) *sister* [KL1, L4]
germānus, -ī (m) *brother* [KL1, L4]
germinō (1) *I sprout forth, bud, put forth* [KL3, W4]
gerō, -ere, gessī, gestum *I bear, carry on;* **bellum gerō** *I wage war* [KL1, L28]
gigās, gigantis (m) *giant* [KL1, L15]
gignō, -ere, genuī, genitum *I beget, create (in pass., I am born)* [KL2, L9]
gladius, -ī (m) *sword* [KL1, L4]
glōria, -ae (f) *fame, glory* [KL1, L15]
Gorgō, -onis (f) *a Gorgon* [KL2, W6]
grabātus, -ī (m) *pallet, mat, low couch* [KL3, W5]
gracilis, -e *slender, thin* [KL2, L5]
Graeae, -ārum (f, pl) *the Graeae (Gray Sisters)* [KL2, W6]
Graecus, -a, -um *Greek* [KL3, L6]
Graecus, -ī (m) (as noun) *a Greek* [KL3, L6]
grāmen, grāminis (n) *grass, greenery* [KL1, L13]
grandō, -dinis (f) *hail* [KL2, W9]
grātia, -ae (f) *grace, favor, kindness, thanks;* **grātiās agō (+dat.)** *I give thanks, I thank* [KL1, L27]
grātus, -a, -um *grateful, pleasing* [KL1, L27]
gravis, -e *heavy, burdensome* [KL3, L6]
gravitās, -tātis (f) *weight, heaviness* [KL3, W2]
grex, gregis (m) *flock, herd* [KL1, L31]
gubernō (1) *I steer, direct, govern* [KL1, L25]

H

habēna, -ae (f) *rein, strap* [KL3, W8]
habeō, -ēre, -uī, -itum *I have, hold* [KL1, L9]
habitō (1) *I live, dwell, inhabit* [KL1, L3]
haereō, -ēre, haesī, haesum *I cling, stick* [KL3, W3]
hara, -ae (f) *pig-sty* [KL1, W25]
harēna, -ae (f) *sand, beach* [KL1, L3]
hasta, -ae (f) *spear* [KL1, L3]
haud *not at all, by no means* [KL3, L1]
hauriō, -īre, hausī, haustum *I draw up, draw out, drink up* [KL2, W12]
herī *yesterday* [KL1, L6]
Hesperidēs, -um (f, pl.) *the Hesperides* [KL2, W6]
heu (ēheu) *alas! oh! (expresses grief or pain)* [KL1, L22]
hic, haec, hoc *this, (pl.) these* [KL1, L30]
hīc *here, in this place* [KL2, L11]
hinc *from here, hence, from/on this side* [KL2, L11]
Hierusalem (indecl.) *Jerusalem*
hodiē *today* [KL1, L2]
homicīda, -ae (m/f) *murderer/murderess), homicide, manslayer* [KL3, L13]
homō, hominis (m) *man, human being* [KL1, L12]
hōra, -ae (f) *hour* [KL1, L31]
horrendus, -a, -um *dreadful, awful, fearful* [KL1, L13]
horreum, -ī (n) *barn, granary, storehouse* [KL2, W14]
hortus, -ī (m) *garden* [KL2, W6]
hospes, -pitis (m) *guest* [KL2, W6]
hostis, -is (m) *enemy (of the state)* [KL1, L18]
hūc *to this place, hither* [KL2, L11]
hūmānus, -a, -um *human, humane, cultured* [KL3, W2]
humilis, -e *humble, low(ly)* [KL2, L5]
humus, -ī (f) *ground, soil, earth* [KL2, L14]
hydria, -ae (f) *jug* [KL2, W12]
hyacinthinus, -a, -um *blue, purplish-blue, violet* [KL1, L17]
hydrus, -ī (m) *sea serpent* [KL1, W12]
hydrum, -ī (m) *sea serpent* [KL2, W4]
hypocrita, -ae (m) *hypocrite* [KL2, W14]

I

iaceō, -ēre, -uī, —— *I lie (flat), lie down* [KL1, L9]
iaciō, -ere, iēcī, iactum *I throw, cast, hurl* [KL1, L31]
iactūra, -ae (f) *a throwing (away/over)* [KL2, W7]
iam *now, already;* **nōn iam** *no longer* [KL1, L15]
ibī *there, at that place; then* [KL1, L5]
ictus, -ūs (m) *blow, stroke* [KL3, W5]
īdem, eadem, idem *the same* [KL3, L2]
ideo *therefore, for that reason* [KL2, L14]
īdōlum, -ī (n) *image, form, idol* [KL3, L7]
iēiūnium, -iī (n) *a fast, fasting, fast-day* [KL3, W10]
iēiūnō (1) *I fast, abstain from* [KL3, W10]
Iēsus, -ūs (m) *Jesus* [KL1, L25]
igitur *therefore, then* [KL2, L9]
ignis, ignis (m) *fire* [KL1, L18]
ignōrō (1) *I do not know, am ignorant of* [KL2, L15]
ille, illa, illud *that, (pl.) those; that famous* [KL1, L30]
illīc *there, in that place* [KL2, L11]
illinc *from there, thence, from/on that side* [KL2, L11]
illūc *to that place, thither* [KL2, L11]
illūminō (1) *I light up, give light, illuminate* [KL3, W4]
imāgō, -ginis (f) *image, likeness* [KL3, L4]

imber, -bris (m) *rain(storm), shower* [KL2, W9]

immānis, -e *enormous, monstrous, immense* [KL3, L7]

immemor, -oris *unmindful, heedless, not thinking* [KL2, W6]

immō *nay rather, on the contrary, no indeed* [KL3, W7]

immortālis, -e *immortal* [KL2, W6]

immundus, -a, -um [or inmundus etc.] *unclean, dirty, foul* [KL3, L5]

impediō, -īre, -īvī, -ītum *I hinder* [KL1, L29]

imperium, -iī (n) *command, authority, empire* [KL2, L13]

imperō (1) *I command, order* (alicuī aliquid) [KL3, L10]

impetus, -ūs (m) *attack, onset, impetus* [KL3, L9]

impietās, -tātis (f) *impiety, irreverence, ungodliness* [KL3, W7]

impius, -a, -um *irreverent, wicked, impious* [KL3, L1]

impleō, -ēre, -plēvī, -plētum *I fill up, satisfy, complete* [KL2, L7]

implicō (1) *I entwine, entangle* [KL3, W5]

impōnō, -ere, -posuī, -positum *I put on, establish* [KL2, W13]

importō (1) *I carry in, import* [KL3, W2]

impositiō, -ōnis (f) *a putting on, laying on* [KL3, W7]

improbus, -a, -um *wicked* [KL1, L29]

impudīcitia, -ae (f) *sexual immorality* [KL3, W9]

īmus, -a, -um *lowest, deepest* [KL2, L5]

in (+acc.) *into, against;* **(+abl.)** *in, on* [KL1, L3]

Īnachus, -ī (m) *Inachus (god of the Inachus River in Argos)* [KL1, W21]

inānis, -e *empty, void* [KL3, W4]

incarcerō (1) *I imprison, incarcerate* [KL2, W4]

incendō, -ere, -cendī, -censum *I kindle, set on fire* [KL2, W13]

incertus, -a, -um uncertain, unsure [KL2, W11]

incipiō, -ere, -cēpī, -ceptum *I begin, commence* [KL1, L31]

incircumcisus, -a, -um *uncircumcised* [KL1, W32]

inclūdō, -ere, -clūsī, -clūsum I shut in/up, enclose [KL3, W6]

incolō, -ere, -coluī, -cultum *I dwell in, inhabit, cultivate* [KL3, L2]

incolumis, -e *safe, unhurt, uninjured* [KL3, W2]

inde *from there, thence* [KL2, L10]

indīcō (1) *I declare, show, make known* [KL3, L11]

indigeō, -ēre, -diguī, —— (+ gen./abl.) *I need, require, lack* [KL2, W14]

indīgnitās, -tātis (f) *unworthiness, indignity* [KL2, W15]

induō, -ere, -duī, -dūtum *I put on, clothe, wear* [KL2, L14]

ineō, -īre, -iī (-īvī), -ītum *I go in(to), enter, begin* [KL3, L4]

īnfāns, -fantis (adj. & noun, m/f) *baby, infant* [KL1, W31; KL3, L12]

infēlix, (gen.) -līcis *unlucky, unfortunate, miserable* [KL1, L19]

īnfēnsus, -a, -um *enraged, hostile* [KL2, W15]

īnferior, -ius *lower* [KL2, L5]

inferō, -ferre, intulī, illātum (+dat. or + ad/ in +acc.) *I bring in, carry in* [KL3, L2]

īnferus, -a, -um *below* [KL2, L5]

inficiō, -ere, -fēcī, -fectum *I put/dip in, dye* [KL3, W2]

infīgo, -ere, -fixī, -fixum *I fix in, fasten in* [KL1, W32]

īnfimus, -a, -um *lowest, deepest* [KL2, L5]

infīnītus, -a, -um *boundless, infinite* [KL3, W2]

īnfīrmitās, -tātis (f) *infirmity, sickness, weakness* [KL3, W5]

īnfīrmus, -a, -um *feeble, weak, infirm* [KL3, W5]

īnfrā (adv. and prep. +acc.) *below, under* [KL3, W16]

infundō, -ere, -fūdī, -fūsum (+dat.) *I pour in(to)* [KL3, W9]

ingēns, (gen.) -entis *huge, vast, enormous* [KL1, L19]

ingredior, -gredī, ——, -gressus sum *I go in, advance, undertake* [KL2, L6]

iniciō, -ere, -iēcī, -iectum *I throw in/on, put in/on, cast in/on* [KL2, W15]

inimīcus, -ī (m) *(personal) enemy* [KL1, L10]

inīquitās, -tātis (f) *injustice, unfairness, iniquity* [KL2, L10]

initium, -iī (n) *beginning, commencement, entrance* [KL3, L7]

iniūstus, -a, -um *unjust, unreasonable* [KL3, W16]

inmeritus [imm-], -a, -um *undeserved, undeserving, innocent* [KL3, W16]

innoxius, -a, -um *harmless* [KL3, W3]

innumerus, -a, -um *innumerable, countless* [KL3, W16]

inperitus, -a, -um *unskilled, inexperienced, ignorant* [KL2, W9]

insānia, -ae (f) *insanity, madness* [KL3, W6]

insānus, -a, -um *insane, mad* [KL3, W3]

īnscius, -a, -um *not knowing, ignorant* [KL3, W16]

īnsidiae, -ārum (f, pl) *ambush, plot* [KL2, L15]

īnsōmnium, -iī (n) *dream* [KL2, W13]

īnsonō, -āre, -uī, -ītum *I resound, echo* [KL2, W6]

īnsula, -ae (f) *island* [KL1, L3]

īnstar (indecl) *likeness, appearance, worth* [KL2, W13]

īnstō, -āre, -stitī, -stātum *I press on, urge forward* [KL2, W6]

intāctus, -a, -um *untouched, uninjured* [KL2, W15]

integer, -tēgra, -tēgrum *whole, fresh, untouched* [KL3, W2]

intellegō, -ere, -lēxī, -lēctum *I understand, perceive* [KL3, L2]

inter (+acc.) *between, among* [KL1, L19]

intereā *in the meantime, meanwhile* [KL2, L12]

interficiō, -ere, -fēcī, -fectum *I kill, slay, destroy* [KL1, L31]

interim *meanwhile, in the meantime* [KL1, L9]

interior, -ius (gen. -teriōris) *inner, interior* [KL3, W2]

interrogō (1) *I ask, interrogate* [KL2, W8]

intervāllum, -ī (n) *interval, distance [of space or time]* [KL3, W2]

intonō, -āre, -uī/-āvī, —— *I thunder, make a noise* [KL3, W3]

intrā (prep. +acc.; adv.) *within, inside, inwardly* [KL2, L15]

intrō (1) *I enter* [KL1, L9]

inveniō, -īre, -vēnī, -ventum *I come upon, find* [KL1, L29]

invicem *reciprocally (i.e., "[to] one another")* [KL1, W26]; *in turn, by turns; one another, each other* [KL2, L12]

invīctus, -a, -um *unconquered, invincible* [KL3, W13]

invideō, -ēre, -vīdī, -vīsum *I envy* [KL1, W29]

invidus, -a, -um *envious, unfavorable (to)* [KL2, W11]

inviolātus, -a, -um *unharmed, unhurt* [KL3, W1]

involvō, -ere, -volvī, -volutum *I wrap (in)* [KL2, W9]

Īō, -ōnis (f) *Io (a beautiful nymph and daughter of Inachus)* [KL1, W21]

ipse, ipsa, ipsum *himself, herself, itself; the very* [KL2, L3]

īra, -ae (f) *anger* [KL1, L2]

īrāscor, -scī, ——, īrātus sum *I am angry, am in a rage* [KL3, W9]

īrātus, -a, -um *angry, wrathful* [KL1, L15]

is, ea, id *he, she, it, they; this, that* [KL1, L17]

Isai (indecl.) *Jesse* [KL1, W32]

Israhel (indecl.) or Israhel, -is *Israel* [KL1, W32; KL2, W3]

Israhelita, -ae (m) *Israelite* [KL1, W32]

iste, ista, istud *that (of yours); such (sometimes used with tone of contempt)* [KL1, L30]

ita *so, thus, therefore* [KL2, L6]

Ītalia, -ae (f) *Italy* [KL1, W8; KL2, W5]

itaque *and ēo, therefore* [KL1, L2]

iter, itineris (n) *journey, road, route, trek* [KL1, L13]

iterum *again, a second time* [KL1, L25]

iubeō, -ēre, iūssī, iūssum *I order, command* [KL3, L2]

Iudaeus, -a, -um *Jewish* [KL2, W3]

iūdex, -dicis (m) *judge* [KL1, W28; KL3, L1]

iūdicium, -ī (n) *judgment, decision, trial* [KL2, L9]

iūdicō (1) *I judge, decide* [KL2, L14]

Iūlia, -ae (f) *Iulia or Julia* [KL1, W11]

Iūlius, -iī (m) *Iulius or Julius* [KL1, W19]

iūmentum, -ī (n) *beast (of burden)* [KL3, W4]

iungō, -ere, iūnxī, iunctum *I join, unite, yoke* [KL1, L27]

Iūnia, -ae (f) *Iunia or Junia* [KL1, W11]

Iūno, -ōnis (f) *Juno (queen of the gods and wife of Jupiter)* [KL1, W21; KL3, W3]

Iuppiter, Iovis (dat. Iovī, acc. Iovem, abl. Iove) (m) *Jupiter/Jove (king of the gods)* [KL1, W21; KL2, W6]

iūrō (1) *I swear, vow, take an oath* (**iūs iūrandum** [*or as one word,* **iūsiūrandum**] *an oath*) [KL2, L15]

iūs, iūris (n) *justice, right, duty* [KL2, L15]

iūstitia, -ae (f) *justice, righteousness* [KL3, L12]

iūstus, -a, -um *just, right, fair, righteous* [KL1, L7; KL3, L7]

iuvenis, -e *young* [KL2, W2]

iuvenissimus, -a, -um *youngest* [KL1, W19]

iuventūs, -tūtis (f) *youth* [KL2, W15]

iuvō, -āre, iūvī, iūtum *I help* [KL1, L22]

iūxta (adv. & prep. +acc.) *near (to), close to/by* [KL1, L28]

L

lābor, -ī, ——, lapsus sum *I slip, fall, glide* [KL2, L6]

labor, labōris (m) *work, toil, labor, hardship* [KL1, L12]

labōrō (1) *I work* [KL1, L22]

lābrum, -ī (n) *lip* [KL3, W2]

labyrinthus, -ī (m) *labyrinth, maze* [KL1, W30]

lac, lactis (n) *milk* [KL1, L13]

lācrima, -ae (f) *tear* [KL3, L9]

lacus, -ūs (m) *lake, tub, hollow* [KL1, L27]

laedō, -ere, laesī, laesus *I wound, offend* [KL3, W6]

laetitia, -ae (f) *joy, gladness* [KL3, L7]

laetus, -a, -um *happy, joyful, glad* [KL1, L7]

lambō, -ere, lambī, lambitum *I lick (up), touch* [KL3, W3]

lapis, -idis (m) *stone* [KL1, W27; KL2, L14]

lassus, -a, -um *tired, weary, faint* [KL3, W3]

Latīnus, -a, -um *Latin, of Latium* [KL2, W13]

lātitūdō, -dinis (f) *width, extent, latitude* [KL2, W9]

lātus, -a, -um *wide, broad* [KL1, L20]

latus, -eris (n) *side, flank* [KL3, L6]

laudō (1) *I praise* [KL1, L1]

laurus, -ī (m) *laurel-tree* [KL1, W20]

laus, laudis (f) *praise* [KL1, L15]

lavō, -āre, lāvī, lōtum/lavātum *I wash, bathe* [KL1, W27; KL2, L11]

lea, -ae (f) *lioness* [KL2, W11]

lectiō, -ōnis (f) *a reading, text* [KL3, W9]

lectulus, -ī (m) *bed, small couch* [KL3, W5]

lēgātus, -ī (m) *ambassador, envoy, lieutenant* [KL2, L15]

legiō, -ōnis (f) *legion* [KL3, W2]

legō, -ere, lēgī, lectum *I read, choose* [KL1, L28]

leō, leōnis (m) *lion* [KL1, L12]

lepus, -oris (m) *hare* [KL3, W2]

levis, -e *light* [KL2, W6]

leviter *softly, lightly* [KL2, W6]

levō (1) *I lift up, raise* [KL3, W1]

lēx, lēgis (f) *law, covenant* [KL2, L10]

liber, librī (m) *book* [KL1, L11]

līberī, -ōrum (m, pl) *children* [KL1, L10]

līberō (1) *I set free* [KL1, L1]

licet, licuit, -(impers. +dat./acc.) *it is permitted/lawful/allowed* [KL1, W26; KL3, L1]

līgneus, -a, -um *wooden* [KL3, W6]

lignum, -ī (n) *wood, tree* [KL2, L13]

ligō (1) *I bind (up/together), tie* [KL3, W16]

līlium, -iī (n) *lily* [KL3, W13]

līmen, -minis (n) *threshold, doorway, house* [KL3, L3]

limpidissimus, -a, -um *very bright, very clear* [KL1, W32]

linea, -ae (f) *line, string* [KL3, W9]

lingua, -ae (f) *language, tongue* [KL1, L26]

līnum, -ī (n) *flax* [KL3, W1]

līquidus, -a, -um *liquid, flowing, pure* [KL3, W16]

littera, -ae (f) *letter of the alphabet; (pl) letter, epistle* [KL1, L26]

lītus, lītoris (n) *shore, shoreline* [KL1, L13]

locus, -ī (m) *place*; **loca, -ōrum (n, pl)** *places [geographic]* [KL2, L7]; **locī, -ōrum (m, pl)** *places, passages, topics [in a book]* [KL2, L7]

longē *a long way off, far off* [KL3, L3]

longinquus, -a, -um *distant, far away* [KL1, L7]

longus, -a, -um *long* [KL1, L20]

loquor, -quī, ——, locūtus sum *I say, speak* [KL2, L6]

lūceō, lūcēre, lūxī, —— *I shine, am bright* [KL1, L11]

lūctus, -ūs (m) *grief, sorrow, mourning* [KL3, W13]

lūdō, lūdere, lūsī, lūsum *I play, tease, trick* [KL1, L26]

lumbus, -ī (m) *loin* [KL2, W9]

lūmen, -minis (n) *light, lamp* [KL3, L11]

lūmināre, -āris (n) *light(-giver), heavenly body, luminary* [KL3, W4]

lūna, -ae (f) *moon* [KL1, L2]

lutum, -ī (n) *mud, clay* [KL3, W8]

lux, lūcis (f) *light* [KL1, L12]

lyra, -ae (f) *lyre* [KL1, W28]

M

māchina, -ae (f) *machine, device, (military) engine* [KL3, W6]

magis *more, rather* [KL2, L7]

magicus, -a, -um *magic, magical* [KL2, W2]

magister, -strī (m) *teacher (male)* [KL1, L6]

magistra, -ae (f) *teacher (female)* [KL1, L6]

magistrātus, -ūs (m) magistrate [KL3, W5]

magnanimus, -a, -um *brave, bold, noble* [KL1, W9]

magnoperē *greatly, very much* [KL1, L29]

magnus, -a, -um *large, big, great* [KL1, L7]

māior, māius (gen. māioris) *greater, older* [KL1, W31; KL2, L5]

male *badly, ill, wrongly* [KL1, L1]

maledīcō, -ere, -dīxī, -dictum (+dat.) *I speak ill, curse, slander* [KL1, W30; KL3, L4]

malignus, -a, -um *evil, wicked, malicious, malignant* [KL3, L13]

malitia, -ae (f) *malice, wickedness* [KL2, L14]

malus, -a, -um *bad, evil* [KL1, L7]

mālō, mālle, māluī, —— *I prefer, want more/ instead* [KL2, L14]

mandātum, -ī (n) *command(ment), order* [KL2, L10]

mandō (1) *I order, command; commit, entrust* (alicuī aliquid) [KL3, L10]

mandūcō (1) *I chew, eat* [KL1, L6]

māne *in the morning, early* [KL1, W19; KL2, L6]

maneō, -ēre, mansī, mansum *I remain* [KL1, L10]

manifestō (1) *I reveal, make clear, manifest* [KL2, W8]

manifestus, -a, -um *manifest, evident* [KL3, W1]

mānō (1) *I flow, trickle, drop* [KL3, W16]

manus, -ūs (f) *hand* [KL1, L25]

mappa, -ae (f) *starting flag (lit., "napkin")* [KL1, W23]

mare, maris (n) *sea* [KL1, L18]

maritimus, -a, -um *of/belonging to the sea* [KL3, W2]

marmoreus, -a, -um *(made of) marble, marble-like* [KL3, W16]

Mars, Martis (m) *Mars* [KL2, W13]

masculus, -a, -um *male* [KL3, W4]

māter, mātris (f) *mother* [KL1, L12]

māteria, -ae (f) *material, timber* [KL3, W2]

māternus, -a, -um *of/belonging to a mother, maternal* [KLS, W16]

mātrimōnium, -ī (n) *marriage* [KL1, L20]

mātūtīnus, -a, -um *of the (early) morning, early* [KL3, W9]

māximē *most, especially, very* [KL2, L7]

māximus, -a, -um *biggest, greatest* [KL1, W31; KL2, L5]

mediōcris, -e *ordinary* [KL1, L19]

mediterrāneus, -a, -um *inland* [KL3, W2]

medius, -a, -um *middle (of), midst (of)* [KL1, L26]

melior, -ius *better* [KL1, W28; KL2, L5]

melius *better* [KL2, L7]

memor, -oris *mindful, remembering* [KL3, L9]

memoria, -ae (f) *memory, remembrance* [KL3, L2]

mendācium, -iī (n) *lie, falsehood, counterfeit* [KL3, L6]

mendāx, -dacis (m/f) *liar* [KL3, L6]

mendicō (1) *I beg (for)* [KL2, W8]

mendicus, -ī (m) *beggar* [KL2, W8]

mensa, -ae (f) *table* [KL1, L31]

mensis, -is (m) *month* [KL3, L10]

mēnsūra, -ae (f) *measurement, measure* [KL2, L14]

mentior, -īrī, ——, -ītus sum *I lie, deceive, say falsely* [KL3, L6]

Mercurius, -ī (m) *Mercury (the messenger god)* [KL1, W21; KL2, W6]

mereō, -ēre, -uī, -itum *I deserve, earn, am worthy of* [KL1, L15; KL3, W6]

merīdiēs, -ēī (m) *noon* [KL1, L28]

Messīā(s), -ae (m) *Messiah, Anointed One* [KL2, W12]

-met (intensifying suffix on personal pronouns) *-self* [KL3, L7]

mēta, -ae (f) *turning-post, goal* [KL1, W23]

mētior, -īrī, ——, mēnsus sum *I measure, traverse* [KL2, L14]

metō, -ere, messuī, messum *I reap, harvest* [KL2, W14]

metuō, -ere, -uī, -ūtum *I fear, am afraid of, revere* [KL3, L15]

metus, -ūs (m) *fear, dread* [KL1, L26]

meus, -a, -um *my, mine* [KL1, L11]

micō, -āre, -uī, —— *I glitter, flash* [KL3, W3]

Midās, -ae (m) *Midas (king of Phrygia)* [KL1, W27]

mīles, mīlitis (m) *soldier* [KL1, L12]

mille *one thousand* [KL1, L21]

mīllēsimus, -a, -um *one thousandth* [KL1, L23]

Minerva, -ae (f) *Minerva* [KL3, W6]

minimē *least, not at all* [KL2, L7]

minimus, -a, -um *least, younger* [KL1, W31; KL2, L5]

minister, -strī (m) *attendant, servant, minister* [KL3, L10]

minor, -ārī, ——, -ātus sum *I threaten, menace* [KL2, W5]

minor, minus *smaller* [KL2, L5]

Mīnōs, -ōnis (m) *Minos* [KL1, W30]

Mīnōtaurus, -ī (m) *the Minotaur* [KL1, W30]

minus *less* [KL2, L7]

minūtātim *gradually, bit by bit* [KL1, L20]

mīrābilis, -e *marvelous, wonderful* [KL3, L3]

mīror, -ārī, ——, mīrātus sum *I marvel at, am amazed at, admire* [KL2, L6]

mīrus, -a, -um *strange, wonderful* [KL1, L7]

miser, -era, -erum *unhappy, wretched, miserable* [KL1, L7]

misereor, -ērī, ——, misertus sum (+ gen.) *I pity, have mercy on* [KL2, L6]

miseria, -ae (f) *misery, distress, suffering* [KL3, W9]

misericordia, -ae (f) *mercy, pity* [KL2, L10]

mītigō (1) *I calm, soothe, pacify* [KL3, W7]

mītra, -ae (f) *turban* [KL1, W28]

mittō, -ere, mīsī, missum *I send, let go* [KL1, L26]

modicus, -a, -um *moderate, ordinary, little* [KL2, L14]

modus, -ī (m) *measure, way, manner, sort* [KL3, L7]

modo *only, just, merely, now, but* [KL1, L27]

moenia, -ium (n, pl) *fortifications, city walls* [KL1, L18]

mōlior, -īrī, ——, mōlītus sum *I labor, build, undertake* [KL2, L6]

monachus, -ī (m) *monk* [KL3, W7]

monastērium, -iī (n) *monastery* [KL3, W7]

moneō, -ēre, -uī, -itum *I warn* [KL1, L9]

mōns, montis *mountain* [KL1, L18]

mōnstrum, -ī (n) *monster* [KL1, W30]; *omen, portent* [KL3, W3]

monumentum, -ī (n) *monument, memorial* [KL2, W11]

mordeō, -ēre, momordī, morsum *I bite, sting* [KL1, L9]

morior, morī, ——, mortuus sum *I die* [KL2, L6]

mors, mortis (f) *death* [KL1, L18]

mortālis, -e *mortal* [KL2, W6]

mortuus, -a, -um *dead* [KL2, L3]

mōrus, -ī (f) *mulberry tree* [KL2, W11]

mōs, mōris (m) *manner, custom; (pl.) character, morals* [KL2, L13]

moveō, -ēre, mōvī, mōtum *I move* [KL1, L14]

mox *soon* [KL1, L15]

mulier, mulieris (f) *woman* [KL1, L22]

multiplicō (1) *I multiply, increase* [KL3, W20]

multitūdō, -tudinis (f) *multitude, crowd* [KL2, L12]

multum *much* [KL2, L7]

multus, -a, -um *much, many* [KL1, L7]

mundō (1) *I clean, cleanse* [KL3, L5]

mundus, -a, -um *clean, neat, elegant* [KL3, L5]

mundus, -ī (m) *world, universe* [KL1, L6]

mūnītiō, -ōnis (f) fortification, bulwark [KL3, W2]

mūnus, -neris (n) *office, duty, gift* [KL2, L15]

mūrus, -ī (m) *wall* [KL2, L11]

musicus, -ī (m) *musician* [KL1, W28]

mūtō (1) *I change* [KL1, L20]

mūtus, -a, -um *mute* [KL3, W1]

N

nam *for; certainly* [KL1, W32; KL2, L9]

narrō (1) *I tell, relate, recount* [KL1, L2]

nāscor, -scī, ——, nātus sum *I am born, am begotten, arise* [KL2, L12]

natātōria, -ae (f) *pool, place for swimming* [KL2, W8]

nātīvitās, -tātis (f) *birth, nativity* [KL2, W8]

naufragium, -ī (n) *wreck, crash (lit., shipwreck)* [KL1, W23]

nauta, -ae (m) *sailor* [KL1, L3]

nāvicula, -ae (f) *boat* [KL1, W31]

nāvigō (1) *I sail* [KL1, L4]

nāvis, -is (f) *ship* [KL1, L18]

-ne *interrogative enclitic indicating a simple yes/no question* [KL2, L7]

nē (adv.) *not, no* [KL3, L4]

nē (conj.) *that not, lest* [KL3, L4]

nec (neque) *and not, nor;* **nec...nec** *neither....nor* [KL1, L14]

necesse (n, indecl.) *necessary, unavoidable*; **necesse est (impers. +dat./acc.)** *it is necessary* [KL3, L1]

necō (1) *I kill, slay* [KL1, L1]

nefās (n, indecl.) *sin, crime*; **(when transl. as adj.)** *forbidden* [KL3, L2]

negō (1) *I say no, deny (often used instead of* nōn dicō*)* [KL3, L3]

negōtium, -iī (n) *business, occupation* [KL3, W9]

nēmō, neminis (m/f) *no one, nobody* [KL2, L4]

neō, nēre, nēvī, nētus *I spin, weave* [KL2, W14]

nepōs, -pōtis (m/f) *descendant, grandson/granddaughter, nephew/niece* [KL2, L13]

Neptūnus, -ī (m) *Neptune* [KL2, W7]

nequaquam *by no means, not at all* [KL2, W8]

neque (nec) *and not, nor;* **nec...nec** *neither....nor* [KL1, L14]

nesciō, -īre, -īvī, -ītum *I do not know, am ignorant (of)* [KL1, L30; KL3, L3]

neuter, -tra, -trum *neither* [KL2, L15]

nex, necis (f) *(violent) death, slaughter, murder* [KL3, W10]

niger, -gra, -grum *(shining) black, dark-colored* [KL1, L17]

nihil (n. indecl.) *nothing;*

nihil (adv.) *not at all* [KL1, L6]

nimis (adv.) *too (much), excessively* [KL3, L4]

nimium *too much, too, excessively* [KL2, W13]

nisi *if not, unless, except* [KL3, L11]

nix, nivis (f) *snow* [KL2, L9]

nō (1) *I swim* [KL1, L14]

nōbilis, -e *noble, famous* [KL2, W15]

nocēns, -ntis *harmful, injurious* [KL2, W11]

nōlō, nōlle, nōluī, —— *I do not wish, do not want, am unwilling* [KL2, L14]

nōmen, nōminis (n) *name* [KL1, L13]

nōminō (1) *I name, give a name to, call* [KL3, W13]

nōn *not* [KL1, L1]

nōndum (adv.) *not yet* [KL3, L7]

nōnne *interrogative adverb expecting a yes answer* [KL2, L7]

nōnus, -a, -um *ninth* [KL1, L23]

nōs (pl.) *we* [KL1, L17]

noscō, -ere, nōvī, nōtum *I learn, get to know; pf. tense, I know* [KL2, L9]

noster, -stra, -strum *our, ours* [KL1, L11]

novem *nine* [KL1, L21]

noverca, -ae (f) *step-mother* [KL1, W22]

novus, -a, -um *new* [KL1, L26]

nox, noctis (f) *night* [KL1, L18]

nūbes, nūbis (f) *cloud, gloom* [KL1, L18]

nūbō, -ere, nūpsī, nūptum *I marry, am married to (of a bride)* [KL3, W2]

nūdus, -a, -um *naked, bare, exposed* [KL3, W7]

nūllus, -a, -um *no, none, not any* [KL2, L4]

num *interrogative adverb expecting a no answer* [KL2, L7]

nūmen, -minis (n) *divinity, god, divine will* [KL2, L7]

numerus, -ī (m) *number* [KL3, L2]

nummus, -ī (m) *coin* [KL1, W22]

numquam *never* [KL1, L5]

numquid (emphatic form of num) *interrogative adv. expecting a no answer (can be translated "surely...not? is it really possible that...?" etc.)* [KL2, L9]

nunc *now* [KL1, L1]

nuntiō (1) *I announce, declare* [KL1, L14]

nuntius, -ī (m) *messenger* [KL2, L12]

nūptiālis, -e, *of a wedding, wedding (adj.), nuptial* [KL2, W2]

nūtō (1) *I nod, shake, sway to and fro* [KL3, W7]

nympha, -ae (f) *nymph* [KL1, W20; KL2, W6]

O

ob (+acc.) *on account of, for; in front of* [KL2, L3]

obcaecō (1) *I (make) blind, darken, conceal* [KL3, W12]

oblīvīscor, -vīscī, ——, oblītus sum (+ gen.) *I forget* [KL2, L7]

oboediō [obediō], -īre, -īvī, -ītum (+dat.) *I obey, serve, heed* [KL3, W5]

obsecrō (1) *I beseech, beg, implore;* [tē/vōs] obsecrō *please, pray* [KL3, L13]

observō (1) *I observe, watch, keep, guard* [KL3, W11]

obsideō, -ēre, -sēdī, -sessum *I besiege, remain near* [KL1, L10]

obsidiō, -ōnis (f) *siege, blockade* [KL2, W15]

obsistō, -ere, -stitī, -stitum *I oppose, withstand, resist* [KL3, W7]

obstō, -stāre, -stitī, -stātūrum (+dat.) *I stand in the way, hinder, obstruct* [KL2, W11]

obumbrō (1) *I overshadow, cover, cast a shadow (on)* [KL3, W4]

obviam (adv.) *in the way, against* [KL3, W7]

occāsiō, -ōnis (f) *occasion, opportunity* [KL3, W10]

occīdō, -ere, -cīdī, -cīsum *I kill, cut down, slay* [KL1, L30]

occultō (1) *I hide, conceal* [KL1, L22]

occupō (1) *I seize* [KL1, L6]

Ōceanus, -ī (m) *ocean, [the deity] Ocean* [KL3, W6]

ōceanus, -ī (m) *ocean* [KL1, L4]

octāvus, -a, -um *eighth* [KL1, L23]

octō *eight* [KL1, L21]

oculus, -ī (m) *eye* [KL2, L3]

ōdī, ōdisse, [fut. prt.] ōsūrum [defective] *I hate, dislike* [KL3, L6]

odium, -iī (n) *hatred, disgust* [KL3, L4]

offerō, offerre, obtulī, oblātum *I offer, bring/carry to* [KL2, L11]

oleum, -ī (n) *oil, olive oil* [KL3, L14]

ōlim *once upon a time, formerly, then* [KL1, L6]

omnīno *altogether, wholly, at all* [KL3, L5]

omnipotēns, -tentis *omnipotent, all-powerful, almighty* [KL3, W2]

omnis, -e *every, all* [KL1, L19]

onus, oneris (n) *burden, load, weight* [KL1, L13; KL3, L3]

operor, -ārī, ——, operātus sum *I work, labor, am busy* [KL2, L6]

oportet, -ēre, -tuit, -tuitum (impers. +acc.) *it is proper, necessary* [KL3, L1]

oppidum, -ī (n) *town* [KL1, L5]

oppugnō (1) *I attack* [KL1, L4]

optimē *best* [KL2, L7]

optimus, -a, -um *best* [KL2, L5]

optio, optiōnis (f) *choice* [KL1, W12]

opus, operis (n) *work, deed* [KL2, L3]

ōra, -ae (f) *shore* [KL1, L13]

ōrāculum, -ī (n) *oracle, prophecy* [KL1, W31; KL2, W6]

orba, -ae (f) *orphan (female)* [KL1, L22]

orbus, -a, -um *deprived of parents or children, bereft* [KL1, L22]

orbus, -ī (m) *orphan (male)* [KL1, L22]

ōrdō, -dinis (m) *line, row, order* [KL2, L15]

orior, -īrī, ——, ortus sum *I (a)rise, am born/created* [KL2, L6]

ornātus, -ūs (m) *preparation, furnishing, adornment, ornament* [KL3, W6]

ōrō (1) *I pray, speak (takes double acc.)* [KL1, L6]

ōs, ōris (n) *mouth* [KL1, L13]

os, ossis (n) *bone* [KL3, L15]

ōsculum, -ī (n) *a kiss* [KL2, W11]

ostendō, -ere, -dī, -sum/tum *I show, point out, declare* [KL3, L5]

ōstium, -iī (n) *door, gate, entrance* [KL2, L4]

Oswaldus, -ī (m) *Oswald* [KL1, W19]

ovis, ovis (f) *sheep* [KL2, L3]

P

Pactōlus, -ī (m) *Pactolus (a river in Lydia in Asia Minor)* [KL1, W27]

paene (adv.) *almost* [KL1, L19]

paenitentia, -ae (f) *repentance, penitence* [KL3, W5]

pactus, -a, -um *agreed upon, covenanted, appointed* [KL2, L13]

palleō, -ēre, -uī, —— *I am/grow pale* [KL3, W7]

pallium, -ī (n) *cloak, cover(ing)* [KL3, W7]

Pallas, -adis (f) *(Pallas) Athena* [KL3, W6]

palma, -ae (f) *hand* [KL1, W14]

palus, palūdis (f) *swamp* [KL1, W13]

Pān, Pānos (acc. Pāna) (m) *Pan (god of woods, shepherds, and flocks)* [KL1, W28]

pānis, -is (m) *bread* [KL1, L29]

parcō, -ere, pepercī, parsūrum (+dat.) *I spare* [KL2, L13]

parēns, -ntis (m/f) *parent, father, mother* [KL1, W11; KL2, W8]

pariō, -ere, peperī, par(i)tum *I bring forth, give birth to, beget* [KL3, L13]

pariter *equally* [KL3, L1]

parō (1) *I prepare* [KL1, L14]

pars, partis (f) *part; side, direction* [KL2, L3]

parum *(too) little, not enough* [KL2, L7]

parvus, -a, -um *little, small, unimportant* [KL1, L7]

pascō, -ere, pāvī, pastum *I feed, pasture* [KL1, W32; KL2, W14]

passim *everywhere, far and wide* [KL2, L13]

pastor, pastōris (m) *shepherd* [KL1, L20]

pastorālīs, -e *of/belonging to a shepherd, pastoral* [KL1, W32]

pater, patris (m) *father* [KL1, L12]

patior, -ī, ——, passus sum *I suffer, endure* [KL2, L6]

patria, -ae (f) *native land* [KL1, L3]

pātrō (1) *I bring to pass, accomplish* [KL3, W4]

patruēlis, -is (m/f) *cousin (on the father's side)* [KL1, L22]

patruus, -ī (m) *uncle (father's brother)* [KL1, L22]

paucī, -ae, -a (pl) *few* [KL1, L7]

paulātim *little by little, gradually* [KL3, W7]

pauper, -eris *poor* [KL3, L9]

paveō, -ēre, pavī, —— *I dread, fear, tremble* [KL3, L15]

pāvo, -ōnis (m) *peacock* [KL1, W21]

pāx, pācis (f) *peace* [KL1, L15]

peccātor, -ōris (m) *sinner* [KL3, L5]

peccātrix, -trīcis (f) *sinner* [KL3, L5]

peccātum, -ī (n) *sin, fault, offense* [KL3, L11]

peccō (1) *I sin, offend, transgress* [KL3, L11]

pecūnia, -ae (f) *money* [KL1, L3]

pecus, -coris (n) *cattle, herd* [KL3, L2]

pēior, pēius *worse* [KL2, L5]

pēius (adv.) *worse* [KL2, L7]

pellis, -is (f) *skin, hide* [KL3, W2]

penātēs, -ium (m, pl) *the Penates* [KL3, W3]

pendō, -ere, pependī, pensum *I weigh, suspend, ponder* [KL3, L10]

penna, -ae (f) *feather*; in pl., *wing(s)* [KL3, W16]

pennātus, -a, -um *winged* [KL2, W6]

per (+acc.) *through* [KL1, L3]

pēra, -ae (f) *bag, satchel* [KL1, W32]

percutiō, -ere, -cussī, -cussum *I strike down/through, cut down, beat, pierce* [KL1, W32; KL2, L3]

perdō, -ere, perdidī, perditum *I destroy, ruin, lose* [KL1, L27]

perficiō, -ere, -fēcī, -fectum *I complete, finish* [KL1, W23; KL3, L14]

perfundō, -ere, -fūdī, -fūsus *I pour over, drench* [KL3, W6]

perīculum, -ī (n) *danger* [KL1, L5]

permaneō, -ēre, -mansī, -mansum *I remain, continue, abide (in)* [KL3, L7]

permittō, -ere, -mīsī, -missum *I permit, allow* [KL1, W30]

perpetuō, *forever* [KL2, W2]

persequor, -sequī, ——, -secutus sum (deponent) *I pursue (with hostile intent), hunt down* [KL1, W32; KL2, W6]

perspiciō, -ere, -spēxī, -spectum *I perceive, ascertain* [KL3, W2]

persuādeō, -ēre, -suāsī, -suāsum (+dat.) *I persuade* [KL1, W15; KL3, L10]

pertūsus, -a, -um *leaky* [KL1, W29]

perveniō, -īre, -vēnī, -ventum *I arrive, come through to, reach* [KL2, L11]

pēs, pedis (m) *foot* [KL3, W3]

pessimē *worst* [KL2, L7]

pessimus, -a, -um *worst* [KL2, L5]

petītiō, -ōnis (f) *petition, request* [KL3, W16]

petō, -ere, -īvī, -ītum *I shoot* [KL1, W20]; *I seek, ask (for); attack* [KL2, L12]

Pharisaeus, -ī (m) *Pharisee* [KL2, W3]

Philistheus, -ī (m) *Philistine* [KL1, W32]

phoenīx, -nīcis (m) *phoenix* [KL3, W3]

Phrygia, -ae (f) *Phrygia (a land in Asia Minor)* [KL1, W27]

pietās, -tātis (f) *duty, piety, loyalty* [KL2, W13]

pila, -ae (f) *ball* [KL1, W30]

pinguis, -e *fat* [KL1, W25]

pīnus, -ī (f) *pine (tree), fir (tree)* [KL3, W7]

pīrāta, -ae (m) *pirate* [KL1, L2]

piscātor, -ōris (m) *fisherman* [KL3, W6]

piscis, -is (m) *fish* [KL1, L19]

piscor, -ārī, ——, -ātus sum (deponent) *I fish* [KL1, W29]

placeō, -ēre, -cuī, -citum *I please, am pleasing (often impers.* placet/placuit *[+dat.]; rarely, a first conjugation verb)* [KL3, L1]

placidus, -a, -um *calm, quiet* [KL1, W29]

placitum, -ī (n) *principle, agreement* [KL3, W9]

placitus, -a, -um *pleasing, agreeable* [KL3, W12]

plāga, -ae (f) *a blow, wound; plague, destruction* [KL3, L14]

planctus, -ūs (m) *lamentation, wailing* [KL3, W8]

platēa, -ae (f) *street, broad way* [KL3, L1]

plēnus, -a, -um *full, plump, abundant* [KL2, L4]

plērumquē (adv.) *generally, for the most part* [KL3, W7]

plumbeus, -a, -um *leaden, of lead* [KL1, W20]

plumbum, -ī (n) *lead* [KL3, W2]

plūrimum *most* [KL2, L7]

plūrimus, -a, -um *most* [KL2, L5]

——, plūs *more* [KL2, L5]

Plūto, -tōnis (m) *Pluto* [KL2, W6]

pluvia, -ae (f) *rain* [KL2, L9]

poena, -ae (f) *penalty, punishment;* **poenās dō** *I pay the penalty* [KL1, L27]

poēta, -ae (m) *poet* [KL1, L2]

polliceor, -ērī, ——, pollicitus sum *I promise, offer, declare* [KL3, L7]

Polyphēmus, -ī (m) *Polyphemus* [KL2, W4]

pōmum, -ī (n) *fruit, apple* [KL3, W11]

pōmifer, -era, -erum *fruit-bearing* [KL3, W6]

pōnō, -ere, posuī, positum *I put, place* [KL1, L26]

pōns, pontis (m) *bridge* [KL1, W19]

populus, -ī (m) *people, nation* [KL1, L11]

porcus, -ī (m) *pig* [KL1, L10]

porta, -ae (f) *door, gate* [KL1, L31]

porticus, -ūs (f) *portico, porch, colonnade* [KL3, W5]

portō (1) *I carry* [KL1, L4]

postquam *after* [KL2, L10]

postulō (1) *I ask, demand, desire* (aliquid ab/dē aliquō; aliquem aliquid) [KL3, L10]

portus, -ūs (m) *harbor, port* [KL1, L25]

poscō, -ere, pōposcī, —— *I request, ask earnestly* [KL3, W12]

possum, posse, potuī, —— *I am able, can* [KL1, L11]

post (+acc.) *after, behind* [KL1, L17]

postea *afterwards* [KL1, L28]

postnatus, -ī (m) *oldest [son]* [KL1, W19]

postquam (conj.) *after* [KL1, W15]

potēns, (gen.) -entis *powerful* [KL1, L19]

potius (adv.) *more, rather* [KL3, L7]

pōtō, -āre, -āvī, pōtātum or pōtum *I drink, drink heavily* [KL1, L6]

prae (adv. & prep. +abl.) *below* [KL2, L5]

praebeō, -ēre, -uī, -ītum *I give, show, expose* [KL3, W7]

praecīdō, -ere, -cīdī, -cīsum *I cut off, lop* [KL1, W32; KL2, W6]

praecipiō, -ere, -cēpī, -ceptum *I anticipate, warn, command* [KL3, W5]

praeda, -ae (f) *spoil, booty, plunder* [KL2, L15]

praedīcō (1) *I proclaim, preach, declare* [KL3, W7]

praedīcō, -ere, -dīxī, -dictum *I predict, prophesy* [KL1, W31]

praeferō, -ferre, -tulī, -lātum *I seek after, prefer* [KL2, W11]

praemium, -ī (n) *reward* [KL1, W27]

praeter (prep. +acc.) *beside, beyond, past* [KL2, L13]

prātum, -ī (n) *meadow, plain* [KL2, W15]

premō, -ere, pressī, pressum *I press, crush, overpower* [KL2, L10]

pretiōsus, -a, -um *expensive* [KL2, W2]

prīmum/prīmō *(at) first* [KL2, L7]

prīmus, -a, -um *first* [KL1, L23]

prīnceps, -cipis (m) *leader, chief, prince* [KL2, L3]

prīncipium, -iī (n) *beginning, origin* [KL3, L4]

prior, prius *former, before* [KL2, L5]

priusquam (conj.) *before, sooner, rather, until* [KL3, L15]

prō (+abl.) *before, in front of; for (the sake of), instead of* [KL1, L18]

probō (1) *I try, examine, test, prove, approve (of)* [KL3, L14]

procul *at/from a distance, (a)far* [KL2, L11]

prōdeō, -īre, -iī, -itum *I go/come forth* [KL3, L12]

prōdigium, -iī (n) *prophetic sign, wonder, portent* [KL3, W5]

prōdūcō, -ere, -dūxī, -ductum *I lead forth, bring forth, produce* [KL3, W4]

proelium, -ī (n) *battle* [KL1, L15]

proficīscor, -ficīscī, ——, -fectus sum *I start, set out* [KL2, L7]

profundum, -ī (n) *depth, chasm* [KL3, W9]

prōmittō, -ere, -mīsī, -missum *I send forth, let grow* [KL3, W2]

prope (adv./prep. +acc.) *near, next to* [KL1, L19]

properō (1) *I hurry, rush* [KL1, L20]

prophēta, -ae (m) *prophet, soothsayer* [KL3, L4]

propior, -ius *nearer* [KL2, L5]

propinquō (1) (+dat./acc.) *I approach, come near* [KL2, W3]

propitiātiō, -ōnis (f) *propitiation, atonement* [KL2, W11]

prōpositiō, -tiōnis (f) *a setting forth, proposition, resolution* [KL3, W1]

propter (+acc.) *because of, on account of, near* [KL1, L25]

propterea *meanwhile* [KL2, L10]

prōra, -ae (f) *prow* [KL2, W13]

prōrumpō, -ere, -rūpī, -ruptum *I break forth, burst forth* [KL2, W9]

prōvidentia, -ae (f) *providence, provision, forethought* [KL2, W9]

prōvincia, -ae (f) *province, territory* [KL3, W10]

provocō (1) *to challenge* [KL1, W32]

proximus, -a, -um *next, nearest* [KL2, L5]

puella, -ae (f) *girl* [KL1, L3]

puer, puerī (m) *boy* [KL1, L5]

pugna, -ae (f) *fight, battle* [KL2, W9]

pugnō (1) *I fight* [KL1, L1]

pulcher, -chra, -chrum *beautiful, handsome* [KL1, L7]

pulsō (1) *I strike, knock* [K2L, W14]

purpureus, -a, -um *purple; dark-red, dark-violet, dark-brown* [KL1, L17]

puteus, -ī (m) *a well, pit* [KL2, L12]

putō (1) *I consider, think, suppose* [KL3, L3]

pseudoprophēta, -ae (m) *false prophet* [KL3, W14]

pyra, -ae (f) *funeral pyre* [KL1, W8]

Q

quadrīgae, -ārum (f, pl) *four-horse chariot* [KL1, W23]

quaerō, -ere, quaesīvī, quaesītum (-situm) *I ask, seek, inquire* [KL2, L3]

quālis (interrog. adj.) *of what sort, what kind of*; **(rel. adj.)** *of such a sort, such as, as* [KL3, L9]

quam *as, than, how* [KL1, L28]

quamdiu *how long?; as long as, until* [KL3, L9]

quandō *when (?), ever; since, because* [KL1, L12]

quantō (adv.) *(by) how much* [KL2, W14]

quantus, -a, -um *how much, how many, how great* [KL2, W13]

quārē *by what means? how? why? wherefore (?)* [KL3, L9]

quārtus, -a, -um decimus, -a, -um *fourteenth* [KL1, L23]

quārtus, -a, -um *fourth* [KL1, L23]

quasi *as if, just as; almost, nearly, about* [KL3, L11]

quassō (1) *I shake violently, batter* [KL3, W1]

quatiō, -ere, quassī, quassus *I shake, brandish* [KL3, W5]

quater (adv.) *four times* [KL3, W6]

quattuor *four* [KL1, L21]

quattuordecim *fourteen* [KL1, L21]

-que, (enclitic) *and* [KL1, L10]

quemadmodum (adv.) *how, in what manner* [KL3, L9]

quī, quae, quod *who, what, which, that* [KL2, L3]

quī? quae? quod? (interrog. adj.) *what (kind of)? which?* [KL2, L9]

quia (conj.) *because, since, that* [KL1, L18]

quīcumque, quaecumque, quodcumque *whoever, whichever, whatever; whosoever, etc.* [KL2, L12]

quid *what?* [KL1, W19]

quīdam, quaedam, quiddam (pron.) *a certain one/thing; someone, something* [KL2, L12]

quīdam, quaedam, quoddam (adj.) *a certain; some* [KL2, L12]

quidem *indeed, certainly, even* [KL2, L3]

quiēscō, -ere, quiēvī, quiētum *I rest, keep quiet* [KL3, W7]

quīndecim *fifteen* [KL1, L21]

quīngentēsimus, -a, -um *five hundredth* [KL1, L23]

quīngentī *five hundred* [KL1, L21]

quīnquāgēsimus, -a, -um *fiftieth* [KL1, L23]

quīnquāgintā *fifty* [KL1, L21]

quīnque *five* [KL1, L21]

quīntus, -a, -um decimus, -a, -um *fifteenth* [KL1, L23]

quīntus, -a, -um *fifth* [KL1, L23]

quis *who?* [KL1, W31]

quis, quid (interrog. pron.) *who? what?; why?* [KL2, L9]

quisquam, quidquam/quicquam *anyone, anything, someone, something* [KL3, L1]

quisque, quaeque, quidque (pron.) and quodque (adj.) *each (one), every(one)* [KL3, L2]

quisquis, quidquid (quicquid) (pron.) *whoever, whichever, whatever* [KL2, L12]

quō *in/to what place (?), in/to which place (?), whither (?), where (?); why; in order that* [KL2, L11]

quoad *until* [KL2, W15]

quod *because, that* [KL1, L10]

quōmodo *how, in what way* [KL1, L25]

quondam *ever, once, formerly* [KL2, L13]

quoniam *because, since* [KL1, L26]

quoque *also, too* [KL1, L29]

R

rādō, -ere, rāsī, rāsum *I shave* [KL3, W2]

rapiō, -ere, rapuī, raptum *I snatch, seize, carry (off)* [KL1, L31]

raptus, -ūs (m) *kidnapping, abduction* [KL1, W31]

rārus, -a, -um *thin, scattered* [KL3, W2]

recēns, -centis *fresh, recent* [KL2, W11]

recipiō, -ere, -cēpī, -ceptum *I take back/again, receive* [KL3, L11]

redeō, -īre, -iī, -itum *I go back, come back, return* [KL3, L2]

referō, -ferre, -(t)tulī, -(l)lātum *I bring/take back, apply* [KL3, W9]

reficiō, -ere, -fēcī, -fectum *I repair, remake* [KL1, W29; KL3, W2]

rēgālis, -e *royal, regal, kingly* [KL3, W10]

rēgia, -ae (f) *palace* [KL1, L2]

rēgīna, -ae (f) *queen* [KL1, L2]

regiō, -ōnis (f) *boundary, territory, region* [KL3, W2]

regnō (1) *I rule, govern, reign* [KL1, L6]

regnum, -ī (n) *kingdom* [KL1, L5]

regō, -ere, rexī, rectum *I rule* [KL1, L26]

regredior, -gredī, ——, -gressus sum *I go back, return* [KL3, L10]

rēgula, -ae (f) *rule, example, pattern* [KL3, W9]

rēiciō, -ere, -iēcī, -iectum *I throw back, fling back* [KL3, W7]

religiō, -ōnis (f) *religion, reverence* [KL3, W7]

religō (1) *I bind (back/up), fetter* [KL3, W16]

reliquus, -a, -um *remaining, rest (of)* [KL2, L6]

relinquō, -ere, -līquī, -lictum *I abandon, leave behind* [KL1, L28]

remissiō, -ōnis (f) *remission, forgiveness* [KL3, W5]

remittō, -ere, -mīsī, -missum *I send back, remove, forgive* [KL3, L11]

removeō, -ēre, -mōvī, -mōtum *I remove, take away* [KL1, L14]

rēmus, -ī (m) *oar* [KL2, W5]

reor, rērī, ——, ratus sum *I think, suppose, imagine* [KL3, W16]

repellō, -ere, reppulī, repulsum *I drive back, push back, repel* [KL3, W2]

repentē *suddenly* [KL1, L10]

repetō, -ere, -īvī/-iī, -ītum *I repeat, seek again* [KL3, W9]

rēpleō, -ēre, -plēvī, -plētum *I fill (up), fill again, complete* [KL3, L5]

reprehendō, -ere, -hendī, -hensum *I hold back, rebuke, censure, find fault with* [KL3, W13]

reprimō, -ere, -pressī, -pressum *I hold/keep back, restrain* [KL3, W9]

reprōmissiō, -ōnis (f) *(formal) promise, guarantee, counter-promise* [KL3, W12]

reptilis, -e *creeping, reptile* [KL3, W4]

reptō (1) *I crawl, creep* [KL1, L14]

requiēscō, -ere, -quiēvī, -quiētum *I rest* [KL3, L4]

rēs, reī (f) *thing* [KL1, L28]

resistō, -ere, -stitī, —— *I stand back/still, halt* [KL3, L2]

rēspiciō, -ere, -spēxī, -spectum *I look back, regard* [KL2, L14]

respondeō, -ēre, -spondī, -sponsum *I answer, respond* [KL1, L9]

rēstinguō, -ere, -stinxī, -stinctum *I put out, exstinguish* [KL3, W3]

restituō, -ere, -stituī, -stitutus *I restore, revive* [KL3, W1]

resūmō, -ere, -sūmpsī, -sūmptum *I resume, take up again, take back* [KL3, W16]

resupīnus, -a, -um *backwards, lying on one's back, supine* [KL3, W7]

resurgō, -ere, -surrēxī, -surrēctum *I rise again* [KL1, L29]

retrō *back(ward), behind* [KL1, W23; KL3, W3]

revēlō (1) *I unveil, reveal, disclose* [KL3, W9]

revertor, -vertī, ——, reversus sum *I turn back, return, go back (not always deponent)* [KL2, L6]

revocō (1) *I call back, call again* [KL3, W2]

rēx, rēgis (m) *king* [KL1, L12]

rīdeō, -ēre, rīsī, rīsum *I laugh, smile* [KL1, L9]

rīma, -ae (f) *crack, fissure* [KL2, W11]

rogō (1) *I ask (takes double acc. or phrase with* dē*)* [KL1, L6]

Rōma, -ae (f) *Rome (capital city of ancient and modern Italy)* [KL2, L14]

Rōmānus, -a, -um *Roman*; **(subst.)** *a Roman* [KL2, L15]

rōs, rōris (m) *dew* [KL2, W9]

ruber, -bra, -brum *red, ruddy* [KL1, L17]

rūfus, -a, -um *red, ruddy* [KL1, W32]

rumpō, -ere, rūpī, ruptum *I burst, break* [KL2, L12]

ruō, -ere, ruī, rutum [but ruitūrus] *I fall down (violently), rush (down), hurl down* [KL3, L4]

rursum/rursus *back(wards), again* [KL3, L3]

rūs, rūris (n) *country, farm* [KL2, L14]

rusticus, -a, -um *of the county, rustic, rural;* **(as noun)** *a countryman, rustic, peasant* [KL3, W7]

S

sabbata, -ōrum (n, pl) *Sabbath* [KL1, W26]

sabbatum, -ī (n) *the Sabbath (often plural with singular meaning)* [KL3, L1]

saccus, -ī (m) *sack, bag* [KL2, W6]

sacer, -cra, -crum *holy, sacred* [KL2, L3]

sacerdōs, -dōtis (m) *priest* [KL2, L3]

sacrificium, -iī (n) *sacrifice, offering* [KL2, L4]

saeculum, -ī (n) *generation; the spirit of the age, times* [KL1, L6]

saepe *often* [KL1, L6]

saevus, -a, -um *savage, cruel, fierce* [KL2, W11]

sagitta, -ae (f) *arrow* [KL1, L3]

saliō, -īre, -uī, saltum *I jump, leap, spring* [KL1, W29; KL2, W12]

saltem *at least, anyhow* [KL3, W5]

sālum, -ī (n) *the (salt) sea* [KL3, W6]

salūs, -ūtis (f) *salvation, deliverance, health, safety* [KL3, L7]

salvātor, -ōris (m) *savior, redeemer* [KL3, L5]

salveō, -ēre, ——, —— *I am well;* **salvē(te)**, *Good day! Be well!* [KL1, L9]

salvus, -a, -um *safe, saved, well, sound* [KL1, L25]

sanctificō (1) *I make holy, sanctify* [KL3, L4]

sanctus, -a, -um *holy, sacred, consecrated* [KL1, L25]

sanguis, -guinis (m) *blood* [KL2, L3]

sānus, -a, -um *healthy* [KL3, W1]

sapiēns, -entis *wise* [KL2, L4]

sapientia, -ae (f) *wisdom* [KL2, L10]

Satanās, -ae (m) *Satan* [KL3, W1]

satis (adv. & indecl. adj./noun) *enough, sufficient(ly)* [KL1, L30]

satrapa, -ae (m) *satrap, governor* [KL3, W10]

Saul (indecl.) *Saul* [KL1, W32]

saxum, -ī (n) *rock* [KL1, L29]

scandalum, -ī (n) *stumbling block, temptation, cause of offense* [KL3, L12]

scelus, -leris (n) *crime, sin* [KL3, L6]

schisma, -matis (n) *schism, division* [KL2, W8]

scīlicet *of course, naturally, it is clear* [KL3, L6]

scindō, -ere, scidī, scissum *I cut, tear, rend* [KL3, L10]

sciō, -īre, sciī (scīvī), scītum *I know* [KL1, L29]

scopulus, -ī (m) *cliff* [KL1, W30]

scrība, -ae (m) *scribe, clerk, secretary* [KL3, L10]

scrībō, -ere, scrīpsī, scrīptum *I write* [KL1, L26]

scūtum, -ī (m) *shield* [KL1, L10]

sē (acc. reflexive pronoun) *himself, herself, itself* [KL1, W8]

sēcēdō, -ere -cessī, -cessum *I withdraw, go apart* [KL3, W1]

sēcrētum, -ī (n) *secret* [KL1, W28]

secundum (adv. & prep. +acc.) *after; according to* [KL1, L28]

secundus, -a, -um *second* [KL1, L23]

sed *but* [KL1, L1]

sēdecim *sixteen* [KL1, L21]

sedeō, -ēre, sēdī, sessum *I sit* [KL1, L9]

sēdūcō, -ere, -dūxī, -ductum *I lead aside/astray, seduce, deceive* [KL3, W11]

sella, -ae (f) *seat, chair* [KL1, L31]

sēmen, -minis (n) *seed, offspring, origin* [KL3, W4]

semper *always* [KL1, L5]

senātus, -ūs (m) *senate* [KL3, W15]

senex, senis (m) *old man* [KL1, L14]

senior, -ōris (adj.) *older, elder*; **(as noun)** *an elder* [KL3, L5]

sensus, -ūs (m) *sense, feeling, understanding* [KL2, L15]

sententia, -ae (f) *thought, opinion, sentence* [KL3, L9]

sentiō, -īre, sēnsī, sēnsum *I feel, realize, perceive* [KL3, L3]

sepeliō, -īre, -īvī, sepultus *I bury* [KL3, W5]

sepulcrum (sepulchrum), -ī (n) *grave, tomb* [KL2, L13]

septem *seven* [KL1, L21]

septendecim *seventeen* [KL1, L21]

septimus, -a, -um decimus, -a, -um *seventeenth* [KL1, L23]

septimus, -a, -um *seventh* [KL1, L23]

sequor, sequī, ——, secūtus sum (deponent) *I follow* [KL1, W30; KL2, L6]

sermō, -ōnis (m) *speech, talk, conversation* [KL2, L9]

serō, -ere, sēvī, satum *I sow, plant* [KL2, W11]

sērō, sērius, sērissimē (adv.) *late* [KL2, L11]

serpēns, -pentis (m/f) *serpent, snake* [KL2, W2]

serva, -ae (f) *female slave, servant* [KL1, L4]

serviō, -īre, -īvī, -ītum (+dat.) *I serve, am a slave to* [KL2, L10]

servō (1) *I save* [KL1, L6]

servus, -ī (m) *male slave, servant* [KL1, L4]

sēū (sīve) *or;* **sēū…sēū** *whether…or* [KL1, L30]

sex *six* [KL1, L21]

sextus, -a, -um decimus, -a, -um *sixteenth* [KL1, L23]

sextus, -a, -um *sixth* [KL1, L23]

sī (conj.) *if* [KL1, L18]

sībilus, -a, -um *hissing, whistling* [KL3, W6]

Sibylla, -ae (f) *the Sibyl* [KL2, W13]

sīca, -ae (f) *dagger* [KL1, L3]

sīc *so, thus* [KL2, L4]

Sicilia, -ae (f) *Sicily* [KL2, W5]

sīcut *as, just as, like* [KL1, L20]

sīdus, sīderis (n) *constellation, star, heavenly body* [KL3, L15]

sīgnō (1) *I mark out, point out* [KL3, W3]

sīgnum, -ī (n) *sign, signal, miracle* [KL3, L4]

silentium, -iī (n) *silence, stillness* [KL3, W9]

Sīlēnus, -ī (m) *Silenus (pudgy old fellow [usually drunk], former tutor and longtime companion of Bacchus)* [KL1, W27]

sileō, -ēre, -uī, —— *I am silent, keep silent* [KL3, W10]

silva, -ae (f) *forest* [KL1, L3]

similis, -e *similar, like* [KL2, L5]

similitūdō, -dinis (f) *likeness, resemblance* [KL3, W4]

simul *together, at the same time;* **simul atque/ac** *as soon as* [KL2, L9]

simulācrum, -ī (n) *statue, likeness, image, idol* [KL1, W25; KL3, L6]

sine (+abl.) *without* [KL1, L9]

singulī, -ae, -a *one at a time, single, separate* [KL2, L13]

sinister, -stra, -strum *left(-handed); inauspicious* [KL1, L30]

sinō, -ere, sīvī, situs *I let, allow* [KL2, W13]

sitiō, -īre, -īvī, —— *I thirst (for), am thirsty* [KL2, W12]

sive *whether* [KL3, W1]

sīve (sēū) *or;* **sīve…sīve** *whether…or* [KL1, L30]

societās, -tātis (f) *society, fellowship, community* [KL3, W11]

socius, -iī (m) *ally, companion* [KL2, L13]

sōl, sōlis (m) *sun* [KL1, L12]

solea, -ae (f) *sandal* [KL2, W6]

soleō, -ēre, ——, solītus sum (semi-deponent) *I am accustomed (to), am in the habit of* [KL3, L9]

solidō (1) *I make firm, strengthen* [KL2, W9]

sōlitūdō, -dinis (f) *solitude, loneliness* [KL3, W9]

solium, -iī (n) *throne, seat* [KL3, W10]

sollicitus, -a, -um *anxious, troubled* [KL2, W14]

sōlum (adv.) *only, alone, merely* [KL3, L7]

sōlus, -a, -um *only, single* [KL1, W12; KL2, L4]

solvō, -ere, solvī, solūtum *I loose, set free, pay* [KL2, L10]

somniō (1) *I dream* [KL1, W18]

somnus, -ī (n) *sleep* [KL2, W13]

sonitus, -ūs (m) *noise, sound* [KL3, W3]

sopor, -ōris (m) *(deep) sleep* [KL3, W6]

soror, sorōris (f) *sister* [KL1, L12]

sors, -rtis (f) *lot, oracle, chance, destiny* [KL3, L6]

spargō, -ere, sparsī, sparsum *I scatter, sprinkle* [KL2, W9]

speciēs, -ēī (f) *appearance, likeness, species* [KL3, W4]

spectō (1) *I look at, watch* [KL1, L1]

spēlunca, -ae (f) *cave* [KL1, L3]

spērō (1) *I hope, expect* [KL3, L1]

spēs, speī (f) *hope* [KL1, L28]

spīca, -ae (f) *point, head (of grain), ear (of corn)* [KL3, W1]

spīna, -ae (f) *barrier (lit., "spine," the wall dividing a race course in half lengthwise)* [KL1, W23]

spīra, -ae (f) *coil, fold* [KL3, W6]

spīrō (1) *I breathe, blow* [KL2, W3]

spīritus, -ūs (m) *spirit, breath* [KL1, L25]

spūmō (1) *I foam, froth, spray* [KL3, W6]

spurius, -a, -um *spurious* [KL1, W32]

squāmeus, -a, -um *scaly* [KL3, W6]

statim *immediately* [KL1, L13]

statuō, -ere, -uī, -ūtum *I cause to stand, set (up), place* [KL2, W7]

stella, -ae (f) *star* [KL1, L11]

sternō, -ere, strāvī, strātum *I spread (out), scatter, extend* [KL2, L13]

stīpendium, -iī (n) *pay, stipend, tax* [KL2, W15]

stō, stāre, stetī, statum *I stand* [KL1, L1]

strātum, -ī (n) *covering, blanket* [KL3, W10]

stringō, -ere, strinxī, strictum *I draw (out), pull* [KL3, W7]

stultitia, -ae (f) *foolishness, folly* [KL1, W27]

stultus, -a, -um *foolish* [KL1, L7]

stupeō, -ēre, -uī, —— *I am stunned, am astonished, am stupefied* [KL3, W16]

stupor, -ōris (m) *amazement, astonishment* [KL1, W28]

suādeō, -ēre, suāsī, suāsum *I persuade, exhort* [KL3, W13]

sub (+acc.) *under, up under, close to;* **(+abl.)** *below, under(neath), at the foot of* [KL1, L14]

subdūcō, -ere, -dūxī, -ductum *I draw up, haul up* [KL2, W2]

sūbiciō, -ere, -iēcī, -iectum *I throw/place under, subdue* [KL3, W4]

subitō/subitum *suddenly, unexpectedly, immediately* [KL3, L3]

subitus, -a, -um *sudden, unexpected* [KL3, W3]

substantia, -ae (f) *substance, essence; property, fortune, worldly goods* [KL3, L13]

subsistō, -ere, -stitī, —— *I halt, stand still, pause* [KL3, W6]

subvertō, -ere, -vertī, -versus *I overturn, overthrow, ruin* [KL3, W7]

succedō, -ere, -cessī, -cessum *I succeed, replace* [KL3, W2]

sufficiō, -ere, -fēcī, -fectum *I am sufficient, suffice* [KL2, W14]

——, suī (3rd person reflexive pron.) *himself, herself, itself, themselves* [KL3, L2]

sum, esse, fuī, futūrum *I am* [KL1, L3]

summa, -ae (f) *top, main point, sum(mary)* [KL2, W10]

summitās, -tātis (f) *top, tip, summit, height* [KL2, W10]

summus, -a, -um *highest, greatest* [KL2, L5]

sūmō, -ere, sūmpsī, sūmptum *I take (up), assume* [KL2, L10]

super (+acc. /+abl.) *over, above, beyond* [KL1, L26]

superbia, -ae (f) *pride, arrogance* [KL3, L12]

superbus, -a, -um *proud, haughty* [KL1, W18; KL2, L4]

superior, -ius *higher* [KL2, L5]

superō (1) *I conquer, defeat* [KL1, L2]

superus, -a, -um *above, high* [KL2, L5]

suprā (adv. & prep. +acc.) *above, over* [KL1, L14]

suprēmus, -a, -um *highest, greatest* [KL2, L5]

surgō, -ere, surrēxī, surrēctum *I (a)rise* [KL1, L28]

suscitō (1) *I raise up [from the dead], awaken, stir up* [KL3, W5]

suspendō, -ere, -pendī, -pensum *I hang (up), suspend* [KL3, W5]

suspīciōsus, -a, -um *suspicious* [KL1, W21]

susurrō (1) *I whisper* [KL1, W28]

suum negōtium agō *(idiom) I mind my own business* [KL1, W29]

suus, -a, -um (3rd person reflexive possessive adj.) *his (own), her (own), its (own)* [KL1, W31; KL3, L2]

synagōga, -ae (f) *synagogue* [KL1, W26]

T

tabernāculum, -ī (n) *tent* [KL1, W32]

taceō, -ēre, -uī, -itum *I am silent* [KL1, W26]

tactus, -ūs (m) *touch* [KL1, W28]

tālāria, -ium (n, pl) *winged sandals/shoes; ankles* [KL3, W16]

tālis, -e *such* [KL3, L5]

tam *so, so much;* **tam...quam** *so...as* [KL3, L5]

tamen *yet, nevertheless, still* [KL1, L30]

tandem (adv.) *finally, at last* [KL3, L15]

tangō, -ere, tetigī, tactum *I touch, strike* [KL1, L27]

tantum (adv.) *only, merely, but; so, so much/greatly* [KL3, L14]

tantus, -a, -um *so/such great, of such size* [KL3, L5]

taurus, -ī (m) *bull* [KL3, W6]

tellūs, tellūris (f) *the earth, ground, land* [KL1, L14]

tēlum, -ī (n) *weapon* [KL3, L6]

temere *rashly, at random, by chance* [KL3, W15]

tempestās, -tātis (f) *weather, storm* [KL1, L26]

templum, -ī (n) *temple, shrine* [KL1, W25; KL2, L10]

temptō (1) *I attempt, try, handle* [KL1, W27; KL3, L7]

tempus, temporis (n) *time* [KL1, L13]

tendō, -ere, tetendī, tentum *I stretch; hasten, strive; aim* [KL2, L4]

tenēbrae, -ārum (f, pl) *darkness, gloomy place, shadows* [KL1, L11]

tenēbrōsus, -a, -um *gloomy, dark* [KL2, W15]

teneō, -ēre, tenuī, tentum *I hold, possess* [KL1, L9]

tenuis, -e *thin, slender* [KL2, L11]

tepidus, -a, -um *warm, tepid* [KL3, W16]

ter *three times, thrice* [KL3, W5]

tergum, -ī (n) *back, rear* [KL3, L6]

terminus, -ī (m) *limit, bound(ary), end* [KL3, L15]

terra, -ae (f) *earth, land* [KL1, L4]

terreō, -ēre, -uī, -itum *I frighten, terrify* [KL1, L9]

tertius, -a, -um decimus, -a, -um *thirteenth* [KL1, L23]

tertius, -a, -um *third* [KL1, L23]

testificor, -ārī, ——, -ātus sum *I testify, bear witness* [KL3, W14]

testimōnium, -ī (n) *testimony, evidence, witness* [KL2, L10]

testis, -is (m) *witness* [KL3, L5]

testor, -ārī, ——, -ātus sum *I testify, bear witness* [KL3, W11]

thēsaurus, -ī (m) *treasure, hoard* [KL3, L11]

Thēsēūs, -eī (m) *Theseus* [KL1, W30]

tigris, tigridis (m/f) *tiger* [KL1, L12]

timeō, -ēre, -uī, —— *I fear* [KL1, L9]

timor, -ōris (m) *fear* [KL3, L14]

Tmōlus, -ī (m) *Tmolus (a god and a mountain in Lydia)* [KL1, W28]

tollō, -ere, sustulī, sublātum *I lift up, raise up; take away, destroy* [KL1, W25; KL2, L13]

tonitrus, -ūs (m) *thunder* [KL1, L25]

tonsor, -ōris (m) *barber* [KL1, W28]

torrens, -ntis (m) *a torrent, stream* [KL1, W32]

torreō, -ēre, torruī, tostum *I burn, parch, dry up* [KL1, L17]

tot (indecl. adj.) *so many, so great a number* [KL3, L9]

tōtus, -a, -um *all, every, whole* [KL2, L3]

trabēs, -is (m) *tree trunk, beam* [KL2, W14]

trādō, -ere, -didī, -ditum *I hand over, surrender; hand down, teach* [KL1, W13; KL2, L4]

tragoedia, -ae (f) *tragedy* [KL1, W4]

trahō, -ere, trāxī, trāctum *I draw, drag* [KL1, L30]

tranquillus, -a, -um *quiet, calm* [KL3, W9]

trāns (+acc.) *across* [KL1, L11]

trānseō, -īre, -iī, -itum *I go across/over, cross (over), pass (by/over)* [KL2, L15]

trānsferō, -ferre, -tūlī, -lātum *I carry/bear/bring across/over, transfer, translate* [KL3, L13]

tredecim *thirteen* [KL1, L21]

tremō, -ere, -uī, —— *I tremble, quake* [KL1, W25; KL3, W6]

trēs, tria *three* [KL1, L21]

tribūnal, -ālis (n) *judgment seat, tribunal* [KL2, W15]

tribūtum, -ī (n) *tribute, tax* [KL1, W30]

trīstis, -e *sad, gloomy, dismal* [KL1, L20; KL2, L3]

triumphō (1) *I triumph, exult, rejoice exceedingly* [KL3, W9]

Troia, -ae (f) *Troy* [KL2, W4]

Trōianus, -a, -um *Trojan, of Troy* [KL2, W5]

tū (sg.) *you* [KL1, L17]

tum *then, at that time; next, thereupon* [KL1, L15]

tumulus, -ī (m) *tomb, grave mound* [KL2, W11]

tunc *then, thereupon, at that time* [KL2, L4]

turba, -ae (f) *crowd, mob, throng* [KL1, L2]

turbō (1) *I disturb, trouble* [KL2, W13]

turbō, -binis (m) *whirlwind* [KL2, W9]

turbulentus, -a, -um *restless, stormy, turbulent* [KL3, W9]

turpitūdō, -dinis (f) *ugliness, shame, dishonor* [KL3, W9]

turris, turris (f) *tower, turret* [KL1, L18]

tūtus, -a, -um *safe, secure* [KL3, L7]

tuus, -a, -um *your (sg), yours* [KL1, L11]

U

ūber, -eris *rich, fruitful, abundant* [KL2, W11]

ubi *where (?), when* [KL1, L12]

ubīque *everywhere* [KL1, W29]

Ulixēs, -is (m) *Ulysses (Odysseus)* [KL2, W5]

ūllus, -a, -um *any; anyone, anything* [KL1, W27; KL2, L4]

ulterior, -ius *farther* [KL2, L5]

ultimus, -a, -um *farthest* [KL2, L5]

ultrā (adv.) *beyond, farther* [KL2, L5]

ululātus, -ūs (m) *howling, shrieking, wailing [of mourning]* [KL3, W10]

ululō (1) *I howl, scream* [KL1, L6]

umbra, -ae (f) *shadow, shade, ghost* [KL3, L3]

umerus, -ī (m) *shoulder, upper arm* [KL3, W3]

umquam (adv.) *ever, at any time* [KL3, L14]

ūnā *together, in one* [KL1, L29]

ūnctiō, -ōnis (f) *anointing, ointment* [KL3, W12]

uncus, -a, -um *hooked, curved* [KL3, W16]

unda, -ae (f) *wave* [KL1, L10]

unde *from where (?), whence (?)* [KL2, L11]

ūndecim *eleven* [KL1, L21]

ūndecimus, -a, -um *eleventh* [KL1, L23]

ūndēvīcēsimus, -a, -um *nineteenth* [KL1, L23]

ūndēvīgintī *nineteen* [KL1, L21]

undique *on/from all sides, from every direction* [KL1, L30; KL2, L15]

ūnicus, -a, -um *one, only, sole* [KL1, W22]

unigenitus, -a, -um *only-begotten, only* [KL2, W3]

ūniversus, -a, -um *all together, whole, entire* [KL3, L4]

ūnus, -a, -um *one* [KL1, L21]

urbānus, -a, -um *polite* [KL1, W29]

urbs, urbis (f) *city* [KL1, L18]

urna, -ae (f) *urn* [KL2, W11]

ursus, -ī (m) *bear* [KL1, W32]

usquam *anywhere, at/in any place* [KL3, L9]

usque (adv.) *continuously, constantly;* **(prep. +acc.)** *all the way up to, as far as* [KL3, L4]

ut (conj. +indic.) *as, when, how;* **(+subj.)** *(so) that, in order that/to, to* [KL3, L5]

uter, utra (ūtra), utrum (ūtrum) (interrog.) *which (of two)?;* **(relat.)** *whichever (of two), the one which;* **(indef.)** *either, one (of two)* [KL2, L15]

uterus, -ī (m) *womb, belly* [KL2, W9]

utinam *would/oh that! if only! I wish that!* [KL3, L13]

utique *certainly, surely* [KL3, L12]

ūtor, ūtī, ——, ūsus sum (+abl.) *I use, enjoy* [KL3, L2]

ūtrum (adv.) *whether (translated by tone of voice in direct questions)* [KL3, L9]

uxor, -ōris (f) *wife* [KL1, L30]

V

vacuus, -a, -um *empty, vacant, void* [KL3, W4]

vādō, -ere, vāsī, —— *I go, proceed* [KL2, L9]

valde *very, exceedingly* [KL2, L10]

valeō, -ēre, -uī, -itum *I am well/strong;* **valē(te)** *Goodbye! Be well!* [KL1, L9]

valles, vallis (f) *valley, vale* [KL1, L18]

vās, vāsis; pl. vāsa, -ōrum (n) *vessel, equipment* [KL3, W1]

vastō (1) *I devastate, lay waste* [KL1, L14]

vastus, -a, -um *vast, enormous, desolate* [KL2, L6]

vātēs, -is (m/f) *prophet/prophetess* [KL1, W31]

vehemens, -mentis *violent, vehement* [KL2, W9]

vehō, -ere, vexī, vectum *I carry, ride, convey* [KL1, L27]

vel *or, or rather* [KL2, L9]

vēlāmen, -minis (n) *veil, covering* [KL2, W11]

vellō, -ere, vulsī/vellī, vulsum *I pluck, pull* [KL3, W1]

vēlum, -ī (n) *sail* [KL1, W30]

vendō, -ere, -didī, -ditum *I sell* [KL3, W9]

venēnum, -ī (n) *venom, poison* [KL1, L10; KL3, W6]

venia, -ae (f) *mercy, pardon, forgiveness* [KL3, W12]

veniō, -īre, vēnī, ventum *I come* [KL1, L29]

ventus, -ī (m) *wind* [KL1, W28; KL3, W16]

verbum, -ī (n) *word* [KL1, L5]

vereor, -ērī, ——, veritus sum *I respect, reverence, fear* [KL2, L6]

vēritas, -tātis (f) *truth* [KL1, L27]

vērō *truly, certainly [can also be used to say "yes"]* [KL2, L15]

versus, -ūs (m) *row, line (of poetry), furrow* [KL1, L27]

vertō, -ere, vertī, versum *I turn, change* [KL1, L28; KL2, L11]

vērumtamen *however, nevertheless* [KL3, L13]

vērus, -a, -um *true* [KL1, L22; KL2, W13]

vesper, vesperis (m) *evening, evening star, west* [KL1, L14]

vester, -stra, -strum *your (pl), yours (pl)* [KL1, L11]

vestīgium, -iī (n) *footstep, footprint, track* [KL2, W11]

vestīmentum, -ī (n) *clothing, garment* [KL2, L14]

vestis, vestis (f) *clothing, garment* [KL1, L18]

vetō, -āre, vetuī, vetitum *I forbid, prevent* [KL3, W11]

vetus, (gen.) -teris *old* [KL1, L30]

vexō (1) *I vex, ravage, annoy* [KL1, L19]

via, -ae (f) *road, way* [KL1, L11]

vibrō (1) *I vibrate, flicker* [KL3, W6]

vīcēsimus, -a, -um prīmus, -a, -um *twenty-first* [KL1, L23]

vīcēsimus, -a, -um *twentieth* [KL1, L23]

vīcīnus, -a, -um *neighbor(ing), near(by)* [KL3, L9]

victor, -toris (m) *victor, conqueror* [KL2, W13]

victōria, -ae (f) *victory* [KL1, L11]

videō, -ēre, vīdī, visum *I see* [KL1, L9]

vidua, -ae (f) *widow* [KL1, L22]

viduō (1) *I deprive of* (**viduāta, -ae** *widowed)* [KL1, W19]

vīgintī *twenty* [KL1, L21]

vīgintī ūnus, -a, -um (ūnus et vīgintī) *twenty-one* [KL1, L21]

vīlis, -e *cheap, worthless* [KL2, W15]

villa, -ae (f) *farmhouse, country house* [KL1, L2]

vinciō, -īre, vinxī, vinctum *I bind, tie* [KL1, L30]

vincō, -ere, vīcī, victum *I defeat, conquer* [KL1, L26]

vīnum, -ī (n) *wine* [KL1, L5]

violō (1) *I violate, profane, dishonor* [KL3, W1]

vir, virī (m) *man* [KL1, L4]

virga, -ae (f) *branch, rod, staff* [KL3, L10]

virgō, virginis (f) *maiden, young woman* [KL1, L12]

vīridis, -e *green; fresh, young, vigorous* [KL1, L17]

virtūs, virtūtis (f) *manliness, courage, strength* [KL1, L12]

vīs, vīs (f) *strength, force, power, violence* [KL3, L5]

vīscus, -eris (n) *internal organs, entrails, inward parts; (metaphorically) heart* [KL3, L13]

vīta, -ae *life* [KL1, L11]

vītō (1) *I avoid, shun* [KL1, L30]

vitrum, -ī (n) *woad* [KL2, W2]

vīvō, -ere, vīxī, victum *I live* [KL1, L27]

vīvus, -a, -um *living* [KL1, L20]

vix *scarcely, hardly* [KL3, L3]

vocō (1) *I call, summon, invite* [KL1, L1]

volātilis, -e *flying, winged* [KL3, W4]

volō (1) *I fly* [KL1, L10]

volō/velle, voluī, ——, —— *I wish, want, will* [KL2, L14]

voluntās, -tātis (f) *will, wish, desire* [KL3, L12]

voluptās, -tātis (f) *pleasure, enjoyment* [KL3, W2]

volvō, -ere, volvī, volūtum *I roll, turn around/over* [KL3, W1]

vōs (pl.) *you* [KL1, L17]

vox, vōcis (f) *voice* [KL1, L14]

vulnerō (1) *I wound* [KL1, L1]

vulnus, vulneris (n) *wound* [KL1, L13]

vultus, -ūs (m) *face, expression* [KL1, L25]

Z

zēlus, -ī (m) *zeal, jealousy* [KL3, W7]

APPENDIX D

Sources and Helps

Bennett, Charles E. *New Latin Grammar.* Wauconda, IL: Bolchazy-Carducci Publishers, 1998. A good resource for your grammar questions.

Biblia Sacra Vulgata. Stuttgart, Germany: Deutsche Bibelgesellschaft, 1994. If you have extra time, read a bit from the Vulgate every day to improve your Latin skills.

Davis, William Stearns. *A Day in Old Rome.* New York: Biblo and Tannen, 1962.

Gildersleeve, B. L. and Lodge, G. *Gildersleeve's Latin Grammar.* Mundelein, IL: Bolchazy-Carducci Publishers, 2012. This is another helpful and very thorough Latin grammar. It is organized a little differently than Bennett's *New Latin Grammar* and *Allen and Greenough's*, which can be helpful for looking at grammar concepts in a new way.

Glare, P. G. W. *The Oxford Latin Dictionary.* Oxford: Oxford University Press, 1983. The *OLD* is of course "the" standard for all Latin dictionaries, although occasionally I have found nuggets in *Lewis and Short* that were not in the *OLD.*

Greenough, J. B., et al., ed. *Allen and Greenough's New Latin Grammar.* Newburyport, MA: Focus Publishing, R. Pullins & Company, 2001. A fantastic resource; I referred to it frequently regarding grammar concepts of all kinds.

Jenney, Charles Jr., et al. *Jenney's First Year Latin.* Newton, MA: Allyn and Bacon, 1987. I consulted this text for the order of teaching various grammatical concepts. I studied Latin from it back in my junior high days, and have always been fond of it (although it is a little too addicted to Caesar for my liking). Although short on explanations, it contains plenty of exercises and translations to practice each concept.

LaFleur, Richard A. *Love and Transformation: An Ovid Reader.* Glenview, IL: Scott Foresman-Addison Wesley, 1999. I referred to this Latin text (in addition to online texts) for some of the myths in the Latin to English translations.

The Latin Library: http://www.thelatinlibrary.com/. This website has numerous Latin texts and I used it for some of the Latin to English passages.

Latin Vulgate: http://www.latinvulgate.com/. This website is helpful because it has side-by-side translations from the Vulgate. Although most of us are familiar with Biblical texts and stories, sometimes the Vulgate has completely different wording than what we are used to.

Lee, A. G., ed. *Ovid: Metamorphoses, Book I.* Wauconda, IL: Bolchazy-Carducci Publishers, 1988. I also referred to this book (in addition to online texts) for some of the myths in the Latin to English translations.

Lewis, Charlton T. and Short, Charles. *A Latin Dictionary.* Oxford, United Kingdom: Oxford University Press, 1958. Lewis and Short's dictionary is a standard resource and has helpful examples and commentary on many entries. You can also access it online at http://www.perseus.tufts.edu/hopper/text?doc=Perseus%3atext%3a1999.04.0059.

Martin, Charles, trans. *Ovid: Metamorphoses.* New York: W. W. Norton & Company, 2004. I consulted this English translation as well as Latin texts for some of the myths found in the Latin to English translations.

Mountford, J. F., ed. *Bradley's Arnold Latin Prose Composition.* Wauconda, IL: Bolchazy-Carducci Publishers, 2006. This book is great for practicing English-to-Latin composition, especially when using advanced grammar concepts.

Simpson, D. P. *Cassell's New Latin Dictionary.* New York: Funk & Wagnall's, 1959. I picked this up at a used bookstore (always check out the language section for Latin books!), and it has an especially helpful English to Latin section.

Smith, William and Hall, Theophilus D. *A Copious and Critical English-Latin Dictionary.* Nashville, TN: Wimbledon Publishing Company Ltd., 2000. This is a very thorough English-to-Latin dictionary, besides having a fabulous title.

Stelten, Leo F. *Dictionary of Ecclesiastical Latin.* Peabody, MA: Hendrickson Publishers, 1995. I consulted this dictionary for the translations adapted from the Vulgate, since some dictionaries don't include ecclesiastical words.

Wheelock, Frederic M.; revised by Richard A. LaFleur. *Wheelock's Latin*, 6th ed. rev. New York: HarperCollins Publishers, 2005. I have taught out of this book for several years and referred to it for some grammar matters as well as researching in what order grammatical concepts were presented. It is a good standard text and resource, but not the best for someone trying to teach himself Latin.

Whitaker, William. "Words." http://www.archives.nd.edu/cgi-bin/words.exe. This website (from which you can also download a program) has Latin to English and English to Latin search engines. You can type in any form of a Latin word and it will parse it for you and give you the meaning—pretty handy! All students seem to know about this, so it's best to face it head on. I told my students they were welcome to use it, but that they not become dependent upon it (and of course they shouldn't use it to "cheat" on parsing exercises). It's best to use it when you are stumped by a particular form and need to look it up. The English to Latin search can be very helpful when writing stories or sentences.

Vulgate Frequency: http://www.intratext.com/IXT/LAT0001/_FF1.HTM. This website tells you which words appear the most often in various Latin texts. Since I'm especially fond of the Vulgate and Vergil, I consulted this site to see which words from those sources needed to be incorporated into the vocabulary lists.

APPENDIX E

Verb Formation Chart

Which principal part is used for which tense, voice, and mood? Keep this handout all year, and fill it in as you learn the various verb forms. The principal parts of *necō* (I kill) are provided as an example.

	FIRST	SECOND	THIRD	FOURTH
	necō	necāre	necāvī	necātum
DEFINITION/ FUNCTION				
INDICATIVE				
IMPERATIVE				
INFINITIVE				
SUBJUNCTIVE				
PARTICIPLE				

www.ingramcontent.com/pod-product-compliance
Lightning Source LLC
Chambersburg PA
CBHW080222170426
43192CB00015B/2714
* 9 7 8 1 9 4 7 6 4 4 3 6 6 *